3

mergers

Peter O. Steiner

mergers

motives, effects, policies

Ann Arbor   University of Michigan Press

Published with the assistance of a grant from the
Horace H. Rackham School of Graduate Studies and with
the aid of funds derived from the gifts to The University
of Michigan by William W. Cook.

To p.o.s.

Preface

THE GENESIS of this book was a conference that took place at the University of Chicago in October 1969 on the legal and economic aspects of conglomerate mergers. Harold Demsetz had asked me to talk on "The Public Interest in Conglomerate Mergers." The central theme of my remarks was that while it was possible to define the question narrowly, as merely the effect on economic efficiency, there was nothing inherently compelling in such a narrow definition. The discussant of my paper, Richard A. Posner, disagreed. He failed to understand, he said, how that was sensible and indeed felt that since a purely conglomerate acquisition increased power in no market, its effects on efficiency could be presumed to be beneficial, or at worst neutral. In his view the problems I alluded to merited a good deal less discussion than I had given them. If Posner's attitude made a longer exposition necessary, the Brookings Institution made it possible: That winter I accepted its invitation to write "a brief monograph on conglomerate mergers, of a hundred pages or so, to serve as a background paper for a conference of experts and representatives of different interests."

When the merger wave collapsed, the public curiosity (as distinct from the public interest) in the problem began to fade. My interest shifted from how best to cope with the phenomenon of a merger wave to the question of understanding what had happened. I was particularly struck by the harsh test imposed by the change of events on the many theories that had so readily been used to predict the accelerating merger rate. By imperceptible stages, the short background paper became a long book, and research on a current problem became a retrospective analysis of an episode in economic history.

The title of this work may be misleading in one important sense. The research and focus were always on the question of the *conglomerate* merger, not all mergers. It was originally titled "Conglomerate Mergers: A Retrospective Analysis." Yet the framework for analysis and for policy seems so closely related to mergers more generally that it seems fitting to use the broader title *Mergers: Motives, Effects, Policies.*

My debts are many, and I should like to acknowledge the major ones. At the financial level, the work on this volume was generously supported by: The Brookings Institution under its program of Studies in the Regulation of Economic Activity, financed by a grant from the Ford Foundation; The University of Michigan Law School, with the aid of funds derived from gifts of William W. Cook to the University; the Horace H. Rackham School of Graduate Studies, through the Rackham Publication Fund. None of them, their officers, trustees, or other staff members, is in any way responsible for the views expressed here, except in having made their development and expression possible.

At different stages several research assistants contributed greatly to the enterprise. Alan Beckenstein, now teaching economics at the University of Virginia, served as a research assistant during the first year and a half of the project and contributed greatly to my digestion of a large economic and econometric literature. His influence is particularly great in chapters 4 and 8. At a later stage, Kenneth Mayfield spent many dreary hours collecting and analyzing data on prices, earnings, and assets of merger partners. Nelson Leavitt painstakingly checked the footnotes and bibliography.

Denis Binder, now teaching law at Ohio Northern University, was never a research assistant, but while a graduate student preparing an S.J.D. thesis here at Michigan, he introduced me to the complex world of security law and regulation, and his research on contested tender offers proved invaluable to my understanding of merger motivations. Chapters 5 and 7 owe much to him and the data he developed in the course of reading ten years of the *Wall Street Journal.*

Because this book strives to deal with the problem from a legal point of view as well as an economic one, I (who am not a lawyer) am particularly grateful to law students, law school colleagues, and practicing lawyers for educating me, and for helping me eliminate grievous gaffes in legal interpretation. Among my law colleagues, Professors Thomas Kauper, Charles Donahue, Jr., and Edward Cooper were particularly helpful. Richard Sayler, Robert Kheel, Dana Trier, and Darryl Snider each wrote seminar papers on some aspect of the conglomerate problem that furthered my thinking. Hammond Chaffetz, Reuben Hedlund, and William Jentes of Kirkland & Ellis all fostered my education. None of them should be assumed to share my conclusions.

After a first draft manuscript was completed, I benefited measurably, although hardly painlessly, from the searching critiques of a number of readers of the manuscript. Two of these remain anonymous but they will see how much I benefited from their comments. Professors Donald Turner of Harvard, Lee Preston of Buffalo, and Leonard Weiss of Wisconsin each read the whole manuscript and improved the final draft enormously by their comments. Edward Cooper's comments on the reciprocity chapter transformed it, and Dana Trier forced me into a major rethinking of my views on potential competition.

The almost endless typing, retyping, and manuscript management chores were handled efficiently and cheerfully by Nicole Wing and Gail Klein.

To all of the above I am indebted; they deserve much of the credit for whatever merit exists, and are responsible for none of the errors of omission or commission.

My greatest debt is to Patricia O. Steiner, the "p.o.s." to whom this book is dedicated. Her contribution began in 1968 with a remarkably insightful clipping of interesting items about conglomerates that appeared in the *New York Times,* and ended only with the preparation of the Index. Most importantly, she has sustained me in the project all those years in between.

PETER O. STEINER

Contents

CHAPTER ONE

Conglomerate Mergers and the Merger Wave of the 1960s

IT WAS once fashionable to seek biological analogies in discussing behavior of industrial firms.[1] Firms, some suggested, might fruitfully be viewed as having a life cycle of birth, growth, maturity, and death; the economic environment might be viewed as encouraging evolution by natural selection, and so on. In that tradition mergers might have been (but were not) analogized to marriages and variations in the merger rate analogized to the biological and cultural causes of marriages. I do not wish to revive that literature, only to toy with it for a moment.

The analogy of a merger to a marriage is superficially attractive. A merger is like a marriage in that it almost always takes at least two parties to agree. In perhaps the great majority of cases analyzing the motives of the two primary partners is all that is required, within the constraints (legal and other) imposed by the external world. But in some cases, views of other interested parties may prove decisive in either forcing a union, or preventing one. Marriages and mergers both may respond to a variety of individual motives and in aggregate be subject to cyclical and secular influences. In either case one may be interested in who the partners are and in what (if any) alternatives exist. Further, it is worth asking whether the institution itself warrants public support, control, or condemnation. And so on.

This analogy is, however, more than usually deceptive. One can argue that the biological and sociological incentives to marriage are well understood and widely accepted, that variations in the marriage rate occur gradually and are relatively easily linked to underlying causal factors. Moreover, any "externalities" of individual unions are likely to be widely diffused. None of this is true of mergers. Motives are multiple, complex, and much in controversy. The merger rate is potentially an explosive variable: The rate of asset acquisition, which had held steady at just over 1 percent per year from 1961 to 1966,

---

1. For a critical discussion see Edith Penrose, "Biological Analogies in the Theory of the Firm," *American Economic Review* 42, no. 5 (December 1952): 804–19.

doubled in 1967 and tripled in 1968.[2] This kind of change threatened a major transformation of the industrial landscape, and (arguably) of the nature and quality of the society itself.

The great merger wave of the late 1960s spawned several massive and diverse literatures: economic, theoretical, econometric, legal, and policy prescriptive. What was novel was not the mergers per se, but the sudden acceleration in the merger rate and the fact that so many of these mergers were "conglomerate" rather than the more readily understood horizontal or vertical acquisitions.

This monograph is, in the first instance, an attempt at review and evaluation of those literatures. The plural is stressed because their joint discussion is a principal aim of the study. The dominant conclusion of that review is that the whole is a good deal less than the sum of the parts. The state of our knowledge reveals the frontiers of our ignorance and a major objective of the monograph is to provide constructive suggestions for future research that *will* show promise of cumulatively reducing our ignorance.

Does it really matter very much? The merger explosion of 1965–68 proved a wave and receded as sharply as it rose. Its effects, as will be seen, hardly transformed the industrial landscape, and while its political and financial implications were not negligible, they too were minor rumbles rather than major quakes.

I believe that it *does* matter, and that a review of the phenomena and our failure to explain them is much more than a footnote to economic history. Mergers are transactions in the market for corporate control. If we come to understand them it has more general implications for and about the behavior, and control, of large corporate firms in an economy in which such firms are dominant elements. The merger wave of the 1960s provided a severe—often destructive—test of theories of economic cause and effect, and of legal theories of avenues for regulation and control.

The primary focus of this book is the conglomerate merger. It concerns what we know about the motivations that lead to such mergers and what accounts both for their relative rise in importance in the American economy and for the incredible conglomerate merger spurt in the late 1960s. It also concerns what effects they have had (or may have had) and the emergence of legal policies toward them. This

---

2. See table 1–2. The particular measure used is assets acquired as a percentage of assets held, all large manufacturing and mining corporations.

is also a book about mergers in general, and about the merger wave of the 1960s of which conglomerates were but a part.

It would be unwise to treat conglomerate mergers out of the context of all mergers, even if it were technically possible. A first reason is that the motives that impel firms (and men) are toward substantive things such as profits, or power, or capital gains, rather than toward forms of organization, such as conglomerate corporations. Such organizations, and the mergers that create them, are, and can only be understood as, means toward more proximate ends. The general motivational framework required to account for conglomerate mergers is necessarily the same as that required to deal with horizontal or vertical mergers, or indeed internal expansion of a firm, because these alternative forms of economic activity are part of a single choice set. Which elements of the set—which forms of activity—prove attractive at a given time depends upon the strength of the motivations, the ability of different forms to achieve desired ends, and the constraints imposed by law or by markets on the realization of the ends.

A second reason for dealing with conglomerate mergers in the context of all mergers is that in terms of economic effect, as well as of law, "all mergers must be tested by the same standard, whether they are classified as horizontal, vertical, conglomerate, or other."[3] It might, of course, be a valid *conclusion* that conglomerates are so different that they can be treated as a separate class either in law or in economics, but it cannot be an initial *assumption*. Third, the conglomerate may be defined as a more or less inclusive subset of all mergers, and the relevant definition varies from problem to problem.

The conglomerate problem is inextricably intertwined with the experience of the 1960s not because that was exclusively a conglomerate phenomenon (it was not) but because that period provides most of our experience with the conglomerate merger. The rapid rise and sudden fall of the conglomerate phenomenon over the decade of the sixties provide the variance required to formulate and test alternative explanations of the conglomerate movement. Helpfully much of the theorizing was done before the fall, and the data permit a stern test.

The plan of this study is as follows. Chapter 1 sets the stage by describing the merger movement of the 1960s and the place of conglomerates therein. The next six chapters are concerned with merger motivation. Chapter 2 provides an analytic framework for a multiple-

---

3. *FTC v. Procter & Gamble,* 386 U.S. 568 (1967) at 577.

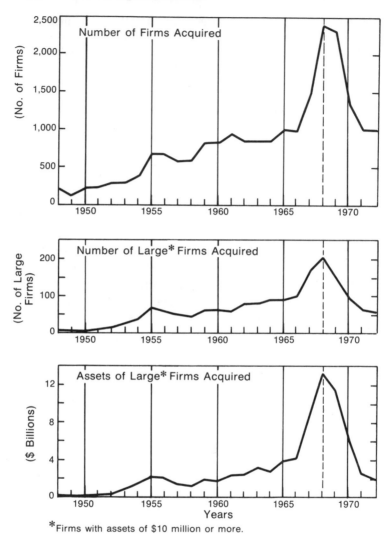

*Firms with assets of $10 million or more.

Source: Federal Trade Commission, Bureau of Economics, *Current Trends in Merger Activity, 1971,* Statistical Report No.10 (Washington, D.C., May 1972), p. 6, and *Report on Mergers and Acquisitions* (Washington, D.C., October 1973), p. 147.

Fig. 1–1.   Manufacturing and mining firms acquired 1948–72.

cause merger hypothesis. It treats the merger as a market transaction and asks what considerations may lead both sellers and buyers to want a merger. Each chapter from 3 through 7 looks with some care at the forces in the economy that conduced to—or inhibited—merger activity. Chapters 8 through 11 are concerned with effects, first in terms of a review of the econometric evidence, and second with an evaluation of the alleged economic and socio-economic effects that are shaping contemporary policy. While policy issues are discussed at many earlier stages, the concluding chapter 12 attempts to provide some premises to guide future policy discussions.

The Merger Wave of the 1960s

AN OVERVIEW

Figure 1–1 is the summary chart published by the Federal Trade Commission (FTC) to reflect current trends in merger activity. Even casual inspection of it shows a sharp, well-defined cycle that took off after 1965, crested in 1968, and has ended. Note at the outset that much of the interest in and attention to the merger wave of the 1960s arose during 1967 and 1968. From the vantage point of 1968, the phenomenon did look alarming, as can be seen by truncating figure 1–1 at the dashed line. Much of the attention was to explain the sudden acceleration in merger activity. The implicit questions were first how long could the economy stand an accelerating merger rate, and second what public policies could be used to reverse the new "trend" in acquisitions.

What might have been a trend proved to be a cycle. While the decline in merger activity has decreased some of the popular interest in the merger phenomenon, the problem is more interesting to study in 1972 than it was from the perspective of 1968 from the scientific point of view. One needs to explain the abrupt reversal in the merger rate as well as its sharp takeoff.

Figure 1–2 attempts to place the sixties into a broader historical perspective. Despite certain limitations in the data available for such long-term comparisons,[4] the merger wave of the late sixties appears

---

4. The source for this chart is Ralph L. Nelson, *Merger Movements in American Industry 1895–1956,* National Bureau of Economic Research, General Studies No. 66 (Princeton, 1959), table C–7, updated by FTC merger data presented in table 2–1. Two very different series have been

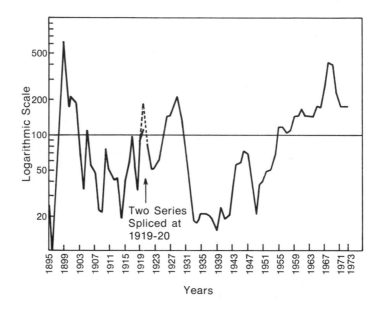

Sources: Nelson, *Merger Movements,* table C-7; FTC, *Current Trends,* 1971; FTC, *Report on Mergers and Acquisitions,* 1973.

Fig. 1–2.   Index of merger activity (indexes 1919–20 = 100) based on number of mergers 1895–1972.

(from the vantage point of 1974) to mark the capstone of the third great merger movement in American history, the first two covering the periods 1897–1901 and 1925–30. It is of course too early to tell whether the merger rate for the seventies will fall below the level of the sixties. There was a steady upward movement in merger activity from 1949 to 1959, and some commentators regard this as a merger wave of major proportions in and of itself. Whether the 1950s should properly be regarded as (*a*) a recovery from the abnormally low merger rate of the immediate postwar period, (*b*) the first stages in a merger wave that will ultimately be dated 1949–197?, or (*c*) the be-

---

spliced by me at 1919–20. Nelson discusses the limitations of these data in chapter 2 of his study and *he* does not splice them. The indexes (1919–20 = 100) are plotted on a log scale, to focus on percentage changes. Use of this chart to do more than form a general impression of the trends and cycles in merger activity is not necessarily warranted. *Caveat emptor.*

ginning of a long-term trend to increasing acquisitions will not be clear for a decade or more.

FURTHER DETAIL

The common pattern suggested in figure 1–1 is not a mere artifact of a particular merger series as figure 1–3[5] and table 1–1[6] make clear. Whether attention is directed to all mergers or to mining and manufacturing, to assets or to numbers, to the largest 200 firms, or to "large mergers," the same sharp, well-defined cycle is evident. As a general merger index for the subsequent comparisons I shall somewhat arbitrarily use asset values in large manufacturing and mining mergers— reflected in the heavier line of figure 1–3.[7]

Figure 1–4 compares this index of the merger rate to three widely used business indicators (again on a log scale). The *amplitude* of the

---

5. Figure 1–3 is plotted on a semi-log scale which gives equal percentage changes equal emphasis. It is the *slopes* of the curves, not their *level,* that is of interest in this figure.

6. In addition to the series presented in table 1–1, W. T. Grimm and Company publishes an annual merger survey that deals with a count of merger *proposals.* For a critique of this series see B. B. Carr and S. J. Browne, "Method vs. Myth in Measuring Merger Activity," *Mergers and Acquisitions, The Journal of Corporate Venture* 6, no. 3 (Fall 1971): 5–15. Notwithstanding all the biases in the Grimm series if used to measure actual acquisitions, it too shows a pattern broadly similar to that of other series.

7. The restriction of attention to mining and manufacturing is usually justified on the grounds that it avoids a major heterogeneity. Total assets are regarded as an adequate proxy for size of company within manufacturing and mining, services, banks, or insurance sectors, but not among them. As we shall note below the restriction to manufacturing and mining introduces some bias into certain merger statistics, but it does not appear to distort the basic outlines of the merger cycle. See the top two lines in figure 1–3. Mergers in manufacturing and mining appear to have peaked somewhat earlier than in the service and financial sectors. Many of the data available are further limited to the relatively small number of "large" mergers, defined to involve acquisition of a company with assets of $10 million or more. The top four lines in figure 1–3 reflect simple counts of number of firms acquired. Since less than 5 percent of all mergers by *number* were made by the 200 largest firms, and less than 10 percent of all acquisitions were large acquisitions, the similarity of these different indicators is striking.

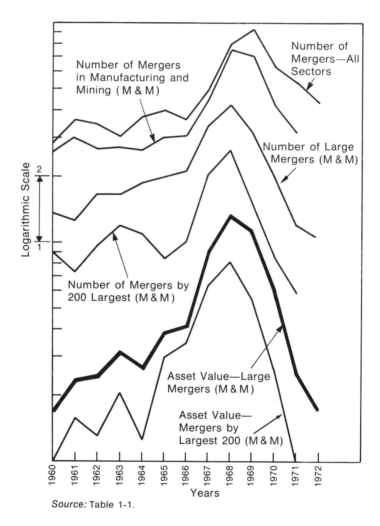

Source: Table 1-1.

Fig. 1–3.   Alternative merger indexes 1960–72.

changes in merger activity is very much greater than for the economy as a whole, or the stock market in particular. This was not a period of violent economic fluctuations which makes this violent merger movement the more atypical.

The merger wave of the sixties has sometimes been characterized as special in the size of the companies acquiring and being acquired.

TABLE 1–1

MERGER ACTIVITY 1960–72

		NUMBER OF ACQUISITIONS			VALUE OF ASSETS ACQUIRED (MILLIONS OF DOLLARS)	
Year	*Total Recorded*	*All Manufacturing and Mining (M & M)*	*Large* M & M Acquisitions*	*Large M & M Acquisitions by 200 Largest Firms†*	*Large* M & M Acquisitions*	*Large M & M Acquisitions by 200 Largest Firms†*
1960	1,345	844	64	32	1,729	1,013
1961	1,724	954	60	25	2,356	1,565
1962	1,667	853	80	33	2,448	1,301
1963	1,479	861	82	41	3,148	2,051
1964	1,797	854	91	38	2,728	1,248
1965	1,893	1,008	91	29	3,845	1,928
1966	1,746	995	101	35	4,171	2,468
1967	2,384	1,496	168	73	9,091	6,287
1968	3,932	2,407	207	94	13,297	8,209
1969	4,542	2,307	155	52	11,353	5,543
1970	3,089	1,351	98	30	6,346	2,672
1971	2,633	1,011	66	19	2,544	989
1972‡	2,113	1,036	56§	n.a.‖	1,749§	n.a.‖

SOURCE: Federal Trade Commission, Bureau of Economics, *Current Trends in Merger Activity, 1970 and 1971,* Statistical Report Numbers 8 (March 1971) and 10 (May 1972); FTC, *Report on Mergers and Acquisitions* (October 1973).

* Acquired firms with assets of $10 million or more.

† Ranked by 1970 total assets.

‡ Preliminary.

§ Excludes companies for which data not publicly available. The FTC is now revising all series to exclude such companies. The exclusion does not alter the trends.

‖ Not available.

Table 1–2 looks in three ways at the large acquisitions. While the large acquisitions were relatively few in number they accounted for a lot of assets. Although there are hundreds of thousands of manufacturing and mining companies, and only about 3,000 with assets of $10 million or more, these 3,000 large corporations accounted for roughly 86 percent of all assets of manufacturing and mining companies.

The first column shows that whereas in the first half of the decade, assets of acquired companies represented roughly 1 percent

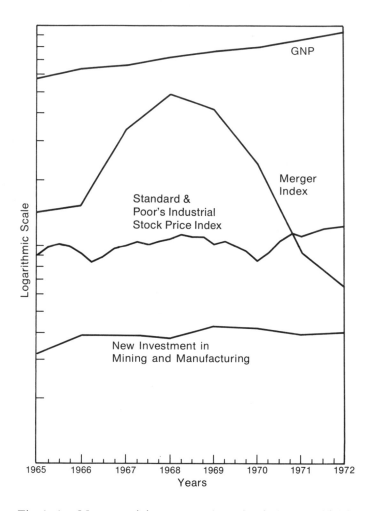

Fig. 1–4.   Merger activity compared to other indexes 1965–72.

of the assets outstanding each year, this rose to a peak of 3.33 percent in 1968. Over the three peak years of merger activity (1967–69) total acquired assets in large mergers were roughly 8 percent of the outstanding assets of 1968. Clearly large acquisitions were playing a more significant role in absolute amount. This was due (as column 2 shows) in part to the fact that the average size of the acquired firms (relative to all large firms) was larger during the merger boom than earlier—or later. (Of course, on the average, it was still smaller-than-average size firms that were acquired.) While these facts are indis-

TABLE 1–2

<small>LARGE MANUFACTURING AND MINING ACQUISITIONS AND LARGE M & M CORPORATIONS: THREE COMPARISONS</small>

Year	Assets Acquired as a Percentage of Assets Held (Percentage) (1)	Relative Size of Average Assets: Firms Acquired/ All Firms (Percentage) (2)	Assets Acquired as a Percentage of Total Increase in Assets Held* (Percentage) (3)
1961	1.06	37.0	15.6
1962	1.03	28.0	22.2
1963	1.26	34.6	20.4
1964	1.03	26.2	13.1
1965	1.35	35.6	11.1
1966	1.30	32.5	11.1
1967	2.54	40.3	21.9
1968	3.33	42.6	25.2
1969	2.51	45.4	21.5
1970	1.26	37.6	18.9
1971	0.47	21.2	6.1
1972†	0.36	16.0	n.a.‡

SOURCE: Computed from data in FTC, *Current Trends, 1971* (May 1972), table 7, except for 1972 data, which came from FTC, *Report on Mergers and Acquisitions* (October 1973).

* $\dfrac{\text{assets acquired in year t}}{\text{assets held in year t} + 1 - \text{assets held in year t}}$.

† Preliminary.

‡ Not available.

putable, they do *not* support a suggestion often drawn from them— that this period witnessed an ever-greater swallowing up of the assets of large companies by larger ones—for the stock of assets held by large companies was growing rapidly over the period. What then was the significance of the accelerating acquisitions?

Column 3 of table 1–2 compares assets acquired in large mergers to this growth. The total assets of large mining and manufacturing companies might grow in any or all of the following ways: (1) acquisition of companies with assets of less than $10 million; (2) acquisition of non-mining and manufacturing companies; (3) new investment by large companies; (4) growth of previously small companies to large status; (5) upward revaluations of assets held. Notice, however, that acquisition of large mining and manufacturing companies by other large companies would *not* increase the total. Thus, absent growth, the percentages shown in column 3 could approach infinity. Relative to growth, the acquisition of assets was not significantly greater during the peak of the merger boom than it had been in 1962 or 1963.

A significant feature of the merger boom was the rise in acquisitions of very large companies. The acquisition of companies with assets of over $100 million, which had averaged only 1.3 per year from 1948 to 1960, and 5 per year from 1961 to 1966, rose to 24 in 1967, 31 in 1968, 20 in 1969, 12 in 1970, before falling back to 5 each year in 1971 and 1972. Over the decade there were 117 acquisitions in the over $100 million class involving $31 billion in assets. Indeed 13 of these large acquirees had assets in excess of $500 million, and these 13 accounted for $11 billion in assets. Moreover, 12 of these very large acquisitions occurred from 1967 on. Therein lay the source of much concern. Clearly if the sudden pattern of large acquisitions that started in 1967 to 1969 presaged a long-lived trend, these concerns would be merited. This topic is subject to detailed attention in chapter 11 in the context of what is called "macro-concentration."

As to the average size of *acquiring* companies, the median size of acquiring companies has been between $29 and $41 million for every year since 1963, with no marked cycle during the merger boom. Figure 1–5 suggests that while there was a slight rise in the typical size of acquiring companies over the decade, the change was small—probably no larger than one would expect as a result of the inflation.

Nevertheless what gave the merger movement of the sixties its distinctive flavor were the repeated acquisitions by a small number of companies that were to become well known in the process. Table 1–3 reflects this phenomenon. The list is dominated by two groups: well-known conglomerates and the oil companies.[8]

What of the *relative* size of acquired and acquiring companies?[9] A detailed examination of the cross-tabulation of sizes of acquiring and acquired companies shows that there is a positive relationship

---

8. From the perspective of the next decade, it may well be that the significant aspects of the mergers of the sixties will prove to be the acquisitions by oil companies of other fuel producers—including importantly coal mining companies. This occurred dramatically while public attention focused on the conglomerates.

9. Mr. David W. Penn of the FTC staff has most kindly made available to me a cross-tabulation of size of acquirer and acquiree, by year,

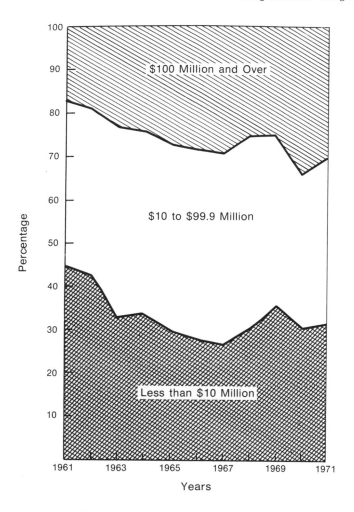

Source: Computed from FTC, *Currrent Trends,* 1971 (May 1972), table 4.

Fig. 1–5. Size distribution of acquiring company (asset size).

between sizes of acquirer and acquiree, that firms tend to acquire firms smaller than themselves, and that both acquirers and acquirees tended to be larger in the period 1966–69 than during the rest of the period 1948–71. All of this was known before. The basic finding is thus

from 1948 to 1971. This paragraph is based on that tabulation. Summary tables from that tabulation will be made available on request. The definition of acquirer and acquiree is, to a degree, arbitrary in some mergers. I have had no recourse but to accept the FTC classification in all cases.

TABLE 1-3

ASSETS ACQUIRED BY 25 MOST ACTIVE ACQUIRING COMPANIES
AMONG THE 200 LARGEST* MANUFACTURING CORPORATIONS 1961–68

Company	Number	Total Assets of Acquired Companies (Millions of Dollars)
	ACQUISITIONS 1961–68 INCLUSIVE†	
Gulf & Western Industries, Inc.	67	$2,882
Ling-Temco-Vought, Inc.	23	1,901
International Telephone & Telegraph Corp.	47	1,487
Tenneco, Inc.	31	1,196
Teledyne, Inc.	125	1,026
McDonnell Douglas Corp.	8	864
Union Oil Company of Cal.	11	825
Sun Oil Company	3	808
Signal Companies, Inc.	10	770
Occidental Petroleum Corp.	15	767
Continental Oil Co.	19	686
General Telephone & Electronics Corp.	40	679
U.S. Plywood-Champion Papers, Inc.	27	649
Litton Industries, Inc.	79	609
Atlantic Richfield Co.	9	543
North American Rockwell Corp.	6	534
FMC Corp.	13	497
Studebaker-Worthington, Inc.	13	480
General American Transportation Corp.	4	453
Textron, Inc.	50	453
White Consolidated Industries, Inc.	28	443
Phillips Petroleum Co.	11	440
Colt Industries, Inc.	9	437
Radio Corporation of America	2	402
Georgia-Pacific Corp.	45	396
Total 25 companies	695	$20,227

SOURCE: Federal Trade Commission, Bureau of Economics, *Economic Report on Corporate Mergers* (Washington, D.C., 1969), pp. 260–61.

* Ranks refer to the FTCs ranking of the 200 largest manufacturing companies by asset size.

† It should be emphasized that the data shown are compilations based on publicly announced acquisitions of United States and Canadian companies. Foreign acquisitions are not included and asset data are not available for many smaller acquired companies.

negative: no major structural changes in the relative sizes of merger partners occurred during the merger wave of the sixties.

Perhaps the most visible detail about the merger wave was the rising importance of conglomerate mergers. This merits a detailed look.

The Conglomerate Phenomenon

THE HISTORICAL NEGLECT OF THE PHENOMENON

The traditional way to define conglomeration is as a residual category; a "not elsewhere classified" ("n.e.c.") after all relatively sensible distinctions have been made. Thus, for example, conglomerate mergers are defined in the Department of Justice Guidelines as "mergers that are neither horizontal nor vertical as those terms are defined." While this is easy, it is not very helpful, for this kind of residual is too heterogeneous for analytic purposes.

The historical neglect of the conglomerate phenomenon and its relegation to an "n.e.c." category are understandable enough. In the first place (as we shall see) conglomeration was relatively unimportant before the 1960s. In the second place, the market and competitive impact of the sorts of unrelated activities that characterize the truly conglomerate merger has traditionally seemed relatively small compared to the horizontal or vertical acquisition and thus, until very recently, of not much interest in the context of antimonopolistic (or procompetitive) policy making. In the third place, a product-and-market oriented *theory* of corporate behavior found conglomeration an uncomfortable phenomenon to explain because of the absence of the compelling natural advantages that could be argued (at least ex post) to account for more conventional acquisitions. What is infrequent, benign, and hard to explain is easy to ignore.

The previous paragraph oversimplifies. Competitive harm was never the only strand in American concern with industrial structure. Populism and fear of size per se crop up periodically on the American scene. They were there in Berle and Means's classic of 1932[10] in the TNEC's concerns with power groups later in the decade, and they reappear in the legislative history of the 1950 Amendments to the

---

10. A. A. Berle and G. C. Means, *The Modern Corporation and Private Property* (New York, 1932).

Clayton Act, known as the Cellar-Kefauver Act. While these concerns that bloomed in the thirties tended to fade during the fifties, they were never far below the surface. Wright Patman and Hugo Black among others expressed the populist view regularly in Congress and on the Supreme Court. When, partly as a consequence of the Cellar-Kefauver Act (1950) and a series of Court decisions which increasingly limited horizontal or vertical acquisitions, the trend toward conglomerate acquisitions developed, this latent concern was newly aroused. What became visible was the rapid and dramatic change in size of some large firms, a change achieved by large acquisitions, many of which fell into the conglomerate category.

Interestingly, here unlike the horizontal area, a major distinction exists between the conglomerate firm (as an operating entity) and the merger that brings it about. A horizontal merger which leads to the elimination of a competitor, to an increase in the market share of the acquiring firm, and to an increase in the degree of concentration of the industry has been regarded as undesirable *because of* the large firm, and/or the more concentrated industry it brings about. A monopoly position (or an oligopolistic one) is the economic evil that is feared.[11] Economists, at least, have not cared very much whether substantial market power was largely achieved by maintaining a dominant position from the start as with ALCOA, by internal growth and the gradual withering away of competitors as in the case of GM, or whether the dominant market position was achieved primarily by merger as in the cases of U.S. Steel and of Peabody Coal Company. Most economists regard means as incidental, and focus on market structure, however achieved.

In contrast, even today the large diversified conglomerate company is not much criticized—unless the method of its creation was that of acquisition. Indeed contemporary policy regards the alternative to acquisition by merger open to the conglomerate firm as the *de novo* or toehold entry into precisely the same industries it has entered by merger. Thus it is the merger—the means—not the diversified corporation—the end—that is regarded with suspicion.

---

11. While the legal bases for attacking the horizontal merger are different from those for attacking the comparable market positions achieved by internal expansion, or by predatory tactics, the underlying problem is the same.

Part of the reason is that the sort of populist concern I have referred to seems to be triggered by *changes in* rather than *levels of* asset concentration, and it is mergers that bring dramatic changes. Another part is that diversification is not generally regarded as undesirable, and the conglomerate corporation is certainly diversified. But while diversification may be justified, even applauded, it has often been argued that legitimate diversification objectives can almost always be achieved by other means, and thus it is only illegitimate motivations that are likely to be discouraged by attacking the conglomerate acquisition as a means of diversification.

PROBLEMS IN DEFINITION:
CONGLOMERATION VERSUS DIVERSIFICATION

As attention turned to the conglomerate merger, and a desire to understand it and control it, definition became more important.

It is clear that a conglomerate firm is *not* one which specializes exclusively or primarily in the production of a single final product for distribution in a single market. But that does not take us very far. Is the single product, multimarket cement firm a conglomerate firm? Is the multiproduct single major industry firm (e.g., General Foods, any large chemical company, Procter & Gamble) a conglomerate firm? Is every multimarket, multiproduct, multiindustry firm (e.g., General Motors) a conglomerate firm?

Clearly conglomeration means something different from diversification. While many of the nation's largest firms are diversified, for some the diversification is largely intraindustry, or intratechnology, or incidental. For others the diversification is dominant and the nature of their particular product-mix seems potentially elusive.

Using product-mix to define the conglomerate category might be sensible from either of two points of view: first, identifying a set of firms that are in close and recognized competition with one another; second, predicting probable kinds of acquisitions.

Many diversified firms have the great bulk of their activities devoted to products that fall into few industries, among which the technology is relatively constant. Others utilize the common techniques involved in efficient distribution to find areas for diversification in which they possess some sort of natural advantage. *In any of these cases, what is true for one firm is often true for many, and many*

*diversified firms have well-defined and similarly diversified compet-
itors.* I do not regard General Motors as a conglomerate firm notwithstanding its ownership of some subsidiaries that are significantly
removed from the manufacture, distribution, sale, and financing of
automotive products. Its primary impact on the economy is in a limited
set of industries and its competitors are well defined. The same is true,
though perhaps in a different degree, of General Foods and Monsanto.
In contrast are firms such as Textron, General Dynamics, LTV, ITT,
Northwest Industries, Gulf and Western, and Litton Industries. None
of these faces a relatively well-defined technology, an easily identified
set of major competitors, or a by-and-large stable place in a well-
defined industry group. If they are in competition with one another it
is in an elusive "market for corporate acquisitions." Thus a distinction
seems useful.

From the viewpoint of predictability, soup, catsup, and corn-
flakes are perhaps less baffling to account for under one corporate roof
than are fire sprinklers, rental cars, a baking company, and a manufacturer of telephone switching equipment. One might attempt to
define a conglomerate firm in terms of the absence of a well-defined
interconnection among the products or services it provides that could
be used to predict which products it might add to its line. For General
Motors (supposing it was seeking new firms to acquire and had no
legal impediment in its way) I believe one would have little difficulty
distinguishing a set of plausible acquirees (e.g., a parts manufacturer, a
trailer company, an auto leasing service, etc.) from a set of improbable
acquirees (e.g., a coal mine, a pipeline, or a chain of French restaurants).

For the conglomerate firm, in contrast, there seems no natural
ambit. It would seem farfetched for GM but not ITT to have acquired
(all of) a chain of restaurants, a consumer credit agency, a manufacturer of pumps, a hotel firm, an airport parking company, and a
builder of homes.[12]

Conversely, what acquisition might appear plausible for GM but
farfetched in terms of product characteristics for ITT? I think of none!
Extreme cases are often easier than intermediate cases. If General
Foods was unlikely to acquire Firestone, was it likely or unlikely to
acquire Clorox, Gillette, or SOS?[13]

---

12. All of these are or were ITT subsidiaries.
13. It acquired only the last listed.

But if this kind of guidance is not simple, it is roughly helpful in many cases. Thus, looking at its product-mix gave no clue that ITT would acquire Canteen rather than to seek to purchase Braniff Airlines or Neiman-Marcus—each recent acquirees of someone. In contrast, once the department store chain of Broadway-Hale began acquiring independent specialty and department stores, it might well have been predicted to attempt the acquisition of Neiman-Marcus and/or Bergdorf Goodman. ITT is easily classified as a conglomerate and distinguished from Broadway-Hale, using this criterion.

Implicit in the product line characterization is the assumption that there is a distinguishable rationale when similar products are involved. This seems justified. Product similarity, which may lead to economies of scale in production, distribution, or marketing, is useful in predicting "nonconglomerate" acquisitions. Of course there may be equally good predictors of conglomerate acquisitions, such as the search for economies in the use of capital or of management. ITT, predictably, sought firms to acquire with a high service component in their outputs, whose demand would grow secularly with population, with high cash flow, and/or relatively old-fashioned managements. It is the likelihood of finding a difference in predictors that justifies distinguishing conglomerates from other acquisitions. Of course, once on this route, it may quickly develop that a much more complex set of categories is required because conglomerates themselves prove to be a heterogeneous class. Definitions are meant to be useful, rather than to be aspects of revealed truth, and some distinction among firms according to the nature of their products is useful. For the range of phenomena I want to consider it does not seem to me that General Motors, General Foods, or General Chemical are conglomerate firms in the same sense as are ITT or Textron. A definition of "conglomerates" is thus a useful step—albeit only a first step—in understanding both behavior and effect.

A PRAGMATIC DEFINITION

Data compilations for the last two decades (limited to large mergers in mining and manufacturing) utilize the following five-way subdivision of mergers:

1. Horizontal mergers
2. Vertical mergers

3. Product extension mergers
4. Market extension mergers
5. Pure conglomerate mergers

While FTC practice is to regard categories 3, 4, and 5 as all subparts of "conglomerate" mergers, a careful review of the actual mergers and the way they are classified[14] suggests that for our purposes this is less appropriate than a different aggregation. Market extension mergers are not the same as horizontal mergers, but such mergers are surely more nearly horizontal than conglomerate in terms of product classification and the predictability of acquisition. A great many of them took place in four industries: dairies, beer, cement, and oil. The motivations behind them seem very similar to those in many horizontal mergers. Because the probable results of these mergers seemed likely to affect competition in the industries involved in much the same way as horizontal mergers, the Justice Department and the Supreme Court have been steadily eroding the distinction for antitrust purposes between market extension mergers and horizontal mergers in the period since 1965 (see chap. 7). In any event for the focus of this study, the mergers between (to list a few haphazardly) Ideal Cement and Pacific Portland Cement, Purity Bakeries and American Bakeries, Schlitz and Burgermeister Breweries, Standard Oil of California and Standard Oil of Kentucky, Atlantic Oil and Richfield Oil, Phillips and Tidewater Oil Companies, or Olivetti and Underwood, seem worth excluding from the conglomerate category. Each of these was classified as a market extension conglomerate by the FTC.

Product extension mergers (category 3) are more troublesome. Some—like American Metal Climax's acquisition of Apex Smelting Company, Honeywell's acquisition of Computer Control, Stauffer Chemical's acquisition of Cowles Chemical, or Emerson Electric's acquisition of Fisher Radio Corporation—seem to have a product, marketing, or technological logic that makes them more nearly vertical or horizontal than conglomerate. Yet many other category 3 acquisitions—such as ITT's acquisition of Grinnell—are clearly con-

---

14. The Bureau of Economics of the Federal Trade Commission, in *Large Mergers in Manufacturing and Mining 1948–71,* Statistical Report No. 9 (May 1972), gives a complete listing of all large mergers for which public data is available. In a typical year such mergers constitute over 80 percent of all large mergers by number, and over 90 percent by total assets.

glomerate in spirit. Indeed, for my purposes one of the defects in the classification procedure used by the FTC is that too little attention was paid to the identity of the acquirer. ITT over the period since 1965 has been above all else a conglomerate firm. Yet only six of the eleven ITT acquisitions listed in the FTC sample are treated as pure conglomerates. Four of them are "product extension" and the remaining one, vertical. Similarly between 1968 and 1970 Litton had seven product extension acquisitions and Textron three in the FTC sample—yet each of these acquirers seem to be clearly conglomerates in the meaning usually assigned to that term.

Rather than attempt my own reclassification of particular mergers, it seems desirable to stay with the FTC-defined subclasses. Perhaps the best single index of conglomerate activity for my purposes includes both product extension and pure conglomerate mergers but excludes market extension mergers.[15]

If one regards conglomerate mergers as being ones that do not have a primary direct impact on competition within an economic market—one common use of the conglomerate category—the definition above overstates the size of the conglomerate category by including as conglomerate some product extension mergers of products in competition with one another. It understates it by excluding some market extension mergers that perhaps have no competitive consequences. I suspect the first bias is larger than the second.

This net probable upward bias may be offset in part or in whole by another one. The FTC's limitation of its major statistical compilations to manufacturing and mining mergers—while understandable in terms of data comparability, probably results in an underestimate of the conglomerate portion of the merger movement. This results from the particular importance of financial and service companies as acquirees by the leading conglomerate acquirers. This bias is nicely illustrated by the fact that ITT's acquisitions of Canteen Corporation and Hartford Insurance, two of the three ITT acquisitions that were regarded by the Justice Department as key test cases of its ability to deal with the conglomerate phenomenon under existing law, are not in the FTC large merger series. During the period 1961–68 ITT acquired 47 companies with assets of nearly $1.5 billion, only 10 of these, with less than half the total assets, were included in

---

15. We are not of course required to use but a single index, and I shall be concerned with certain market extension mergers at a later point.

the FTC sample. Some of these exclusions were due to acquirees being small, but many were due to the limitation to manufacturing and mining. When a manufacturing or mining company acquires vertically or horizontally it is almost always acquiring a manufacturing or mining company. When a manufacturing or mining company makes a conglomerate acquisition the acquiree may or may not be in the manufacturing and mining category, and this is particularly true of the pure conglomerate acquisition. Thus a disproportionate number of excluded mergers will tend to be conglomerate. Since, as we shall see, there *are* special incentives for conglomerate companies to acquire both service-oriented companies and insurance companies, this potential bias is likely to be real.

THE TENDENCY FOR CONGLOMERATE ACQUISITIONS

The long-term trend.   Table 1–4 presents such data as are available about the distribution of assets acquired in large mergers by type over the period since 1948. The solid lines in figure 1–6 show how the

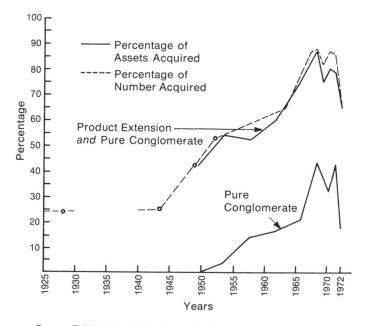

Source: Table 1-4 and FTC, *Economic Report on Corporate Mergers*, p. 63.

Fig. 1–6. Large conglomerate mergers as a percentage of all large mergers.

importance of conglomerate mergers has increased since 1950; a date whose significance lies in the passage of the Cellar-Kefauver Amendments to the Clayton Act, which put real teeth into the antimerger provisions of Section 7 of that Act. Fragmentary data on *numbers* of mergers by type go back to the period 1926–30[16] and cover the period 1940–47[17] as well. These data are shown by the dashed line in figure 1–6. Evidently "numbers" and "assets" reflect the same phenomenon. The fact that the levels of the two lines are so similar suggests that the size of conglomerate acquisitions is roughly the same as the size of other acquisitions. The emergence of the pure conglomerate acquisition seems to be a post-1950 phenomenon, although detail is not available in the earlier data.

Unmistakably the conglomerate trend was upward during the 1960s for reasons that occupy us at length subsequently. This trend was clearly evident before the onset of the merger wave, and was little affected by it. Superimposed on this trend was a wave in conglomerateness as well as in merger activity.

The cyclical evidence. Figure 1–7 suggests at a glance that while the merger wave of the late 1960s was more a conglomerate phenomenon than a nonconglomerate one, it was not exclusively conglomerate. Nonconglomerate as well as conglomerate acquisitions were above the 1960–65 base level from 1966 to 1970, and rose to a peak in 1968 that was well above the earlier levels. For the period 1960–65 nearly 40 percent of all assets acquired were in horizontal, vertical, or market extension mergers.

Figure 1–8 provides a bit more detail. The absolute data on numbers and amount of assets involved in these mergers are given in table 1–5, which should be looked at along with the indexes portrayed in the figure.[18] Each of the four merger types portrayed in figure 1–8 exhibited roughly the same cyclical pattern, although at the end of the period only the pure conglomerate category was significantly above the level at which it started. (By 1972 even the pure conglomerates were back to pre-1965 levels.) The differences in *level* seem to me

---

16. The basic work is the dissertation of Carl Eis, "The 1919–1930 Merger Movement in American Industry," (Ph.D. diss., CUNY, 1968).

17. Federal Trade Commission, Bureau of Economics, *Report of the FTC on the Merger Movement: A Summary Report* (Washington, D.C., 1948).

18. Combining horizontal and market extension mergers is necessary because of the small number of the latter.

TABLE 1-4

DISTRIBUTION OF ASSETS ACQUIRED IN LARGE MERGERS BY TYPE AND PERIOD
(PERCENTAGES)

	1948–51	1952–55	1956–59	1960–63	1964–67	1968	1969	1970	1971*	1972†
Horizontal	38.8	36.6	27.3	13.3	11.4	4.2	19.4	15.2	20.4	30.0
Market extension	—	2.7	5.0	8.0	8.7	5.9	3.1	4.2	2.2	0.0
Vertical	23.8	11.5	20.1	23.8	8.9	7.2	7.7	4.5	3.2	7.6
Subtotal	62.6	50.8	52.4	45.1	29.0	17.3	30.2	23.9	25.8	37.6
Product extension	37.5	45.7	33.5	37.8	49.9	39.0	31.7	43.6	30.8	44.5
Pure conglomerate	—	3.6	14.2	17.1	21.2	43.6	38.1	32.5	43.4	17.9
Subtotal	37.5	49.3	47.7	54.9	71.1	82.6	69.8	76.1	74.2	62.4
Total‡	100.0	100.0	100.0	100.0	100.0	100.0	100.0	100.0	100.0	100.0

SOURCES: FTC, *Economic Report on Corporate Mergers*, p. 673; FTC, *Current Trends, 1970*, table 12; FTC, *Current Trends, 1971*, table 11; FTC, *Report on Mergers and Acquisitions*, table 14.

* Preliminary.
† Excludes companies for which data not publicly available. The FTC is now revising all series to exclude such companies. The exclusion does not alter the trends.
‡ Details do not always add to totals due to rounding.

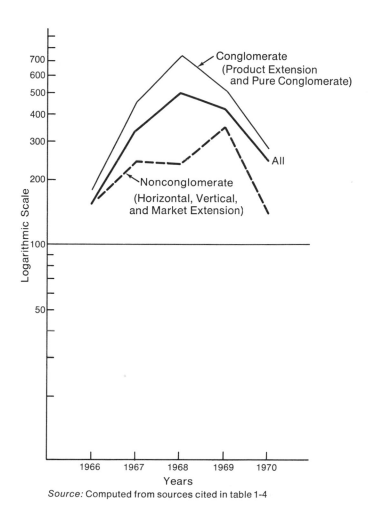

Fig. 1–7.   Conglomerates versus nonconglomerates (indexes 1960–65 = 100) 1966–70.

almost wholly explained by the antitrust climate. Large vertical mergers had become very vulnerable by the late sixties. The same was true for horizontal and market extension mergers in general, but the willingness of the Justice Department to permit major mergers among leading oil companies was an important exception. Thus the only large mergers that were not relatively sure to invite Justice De-

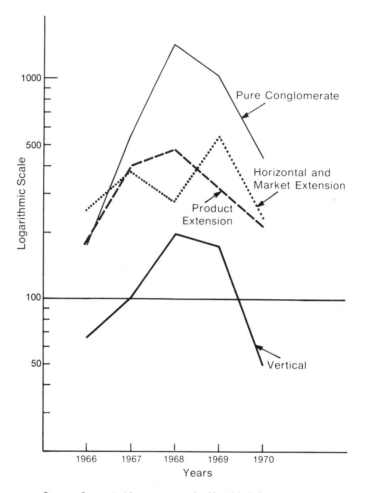

Source: Computed from sources cited in table 1-4.

Fig. 1–8.   Merger activity by type (indexes 1960–65 = 100) 1966–70.

partment response were in the conglomerate categories—and the purer the better.[19]

___

19. These matters are discussed in chapter 7. In brief, some product extension mergers were arguably horizontal for antitrust purposes after the decisions in Continental Can and ALCOA (Rome Cable), see p. 155. Thus more helpful (to the plaintiff) market definition tended to apply the stricter standards of horizontal acquisitions to what in an earlier period might have been regarded as conglomerate acquisitions.

TABLE 1-5

ACQUISITIONS OF LARGE MINING AND MANUFACTURING FIRMS, BY TYPE OF ACQUISITION 1966–70

(ASSET ACQUISITIONS IN MILLIONS OF DOLLARS)

Type of Acquisition	1966		1967		1968		1969		1970	
	No.	$	No.	$	No.	$	No.	$	No.	$
Horizontal	11	301	11	1,096	14	525	14	2,140	6	828
Market extension	2	872	1	706	1	749	6	340	7	229
Vertical	11	328	17	501	19	979	15	851	3	244
Product extension	52	1,960	99	4,424	122	5,145	67	3,497	38	2,374
Pure conglomerate	22	692	39	2,363	50	5,912	50	4,209	34	1,772

SOURCE: FTC, *Current Trends, 1970*, table 12.

We noted earlier (see page 12) that a few giant mergers played a highly important role in the merger wave of the late 1960s. Table 1–6 lists the thirteen largest acquisitions of the decade, each of which involved acquisition of assets in excess of $500 million. The list consists roughly half of horizontal or market extension mergers—mostly oil companies—and half of the new-style conglomerates.[20]

TABLE 1–6

VERY LARGE ACQUISITIONS* IN MANUFACTURING AND MINING 1961–70

Year	Acquirer	Acquiree	Assets of Acquiree (Millions of Dollars)
1965	Union Oil-California	Pure Oil Co.	766
1967	McDonnell Co.	Douglas Aircraft	850
1967	Tenneco	Kern County Land	706
1968	Ling-Temco-Vought	Jones and Laughlin	1,093
1968	Glen Alden†	Schenley Industries	571
1968	Sun Oil Co.	Sunray DX Oil	749
1969	General Host	Armour‡	560
1969	Rapid American	Glen Alden†	1,252
1969	Atlantic Richfield	Sinclair Oil	1,851
1969	Lykes Corp.	Youngstown Sheet and Tube	1,027
1970	Greyhound Corp.	Armour‡	607
1970	Standard Oil-Ohio	British Petroleum	627
1970	Honeywell, Inc.	General Electric Computer	548

SOURCE: FTC, *Current Trends, 1971,* table 8.

* $500 million or more in acquired assets.
† Note double counting.
‡ Note double acquisition.

Conclusion

This descriptive review is designed to define the phenomena so widely but often so loosely discussed. In particular it is clear that the so-called merger movement of the late 1960s was a well-defined *cycle*

---

20. In at least two of the horizontal mergers involving Douglas Aircraft and General Electric Computer, the acquired companies were clearly in sufficient financial trouble that their exit from the industry was imminent in any case.

of extraordinary amplitude rather than an upward turn in a secular trend or a sudden upward shift in the long run propensity to merge. Second, the merger wave was significantly but not exclusively a conglomerate one, when that term is used to include "pure conglomerate" and "product extension" acquisitions.

Because the sharp upturn in merger activity in the period 1966–68 was followed by an equally sharp downturn, this period of time provides a laboratory for testing alternative theories of variations in merger activity. A number of forecasting theories that predicted well the upturn in the merger rate failed the sterner test of predicting the subsequent downturn. The empirical evidence will be reviewed in chapter 8. First we shall examine the theory of merger motivation.

CHAPTER TWO

Motives for Mergers:
An Analytic Framework

THIS CHAPTER attempts to provide a coherent theoretical framework for what follows. The basic theoretical strategy is to examine the
decisions of interested parties as to a merger of companies whose
decisions they control, and whose performance affects their economic
well-being.

While our major concern is with mergers in the aggregate, there
are compelling reasons for looking at individual merger motivations.
Even if it were possible accurately to predict aggregate merger rates
using only aggregate predictors (such as the level of GNP or the Dow-
Jones index), it would be desirable to understand individual merger
motivations for what they suggest about the probable effects of particular mergers, and for discriminating among mergers in the design
of public policies. Moreover, aggregate prediction has not proven
notably successful, as we shall see subsequently. A framework suitable
to understanding a particular merger will also be useful in understanding trends or cycles in mergers aggregatively if the forces that impel
particular mergers apply concurrently to a large number of decision
makers in similar situations.

The starting point for this theoretical analysis is to treat the
merger as a market transaction in the market for corporate control.
There is assumed to be a buyer and a seller, and the merger is assumed to occur when the benefits to each of the parties making the
decisions are sufficiently large to outweigh the costs, deterrents, and
inertia that may exist. Even this simple framework becomes complex
because there may be many parties with an interest in and ability
to affect the decision to consummate a particular merger. Where there
are many parties at interest there may be many motivating forces,
and indeed the diffuse literature concerning the recent merger wave
has been replete with suggestions about what it is that leads to mergers.
Each of the following motives has been adduced to explain particular
mergers:[1]

    1. A desire to limit competition or achieve monopoly profits.
    2. A desire to utilize unutilized market power.

---

1. Ansoff, Brandenburg, Portner, and Radosevich, *Acquisition Be-*

3. A response to shrinking opportunities for growth and/or profit in one's own industry due to shrinking demand or excessive competition.
4. A desire to diversify to reduce the risks of business.
5. A desire to achieve a large enough size to realize an economical scale of production and/or distribution.
6. A desire to overcome critical lacks in one's own company by acquiring the necessary complementary resources, patents, or factors of production.
7. A desire to achieve sufficient size to have efficient access to capital markets or inexpensive advertising.
8. A desire to utilize more fully particular resources or personnel controlled by the firm, with particular applicability to managerial skills.
9. A desire to displace an existing management.
10. A desire to utilize tax loopholes not available without merging.
11. A desire to reap the promotional or speculative gains attendant upon new security issues, or changed price earnings ratios.
12. A desire of managers to create an image of themselves as aggressive managers who recognize a good thing when they see it.
13. A desire of managers to manage an ever-growing set of subordinates.

While none of these is inherently absurd and each has surely played some role in some mergers, such a catalog of possible reasons does not help very much. It helps some to classify these into broader categories, such as anticompetitive considerations, search for efficiencies, search for speculative gains, and satisfaction of managerial objectives. But because there are many possible motives, we need more than a classification of them—we need a determination of which motives are decisive in accounting for levels of merger activity, and for changes therein. Let me note at the outset that we do not now have (and I do not end up providing) such a determination. This is the frontier of our ignorance; it is my hope to contribute to piercing it, by identifying a framework for analysis and a strategy for research.

---

havior of U.S. Manufacturing Firms, 1946–1965 (Nashville, Tenn., 1971), report a questionnaire survey of 93 acquirers with substantial support to a dozen or more different motivations. See their table 3–1.

The Nature of the Model

I make the usual economic assumption that men do what promises to advance their own best interests. Initially I assume that the relevant decision makers are the stockholders of the buying and selling companies and that a well-defined notion of profitability can be employed. Subsequently I expand the groups of relevant decision makers and admit the possibility that more complex measures of well-being may be required.

In its simplest form the model defines the conditions that must be met to motivate sellers to sell and buyers to buy. If, but only if, both sets of conditions are met, it is assumed that there exists a mechanism that will effectuate the merger. There are many possible influences that might affect the probability of a particular merger. A theoretical framework should be broad enough to encompass them all; later empirical work may determine that only a subset of them are important enough to worry about.

There is an important issue of point of view that lurks beneath the apparently uncontroversial previous paragraph. One might believe that, while this is indeed a complex world, insight will consist in identifying the one (or few) most important motives for merger, on the assumption that such a dominant cause exists and is likely to apply in a great variety of different circumstances. Theoretically this would imply arguing about which of a set of possible influences is most probable. Empirically it would imply seeking the best predictor on a sample of data and supposing that what is best on the data studied is likely to be the best in other situations as well.

An alternative point of view is that the dominant causes change in a systematic way in response to external changes and that only a multiple-cause framework can capture the diversity of probable outcomes. In this viewpoint one would seek to explain the changing role of different forces, and empirically to wonder what attributes of a particular data set led one predictor to appear dominant. Theoretically here I shall start with the second (multiple-cause) point of view because it embraces the other as a special case. Starting so permits retreat to the other (principal-cause) viewpoint if the evidence warrants, but does not prejudge a central issue.[2]

---

2. Obviously a fully developed understanding of the problem would discriminate between these points of view. Moreover with adequate data one could test these competing hypotheses. Neither our data nor our theory are yet adequate.

One other feature of the model to be developed warrants preliminary comment. It is multiplicative rather than additive in the explanatory variables. The significance of this is that in a multiplicative model even an explanatory variable that is usually of little significance can become decisive if its value approaches zero in some period. Similarly a high product may result as easily from moderately high values of all variables as from very high values of a "key" variable. In a multiplicative model the relative roles of particular variables can readily change as external circumstances change.[3] A multiplicative model is quite compatible with the multiple-cause viewpoint discussed above.[4]

Mergers without Conflicts of Interest: A Formal Analysis[5]

I assume for the present case that the economic interest of a company can be taken to be the economic interest of its stockholders, and that a merger succeeds if, but only if, it is financially attractive to both companies involved. Important questions concern who are the decision makers, for stockholders and managers may have different stakes in the decision, as may different subgroups of either of them. For the

---

3. Either kind of model can be estimated via linear repression of course. If $y = x_1{}^\alpha x_2{}^\beta$, then $\log y = \alpha \log x_1 + \beta \log x_2$. If $y = \alpha x_1 + \beta x_2$ it is directly linear. But knowing which form to estimate is a matter of some importance.

4. Lee E. Preston in "A Probabilistic Approach to Conglomerate Mergers," Conglomerate Mergers and Acquisitions: Opinion and Analysis, 44 ST. JOHN'S LAW REVIEW, Special Edition, 341–55 (Spring 1970), develops a multiplicative model that is similar in form to mine, but is wholly different in spirit. In essence, his model is that even if the probability is high that a particular effect of a conglomerate acquisition will be benign, since there are many markets the chance that it will be benign in all is very small. E.g., suppose the probability of a benign effect in each market is 0.9, but the conglomerate operates in 20 markets and the effect in one market is independent of effects in other markets. Then, since $(0.9)^{20} = 0.12$ there is thus a 0.88 chance than an adverse effect will occur in at least one market. Preston's is a normative attempt to predict "purity," mine is a positive attempt to predict market behavior.

5. Although what follows is not mathematical, it does utilize symbolic notation, and in so doing it becomes technical in ways that some readers will be unable or unwilling to follow. I attempt in the summary of this chapter to state heuristically the important conclusions of the analysis. A reader who is prepared to take these on faith can omit the intervening discussion. I am indebted to Professor John Cross for suggestions which greatly improved my articulation of the model.

moment we neglect such considerations and suppose the owners of the selling (or "target") company are a homogeneous group who have the full power of decision making, and that a similar cohesiveness is present for the buying (or "bidding") company. Conflicts of interest are introduced below.

ASSUMED NATURE OF A MERGER

Visualize a stock acquisition merger which takes place when and if a buying or bidding company, Company B, acquires a controlling share of the stock in a selling or target company, Company S. I assume the form of the merger is to create a combined company, Company C, in which shares in Company C are given to stockholders of Company B on a one-for-one basis, and to stockholders of Company S on an agreed basis that takes the form of a tender offer made and accepted. Such exchanges of stock are assumed for now to be tax exempt. The merger attempt will be said to succeed if Company B acquires the requisite number of shares to control Company S (which I suppose to be a known number of shares) and fails if it does not. If it fails, shares of Company S that have been acquired are disposed of, at a loss to Company B equal to whatever premium was paid to acquire them.

For simplicity assume the whole scenario occurs at a moment of time, and that all values are appropriate present values at the time of merger. This assumption does not neglect future income streams and expectations, but does neglect the fact that tender offers and counter-offers often take a long time to succeed or fail. Further assume the tender offer is not anticipated in advance of its being made, and thus the market prices at the moment preceding the merger reflect the market evaluation of the companies' prospects independent of the particular tender offer.

Suppose just before the tender offer is made, that there are n_S shares of Company S outstanding whose market price is p_S per share, and that n_B and p_B are the number of shares and price per share of Company B. A rough guide to the market value (and also the asset size) of the two companies may be taken to be the aggregate dollar amounts $n_S p_S$ and $n_B p_B$, respectively.

Since the units in which shares are created are essentially arbitrary, I shall with no loss of generality, and with substantial convenience, normalize by assuming that $p_B = p_S = 1$, at the moment of merger. Under this normalization the magnitudes of n_S and n_B are indexes to the size of the two companies.

MARKET PRICE, MARKET VALUE, AND BLOCK VALUES

The prices used above (and then suppressed) are market prices and
reflect the *marginal* conditions of demand and supply in securities
markets at the moment of merger. Tender offers concern large blocks
of stocks and thus we have to be concerned with valuations of such
blocks by different groups. Suppose I own a controlling block of n
shares in Company S, whose price is p_S. I may quite rationally value
my holding at more, or less, than np_S. I will value it at more if I (or
others) consider control worth something. Indeed, if someone attempted to buy stock on the open market in an attempt to wrest
control from me, I would expect his bidding to drive the price up well
above p_S. At the same time, I might have no interest in adding to my
holdings at the market price. Stock market valuations are marginal
valuations, and it is important for what follows to recognize that block
valuations are appropriate *average* valuations, which may differ from
the marginal valuations reflected by market prices.

Unless the market is in sharp disequilibrium, most holders of a
given security will value their holdings at *or above* the market price.[6]

In general, we may denote the value placed by the ith group on
the ownership of n shares of the jth company (at time t) as

$$(1) \qquad V_{ijt} = a_{ijt}n_{jt}p_{jt}$$

and I will follow this practice except that I shall drop the time sub-
script in my instantaneous model.

The multiplier a_{ij} is positive, and is greater or less than unity
accordingly as the ith group values the block of stock at an average
value that is greater or less than the market price. The size of a_{ij} is
itself a function of the size of n_j, among other things. For a very small
holding we would expect it to be in the neighborhood of unity; for
a controlling block it might be well above unity.[7]

---

6. This is not a logically deducible proposition. I may indeed value
my n shares below the market price, but realize that (if my holding is
large) any attempt to sell the stock would seriously depress the price. In
such circumstances, I would be willing to accept a private offer for all
n shares at less than the market price. Similarly, the brokerage costs or
the tax disadvantages of selling one stock and buying another may be
consistent with continuing to hold shares which I value below their market
value.

7. The exceptions noted in footnote 6 apply to this generalization too.

The use of market prices of stocks instead of another measure of value, such as the present value of the company's expected earnings, is designed to retain flexibility. Stock market values are, of course, influenced by company's earnings, and expectations about those earnings, but few would suggest that they are influenced only by these things. Since I wish to incorporate purely speculative motivations for mergers as well as expected earnings, it proves convenient to use stock prices. The a_{ij} multipliers allow for any group incorporating other than market prices in their consideration. The determinants of a_{ij} prove to be complex and important. My purpose in explicitly introducing this term is to avoid the error of assuming it to be unity.

Valuations of the merger target.   Suppose, realistically, that the stock in the target company is valued differently by different people. It is of course always discrepant valuations that lead to mutually satisfactory exchanges. Imagine two frequency distributions of such valuations, one reflecting the present holders of the stock, the other the general stock-buying public. Two illustrative distributions are sketched in figure 2–1. One could derive demand and supply curves for marginal shares of stock from these distributions and I assume that they would indicate p_t as the equilibrium price.

Assume that the right-hand frequency distribution shown represents the controlling block of stock in Company S and that a tender for the block at any price above $\bar{a}_j p$ (the mean of the distribution) will

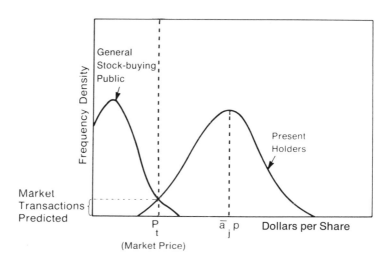

Fig. 2–1.   Valuations of stock of target company.

succeed. The value of $\bar{a}_j$ is not known; but it is revealed to be below the tender offer price if a tender succeeds.

Now let a potential acquirer, Company B, appear on the scene, as if from Mars. It too places a valuation of the share of Company S (which I have not represented on the diagram). Suppose it seeks control of Company S which can be had by acquiring n_S shares. It makes a tender offer for up to n_S shares by offering an exchange of stock that gives sellers more shares in the new combined company than the market prices would warrant. Given our earlier normalization, it offers to exchange kn_S shares in Company C for n_S shares in Company S. If k is greater than unity, this involves a price offer in excess of market price, and if it is sufficiently high (above $\bar{a}_j$) the merger will succeed. For simplicity, I will assume that the bidder gets exactly n_S shares—not more—if the tender offer succeeds, and that if the bidder does not get n_S shares, the merger fails.[8]

The price of Company C's stock. Suppose the tender offer succeeds and that the new company comes into being. The new company has $n_B + kn_S$ shares of stock which are available for trade on stock markets at a price p_C.

Let us designate this immediate post-merger price as

$$(2) \qquad p_C = \alpha \left[\frac{n_B p_B + n_S p_S}{n_B + kn_S} \right] = \alpha \left[\frac{n_B + n_S}{n_B + kn_S} \right]$$

The term in square brackets represents how the market would evaluate the value per share of the new company if it relied on the premerger prices of the shares. α is greater or less than unity according to the stock market's evaluation of the merger. I shall call it the "public synergism coefficient," pronounced "alpha."

The coefficient α might exceed unity for a large number of reasons: real economies of joint operation or management, achievement of monopoly power, of tax advantages, or simply (in certain climates of opinion) an aura of profitability that makes the new company's stock attractive to investors. *The point about α is that it reflects the*

---

8. Assuming $k \geqq 1$ is without loss of generality, since this condition always pertains for one of the two parties to the merger. I am arbitrarily defining as the "buyer" the company which pays the premium.

"public" not the "insider" view of the merger and its effects on the stock's price.[9]

CONDITIONS FOR A SUCCESSFUL TENDER

To Company S's owners.   For a tender to be attractive to the owners of Company S their valuation of their ownership of the new Company C, denoted V_{SC}, must exceed their valuation of the old, V_S, by enough to cover the transactions costs and the risks to them of the exchange. This may be written as

$$(3) \qquad a_{SC} k n_S p_C > a_S n_S p_S (1 + \gamma_S)$$

where γ_S represents the transactions costs and expected value of risks attendant upon the merger as perceived by the sellers. These transactions and risk costs are here expressed on a per-share basis, that is, as a fraction of the total value of stock tendered.

Remembering that $p_S = 1$, this expression may be rewritten as

$$(4) \qquad \frac{a_{SC}}{a_S} \alpha k \left(\frac{n_B + n_S}{n_B + k n_S} \right) > 1 + \gamma_S$$

The right-hand side of expression (4) represents costs to the sellers (per dollar of premerger valuations) of being acquired. The left-hand side represents benefits, in the same units. Since it plays an important role in the subsequent discussion the particular grouping of terms is worth a careful look.

a_{SC}/a_S reflects the selling stockholders' relative valuations *over the stock market prices* of their holdings in the new and old companies. If it is greater than unity, it means that they value stock in the new Company C at a higher premium over the market's valuation than they do their old company's stock. This in turn may be because they have an especially good feeling about the new company (based on insider's information) or a particularly poor feeling about the old (again they may know better than the market just how poor the prospects were for Company S).

---

9. Here and throughout I use the concept of *synergy* to refer to anything that produces a net gain to parties on both sides of a transaction. Thus, it may include real efficiencies and pecuniary ones, monopoly gains, speculative advantages, etc. Other writers sometimes use the phrase more narrowly—to refer to "real economies."

Whereas a_{SC}/a_S represents insider evaluations, α represents *public* evaluations. Expression (4) can usually be satisfied if α is sufficiently larger than unity. That is, real or speculative gains arising as a result of a merger can induce stockholders of Company S to want to be acquired; k is the premium paid to Company S stockholders to induce their acceptance of the tender offer.

The term in parenthesis represents the dilution in stock due to the creation of more shares in Company C than $n_B + n_S$. Since Company S stockholders receive these extra shares *they* are not disadvantaged by the dilution even though, because of dilution, a share in Company C will be worth less than a share in Company B or S, other things being equal.

To the stockholders of the buying company. The buying company ends up with n_B out of the $n_B + kn_S$ shares of the new company. This in turn is advantageous if

(5) $$a_{BC}n_Bp_C > a_Bn_Bp_B(1 + \gamma_B)$$

where all terms are similar to those in expression (3) except for subscripts. This becomes

(6) $$\frac{a_{BC}}{a_B} \alpha \left(\frac{n_B + n_S}{n_B + kn_S}\right) > 1 + \gamma_B$$

It will be helpful for some of the subsequent discussion to simplify these expressions somewhat.

The inhibitions to merger, on the right-hand side of expressions (4) and (6), include both insider and external elements. Let us define:

$$(1 + \gamma_S) = D_S(1 + \gamma), \quad \text{and}$$
$$(1 + \gamma_B) = D_B(1 + \gamma)$$

where $(1 + \gamma)$ are the common, external deterrents borne by all stockholders of the merging companies and D_S, D_B are the insider costs borne by them respectively. D_S and D_B are each assumed greater than or equal to unity. Further define:

$$A_S = \frac{a_{SC}}{a_S}$$

$$A_B = \frac{a_{BC}}{a_B}$$

and

$$Y = \frac{n_B + n_S}{n_B + kn_S} .$$

Y, the dilution constant, will be larger—nearer to unity—the larger is Company B relative to Company S, *ceteris paribus*. We may now rewrite expressions (4) and (6) as

(4′)
$$\frac{A_S}{D_S}\frac{\alpha}{1+\gamma}kY > 1$$

(6′)
$$\frac{A_B}{D_B}\frac{\alpha}{1+\gamma}Y > 1$$

These inequations are the basic motivational expressions in this simple model. It is worth pausing over them for the moment.

First, certain identical terms appear symmetrically in both (4′) and (6′). If external synergies (α) are large enough both parties may be motivated to merge; conversely a sufficiently strong general deterrent (γ) can discourage both parties. The dilution coefficient (Y) which is necessarily less than unity will be less unfavorable to merger the larger is Company B relative to Company S.

Second, note the apparent presence of k in (4′) but not (6′). This is misleading; the effect of k on buyers is through the denominator of Y. As k increases the merger becomes more attractive to sellers and less attractive to buyers.

Third, the insider benefits and costs may be very different for buyers and for sellers. For one example, if the tender offer fails, the owners of Company B will have acquired, at a premium over market value, a number of shares of Company S (less than the required n_S) that they will not be able to use to achieve the benefits they foresaw by acquiring control. Since the premium offered depended on achievement of control, liquidation of these shares is presumed to involve a loss. The expected value of this loss is included in D_B.

Conditions (4′) and (6′) must each be satisfied if the merger is to benefit both groups. If we assume these groups are also the only relevant groups, these two conditions are collectively sufficient for the merger. (The appendix to this chapter derives a single necessary and sufficient condition and explores its implications more formally.) These conditions identify potentially critical elements that enter into merger decisions: the public evaluations of them, reflected in α and in γ, and insider evaluations of them, reflected in the A's and D's. Each of these will be discussed at length in subsequent chapters.

The role of k in these expressions is that of finding satisfactory terms on which to conclude a mutually advantageous merger, not of creating those conditions.[10] It is, of course, quite possible for there to be a range of values of k that work, in which case an element of bargaining enters into the negotiation.[11] What of the fact that a particular company might be the advantageous merger partner of more than one buyer? Both the price of the seller's stock and the a_S coefficient reflect the reservation values attached to the existing Company S. One source of such value is the present value of a future sale.

Conflicts of Interest: Preliminary Consideration

The preceding analysis recognized both "external" and "insider" influences in the motivations of buyers and sellers. But we have not admitted of possible conflicts of interest among the insiders. The large corporation is a complex thing. Its owners include (typically) thousands of small stockholders who individually exercise no control and harbor no thought of making decisions for the firm, but who collectively may have latent power in the rare moments when a proxy fight or a contested takeover occurs. The corporation will often include one or more blocks of large stockholders (individual or institutional) who have a potential for influencing managerial decisions when they feel strongly. The corporation always includes a managerial group (or conceivably groups), and it frequently involves other articulate influences, such as representatives of the financial community. My purpose in noting this diversity is to enable us subsequently to embrace conflicts in valuations and objectives *and* to recognize that *disagreements* may provide significant motivation to either management or owners from being acquired and using the acquiring firm as an ally against the internal "enemy."

Given numerous significant parties to corporate decisions, if all are satisfied, there is presumably the basis for a successful uncontested tender offer. But if one or more parties on each side favor a merger and even one major party is opposed the stage may be set for a contest. A variety of outcomes is possible depending upon the identity of those who oppose the merger, the intensity of their opposition, their financial strengths, the tactics available to them, and so forth.

---

10. This is because increases in k increase the left-hand side of (4') and decrease the left-hand side of (6').

11. One might, but I shall not, include the possibility that for game theoretic reasons, a potential merger partner would refuse an otherwise advantageous merger in order to get the better of some future bargain.

All of this is discussed at length in chapter 6. For the moment it is important to note first that the phrase "insider evaluations" as I have used it can be expanded to embrace a wider variety of actors than in the simple model of the previous section and thus also a wider variety of forces affecting their decisions.[12] This quickly takes us beyond the confines of the simple equilibrium analysis used above. Once conflict situations arise they may change things for parties not directly involved, such as the small stockholders, by raising greatly the costs of the transaction, and affecting the expectations about the success of the companies after the fight is over. Importantly, as we shall see, one outcome to a particular merger contest may be another, different merger.

What the conflict cases add to the simple model is first a much wider set of insider valuations to consider, and second the possibility of *endogenous* changes in some of the key coefficients of (4') and (6'), such as α, γ and k. What remains, as a theoretical framework, is a multiplicative interactional model in which such things, along with the A's and D's, can control the profitability of a merger.

Summary

The analysis above sought to identify the kinds of influences that might lead stockholders of buying and selling companies each to want to consummate a merger. Five sets of influences were singled out and these in turn led to two behavioral inequalities shown as relationships (4') and (6') above.

If both of those conditions are satisfied (and if there are no conflicts of interest within either corporation) the merger will be financially attractive to both sides and is predicted to occur.

The elements entering into these relationships may be summarized in five groups:[13]

1.   External synergies (α), real or pecuniary, may make the stock of a combined company worth more than the sum of its premerger parts. These may embrace among many other possibilities such things as economies of large-scale production or a chance to exploit a

---

12. Indeed, as we shall see, there may be yet other "insiders" such as stockbrokers, bankers, etc., whose interests may affect merger probabilities.

13. For reference purpose the symbolic terms corresponding are indicated in parenthesis.

monopoly position. Because such synergies benefit both buyers and sellers, they appear symmetrically in the relationships and a high enough synergy, other things equal, can motivate both parties to merge.

2. External deterrents (γ), such as the transaction costs of effecting a merger or the likelihood of antitrust prosecution, play an opposite role to synergies. They too enter symmetrically and large enough deterrents can cool the ardor of both sides of a potential merger.

3. "Insider" benefits (A_S) and deterrents (D_S) may exist to the stockholders of the selling company. Included here are all the potential sources of gain or loss to the selling company's owners that are not adequately reflected in the stock market prices of the stocks before and after merger. The ratio of benefits to deterrents may be thought of as an insider benefit/cost ratio and may be greater or less than unity according to whether the selling companies' owners see greater or lesser advantages to them in the new company than in retaining the independence of Company S.

4. Insider benefits (A_B) and deterrents (D_B) to the stockholders of the buying company also may exist. While formally similar to those of the seller, insider gains or losses need not be the same for buyers and sellers, and indeed will typically not be the same.

5. The premium paid by buyers to sellers to induce them to accept the tender offer (k, Y). The premium is the "price" that persuades reluctant sellers to agree to a merger and that thus determines the allocation of advantages accruing from the merger between the parties. In my formulation of the problem, the premium paid takes the form of giving sellers a disproportionate share of the new company by issuing more shares of stock in the new company than the sum of the shares in the buying and selling companies. Buyers pay the premium via the dilution in their holdings.

Each of the elements other than premium offered—external synergies, external deterrents, insider benefits, and costs—concerns us at length in the subsequent chapters.

One more element, not represented in these inequations, also is important. The large corporation is a more complex organism than conventional economic theory represents. Managers, stockholder blocs (and indeed others), may have conflicting goals, and may be or become engaged in struggles for power. While mergers will clearly be attractive to the parties if all groups benefit, the contested takeover is sufficiently common that it cannot be neglected, and may arise if either owners or managers of either company sharply oppose an acquisition beneficial to another group. When they do, the relatively simple structure of relations (4′) and (6′) no longer is sufficient. These matters are discussed in chapter 6.

While I shall not neglect conflict cases, the relatively simpler case of the uncontested takeover seems relevant to a large fraction of all cases. In any event understanding it is an important prerequisite to the more complex conflict situations.

Appendix to Chapter 2: Further Consideration of Relations (4) and (6)

Inequations (4) and (6) in the text defined the conditions required for sellers and buyers respectively to benefit from a merger. By hypothesis if both conditions are satisfied the merger will occur. Another way of saying this is that if there exist one or more positive values of k that permit simultaneous satisfaction of the two conditions, there is a fruitful merger, and it is assumed to occur. (The imposition of antitrust barriers is neglected at this point, although the risk and cost of antitrust consequences are included in γ.) More formally, the pair of inequations (4) and (6) are taken to be necessary and sufficient.

The key conditions in the chapter are most conveniently written now in the form:

Sellers' Condition:

(4)
$$\left(\frac{\alpha}{1+\gamma}\right)\left(\frac{A_S}{D_S}\right) k \left(\frac{n_B + n_S}{n_B + k n_S}\right) > 1$$

Buyers' Condition:

(6)
$$\left(\frac{\alpha}{1+\gamma}\right)\left(\frac{A_B}{D_B}\right)\left(\frac{n_B + n_S}{n_B + k n_S}\right) > 1$$

It is convenient to define the following summary terms:

$N_S = \dfrac{A_S}{D_S}$, the net insider advantage of the sellers.

$N_B = \dfrac{A_B}{D_B}$, the net insider advantage to the buyer.

$Q = \dfrac{\alpha}{1+\gamma}$, the net external synergy.

$\left.\begin{array}{l} S_S = \dfrac{n_S}{n_B + n_S} \\[2ex] S_B = \dfrac{n_B}{n_B + n_S} \end{array}\right\}$ measures of the relative size of the two companies at the time of merger.

All of these expressions are defined to be positive, as is k.

$$S_S + S_B = 1.$$

$$\frac{n_S}{n_B} = \frac{S_S}{S_B}.$$

Substituting these definitions into (4) and (6) and manipulating terms gives, in place of (4) and (6), respectively:

(A1) $$Q\frac{N_S}{S_B} - \frac{S_S}{S_B} > \frac{1}{k} > 0$$

(A2) $$Q\frac{N_B}{S_S} - \frac{S_B}{S_S} > k > 0$$

If (A1) and (A2) are both satisfied for a positive k, a merger is predicted. The symmetry is not surprising since we specified no fundamental difference between Companies S and B. We can relax the text assumption of $k > 1$. If k is greater than 1, Company B acquires Company S. If $k < 1$, Company S should acquire Company B. If $k = 1$ and (A1) and (A2) are both satisfied, the merger might occur spontaneously, or put differently, initiation is not of major concern.

Condition (A1) implies:

(A3) $$Q\frac{N_S}{S_S} > 1 \text{ as a necessary condition.}$$

Condition (A2) implies:

(A4) $$Q\frac{N_B}{S_B} > 1 \text{ as a necessary condition.}$$

Conditions (A1) and (A2) together imply:

(A5) $$Q\frac{N_B}{S_S} - \frac{S_B}{S_S} > k > \frac{1}{Q\frac{N_S}{S_B} - \frac{S_S}{S_B}} > 0,$$

which implies a further necessary condition:

(A6) $$\left[Q\frac{N_B}{S_S} - \frac{S_B}{S_S}\right]\left[Q\frac{N_S}{S_B} - \frac{S_S}{S_B}\right] > 1.$$

Cross-multiplying, and simplifying (A6) leads to:

(A7) $$Q > \frac{S_B}{N_B} + \frac{S_S}{N_S}.$$

It will now be shown that (A7) implies both (A3) and (A4) and is thus alone sufficient. By simple transposition we can rewrite (A7) as:

(A7-a)
$$Q\frac{N_S}{S_S} > \frac{N_S}{N_B}\frac{S_B}{S_S} + 1.$$

Since all the *N*'s and *S*'s are necessarily positive, the right-hand side of (A7-a) is greater than 1 and (A3) is redundant.

Similarly:

(A7-b)
$$Q\frac{N_B}{S_B} > 1 + \frac{S_S}{S_B}\frac{N_B}{N_S} > 1,$$

which shows (A4) to be redundant.

Thus (A7) is both necessary and sufficient. It merits some further examination. Remembering that $1 > S_B$, $S_S > 0$ and $S_B + S_S = 1$, it is immediately apparent that if both N_B, $N_S > 1$, the merger is sure to pay if $Q \geqq 1$. If both N_B, $N_S < 1$, only a Q sufficiently greater than unity will permit the merger to occur.

What can be said if $N_B > 1$ and $N_S < 1$—if, that is, the merger appears desirable to Company B but not to Company S at market prices? Is there a *k* that will permit the merger? This depends upon the relative size of Company S and Company B. To see this quickly, assume $Q = 1$. Then (A7) becomes:

(A8)
$$1 > \frac{S_B}{N_B} + \frac{S_S}{N_S},$$

and substituting $S_B = 1 - S_S$ and transposing gives

(A9)
$$S_S < \frac{1 - \dfrac{1}{N_B}}{\dfrac{1}{N_S} - \dfrac{1}{N_B}}.$$

Since $N_B > 1$ and $N_S < 1$, the right-hand side is positive and there thus exists an S_S greater than zero that makes the merger possible. I.e., there exists an S_S for which there exists a premium *k* at which it pays Company B to make the tender offer and Company S to accept it. Not surprisingly, it is easier to overcome the reluctance of a small company than a large one.

CHAPTER THREE

Synergy I:
Efficiency and/or Monopoly

CHAPTER 2 suggested many things that might motivate a merger of two companies. One of these was a large enough external benefit or "synergy" (represented in my formal treatment as the coefficient α), to assure the attractiveness of the merger.

Not surprisingly many views of the merger problem consist of defining situations when α will be sufficiently high. Recall that alpha reflects the market evaluation of the advantage of owning the stock of the combined company relative to the weighted average of the component companies. If $\alpha = 1$, the market is regarded as being merger-neutral; $\alpha > 1$ indicates a preference for the stock of the merged companies over an appropriate portfolio of the premerger stocks. Things that might lead the *market* to be promerger are our major concern in this chapter and the next two. This chapter is concerned with "real" synergistic elements, that is those that come as a result of the productive, distributive, and sales activities of the firm. Chapters 4 and 5 deal with "pecuniary" advantages motivating a merger, which are defined to be those that provide financial advantages to stock-holders arising *outside* of the basic activities of the firm. For example, the tax laws, accounting rules, stock market institutions, and investor psychology may singly or severally lead to an alpha significantly greater than unity, and thus motivate mergers.

"Monopoly" versus "Efficiency" as Sources of Synergy

Real synergistic effects, of the kind the stock market may be expected to recognize, are usually assumed to be related to the profitability of the merged firm relative to the profitability of its components. Enhanced profits, whatever their source, are likely to be a basis for rising stock market prices. It is convenient for the ensuing discussion to divide increased profits from operations into those that may be regarded as socially (as well as privately) beneficial, which are labeled

47

"economies," and those that may be regarded socially undesirable, which are labeled as aspects of "monopoly" or "monopoly power." These phrases are used in this context as shorthand terms of art to distinguish those synergies that are cost reducing, quality or service improving, and so forth, from those that represent a movement away from competitive results. In the easiest kind of case if Company B acquires Company S for the purpose and with the effect of increasing market power, raising prices, and reducing output in Company S's industry, while at the same time having no effect on costs, this is unambiguously "monopolistic." Similarly where the acquisition is motivated by and has the effect of decreasing costs of production, decreasing price, and increasing output, this seems unambiguously "efficient." Most cases are not of this simple kind. Among many complications that render such a dichotomy of only limited descriptive value are cases where a merger achieves monopoly power but (in a Schumpeterian sense) creates a progressive innovator; where an efficiency results in cost reduction that is not passed on in lower prices but instead is retained by the firm and expended, e.g., in such socially undesirable ways as financing anticompetitive practices; situations in which an increase (decrease) in competition may be socially undesirable (desirable) because of second best considerations, and so forth.

WHY THE DISTINCTION?

My purpose in stressing the dichotomy despite the nondichotomous nature of actual motivations in most cases is not to suggest that actual situations are motivated *either* by efficiency *or* by monopoly considerations, but instead to identify the major and opposing considerations that have made mergers and merger policy controversial at least since the passage of the Clayton Act in 1914. The major policy positions rest (at least in part) on different assumptions about the relative importance of these two sets of influences. The greater, *ceteris paribus,* the tendency for mergers to be the source of economies, the more beneficial (or at least benign) they tend to appear; the greater the tendency for mergers to create or enhance monopoly power, the more socially costly they seem. Men differ about whether mergers are examples of the triumphs or of the failings of the free-market system and the profit motive.

I shall subsequently, albeit briefly, review the kinds of economies and the kinds of competitive harm that mergers may achieve.[1] My point now is to stress that it is these tensions that originally made, and continue to make, merger policy an area where reasonable men can disagree.

MONOPOLY VERSUS EFFICIENCY: THE EARLY HISTORY

The central issues of merger policy arose in a nonmerger context. The year 1890 witnessed both passage of the Sherman Act and the publication of Alfred Marshall's classic *Principles of Economics*. The trusts that Congress legislated against were loose-knit cartels not tight-knit agglomerations of former competitors unless the latter achieved monopolies, and the monopoly problems that appear to have concerned the antitrusters were multilateral cartels and unilateral predatory practices that drove competitors out.[2] On the economics side, while Marshall devoted some space to monopolies, to scale advantages, and to growth of firms it was always in the context of the internal growth of existing competitors, not their merger.

The first of the great American merger movements brought an end to the legal and economic neglect of the merger problem. While mergers were occurring throughout the 1890s, between 1897 and 1905 thousands of mergers occurred, mostly horizontal, that, according to the leading student of the movement, Ralph L. Nelson,

. . . transformed many industries, formerly characterized by many small- and medium-sized firms, into those in which one or a few very large enterprises occupied leading positions. It laid the foundation for the industrial structure that has characterized most of American industry in the twentieth century.[3]

---

1. Briefly because there is a large and well-known literature on this subject. With respect to conglomerate mergers the major classic is Donald Turner, "Conglomerate Mergers and Section 7 of the Clayton Act," 78 HARVARD LAW REVIEW 1313–95 (May 1965).

2. The deadening effect on antitrust activity including potential anti-merger activity of the first Supreme Court antitrust decision perhaps deserves mention. In *United States v. E. C. Knight,* 156 U.S. 1 (1895), the court held that manufacturing was not commerce. This emasculatory notion was soon put to rest. See *Addyston Pipe & Steel Co. v. United States,* 175 U.S. 211 (1899).

3. Ralph L. Nelson, *Merger Movements in American Industry 1895–1956,* National Bureau of Economic Research, General Studies No. 66 (Princeton, 1959), p. 9.

The antitrust history will concern us in chapter 7. What is important here is the Supreme Court's rejection by 1911 of the notion that "every" restraint of trade was illegal and the search for a "rule of reason" to distinguish between naked exercises of monopoly power and restraints that were ancillary to legitimate, efficiency-producing, business activities, and therefore ought to be permitted.[4]

Mergers were all but neglected in legal discussions until the passage in 1914 of the Clayton Act, and were to prove largely unreachable before the 1950 Amendments extended the Clayton Act to asset acquisitions as well as acquisitions of stock.

As of 1950, the central issue of merger policy concerned the effect of *horizontal* acquisitions, the only kind thought to be reachable up to that time. This is illustrated by a debate in 1950 between George Stigler and Joe S. Bain, certainly then as now two of the leading economic students of market behavior. The debate concerned what explained the first great merger wave of a half-century earlier. It had been primarily a horizontal merger movement. Stigler minimized any economies and laid great stress upon the monopolization effects. Bain, although conceding the horizontal aspects of the mergers, argued that they were significantly motivated by attempts to achieve the economies of large-scale production and distribution.[5] In a horizontal acquisition, where buying and selling companies are selling essentially the same product to the same customers, the theoretical possibilities both of economies of combined operations and of increased market and monopoly power are manifest. If one argues that one or the other force is negligible he must do so on empirical not theoretical considerations. One is faced theoretically with potentially large gains in efficiency and potentially large gains in monopoly power. While a balance needs to be struck, it is a balance between potentially large benefits and large costs. The Stigler-Bain debate was part of what then seemed like the central merger issue—striking that balance.

---

4. Part I of Robert Bork's long article "The Rule of Reason and the Per Se Concept: Price Fixing and Market Division" I, 74 YALE LAW JOURNAL 775 (April 1965), is a brilliant if unconventional review of the controversy.

5. Cf. G. J. Stigler, "Monopoly and Oligopoly by Merger," *American Economic Review,* Papers and Proceedings 40, no. 2 (May 1950): 23–34; and J. S. Bain, "Monopoly and Oligopoly by Merger, Discussion," *American Economic Review,* Papers and Proceedings 40, no. 2 (May 1950): 64–66.

As of 1972, it has very largely been resolved. If it is an exaggeration to say that there is today a consensus among economists, lawyers, and courts that horizontal acquisitions by leading firms of genuine competitors have a strong presumption of adverse net effect, it is not much of an exaggeration. The Supreme Court has supported the government in virtually every attack on a horizontal merger. To be sure there is disagreement on details such as how large is a leading company, who is a genuine competitor, what is the relevant market, etc., but these are matters of detail, not of basic principle.[6]

SPECIAL PROBLEMS OF CONGLOMERATE ACQUISITIONS

If the dimensions of the balance between monopoly and efficiency are well drawn in the case of horizontal acquisitions, that is not the case in the conglomerate area. When two firms merge that are in wholly separate industries, producing different products, using different technologies, the existence of potential benefits in terms of efficiencies is less obvious since economies of scale in production and distribution are less likely. But the opportunities for monopolization are also reduced for there is no necessary increase in market share in any market. At least at first glance in the conglomerate case, the balance tends to be struck between small possible benefits and small costs.[7]

More recent discussion has suggested that neither benefits nor costs need be *de minimis,* and that for conglomerate mergers too we need to know the magnitude of their ratio. We have no reason to know a priori that the ratio of benefits to costs is either high or low for conglomerate mergers. Clearly to the extent we can readily distinguish between mergers for which social benefits are large relative to social costs, and cases where the reverse is true, sound policy becomes easy. Whether a sensible basis of distinction is by categories such as "hori-

---

6. The principal dissent from this view comes from those who attack the very foundation of antitrust policy that high concentration is a correlate of anticompetitive behavior. See Yale Brozen, "The Antitrust Task Force Deconcentration Recommendation," 13 JOURNAL OF LAW AND ECONOMICS, no. 2, 279–92 (1970).

7. This fact led a former student of mine (Robert Kheel) to enunciate Kheel's Law: In all arguments about mergers, the greater the potential benefits, the greater the potential detriments. A forensic corollary was previously mistakenly enunciated as the law itself: "To every argument in favor of conglomerate mergers there is an equal and opposite argument against them."

zontal," "vertical," "conglomerate" is a central current issue. Whether, if sensible, it is sufficient is a further issue to which we shall return.

THE NEED FOR GENERAL RULES

The need to generalize for classes of situations rather than make case-by-case determinations was stated in detail by Derek Bok in a seminal paper,[8] and summarized in Donald Turner's classic paper on conglomerate mergers.[9] In essence the argument is that the social costs of making case-by-case determinations are large, and it is worth incurring the risk of some arbitrary and incorrect decisions to avoid such costs.

Accurate determinations of the net balance between potential efficiency gains and market power costs may be all but impossible in any event. Even to the extent that such determinations are possible they would surely absorb substantial resources including the time of economists, of lawyers, of accountants, and of the judicial system even if they did not befuddle the courts in a vast sea of possibilities. Such large transactions costs would necessarily reduce the number of cases that could be brought and would thus result in unbrought cases being approved without careful determination on the merits. Moreover, because the "big case" is likely to be heavily colored by the nature and conditions of a given industry, the ability to generalize any legal holding about economic effect in a particular case to other situations may be small. Perhaps even more important, the delay involved even in the cases investigated may vitiate the possibility of righting any wrong that has been found to occur.[10]

In short, because the judicial system seems unlikely to be able to make quick, infallible, generalizable, and inexpensive decisions on individual cases, there is a disposition to develop general rules for striking the balance between benefits and costs instead of adopting what seems superficially appealing: a neutral Rule of Reason approach.

But what sort of rule? Logically each of the following stances is possible:

a)   A per se rule permitting the merger except when well-defined (and presumably infrequent) conditions are present.

---

8. Derek Bok, "Section 7 of the Clayton Act and the Merging of Law and Economics," 74 HARVARD LAW REVIEW 226 (1960).

9. Turner, "Conglomerate Mergers," p. 1313.

10. See Kenneth G. Elzinga, "The Antimerger Law: Pyrrhic Victories?" 12 JOURNAL OF LAW AND ECONOMICS, no. 1, 43–78 (1969), for a pessimistic view of the adequacy even now of achieving adequate remedies.

b)   A presumption in favor of the merger, but a presumption that is rebuttable by those who would oppose it. The grounds for such opposition need to be well defined, and those seeking to utilize them would have to carry the burden of proof.

c)   A presumption against the merger, but a presumption that is rebuttable by those who propose the merger. The grounds for such a defense need to be well defined, and those seeking to utilize them would have to carry the burden of proof.

d)   A per se rule prohibiting the merger except when well-defined (and presumably infrequent) conditions are present.

Much of the contemporary debate about merger policy has concerned which of these stances ought to be adopted, and that in turn has rested on views of the relative likelihood of efficiencies outweighing competitive harms.

PER SE RULES

A generalized economic theory of when per se rules are appropriate would take us afield. But it is an important question and the solution is not (as many lawyers seem to believe) that such rules are appropriate only when the probability of an incorrect decision is *de minimis*. They are appropriate when the expected value of the costs of wrong decisions under the rules is smaller than the direct and indirect transactions costs required to make an explicit correct decision. The direct costs have already been suggested in the costs of making the determinations and of the delay that is involved. Among the important indirect costs are the encouragement given to conclude "undesirable" mergers in the hope they will not be chosen for attack, and even to litigate cases that are known to deserve to lose. These perverse incentives can occur if the private gains to the proposers promise to be large if the merger succeeds; for then even a small probability of success may give an expected gain that exceeds the expected private cost of defending the merger.

A conviction that the merits are likely to be preponderantly in one direction leads to virtual per se rules. They have been proposed in each direction with respect to conglomerate mergers.

Per se legality.   The contemporary "per se legal" position is taken (more or less explicitly) by a group of economists and lawyers including Robert Bork, Ward Bowman, Ronald Coase, Richard Posner, and George Stigler. Their view, in essence, is that the probability of competitive harm due to nonhorizontal merger is close to zero, but that efficiency benefits may well be achieved.[11] Since the expected value of benefits is positive and the expected value of costs approaches zero, the expected benefit/cost ratio is large indeed. Therefore a per se rule is appropriate.

The following statement by Coase concisely puts the position:

> The acquiring of an enterprise by a firm which has interests in other unrelated enterprises, unlike a horizontal merger, has no direct anticompetitive effects. . . .
>
> It is . . . claimed that these conglomerates will be inefficient. A more likely result is that some will be inefficient and some will be efficient. Competition will sort them out. Those that are inefficient will find resources hard to get and may indeed be forced to dispose of some of their constituent parts. As it is impossible to determine by court proceedings which of those mergers will be efficient and which will not, and competition will in fact do this (and probably in less time than the court proceedings would take), there seems little point in using the efficiency issue as a basis for antitrust actions.
>
> Some support for antitrust action against conglomerate mergers has been based on the fact that the firms might engage in reciprocal buying between constituent units. This practice might, of course, lead to great efficiency (for example, by reducing marketing costs) or it might lead to inefficiency (by substituting a subsidiary's higher cost supplies for an outsider's lower cost supplies). If this practice leads to efficiency, there is no reason to stop it; if it leads to inefficiency, there is no reason why the conglomerate should adopt it (since it would reduce its overall profits).
>
> No convincing case has as yet been made for taking antitrust action against conglomerate mergers.[12]

Because the Coase (et al.) position is boldly stated, it should not be given a simplistic interpretation. It does *not* say that there is no

---

11. Much of the conglomerate debate is an extension of the earlier vertical debate in which Professor Bork urged per se legality of vertical arrangements while the Department of Justice and the Supreme Court positions approximated per se illegality. See the second part of the Bork article cited above, Bork, "The Rule of Reason and the Per Se Concept: Price Fixing and Market Division" II, 75 YALE LAW JOURNAL 375 (1966).

12. Memorandum to the Task Force on Productivity and Competition, dated February 11, 1969. Part of Coase's view is that unconcern about conglomerate acquisitions is simply the continuation of a traditional view, and the burden of proof should be on those who propose a change. In my view however, lack of concern about conglomerate mergers after the merger movement of the 1960s is a very different thing from lack of concern about the conglomerate phenomenon before it occurred.

potential for anticompetitive effect following upon conglomerate mergers. The entrance of B into S's market might lead B to adopt predatory practices and/or seek to monopolize the industry. But these same things might have been done by S on its own, or by B if it had entered S's market *de novo*. Such anticompetitive practices could occur with or without merger, and they are legally proscribed with or without merger. Thus they should form a basis for antimerger rules only if it is shown (*a*) that they are a specially probable consequence of a merger, *and* (*b*) that they are unlikely to occur absent the merger. This, to those holding the position stated above, is an unlikely—and therefore negligible—pair of circumstances.

Per se illegality. The opposite polar view is that, excepting mergers in which the partners are singly and severally so small as to cause no ripples by merging, there is no probability of a gain in efficiency not otherwise attainable, but there is a possible competitive loss. Since the expected value of benefits is zero, but of costs is positive, the expected benefit/cost ratio is zero. Therefore a per se rule is appropriate.

The 1969 FTC *Economic Report* reached this view by distinguishing internal growth and growth by merger:

> . . . Growth accomplished internally, resulting in added product capacity, new and improved products, and new or more efficient techniques of production, clearly confers social gain. The enterprise through these types of investment decisions increases the economy's capacity to serve the customer. On the other hand, the social advantages of growth through acquisition are much more ambiguous. Mergers enable firms to grow without any immediate increase in productive capacity. In addition, through merger the span of private control is extended and the number of independent decision-makers is reduced. Thus, while internal expansion in the first instance tends to intensify competition, merger may diminish it. Private gains obtained from merger can be converted to social gains only if the transaction's harmful effect on competition is minimal and if merger growth ultimately promotes internal growth or improves productive efficiency.[13]

The last sentence leaves ajar the door to a defensible acquisition but it imposes a severe test: *both* minimal harm to competition *and* a positive improvement of efficiency.[14] The crack is soon closed.

---

13. Federal Trade Commission, Bureau of Economics, *Economic Report on Corporate Mergers* (Washington, D.C., 1969), pp. 69–70.

14. Why a conglomerate that achieved a large increase in efficiency but a smaller though nonnegligible harm to competition might not lead to social gains, is not explained in the Report.

The detailed subsequent discussion makes clear that while *some* mergers might meet this test, *conglomerate* acquisitions of large firms are not among them: the benefits do not exist, but the potential harms are inescapable.[15] While these views most directly reflect those of Willard F. Mueller, then director of the FTC's Bureau of Economics, they are in the tradition of two of his predecessors, Corwin Edwards and John Blair. Blair stated the antiefficiency case against conglomerates as follows:

> Of all types of merger activity conglomerate acquisitions have the least claim to promoting efficiency in the economic sense. The lower costs that might result in a horizontal acquisition from the pooling of skills and know-how gained in the production of the same product from different facilities are absent. Likewise the conglomerate acquisition affords little opportunity for the closing down of the less efficient facilities and the centralization of production in the more efficient. Similarly, the gains in a vertical acquisition which might result from the more logical and orderly arrangement of facilities employed in the successive stages of a continuous production process are not present. Because what is involved is the production of unrelated products the conglomerate acquisition provides few opportunities for the securing of economic efficiency in such matters as specialization as between plants, exchange of cost information between plants, savings in handling and reheating, operating with smaller inventories, reductions in the number of styles and sizes, savings in cross freight, etc.
>
> Conglomerate mergers also tend to impair economic efficiency by lessening the dependence of prices upon costs. Even where the conglomerate keeps reasonably accurate cost records, its accounting costs will of necessity reflect some arbitrary method of allocating indirect costs. Or, the conglomerate may even ignore its costs as long as its total return is satisfactory. . . .
>
> In a broader sense, conglomerate mergers may impede the proper allocation of resources by interposing the conglomerate's managers as an intermediary stage between the investing public and the various possible fields of investment. Conceivably, these managers might make as wise a use of capital among the various industries in which the conglomerate is en-

---

15. More recent endorsement of the principle of toehold competition suggests the possibility that there may be cases where the FTC would agree actual procompetitive results might result. But in every case I can find, this is a rhetorical basis for opposing a particular (nontoehold) acquisition, not a basis for approving a merger the FTC finds beneficial. In any case, such arguments rest not on efficiency effects but on a net balance to competition effect.

gaged as would the investors acting independently. But the value of having the decision-making function widely diffused is lost.[16]

The FTC position would not deny the possibility that there may be economies to be achieved in the industry of the acquired firm. But since such economies can readily be achieved by entry of an efficient new producer, achieving such economies is not a benefit of the merger, but of the entry of an efficient firm. Only if it is shown that achievement of such economies is a specially probable consequence of the merger and that they are unlikely to occur absent the merger should they provide a defense of the merger.[17]

Once efficiencies are effectively disposed of, it remains but to demonstrate some competitive harm. The potentials for such harm are several and we shall discuss them subsequently. For the per se position stated above it is necessary only that such harm is expected at a level that is more than minimal. A virtually definitional position is that since the merger (unlike *de novo* entry) necessarily results in the demise of an existing competitive identity, it has at least some adverse impact on the number of actual or potential competitors, and thus, presumably on competition.

Most opponents of conglomerate mergers buttress this kind of probable harm argument with arguments that rest on the adverse effects of large firms in the economy (and the society) generally rather than in specific markets. These macro-concentration concerns are discussed in chapter 11.

Since, in short, the efficiencies can be achieved in other ways, but the potential for harm is present, little would be lost by a per se rule against conglomerate mergers. This is not exclusively an FTC view, and as we shall see below there are arguably traces of it in the Department of Justice's merger guidelines. Moreover, this FTC view was modified in the second (1972) FTC merger report.[18] Perhaps because empirical analysis modifies a priori views, or perhaps because

---

16. John M. Blair, "The Conglomerate Merger in Economics and Law," 46 GEORGETOWN LAW JOURNAL 672, 679–82 (Spring 1958).

17. Notice that this argument is precisely similar in structure to the one enunciated on page 55 with respect to the opposite per se position. See also footnote 7 (Kheel's corollary).

18. Federal Trade Commission, Bureau of Economics, *Economic Report on Conglomerate Merger Performance: An Empirical Analysis of Nine Corporations* (Washington, D.C., 1972).

Stanley E. Boyle replaced Willard Mueller as principal author, the report concludes on a low-keyed note playing down the probable effects for good or ill of the purely conglomerate acquisitions studied.

THE ALTERNATIVE TO PER SE

Can one reject the per se approaches without going to the unworkable alternative of a case-by-case approach? I believe one can.

Per se positions toward conglomerate mergers presume an overall evaluation that *as a class* conglomerate mergers are likely to be ones in which competitive harms clearly outweigh (or are clearly outweighed by) achieved efficiencies. But the class may be divisible into subclasses, stopping well short of a case-by-case *sui generis* approach. If the expected variance in the benefit-cost ratio *within* the conglomerate merger class is associated with the presence or absence of definable characteristics one may be able to formulate rules (or "guidelines") that presume legality (or illegality) unless the presence or absence of the particular characteristics is demonstrated. This is a central policy challenge, and we will return to it in the final chapter. Before then we have much ground to cover. The principal economies that might result from conglomerate acquisitions are considered in this chapter, along with a brief mention of types of competitive effect. The detailed discussion of effects on competition is deferred to chapters 9 to 11.

Real Economies from Conglomerate Acquisitions

The term "real economies" is used in the conventional economic sense: a downward shift in the real opportunity cost of production of goods and services generally. Economies of this kind are defined within the framework of a general-equilibrium system. The link between a particular change in a particular market and the overall efficiency of use of society's resources is not perfect; nevertheless it is helpful to relegate to a lower level of consciousness such things as second-best theorems. For the subsequent discussion we will regard as productive of real economies those things that, in particular markets, have the effect of permitting more or better output for the same expenditure on input, or the same output for a lesser expenditure on inputs.

THE SIGNIFICANCE OF ECONOMIES

Economies may be "short-run" in the sense of overcoming some barriers to efficient use of resources with known technology, or "long-run" in the sense of the discovery and utilization of new, improved technology. Changes of either kind are desirable because they permit the more efficient utilization of the scarce resources that constrain the ability to enjoy by the members of society.

I stress, perhaps even labor, this view of "efficiency" as a desired *end* of economic activity because two other, different views often crop up. The first of these may be labeled the "economies as a sin" syndrome. Its expounders, if faced with a need to choose, prefer preservation of competitors to achievement of the efficiencies that competition is thought to produce. While in one sense this merely reflects a different end, it often confuses means with ends.[19] In its boldest form it is found in the legislative and judicial history surrounding fair trade laws, restrictions on chain stores, unfair competition generally, and some of the concern with price discrimination. This history survives in the Miller-Tydings and McGuire Acts—legislation that is essentially anticompetitive—and in the fact the prohibitions against price discrimination in the Robinson-Patman Act often have anticompetitive side effects. (Some commentators regard these acts as travesties of antitrust. It is worth remembering, however, that historically as well as semantically "antitrust" may be interpreted as "against bigness" as much as "procompetitive.")

A less blatant, but essentially similar, distrust of efficiency arises because of the fear that an efficient firm may trigger undesirable consequences. An example cited by Turner[20] of "not only bad economics but bad law" is the following sentence from the FTC in the Foremost Dairies decision:

. . . the necessary proof of violation of the statute consists of types of evidence showing that the acquiring firm possesses significant power in some markets *or* that its over-all organization gives it a decisive advantage in efficiency over its smaller rivals.[21]

---

19. Concern with goals other than efficiency is perfectly legitimate, and will concern us subsequently. But it seems desirable not to let such concerns obscure the social benefits from efficiency.

20. Turner, "Conglomerate Mergers," p. 1324.

21. *In re Foremost Dairies Inc.,* 60 FTC 944, 1084 (1962).

The Sixth Circuit in 1970 took a similar position in *U.S. Steel Corp. v. FTC:*

> . . . A vertically integrated cement and ready-mix company has decisive cost advantages over non-integrated competitors. Cement manufacturers are burdened with high fixed costs, as well as significant marketing, shipping and distribution costs. Vertical integration creates a more assured level of plant utilization, an elimination of any significant sales and marketing expenses to one's own ready-mix subsidiary, and the ability to integrate the storage and distribution facilities of the cement and ready-mix company into a single urban terminal. All of these factors work to lower overall unit costs of integrated vis-a-vis non-integrated concerns.
>
> However, while unit costs might be used to lower the price of cement to customers generally, they also have the potential of being used as weapons of economic discipline.[22]

The FTC and the Sixth Circuit each regard efficiency as dangerous because it may be used to injure rivals, and (perhaps) competition itself. Without denying that efficiency can be productive of market power and market power can be abused, most economists have little difficulty in agreeing with Turner that such fears should not be allowed to make achieving an efficiency *a reason for opposing* a merger. Abuses flowing from achievement of efficiencies can be dealt with on their merits when they arise.

Society has a stake in achieving real economies. Even if achieving an economy of scale leads to monopolization of an otherwise competitive industry, one can nevertheless regard achieving the economy as socially desirable, and visualize alternative organizational devices—a consent decree, regulation of the industry, public provision of the good, etc.—that retain efficient production but avoid the undesirable monopolistic behavior.

ECONOMIES ATTAINABLE

Clearly, certain economies potentially available for horizontal or vertical acquisitions will be much less likely (and perhaps not likely at all) for the sort of pure conglomerate acquisition that is our concern. This is John Blair's point in the passage cited above (see p. 56). In general, economies that are product oriented, whether arising from the production of the product, distribution of it, or from new product development, are less likely to be achieved by a conglomerate acquisition

---

22. 426 F.2d 592 (1970) at 603.

which combines control of widely disparate products than by a horizontal or vertical acquisition.

But no catalog of particular economies unattainable excludes the possibility of other, attainable ones. These can arise from several sources. Where the outputs of the firm tend to involve *services* rather than *products* the particular forms of know-how, and of "capacity" of a firm, may be readily transferable to other services which fall in industries that have little in common except a service orientation. The rising relative importance of the services sector of the United States economy has, as Neil Jacoby has pointed out, increased the scope for the cross-industry service corporation, and some conglomerates have been heavily service oriented, including, importantly, ITT and Transamerica. Economies in producing services tend to arise from efficient use of certain inputs into production of services, such as credit availability, billing systems, and so forth.

This input (or factor-of-production) feature is a source of economies of larger or integrated operations that is potentially available in all mergers, but perhaps especially in conglomerate ones. It is this that Blair appears to overlook. *Any* factor may be a potential source of economies of larger scale operation, from a research chemist, a skilled lobbyist, an innovative manager, to a patent, a supply of raw materials, or a company image cultivated by decades of reputable operations. For present purposes let me comment on four sources of potential conglomerate economies.

Management. E. A. G. Robinson nearly forty years ago spoke of the optimal size of the firm as determined by a balance of processes.[23] His great insight was to recognize that the minimal efficient level of utilization of different elements in production varied; thus a firm which was to produce with a variety of processes might need to be large. For example, if the minimal efficient scales of machines A, B, and C are 15, 25, and 40 units per period respectively, the firm utilizing them in series would have to achieve an output rate of 600 units per period in order to fully utilize only components operating at efficient sizes. (In the example 40 A's would feed 24 B's which would supply 15 C's.) Robinson was concerned with *plant* size, but his view was readily ex-

---

23. E. A. G. Robinson, *The Structure of Competitive Industry*, rev. ed. (Chicago, 1959). See also Florence, *The Logic of Industrial Organization* (London, 1933).

tended, for example by Bain, to the justification for the multiplant firm arising in terms of economies of distribution and sales promotion.[24] Such distributive considerations are routinely adduced today to account for market and product extensions by existing firms.

Many of the contemporary *managerial* theories of conglomerate growth extend this notion to a key input: managerial talent. In this respect they take an untraditional view of the functions of management. In the earlier literature on the firm, management was usually thought of as the limiting factor in firm growth. But managers may profitably do more than supervise and coordinate activities of their underlings. Key roles may involve search for changing methods, for new investment outlets, for revision of processes and products, and for introduction of known but unutilized new techniques in new areas. In any of these functions, management's services may be not the limiting resources, but the most underutilized potential resources of the firm.

As a theoretical possibility this is evidently true. Suppose, as an example, that a key resource of a firm is a manager whose primary and unique talent is to define the single most profitable new takeover for the company to make each year. His efficient utilization requires such a takeover each year. Theoretical possibilities aside, is there reason to believe that today's managerial role is such as to motivate and require conglomerate growth for efficient utilization?

Neil Jacoby is a believer in and a spokesman for an affirmative answer based on the "revolution" in management science. Hear him:

Radical changes occurred in the science of enterprise management after World War II. These changes had their roots in the wartime efforts of mathematicians to solve complex logistical and military problems by "operations research." Concepts and methods were then developed that were later found to be equally powerful in dealing with the management problems of a civilian economy. Intuitive judgment has been progressively superseded by rational decision-making processes. Such problems as evaluation of investment projects, choice of financing plans, locating facilities, scheduling production and controlling inventories are now solved by mathematical and statistical methods.

The concurrent phenomenal development of electronic computers has promoted and facilitated the expansion of management science. The computer not only does routine accounting with fantastic speed but performs the great volume of calculations involved in solving management

---

24. See Joe S. Bain, "Advantages of the Large Firm: Production, Distribution and Sales Promotion," *Journal of Marketing* 20, no. 4 (April 1956): 336–46.

problems. In 1950 only a few computers were operating in businesses; at the end of 1968 there were more than twenty thousand.

This fundamental development has created opportunities for profits through mergers that remove assets from the inefficient control of old-fashioned managers and place them under men schooled in the new management science. Managers are able to control effectively a larger set of activities. Being of general applicability to business operations, management science makes possible reductions in financial and managerial costs and risks through acquisitions of firms in *diverse* industries. These gains differ markedly from the familiar economies of scale in production, purchasing, or marketing that normally accrue from mergers of firms with *related* products. Thus the new management science is the primary force behind conglomeration.[25]

The Jacoby perspective has the merit of avoiding a mere foreman's role for management (and thus is more compatible with extant rates of managerial compensation). It does not address why the specialized services of management scientists must be embedded in the firm. If scientific management is the input with the largest efficient scale, why is there not general utilization of the services of specialized firms of managerial consultants? Such firms do exist, and such evidence as is available suggests that their productivity is high.[26] This is not too surprising: the productivity of advice given a multimillion dollar corporation is likely to be high relative to its costs if the *sign* of any proposed changes is correct.

Supposing good advice can be had in this way, there seem to be compelling reasons why the very best potential consultants will prefer to operate in line capacities within companies rather than outside of them: (1) Many of the companies most needing managerial consulting advice may be least likely to seek it; old, ineffective, tradition-bound managers are unlikely to spend money on being told that it is their replacement that is imminently required. (2) Even where their advice is sought, consultants may need to spend too much energy persuading existing managers to take the recommended steps, or may

---

25. Neil Jacoby, "The Conglomerate Corporation," *Center Magazine* 2, no. 4 (July 1969): 45.

26. Cf., for example, J. Johnston, "The Productivity of Management Consultants," *Journal of the Royal Statistical Association* 26, pt. 2 (1963): 237–49. Ansoff, Brandenburg, Portner, and Radosevich, *Acquisition Behavior of U.S. Manufacturing Firms, 1946–1965* (Nashville, Tenn., 1971), find that planning has high payoff in their study of mergers and performance, thus confirming Johnston's general finding.

be forced, against their best judgment, to compromise on the steps to be taken. (3) Implementing changes may be too difficult if the consultants do not control the assignments of personnel, and do not supervise the carrying out of the recommended policies. (4) The returns to good advice are the joint product of the advice and the activities to which the advice is applied. Therefore, the "rents" to the advice from consulting will ordinarily have to be shared with those who control the corporation. Where such control is separated from ownership, acquiring the company to achieve control may let the advisors capture more of these rents. (5) Acquisition may permit earning the fees for the salient advice in the form of capital gains, or perquisites of office rather than as ordinary income. (Stock options to business consultants are, of course, theoretically possible; I know of no such use of them.) For all these reasons, and perhaps others, the real economies of management science may not be readily separated from management itself.

Capital economies.   Three kinds of advantages to the large corporation with regard to flows-of-funds are frequently adduced: genuine economies of larger scale use of funds, economies due to avoiding capital market imperfections, and economies due to avoiding tax barriers to the mobility of capital. The third concerns the ability to circumvent taxation of interindustry capital transfers by making them intrafirm and is discussed in the next chapter.

With respect to the other two, I have little to add to what is generally known and frequently said. Obviously there are potential economies that are available to firms large enough to utilize organized securities markets in flotation of securities.[27] Obviously, too, there are advantages in terms of risk avoidance to investors or banks in making loans to large diversified firms rather than to small specialized ones, *ceteris paribus*. This may well mean the large company will pay a lower price for its funding. Similarly, the imperfections that limit the financing of small (particularly very small) companies are well known.

These things do not explain much of the move toward conglomerate acquisitions. First, most of the companies involved in significant acquisitions are already well past the size necessary to achieve prefer-

---

27. Cf. S. H. Archer and L. G. Faerber, "Firm Size and the Cost of Externally Secured Equity Capital," *Journal of Finance* 21, no. 1 (March 1966): 69–83.

ential financing,[28] second, most conglomerates have not used new security flotation or new bank borrowing as a primary source of financing; thus they are not utilizing whatever special borrowing capacity they bring to their acquired companies.

If capital economies play a decisive role it is in the increased ability to channel internally generated and undistributed profits into more profitable endeavors. Here is an important complementary with the economies attainable via efficient management. Capital-budgeting is characteristically a major managerial responsibility; if it is also an art (or science) in which it is possible to perform exceptionally well, access to a large cash flow and a wide variety of investment opportunities can make exceptionally profitable management possible. The conglomerate acquisition can increase both cash flows and investment opportunities.

Promotional expenditures.   Economies in advertising and sales promotion have always been a source of discomfort to economists and lawyers. We are not prepared to say these activities are generally and usually bad, yet they seem somehow less beneficial than achieving economies in distribution or production. Turner's compromise stand is to say that such economies should not be an affirmative ground for invalidating an otherwise legal merger, but that we may wish to regard an efficiency defense as at a lower level of merit if the economies involved are purely promotional.[29]

The relevant economic theorems are twofold: (*a*) anything worth doing is worth doing efficiently; (*b*) not everything that is privately worth doing is socially beneficial. Knowing which one to invoke is the problem.

Much of the discussion of this problem has been in connection with the various decisions in the Clorox case.[30] Although the factual

---

28. A study by the Federal Reserve Board in 1958 (*Financing Small Business Part II*) suggested that $1 million in assets was the size required. As we have noted the typical large conglomerate is acquiring firms much larger than this.

29. Turner, "Conglomerate Mergers," pp. 1332–37.

30. Clorox was acquired by Procter and Gamble in 1957. An FTC hearing examiner found the merger to violate Section 7 in 1960. The case moved in leisurely fashion from the FTC, to the Sixth Circuit, and finally to the Supreme Court. See *FTC v. Procter & Gamble,* 58 FTC 1203 (1961); *In re Procter & Gamble,* 63 FTC 1465 (1963); *FTC v. Procter & Gamble,* 358 F.2d 74 (1966); *FTC v. Procter & Gamble,* 386 U.S. 568 (1967) at 577.

assumptions on which that case was decided—that Procter & Gamble achieved large discounts in its purchases of television advertising time and thus gave Clorox an unfair competitive advantage—have been persuasively challenged,[31] the questions asked were worth asking: (1) Are economies in advertising and promotion achievable? (2) If so, are they "real" economies to society? (3) Are such economies in some sense "unworthy" because they involve expenditures on persuasion rather than production?

The first two questions are answered decisively and affirmatively by Turner, and I have nothing to add:

[Promotional economies] may occur (*a*) because vital advertising media grant substantial quantity discounts, as television networks apparently do; (*b*) because a larger absolute expenditure of funds will buy relatively more efficient promotional techniques; or (*c*) because the acquiring firm has a strong trademark, the pulling power of which is easily transferred to the product of the acquired firm. . . .

To the extent that quantity discounts reflect cost savings to the advertising media, the large firm's advantage is a true economy of scale, and is both a private and a social economy because it reduces the resources necessary to obtain given promotional result. The same must be said when a large expenditure will buy relatively more efficient advertising than a small one, as when a thousand dollar full-page ad in an evening paper will bring in twenty times the added business that would be produced by a hundred dollar distribution of handbills.

Similarly, advertising economies based on the transfer to the new product of an already established trademark also reflect a true economy of scale. There is a more efficient exploitation of a particular asset here just as in the case when a firm economizes in the production of a particular commodity by manufacturing it with facilities that had not been fully utilized in the production of related items.[32]

The third question is more difficult, for it becomes an aspect of the formidable problem of defining public goods.[33] I know of no legal or economic theory that obviates the need for social decision making as to whether advertising expenditures of particular kinds ought to be treated as the equivalent of touting or of education. Ob-

---

31. See John Peterman, "The Clorox Case and the Television Rate Structures," 11 JOURNAL OF LAW · AND ECONOMICS 321–422 (October 1968).

32. Turner, "Conglomerate Mergers," pp. 1332–37.

33. My views on this problem have been explicated at length in P. O. Steiner, "Public Expenditure Budgeting," *The Economics of Public Finance* (Washington, D.C., 1974).

viously not all promotional expenditures have the same purposes or effects. The practical (as well as philosophic) difficulties in drawing workable distinctions between activities that are "persuasive" and those that are "informational"; those that are "deceptive" and those that are "harmless"; those that are "output expanding" and those that are "mutually-canceling" are all but overwhelming. My own disposition is to hold a rebuttable presumption in favor of any real promotional economy. I suspect this is the counsel of cowardice.

A different but related sort of potential promotional economy can arise from extending the use of the acquiring company's reputation. Suppose acquisition of X by RCA extends the implicit guarantee of RCA's reputation to X's activities. If RCA recognizes and honors this trust, this seems to me to be unambiguously a real economy, for it gives X's customers something they value, with no resource cost. I doubt, however, in the area of conglomerate acquisitions, that this is of major importance, although the leading conglomerates have added the parent company's name to subsidiaries' letterheads, advertising, etc.

Diversification.   Is achieving diversification *itself* achievement of a real social economy? It has been so argued. Diversified companies are less likely to fail in response to cyclical and market fluctuations. Moreover, if some division or product line must be liquidated, diversification may make for a more orderly liquidation, and reassignment of personnel and other resources, than would follow the trauma of bankruptcy. The failing company justification for mergers appears to give some official sanction to the notion of diversification as a source of real economy.[34] This argument is not wholly without appeal, particularly with respect to giving companies ability to withstand sudden but temporary and capricious setbacks. Nevertheless, I have doubts about its general cogency.

Avoiding an "unwarranted failure" is a potentially real, but surely infrequent, result of conglomerate acquisitions. Avoiding or delaying the "warranted failure" is an inefficiency and an impediment to resource reallocation. Is is not clear that one can distinguish this result from the previous one.[35] One of the *objections* to conglomerate

---

34. See below, page 330.

35. As we shall see in the next chapter, tax loss carryovers can provide a positive motive for too leisurely liquidation of inefficient or failing companies.

corporations is that they remove many decisions from the test of the free market, and by blurring the public disclosure of division-by-division performance records make the ordinary investor or the serious investigator unable to judge economic performance in particular product markets.[36]

What can be said of diversification to reduce risk as distinct from avoiding unwarranted bankruptcy? Such risk avoidance is a private rather than a public benefit and does not therefore seem to me to yield a real economy.[37] Indeed because it is a private benefit, private companies may by diversification produce social diseconomies while avoiding private costs.[38] Individual owners can reduce their risk by an appropriate diversification of their stock holdings.

Induced economies.   The threat of entry-by-acquisition of a conglomerate corporation into virtually any field may be a source of important economies by amounting to procompetitive entry, by displacing poor management, or by shaking up lethargic management. Entry and the threat thereof have long been regarded as providing significant pressures on existing sellers in particular markets—pressures to find their own survival by matching or exceeding the anticipated performance of the actual or potential entrant. Where takeovers actually occur, the effect of efficiency may be positive through replacement of ineffective personnel, through introduction of new techniques which are copied by other firms, or in myriad other ways.[39]

The threat of expansion by a conglomerate may stimulate more efficient behavior by existing firms in the usual ways (such as putting pressure on existing firms to keep prices and costs low) or additionally in a special one. The conglomerate tender offer and takeover often seek to take over control from an existing management group which

---

36. This is a primary concern of the second FTC study.

37. See the discussion in Steiner, "Public Expenditure Budgeting."

38. This is a matter of current controversy. See H. Levy and M. Sarnat, "Diversification, Portfolio Analysis and the Uneasy Case for Conglomerate Mergers," *Journal of Finance* 25, no. 4 (September 1970): 795–802; and W. Lewellen, "A Pure Financial Rationale for the Conglomerate Merger," *Journal of Finance* 26, no. 2 (May 1971): 521–37.

39. If the industry into which the entry occurs is fettered by any of a number of kinds of inefficiency or monopolistic restriction, the entry of a large newcomer may provide the "cold fresh wind" of competition. Of course precisely the opposite result can also occur: a new entrant can reduce the level of competition by its post-entry behavior.

has failed to realize the profit potential of the resources under its command. Firms in an oligopolistic industry, absent the threat of conglomerate takeover, might be willing to take the risks of tacitly agreeing to forego vigorous competition in order that each may give its managers some of the quiet life that Judge Wyzanski described as one of the fruits of monopoly. The presence of a potential acquirer makes this a dangerous strategy for it invites the unwanted attention of a takeover bid.

Monopoly Power from Conglomerate Mergers

While efficiencies are thus conceptually quite possible, so are adverse competitive effects. No one would deny that a conglomerate acquisition *might* be both necessary to and sufficient for exercise of previously unexercised power in one or more markets, and that such exercise, if it occurred, might be socially undesirable.[40]

In this section I want only to sketch the possibilities of these anticompetitive effects for they are at the heart of the current legal struggles and policy debates about conglomerate mergers, and are discussed at length in that context in chapters 9 through 11.

Mergers that have monopolistic effects must either create new market power in some market or permit exercise of power that previously was unexercised. Such effects may occur in the market of the acquired firm, of the acquiring firm, wholly elsewhere, or in some combination of the above.[41] I will assume for the subsequent discussion that the acquiring firm is large, has some market power in its own market, is profitable and has an aggressive and vigorous managerial group that is motivated to make profits for the firms it manages.

IN THE MARKET OF THE ACQUIRED FIRM

The effect of acquisition on the level of competition in the acquired firm's market will be related to the market structure in that market

---

40. Those whom I have characterized as supporting a "per se legal" view simply think such possibilities are sufficiently unlikely that they can be safely neglected (see pp. 53–55 above).

41. For semantic convenience, I will treat each party to the merger as if it operates in but a single market. By our definition of conglomerates, the product markets of acquired and acquiring firms do not overlap.

and also to the behavior of the acquired firm, and its rivals, prior to acquisition. A few possibilities may be mentioned:

a)   The acquired firm may possess but fail to exercise monopoly power, which the new management may be able and willing to exercise. Is this theoretically, or empirically, an important case? I have no great confidence that it is not. Some (for example those in what I have called the Coase et al. group) might dismiss the possibility on theoretical grounds since it implies widespread and sustained irrational (i.e., nonprofit maximizing) behavior by the premerger managements of the firms in the industry where acquisition occurs. Although agreeing with the implication, it is not clear to me that nonmaximizing behavior is beyond credulity. It might arise as a conscious choice of the quiet life, or in response to an unwarranted fear of the legal consequences of a more monopolistic policy, or simply due to failure to adjust promptly to the changing position of the firm and its products in a dynamic world. Moreover, impediments to entry and to capital flows may well be sufficient to allow chronically inefficient and mismanaged industries to survive and to earn profits for significant periods of time.

Such a situation, if it occurs, is not unlike that in which an inefficient firm becomes a target by virtue of its failure to achieve the lowest attainable levels of cost. But here the social consequences of the takeover—more nearly monopolistic price and output results—may not be desirable.[42]

In any event, it is the change of management, not the acquisition, that is the proximate cause of the effect on competition here. Are there reasons to suppose that conglomerate acquirers are in some sense uniquely or specially available for this sort of takeover? I do not know. But one can put a hypothesis that is similar to the "managerial science" hypothesis, but a good deal less benign. It is that the special talent that the conglomerates have is the ability to create and exercise monopoly power. I see no reason to reject summarily this hypothesis, and to assume that somehow this kind of crime does not pay enough to develop specialists in its practice.

---

42. I say "may" because it is at least arguable that having resources managed by an alert, albeit avaricious, management may be preferable to having them managed by a dull and unresponsive one. In the former case, an appropriate public policy (e.g., antitrust activity) may be able to compel socially desirable and efficient behavior.

b) Acquisition by an outside giant may be the catalyst for transforming a "loose oligopoly" into a tight one, either by providing a focus for agreement (or quasi-agreement), by removing the threat of entry, or by raising the barriers to subsequent entrants. Here again I see no compelling reason to regard this kind of anticompetitive effect as unlikely.[43] It clearly can occur in certain situations. It requires that the conditions in the market of the acquired firm are conducive to loose oligopoly without any natural focus for agreement, and it further supposes the acquiring firm has both a dominant image and some record of or talent for "stabilizing" activities.

c) Acquisition can conceivably convert a formerly competitive industry into a monopolistic one, either by the acquirer realizing some new economy that leads directly to monopolization or by his use of predatory tactics. Neither seems very interesting to pursue in the conglomerate merger context.

It is not impossible that there are industries that are ripe for monopolization by someone's perceiving and exploiting a previously unexploited economy of scale, but if so, there seems no special reason why the conversion should take the form of a takeover of a firm that is, by definition, inefficient. Might not the new entrant more sensibly create a new firm and hire the essential know-how and specialized factors it needs? Even if takeover is of net value, why should it occur in the form of a *conglomerate* acquisition? In any event, the competitive harm, if it occurs, consists not in the rationalization of the industry but in its behavior after it has become efficient.

The most commonly adduced anticompetitive consequence of entry of a large company into a competitive industry is that the acquiring corporation with a "deep pocket" of profits and cash from other ventures is able to engage in predatory behavior and thus either drive out competitors or coerce them into a noncompetitive pattern of behavior. This is discussed more fully in chapter 9. Let me, at this stage, simply associate myself with Turner's conclusion that:

. . . predatory pricing seems so improbable a consequence of conglomerate acquisitions that it deserves little weight in formulating anti-merger rules based on prospective effect.[44]

---

43. The anticompetitive effect rests upon the assumption that the tighter an oligopoly the closer it comes to exercising monopoly power, whether by tacit or overt collusion, or by conscious parallel action, oligopolistic rationale, and so forth.

44. Turner, "Conglomerate Mergers," p. 1346.

IN THE ACQUIRING FIRM'S MARKET

If the acquiring firm possesses significant power in its own market, but is faced with some impediment to its direct use, it is possible that making an acquisition in an unrelated market can be used to avoid the impediment. This will be discussed in substantial detail in chapter 9 with respect to reciprocity. A single example will serve to establish the possibility. Consider a large national defense contractor which sells on contract mainly to the United States government but purchases sufficient quantities of industrial products from a large number of manufacturing firms that it has significant monopsony power in number of markets. Suppose it is unwilling to use this monopsony power *directly* on its suppliers in the form of demanding lower prices. Such reluctance could arise because it was operating on cost plus contracts, or because it was afraid of renegotiation of its contracts if its profit margins per dollar of costs proved too large. Its suppliers too may be reluctant to give direct price concessions, either for fear of being charged with Robinson-Patman violations or because they do not wish to start a price war in their own industry. The monopsonist may be able to use reciprocity to achieve price concessions.[45]

Accepting, for the sake of argument, that this sort of indirect use of market power may be helpful to a firm in gaining the fruits of its market power, is there any reason why this should appear as a conglomerate phenomenon? The answer may well be "yes": the product or products that best serve the purposes of the firm which intends to engage in tying or reciprocity are determined by the characteristics of its customers (in the case of tying) or its suppliers (in the case of reciprocity). Suppose, for illustration, that the conglomerate ITT had wished to find a good or service all of its suppliers utilized. It could hardly have done better than to acquire the Canteen Corporation which provides both vended and manual in-plant food service. Yet such an acquisition is correctly labeled conglomerate because food service (the product of Canteen) is almost entirely unrelated to ITT's other important product lines.[46]

---

45. This may be the correct interpretation of the facts of the General Dynamics-Liquid Carbonic case. See below, p. 222.

46. I do not wish to imply that I believe this was the motive for the Canteen acquisition; indeed, after a lengthy study I am convinced reciprocity played no part. See the opinion of the district court in *United States v. ITT (Canteen)*, 1971 *CCH Trade Cases* ¶73,619 (N.D. Ill. 1971) at

EXERCISING POWER IN OTHER MARKETS OR AREAS

The conglomerate label as applied to mergers rests on the character-istics of the *products* or *services* sold by the merging firms. But these firms operate in other markets as well, especially factor markets, and the merger may affect behavior in those other markets.

As the simplest example, recognize that two firms producing vastly different products may be important purchasers of a common input, and therefore the merger may have anticompetitive effects on factor markets. The merger into a single company of Procter & Gamble, Texaco, Liggett and Meyer, and Ford Motor Company, al-though clearly conglomerate, would represent an awesome increase in the market power vis-à-vis the advertising media. There is nothing special about advertising in this respect: purchases of executive talent, of transportation services, and of the use of money all occur in factor markets where a *conglomerate* acquisition might have horizontal effects.[47]

A different concern involves what has been called development of communities of interest. If one market's leading sellers meet each other in other markets with vertical rather than horizontal relation-ships, or as competitors with very different market shares, they may develop live and let live attitudes and be less willing to compete than a group of wholly independent competitors. This result, if it is sig-nificantly likely to occur, is more likely when many firms are diversify-ing into many markets, by merger or otherwise.

Finally, many worry that the arena in which the conglomerate seeks and achieves power is the political one, where influence takes

---

90, 530, whose conclusions reflect mine. But we are talking about what is possible. My rejection of the reciprocity motive in the Canteen case is based on many other facets of the acquisition.

47. In *United States v. Pennzoil Co.* 252 F.Supp. 962 (W. D. Pa. 1965), the court treated as a horizontal merger the proposed merger be-tween Pennzoil and Kendall Refining Company because of their joint *purchase* of Penn Grade crude oil. The court explicitly rejected the defense that the relevant line of commerce had to be the end product. In this case of course, the products of the two companies were remarkably similar—various refined Penn Grade oil products. While it is not impossible, I doubt that courts would readily treat as horizontal all mergers where the merger partners competed for some factor of production, no matter how disparate the final products, unless the input was a dominant one for each company.

the form of influencing regulatory commissions, congressmen, government officials, or foreign governments. Here the corporation uses its power to change the rules that govern its markets, the taxes it pays, the competitors (foreign and domestic) that it must face—and so on. Whether this sort of thing should be regarded as an anticompetitive phenomenon is perhaps doubtful, but it may be a real phenomenon. Whether it is, in any important sense, a *conglomerate* phenomenon is discussed more fully in chapter 11.

CHAPTER FOUR

Synergy II:
Tax Incentives to Merger

Introduction

CAN A MERGER that is not otherwise motivated become the preferred form of economic activity *because* of the tax laws?[1] It can if the combined company can make more profitable use of the tax laws than the constituent companies, or than their stockholders. As I will show in this chapter and its appendix, this is often possible, and was so particularly before the tax reforms of 1969 limited the tax advantages of exchanging convertible debentures for common stock to finance acquisitions. I regard the availability of such a tax advantage as a synergy because it can benefit both buyers and sellers.

This topic has been extensively discussed in recent years.[2] If there is a concise and clear summary statement of the issues I did not find it, and I hope the present chapter fills that need.

It is hard to talk clearly about the effect of tax incentives on behavior because an incentive exists relative to some base, and confusion in the base for comparison clouds much of the literature. Con-

---

1. Because of the complexity of the tax laws as they apply to individuals, to corporations, to income, and to capital gains, the inclusion of tax considerations into the formal analytic model becomes notationally complex. I attempt in the chapter to state every important proposition but to leave a rigorous formulation and proof to the appendix to chapter 4.

2. See especially the nine articles in 44 ST. JOHN'S LAW REVIEW, Special Edition, 1009–1160 (Spring 1970). N. Sinrich, "Tax Incentives and the Conglomerate Merger: An Introduction"; L. L. Silverstein, "Impact of the Acquisition Indebtedness Provisions of the Tax Reform Act of 1969 on Corporate Mergers"; D. C. Knickerbocker, Jr., "Miching Mallecho: The Tax Reformers' Sneak Attack on Conglomerates"; G. H. Jewell, Jr., "The Tax Legislation Against Conglomerates—The Case Against the Tax Legislation"; L. Lee, "The Tax Reform Act and Convertible Debt Securities"; W. G. Wintrub, R. E. Graichen, and H. W. Keidan, "Tax Aspects of Corporate Acquisitions"; J. D. Shors, "Corporate Reorganizations: Some Current Developments Including the Tax Reform Act of 1969"; R. S. Taft, "Acquiring the Closely-Held Corporation"; J. M. Swenson, "Action Against Conglomerate—Will It Hurt Small Business?".

sider the following quotation from the FTC *Economic Report on Corporate Mergers:*

> Generally speaking, we should strive for a tax system that has a neutral effect on business decision-making and, therefore, on industrial structure. Unfortunately, the present tax system falls far short of this ideal. Considering the massive industrial restructuring resulting from the current merger movement, it is important that existing tax laws be revised to remove incentives for merger activity that are unrelated to economic efficiency. Continued tax subsidies for merger activity bring about an unhealthy distortion of investment resources and entrepreneurial goals.[3]

I am concerned now not with the normative views the quotation expresses, but with the shifting comparison base. The first sentence speaks of the advantages of a neutral tax system, that is, one that would lead to the same allocations of resources as in a tax-free society. The second sentence notes that the existing tax structure is not neutral, not merely in its treatment of mergers. The third sentence refers to the incentives to *merger* within a nonneutral system, and thus impliedly refers not to *any* nonneutrality in favor of corporations, but only to those available to *merging* corporations but not to nonmerging corporations. Yet the sixteen page discussion that this passage concludes has been heavily concerned with advantages not restricted to merging firms.

DEFINITION OF A "TAX INCENTIVE TO MERGER"

Obviously—and unmistakably intendedly—the overall tax system is not neutral in its effect on either personal or business decisions. With respect to business decisions, corporations are taxed differently from proprietorships, dividends differently from interest, income differently from capital gains, distributed profits differently from undistributed ones. All of these things tend to encourage certain kinds of business decisions and discourage others.

A most frequently noted nonneutrality is the different tax treatment of different sorts of capital transactions. One induced incentive is for retention of earnings and internal reinvestment by profitable corporations. Such internal reinvestment reduces the choices of the corporation's stockholders, but it avoids the taxation of dividends that

---

3. Federal Trade Commission, Bureau of Economics, *Economic Report on Corporate Mergers* (Washington, D.C., 1969), p. 158.

would occur if all earnings were distributed. Were neutrality toward use of capital markets truly a preeminent goal of the tax system, the corporate income tax would surely have to be changed. But neutrality in the sense of approximating the allocative results of a system without taxes is clearly not the issue, here or generally.

What activity ought merger be regarded as alternative to? Suppose the desired activity is that the present stockholders of a company in industry X wish to shift part of their investment from the present activities of their company into industry Y. A few of the ways they might do this are:

1. Having sufficient extra dividends paid to stockholders to finance their investment in a company in industry Y. Such distributions would be subject to taxation as personal income. If these stockholders subsequently purchase stock in Y the sellers will be subject to capital gains taxation.

2. Having stockholders sell some of their holdings of the company's stock to acquire funds for investment in stock in Y. Such sales are subject to taxation at appropriate personal rates on any realized capital gains. So are the sales to them by previous owners of stock in industry Y.

3. Having the *company* (not the stockholders) sell some of its assets and purchase assets with which to enter industry Y *de novo*. The asset sales are subject to taxation under the corporate tax law.

4. Having the company use undistributed profits or borrowed funds to finance *de novo* expansion into the industry. No extra taxes are payable because of this transaction.

5. Having the company acquire (or be acquired by) a Y producer (in any of a variety of forms of acquisition). This *merger* may be taxed or untaxed depending upon the form of acquisition.

Which of the previous possibilities is the proper comparison base for the fifth alternative? Clearly because of different kinds of tax treatment the choice among alternatives 1 through 4 (none of which involve merger) is far from neutral under existing tax laws. Alternative 4 seems to me unambiguously the preferred form if the company and its stockholders have been prospering in recent years. Because of this, the net incentive to merger is best measured relative to *de novo* expansion using internally generated funds, or borrowed funds.

If this seems trivially obvious, I should emphasize that the FTC report chooses otherwise. The full report makes it clear that the tax subsidies to merger it deplores are involved in any treatment that does not treat the acquisition of S's assets by B as an open market transaction subject to realized capital gains on any difference between the acquisition value of the assets and their "basis" for tax purposes. (That is, it chooses 2 or 3 as the comparison base.)

As a result the FTC report treats as incentives to *mergers* what are truly incentives only to corporate diversification. These incentives merit a moment's discussion for they surely provide incentives for enlarged economic activities on the part of existing firms, of which mergers are a particular form.

TAX MOTIVATIONS FOR COMPANY
RATHER THAN STOCKHOLDER DIVERSIFICATION

Taxation of dividends to stockholders and taxation of capital gains from the liquidation of their stockholdings unmistakably change the relative attractiveness of different forms of investment. A company whose stockholders wish to invest the cash or profit flow from their present investment in other industries might do so by receiving cash dividends or liquidations and reinvesting them in an efficient firm in the new industry. If they are subject to an effective tax rate T on such distributions their reinvestment will be only $(1 - T)$ times their cash or profit flow. An internal expansion by their own company into new areas would be preferable to them provided that the cost of their company getting established as an efficient competitor is no more than the tax liability they incur. A net incentive to *internal* reinvestment exists, and because internal reinvestment is not likely always to be the most efficient form of investment, such an incentive invites resource misallocation.

If these were the only alternatives, the tax laws could be said to provide some incentive for inefficient diversification. But there is a third alternative which may be more efficient than *de novo* diversification, but with a lower tax liability than stockholder reinvestment: takeover of (or by) an efficient firm in the to-be-entered industry. Like diversification, there is no tax on the shifted resources, but unlike the postulated *de novo* diversification, an efficient producer is acquired at once. To the selling stockholder, there may be a tax advantage of selling out for stock instead of cash.

Such an acquisition, in my view, is not properly regarded as tax induced since the choice between (the tax-free) internal reinvestment of profits in a new industry and (the tax-free) acquisition in that industry (not a tax-affected decision) surely plays the decisive role.

This is not to say that there is not an important issue of tax policy involved. When resources are shifted from one industry to another without paying taxes should this be regarded as a subversion of the intent of the law, or instead should it be regarded as a desirable avoidance of an inefficient and unwanted lock-in of resources? This important issue is not really a *merger* policy question even though a merger may be the most favorable means of achieving a tax-free interindustry (but intrafirm) shift of resources.

More than semantics is at stake because I believe a significant number of conglomerate acquisitions are to be explained in this way.[4] One's view of the merits of such mergers, and thus of the appropriate policy toward them, depends upon the classification and diagnosis. "Utilizing a tax loophole" invites closing the loophole; "efficiently reallocating resources and avoiding a tax inefficiency" seem laudable, and invite no corrective actions if the inefficiency is a by-product of a generally sensible tax law.

Tax Motives for Mergers

MOTIVES UNRELATED TO FORM

Some tax law features provide unambiguous motivations for mergers, independent of the *form* of the merger. The most important is acquisi-

---

4. The General Dynamics-United Electrical Coal Companies merger case decided by the Supreme Court in 1974 is perhaps an almost classic example of this. General Dynamics (GD) with large aerospace and other contracts, was short of cash in a very tight capital market. United Electric Coal Companies (UEC) was receiving a large cash flow from its long-term contracts selling coal to electrical utilities. Most of UEC's existing reserves were already being mined for delivery to particular utility plants under long-term contracts. Because UEC was finding it impossible to acquire suitable additional strip coal mining reserves in its area of operation, the company was faced with the following choices: paying large cash dividends to its stockholders; seeking coal reserves in new areas (e.g., Wyoming) at a higher cost and out of its area of market contacts; entering new ventures for which it lacked know-how and personnel; or being acquired by a company that valued its cash flow very highly. Its principal stockholders preferred the last alternative, and it seems likely they maximized their return by this choice.

tion of unutilized tax-loss carryovers, and I will use it to represent the class of similar incentives.[5]

Corporate tax losses in one year can be carried forward (subject to some limitations) and used to offset future income. But for a firm with large losses and dim future income prospects, or with accumulated losses in excess of what can be offset, there may be an unutilized loss carryover. Acquiring a profit-earning corporation, or being acquired by one, is a means of realizing the potential cash value of the past losses that inhere in the tax laws. Penn Central's accumulation of a tax-loss carryover in excess of $500 million led the *Wall Street Journal* to predict (incorrectly) in April of 1968 that it would become a major conglomerate. Textron is often cited as the classic example of use of tax-loss carryovers to finance a great diversification. Between 1952 and 1959 it paid only $634,000 in corporate income taxes despite an aggregate net income of nearly $55 million: an effective rate of 1.2 percent. During 1960 and 1961 this rose to a rate of 21 percent, still well below the corporate average. According to the FTC,

Operating losses on some of its textile operations were more important sources of tax loss in 1952–54, but most of the subsequent tax losses came from its sales of acquired plants, equipment, and in six instances, entire enterprises which had been acquired. Textron began its diversification program in 1953 with 2 acquisitions; by 1962, it had completed 37 more mergers. In this period, Textron's annual sales increased from $71 million to $550 million. Textron's tax losses were a major factor in motivating its growth by merger, in building up a glamorous reputation for growth of sales and earnings, and in financing many of its mergers.[6]

Tax-loss carryovers are most easily justified in terms of equitable treatment of year to year fluctuations in net income. If T is the appropriate rate of taxation of corporate income, there seems little

---

5. Similar to tax-loss carryovers are unused investment credit carryovers and tax deferrals on credit sales. These seem less important quantitatively, although in particular cases they may prove decisive. The merger of Montgomery Ward and Container Corporation is asserted by the FTC to have been significantly motivated by a large available tax deferral on Ward's credit sales.

6. FTC, *Economic Report on Corporate Mergers,* pp. 152–53. At the end of 1961 Textron still enjoyed $6 million of unused loss carryovers, which it employed to reduce tax liabilities in subsequent years.

reason to tax more heavily companies whose income fluctuates from year to year, with losses in some years, than companies with the same average income stream but a different time profile.

The allowance of tax-loss carryovers can be given an efficiency justification independent of the equitable argument used above. Consider every year's net income of a business venture as a drawing from a probability distribution of rates of return that has a positive mean but sufficient variance so that some portion of the distribution involves losses. A government that wished to be risk neutral would tax outcomes on the basis of the expected income (i.e., the mean of the distribution) not the actual income. A single corporate tax rate, applied positively on income, and negatively on losses, would have that effect in the long run. A tax-loss carryover does approximately the same thing,[7] provided the realized losses are ultimately offset. To the extent that losses are not eventually deductible there is a net disincentive to engage in highly risky ventures—a negative subsidy to risk taking. If, as is usually argued, there is no *public* benefit in private risk aversion, this disincentive is socially undesirable. Any such disincentive is much reduced if large tax losses are salable, as they are via merger.

Salable tax losses may thus be argued to entail equity to stockholders of companies that prove very unlucky, and to incorporate an appropriate neutrality of the government toward risk. *Under present law they are salable now only via the merger route, and this clearly creates a net incentive to a merger that might not have any other justification.*

In principle, one could achieve the equitable and efficiency objectives provided by tax-loss carryovers without motivating a merger. This could be done by applying the corporate income tax negatively as well as positively. The major objection to this is likely to be that "losses" can be easily contrived.[8] But the remedy to that is to redefine taxable net income. As it now stands, such contrived losses are avail-

---

7. Approximately, rather than precisely, because of the deferred nature of the benefits. The present value of a future tax offset is less than the present value of an immediate one.

8. A secondary objection is that the truly losing venture may be kept in production too long if the full burden of its losses is not borne by the company. This assumes it is not loss but bankruptcy that leads to exit.

able for tax offsets to the otherwise profitable firm, and to the unprofitable firm as a merger partner. They are denied only to the unprofitable firm which attempts to stay independent and fight its way back to profitability.

Finally, some mergers involving oil and coal companies may have been motivated by the depletion allowance provisions. Without going into detail the amount of allowable depletion may not exceed the lesser of a percentage of the value of production (e.g., 27½ percent for oil before 1969) *or* 50 percent of net income. If the net income limit applied, firms with unutilized percentage depletion get to use it by acquisition of nonextractive companies with net income, or by merger with another extractive company where the net income limitation did not apply. I have heard the assertion that many oil-coal mergers were affected by this incentive, but I have been unable to verify the assertion.

TAX MOTIVES RELATED TO FORM OF ACQUISITION

The basic model of merger motivation developed in chapter 2 assumed that the stock of Companies S and B could be exchanged for the stock in a new combined Company C with no taxation of the exchanges. This corresponds to the sort of so-called tax-free mergers allowed by Section 368 of the Internal Revenue Code.

In a tax-free exchange of stock the assets of the acquired firm enter the books of the new firm for tax purposes at whatever "basis" they previously had. Stockholders of the selling firm receive stock in the new firm and realize no capital gains until such time as they may liquidate their holdings.

Tax-free mergers may be of three kinds. Type A mergers are statutory mergers, as defined by the relevant state law. They would include, among others, mergers in which one company pays cash for the voting stock or assets of another. Type B are those mergers consummated by exchanges of voting stock, where the acquiring company has, after the transaction, control of at least 80 percent of the acquired company's stock. Type C mergers are those where the acquiring company exchanges voting stock for substantially all of the assets of the acquired corporation. Excluded are cases where the acquiring company achieves insufficient control, and where exchanges of property other than stock (e.g., debentures) are given to stockholders of the selling company. This second exclusion has proven to be an important one.

Tax-free mergers are *easy* to achieve—and over the period 1963–68, roughly 85 percent of all large mergers were tax free in form. What really requires explanation is why so many large mergers did not avail themselves of the tax-free form. The answer paradoxically is that it may be even more profitable to merge by way of a taxable transaction.

Tax advantages of taxable mergers. The explanation of this paradox is that mergers that are tax free to the sellers may benefit sellers less than they will disadvantage the buyer. In a tax-free merger the selling stockholder pays no capital gains either on any premium paid to induce him to merge, or on gains realized because the "book value basis" of his company's assets for tax purposes is below their market value just prior to the merger. (This can be the result of earlier utilization of permitted accelerated depreciation, or of inflation, or both.) But the *buyer* in a tax-free acquisition must carry the newly acquired assets at their old basis, not the price actually paid, and thus forgo depreciation based on the higher value. If the depreciation deduction to the buyer is more valuable than the avoidance of capital gains to the seller, there will be a *net incentive to merge via a taxable rather than a tax-free form.* The critical relationship depends on the rate of tax on current corporate income (against which depreciation is charged) being higher than the rate payable on realized capital gains. This is shown formally in the appendix to this chapter.

Use of convertible debentures. A further important merger inducing feature of the tax laws prior to 1969 concerned debt-equity switching. The acquiring company instead of exchanging stock in the new company for shares of the selling company could give convertible debentures, exchangeable into common stock at some time in the future. Two tax features of this scheme are important: interest payments by the new company on the debentures are deductible from current income, and the capital gains to the seller can be deferred until the debentures are sold or converted. The ability to defer payment of capital gains taxes in effect lowers the effective rate of capital gains tax.

To the acquiring company this form of exchange had the advantages of the taxable[9] acquisition, discussed just above, plus the deductibility of interest. Additionally, if the rate of interest on the debenture is low enough, it has the advantage of requiring payments less than earnings per share on outstanding shares. As we shall see in chapter 5 this may well prove advantageous by raising earnings per share on common stock.

To the seller, the exchange of stock for these convertible debentures is taxable with respect to capital gains, but (effectively) at a lower rate than in a taxable exchange of stock because the tax may be deferred on an installment basis over the life of the debenture or until the debenture is sold or converted. This deferral of tax often is for a great many years. Since the debentures are convertible on a fixed basis for stock in the new company, the stockholders of the selling firm sacrifice none of their rights to subsequent capital gains in the stock of the merged companies.

This *taxable* convertible debenture route provided the greatest incentive to merge relative to the tax-free acquisition.

The appendix to this chapter defines the conditions under which the convertible debenture exchange is beneficial to both sides. The conditions are not simply stated, but before the 1969 changes in the tax laws these conditions were often met.

By way of summary, the tax laws as they existed in the period 1965–68 provided a theoretical incentive to merge, via a taxable reorganization whenever the present value of the extra depreciation to the buyer exceeded the present value of capital gains taxes payable by the seller. Note that the special motivation was not, as the FTC report suggests, in avoiding taxable reorganizations but in using them. The (taxable) convertible debenture route (prior to 1969) tended to be even more advantageous, for it gave both sellers and buyers even lower tax liability than under ordinary taxable reorganizations.

THE IMPORTANCE OF THE TAX INCENTIVES
DURING THE MERGER WAVE

Theoretical possibilities aside, did many mergers get motivated by tax incentives? Table 4–1 permits a preliminary evaluation of the im-

---

9. Such acquisitions become taxable due to the exclusion of convertible debenture exchanges for virtually all of a company's stock from tax-free status.

portance of tax incentives during the peak of the merger wave.[10] It is easier to describe the data than to explain them.

1. The overwhelming percentage of acquisitions did not utilize special tax incentives for merger, but rather utilized the same sort of tax-free status that would be accorded to *de novo* expansion. I have inquired widely, if unsystematically, among securities experts and tax lawyers without achieving a consensus view as to why. I was several times told that psychologically it is undesirable to make a tender offer that generates tax liability to the one who tenders, and that in most cases where stock was widely held it was safer to forgo a net advantage than to incur the public investor's reluctance.[11] Clearly, an interesting area for further research would be a detailed study of this question.

2. Where taxable acquisitions were utilized (in approximately 14–16 percent of the cases) the form changed sharply during the period. The debt-equity exchange route (via convertible debentures) caught on rapidly and by 1968 was a significant form of exchange. Since this form seems to dominate the taxable exchange under a substantial variety of conditions, the shift needs explaining. The "Street" view (to the extent I discovered it) is that it took the boom market of 1967–68 to generate widespread investor acceptance of complex securities ("funny money"), and that until that occurred promoters were slow to see the advantages to them of this means of takeover. The device, once discovered, showed signs of "taking-off" but the prompt revisions in the tax laws combined with a shaky stock market to discourage its continuing use.

But if we are not sure why the tax laws were not more fully taken advantage of, the data suggest the tentative conclusion that general tax incentives do not appear to have played much of a role in explain-

---

10. The data are less than ideal since fewer than 60 percent of all large acquisitions are covered in the tabulation, and the nature of the bias introduced is unknown. But the FTC informs me they are aware of no more comprehensive data.

11. Where the stock was closely held, the tax advantage may actually lie with the tax-free merger because the impact of capital gains taxes was so concentrated. But very few of the large acquisitions studied had this sort of close holding. Thus it appears to be psychological rather than economic explanations that are required. For many small family held firms, in contrast, tax incentives may have been important in their choosing to be acquired.

TABLE 4–1

Tax Treatment of 411 Large Acquisitions* in Mining and Manufacturing

	Number					Percentage of Total†			
	Tax-Free	Taxable	Debt-Equity Exchanges‡	Total in Sample	Total§	Tax-Free	Taxable	Debt-Equity Exchanges‡	Total in Sample
1963–66	145	22	2	169	349	85.8	13.0	1.2	100
1967	101	12	4	117	167	86.3	10.2	3.4	100
1968	104	9	12	125	201	83.2	7.2	9.6	100
Total	350	43	18	411	717	85.2	10.5	4.4	100

SOURCE: Computed from FTC, *Economic Report on Corporate Mergers*, table 2–5, citing CCH *Capital Changes Reporter* as original source; and table 1–1 citing Bureau of Economics, FTC.

* Acquired firms with assets of $10 million or more.
† Detail does not add to total in all cases due to rounding.
‡ Includes mixed treatments which involve some debt-equity switching.
§ Total reported large acquisitions in mining and manufacturing.

ing most large acquisitions. It is clear that tax loss, investment credit, or credit sales carryovers may have provided significant motivation in particular cases. Further, in 1967 and 1968 a nonnegligible number of large acquisitions may have been motivated in significant part by the tax advantages of the treatment of convertible debenture exchanges. But nothing that I have found or that they present even remotely justifies the FTC conclusion that the "tax laws create a significant institutional bias in favor of merger activity."[12]

The FTC view is reachable only by regarding the "tax-free" acquisitions as tax-motivated mergers. *The FTC appears to view the alternative to tax-free merger treatment to have been a fully taxable exchange to the sellers, with no offsetting depreciation of the new asset valuations.* The FTC's estimate that "in 1968 alone, taxes uncollected on the capital gains amounted to at least several hundred million dollars . . . and may have approached or conceivably exceeded $1 billion" is of this sort.[13]

This seems to me to be misleading. It would, of course, be possible to revise the tax code to eliminate tax-free treatment of type A, B, and C acquisitions *and* to insist that assets acquired by merger be depreciated not at their acquisition value but at the old basis on which capital gains had been calculated and taxes paid. In effect this would involve double taxation of capital gains, and would constitute a powerful deterrent to merger, as well as a remarkable new nonneutrality in the tax laws. It does not seem likely to commend itself on grounds of efficiency or equity. Yet nothing short of that would appear to conform to what the FTC report would regard as an unsubsidized scheme, nor to justify its conclusion about effects.

THE 1969 AMENDMENTS

The Tax Reform Act of 1969, among its other provisions, amended the Internal Revenue Code so as to limit the attractiveness of the convertible debenture exchange in mergers.[14] These provisions disallow part of the interest deduction allowed where a corporation incurs excessive debt in making an acquisition. Roughly, if interest is paid in the amount of $5 million or more on convertible bonds the interest is not deductible. As the appendix to this chapter shows, this

---

12. FTC, *Economic Report on Corporate Mergers,* p. 142.
13. FTC, *Economic Report on Corporate Mergers,* pp. 143, 146.
14. See Sec. 411 and 412 of the Act.

provision weakens significantly the tax advantage to large acquirers of using convertible debentures rather than common stocks in tender offers. The Act also took away in some cases the use of the installment method where the seller receives debt instruments that are readily marketable, and thus weakened the incentive to sellers to accept convertible debentures at the very low interest rates that made them attractive to acquirers.

Other things being equal one would have expected these amendments to reverse the shift toward debt-equity switching shown in table 4–1, above. Such a reverse occurred, but the collapse of the merger boom and the decline in the stock market are equally likely explanations.

As of now, it seems to me we must regard the net importance of tax motivations for mergers as unproved historically, and as uncertain for the future. The theoretical possibilities unmistakably exist, but whether the quantitative importance is great enough to matter is unclear.

Appendix to Chapter 4: Tax Incentives to Mergers and the Effect on Taxes of the Form of Acquisition

DEFINITIONS AND NOTATION

This appendix utilizes the notation of chapter 2 and continues the analysis of a situation in which Company B acquires Company S by giving kn_S shares of a new company to acquire the n_S outstanding shares of Company S. Denoting the premerger anticipated annual (pre-tax) income streams of the two companies as $\$I_S$ and $\$I_B$, we shall assume no synergistic or other real advantages of the merger. Thus the new company can expect a pre-tax income stream of $I_S + I_B$.

Such a merger will be neither advantageous nor disadvantageous if, neglecting tax considerations and transactions costs:

(1)
$$I_S = \frac{kn_S}{n_B + kn_S}(I_S + I_B), \text{ and}$$

(2)
$$I_B = \frac{n_B}{n_B + kn_S}(I_S + I_B).$$

These equations require that the aggregate income available to each set of stockholders be the same before and after the merger.

These conditions each imply

(3)
$$\frac{I_B}{n_B} = \frac{I_S}{kn_S} .$$

This type of acquisition will serve as our standard of comparison.

Two other forms of acquisition that were available before the Tax Reform Act of 1969 may provide a tax incentive to consummate the merger:

a)   A so-called *taxable stock transfer* requires stockholders of the selling corporation to pay capital gains taxes on the difference between their receipts from the sale of the stock, and their "basis" for tax purposes, but it also increases the allowable depreciation of the new company. Suppose that the sale of the sellers' stock for kn_S represents sale for $\$kn_S$ of assets that are carried (for tax purposes) on the sellers' books at $\$B$. Let the aggregate taxable gain be designated $G = kn_S - B$.

From the sellers' point of view this gain is now subject to taxation at appropriate capital gains rates. I want to (notionally) convert this lump sum tax liability into an annual stream that may be compared to the annual subsequent incomes receivable.[15] Let the annual capital gains charge be designated $\beta T_j G$ where T_j is the applicable rate of capital gains taxation, and β converts $T_j G$ into an appropriate annual stream.[16]

From the buyer's point of view if the transfer is taxable, the assets of the acquired firm may be entered in its books at the basis, $B + G$, and depreciated at this basis instead of at the original basis B. G may be large not only because of the premium paid to acquire S, but also because inflation (or previously accelerated depreciation) may have made the basis-for-tax purposes of S's assets unrealistically low. Now define a positive fraction g such that gG represents an amount of annual pre-tax income per year that is equivalent to the clearly valuable right to depreciate G on the books of the new company.

b)   Another form of exchange is the *convertible debenture exchange*. Instead of giving the sellers kn_S shares of stock in the new company they are given a like number of dollars' worth of convertible

---

15. Notionally I am capitalizing this cost to the seller of the taxable transaction and amortizing it as an offset to income the transaction will produce.

16. The tax-free acquisition might be regarded as of the same form with $T_j = 0$.

debentures which pay r percent per year interest and which may at any subsequent time be exchanged for kn_s shares of stock. Two tax features of this scheme are important: interest payments by the new company on the debentures are deductible from current income, and the capital gains to the seller can be deferred until the debentures are sold or converted. The ability to defer payment of capital gains taxes in effect lowers the effective rate of capital gains tax.[17]

We now must show the conditions under which either of these forms of acquisition may benefit both sellers and buyers relative to the tax-free reorganization. Since the tax-free reorganization is, by hypothesis, on the margin, any such benefit will constitute a true tax created incentive to merge.

We must define a variety of applicable tax rates.

Let:

> T represent the rate of tax on corporate income.
>
> $\overline{T}_1$ represent the rate of personal income tax paid by stockholders on taxable distributions to them such as dividends or interest. Of course, different stockholders have different effective rates of tax, but I define $\overline{T}_1$ as an appropriate average.[18]

-----

17. Convertibility creates an analytic nuisance. Because the debentures are convertible, debenture holders retain an equity in any undistributed profits of the combined company. This is neglected in the expressions developed below. It could be included by adding an amount (call it F) to expression (9) and subtracting the same amount from (6). F is the present expected value (after taxes) of the debenture holders' right to claim a share of undistributed profits by converting their debentures to common stock. Adding this does not affect any fundamental conclusions, for the buyers' loss is the sellers' gain, and thus the "appropriate" k (which makes the merger) changes to compensate.

18. An "appropriate average" in this context is one that can be substituted for the individual tax rates in decisions and lead to the same decisions with respect to form of acquisition. I have not figured out how to compute such a rate, but notionally it must exist. Proof: If the decision is sensitive to tax rates, varying $\overline{T}_1$ through the interval zero to unity must lead to a different decision in the neighborhood of zero than in the neighborhood of unity. Thus there exists a critical value of $\overline{T}_1$. But this is true for any set of individual values of the tax rates entering into the computation of $\overline{T}_1$.

$\overline{T}_2$ be the effective average[19] rate of capital gains taxes of stockholders of the selling company under so-called taxable exchanges of stock.

$\overline{T}_3$ be the effective average[20] rate of capital gains tax of stockholders of the selling company under exchanges of their stock for convertible debentures.

All of these tax rates fall between 0 and 1, and, in general

$$\overline{T}_1 > \overline{T}_2 > \overline{T}_3.$$

A problem remains. As everyone knows, corporate income is taxed twice: when earned by the corporation and when distributed to stockholders or converted by them into capital gains. The effective present value of stockholders' taxes on their companies' current earnings depends upon both the form and the timing of their receipt of income flows. This affects *our* problem because debenture holders receive payments currently that are taxed as ordinary income, whereas stockholders may receive only a fraction of their share of earnings as current dividends. I will define:

$\overline{T}_4$ as an appropriate average present-value of the tax liability of stockholders on their companies' income after corporate taxes. $\overline{T}_4$ is necessarily less than $\overline{T}_1$. I will assume for simplicity that $\overline{T}_4$ is the same for stockholders of Companies B, S, and C.

In each of the following expressions, the term $(1 - T)$ plays the role of reducing income flows of corporations to an after-tax status and $(1 - \overline{T}_1)$ or $(1 - \overline{T}_4)$ reduces stockholders' shares in income flows to an after-tax status.

AFTER-TAX ANNUAL INCOME TO THE STOCKHOLDERS
OF THE BUYING CORPORATION

After-tax annual income *after tax-free reorganization* is:

(4) $$(1 - T)\left(\frac{n_B}{n_B + kn_S}\right)(I_S + I_B)(1 - \overline{T}_4).$$

The second term reflects the buying firm's share of the combined company. The third term is its income stream.

---

19. The average here is of the same kind as discussed in the previous footnote.
20. See footnote 19 above.

After-tax annual income *after taxable stock transfer* is:

$$(5) \qquad (1 - T)\left(\frac{n_B}{n_B + kn_S}\right)(I_S + I_B + gG)(1 - \overline{T}_4).$$

The term gG reflects the advantage of being able to depreciate the assets of the acquired firm at the purchase price instead of the assets' basis on the books of the acquired firm.

After-tax annual income *after a convertible debenture exchange* is:

$$(6) \qquad (1 - T)(I_S + I_B + gG - rkn_S)(1 - \overline{T}_4).$$

The buying firm has all the equity, but must pay rkn_S of debenture interest, which is tax deductible from its income.

AFTER-TAX ANNUAL INCOME TO THE STOCKHOLDERS OF THE SELLING CORPORATION

After-tax annual income *after tax-free reorganization* is:

$$(7) \qquad (1 - T)\left(\frac{kn_S}{n_B + kn_S}\right)(I_S + I_B)(1 - \overline{T}_4).$$

The second term represents the seller's share in the new company.

After-tax annual income *after taxable stock transfer* is:

$$(8) \qquad (1 - T)\left(\frac{kn_S}{n_B + kn_S}\right)(I_S + I_B + gG)(1 - \overline{T}_4) - \beta\overline{T}_2 G.$$

This is like (5), but the final term recognizes the cost to these stockholders of the annual equivalent of the capital gains tax payable by the seller.

After-tax annual income *after a convertible debenture exchange* is:

$$(9) \qquad (1 - \overline{T}_1)rkn_S - \beta\overline{T}_3 G.$$

The sellers receive income in the form of interest on the debentures, but still have a capital gains liability, although at a lower rate than in the previous case. Notice that receiving debentures relieves these individuals of paying the corporate income tax, but their debenture interest is taxable currently at the rates of tax applicable to ordinary income.

TAX ADVANTAGE OF A TAXABLE ACQUISITION

A sufficient condition for the taxable reorganization to be preferred to the nontaxable one is that both

$$(5) > (4), \text{ and}$$
$$(8) > (7).$$

The buyer prefers the taxable transaction whenever $(5) > (4)$—a condition that is easily met since the tax liability does not fall on him. $(5) > (4)$ implies, for a given value of k:

$$(10) \qquad gG > 0.$$

The buyer is benefited whenever there is a higher basis for him to depreciate on.

The seller will prefer the taxable transfer only if $(8) > (7)$, which requires:

$$(11) \qquad (1 - \bar{T}_4)(1 - T)\left(\frac{kn_S}{n_B + kn_S}\right)gG > \beta\bar{T}_2 G.$$

The left-hand side is the sellers' after-tax share of the gain from the extra depreciation, while the right-hand side reflects the capital gains taxes the sellers will have to pay. The smaller is $\bar{T}_2$ or $\bar{T}_4$, the easier this is to satisfy. If the advantage to the buyer is large enough, there will exist a k that makes it possible to satisfy (11).[21] Thus a pure tax incentive to merger may exist.

THE ADDITIONAL ADVANTAGE OF USE OF CONVERTIBLE DEBENTURES

The principal differences between the taxable acquisition of stock and the uses of convertible debentures are the deductibility of interest and the lowering of the effective capital gains tax through deferral of taxation of such gains. This is sure to provide an advantage for the debenture scheme if for a given k, $(6) > (5)$ and $(9) > (8)$.

The debenture scheme will be preferred to the taxable acquisition *by the buyer* if $(6) > (5)$, which implies:

$$(12) \qquad \frac{I_S + I_B + gG}{n_B + kn_S} > r,$$

---

21. The comparison between equations (5) and (4) and (8) and (7) above assumed a given k value. Once k changes the comparison becomes more complex, but does not alter the conclusions reached above.

which says that the rate of return earned by the new firm (which the buyer gets) is greater than the debenture rate, which he pays.

The debenture scheme will be preferred by the seller if (9) > (8), which implies:

$$(13) \qquad (1 - \bar{T}_1)rkn_S + \beta G(\bar{T}_2 - \bar{T}_3) >$$
$$(1 - T)(1 - \bar{T}_4)\left(\frac{kn_S}{n_B + kn_S}\right)(I_S + I_B + gG).$$

The right-hand side represents selling stockholders' after-tax share of the earnings of the merged firm if they accept stock. The left-hand side represents their after-tax annual debenture interest payment plus the annual equivalent of the saving in capital gains taxation if they accept convertible debentures.

For the merger to be accomplished via a convertible debenture exchange I assume it is necessary to make it preferable to the taxable acquisition to both buyers and sellers. This requires the simultaneous satisfaction of (12) and (13). The implication of this is shown in the following formidable expression:

$$(14) \qquad \frac{1 - \bar{T}_1}{(1 - T)(1 - \bar{T}_4)}r + \frac{\beta G(\bar{T}_2 - \bar{T}_3)}{(1 - \bar{T})(1 - \bar{T}_4)kn_S} >$$
$$\frac{I_S + I_B + gG}{n_B + kn_S} > r.$$

The next to the last term is earnings per share of the new company. For (14) to be satisfied it is necessary to have a set of tax rates that permit the left-hand side to be greater than r. This requires:

$$(15) \qquad \frac{\beta G(\bar{T}_2 - \bar{T}_3)}{kn_S} > r[(1 - T)(1 - \bar{T}_4) - (1 - \bar{T}_1)], \text{ or}$$

$$(16) \qquad \frac{\beta G(\bar{T}_2 - \bar{T}_3)}{kn_S} > r[(\bar{T}_1 - \bar{T}_4) - T(1 - \bar{T}_4)].$$

Since each of the terms in parentheses is nonnegative, this is clearly possible but not necessary. As expression (16) shows, both the installment treatment of capital gains and the deductibility of interest play a role in motivating merger via convertible debentures. The greater the deferral of capital gains to the sellers, the greater is $(\bar{T}_2 - \bar{T}_3)$, and thus the larger the left-hand side. The higher is the corporate tax rate, T, the greater is the value of the deductibility of interest. If it were not deductible, interest would be taxed at rT. Notice that rT enters the right-hand side of (16) with a negative sign. There is thus an additional tax advantage possible through use of convertible debentures.

THE EFFECT OF THE 1969 AMENDMENTS

Suppose the effect of the 1969 amendments was to eliminate entirely the deductibility of debenture interest and reduce (but not eliminate) the capital gains tax deferral to sellers. Condition (6) and all that use it must be modified. Of particular interest are:

(6*) $$[(1 - T)(I_S + I_B + gG) - rkn_S](1 - \overline{T}_4),$$

(12*) $$(1 - T)\left(\frac{I_S + I_B + gG}{n_B + kn_S}\right) > r,$$

(16*) $$\frac{\beta G(\overline{T}_2 - \overline{T}_3)}{kn_S} > r(\overline{T}_1 - \overline{T}_4).$$

Comparing (12) and (12*) it is clear that the buyers' condition for preferring the convertible debenture route is made much stiffer. Only if the *after-tax* profits per share (instead of the pre-tax profits per share) exceeds the debenture rate, will the debenture exchange be preferred by the buyers.

While it is not impossible for (16*) to be satisfied, and thus make the merger attractive to both sides in this form, it is less likely. Since $\overline{T}_1 > \overline{T}_4$, the right-hand side is positive. If there remains *some* deferral of capital gains, $\overline{T}_2 > \overline{T}_3$, the left-hand side can be positive as well. To the extent that the 1969 reforms eliminated most of the differences between $\overline{T}_2$ and $\overline{T}_3$, they effectively removed the tax advantage of the convertible debentures route to acquisitions. They left untouched, however, the potential tax advantages of merger by taxable acquisition shown in expression (11).

CHAPTER FIVE

Synergy III: Speculative and Accounting Motives

IN ADDITION to real synergies discussed in chapter 3 and tax incentives in chapter 4, there is a series of influences that may lead the price of the stock of Company C to rise as a result of the merger without any change in the flows of income, or stocks of assets under the combined control of the merging companies. Stock market psychology, investors' information and beliefs, and accounting practices are all aspects of this kind of potential *pecuniary* incentive, and while they may operate separately, they often interact.

The Stock Market and the Merger Wave

Financial and speculative aspects of the merger wave of the sixties were of double importance: not only did they focus a great deal of attention on the merger movement and on the "new breed" of acquirers called the conglomerators, but they affected the motivations to merge. Before examining the mechanism through which those effects occurred, it is worth looking at the stock market performance during the merger wave, with particular attention to the stocks of the leading conglomerate firms.

In order concisely to discuss behavior of stock market earnings and prices, it is convenient to use certain market averages. I shall use Moody's Industrials index as a general measure of stock market behavior, and the average of the following ten companies as an index of conglomerate acquirers: FMC, Glen Alden, Gulf and Western, ITT, Litton, RCA, Teledyne, Tenneco, Textron, and White Consolidated Industries.[1] Basic data are presented in table 5–1.

---

1. The selection of the ten is subjective, and indeed haphazard. I took a large list of leading acquiring companies and eliminated all those for which (1) data were partially unavailable, (2) I could not accurately adjust for stock splits, or (3) actual losses occurred in some years of the period 1963–71. This last no doubt introduced a bias and surely reduced the variance of my index, but it made it possible to compute price-earnings ratios. In any case I intend "Steiner's Index" to be used only for the very limited purposes of the next few pages; purposes for which it is adequate if not optimal.

TABLE 5–1

Price, Earnings per Share, and PE Ratio, 1963–71
Moody's Industrials (M) and Ten Conglomerates (C)
(1965 = 100 in all indexes)

Year	STOCK PRICE INDEX		EARNINGS PER SHARE INDEX		PRICE EARNINGS RATIO		PRICE EARNINGS INDEX	
	M	C	M	C	M	C	M	C
1963	76.7	64.3	75.7	64.1	17.6	19.3	101.7	100.5
1964	91.0	74.7	87.0	81.2	18.1	17.6	104.6	91.7
1965	100.0	100.0	100.0	100.0	17.3	19.2	100.0	100.0
1966	93.8	121.4	102.2	138.3	15.9	16.8	91.9	87.5
1967	102.0	167.4	96.0	146.1	18.4	22.0	106.3	114.5
1968	111.1	179.1	107.3	164.8	17.9	20.8	103.5	108.3
1969	110.2	141.0	107.6	175.0	17.7	15.5	102.3	80.7
1970	95.3	89.9	93.2	146.9	17.7	11.7	102.3	60.9
1971	112.1	111.9	107.2	146.9	18.1	14.6	104.6	76.0

Sources: *Moody's Handbook of Common Stock,* Quarterly Survey of Current Business, Issues 1963–71 (New York, 1963–71).

Figure 5–1 relates the two indexes of stock prices to the merger index developed in chapter 1.[2] It is clear that stock prices, and particularly conglomerate stock prices, correlate well if imperfectly with changes in merger activity between 1964 and 1970. It is also clear that conglomerate behavior was remarkably more volatile than the Moody's Industrials index, a fact that made them the glamor stocks of the boom, and the disappointments of the post-1968 slump.

Stock market prices are, of course, not unrelated to measured indicia of company performance. Figure 5–2 shows that reported earnings of the conglomerates were higher on average (relative to 1965) than for Moody's Industrials and this partially explains the higher prices. These higher profits are not readily explained in terms of companies acquired. Such evidence as is available suggests that acquired firms were of roughly average profitability relative to all-American industry, and to the industries in which they operated.[3]

2. This is plotted on a log scale. Only the slopes are relevant, not the levels.

3. See especially tables in Federal Trade Commission, Bureau of Economics, *Economic Report on Corporate Mergers* (Washington, D.C., 1969). These tables contain great detail about profitability, by type of acquirer, of the acquirees in the years before the acquisition. Perhaps be-

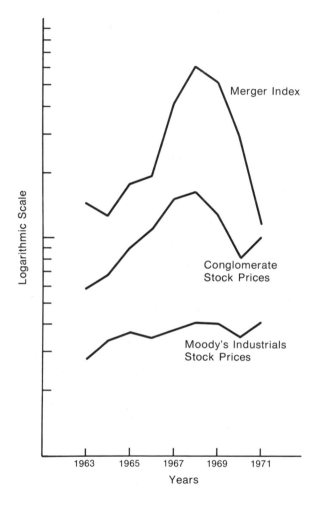

Fig. 5–1. Merger index and two indexes of common stock prices.

But while stock price and earnings indexes are clearly positively correlated, the correlation is neither linear, nor perfect. Prices reflect expectations, and current earnings are but one source of data about future performance. This is illustrated in figure 5–3. For Moody's

cause of the hazards of relying on book values, but perhaps because profitability of the acquiree is but one of many considerations, they do not seem to show very much except that profit rates vary widely.

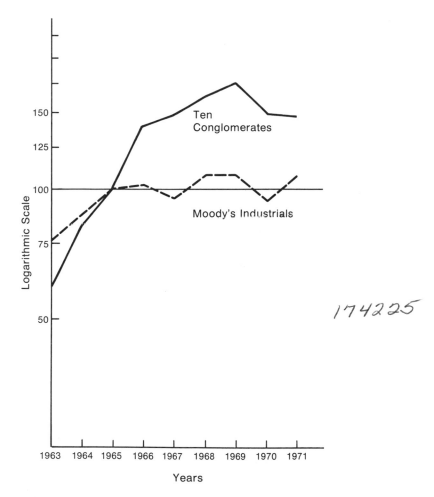

Fig. 5–2.   Indexes of earnings per share (index 1965 = 100).

Industrials as a group, the relationship of price and earnings was close over the entire period. But notice how the market "deglamorized" the conglomerates (as a group) after 1968 notwithstanding their continued high earnings per share. The average price-earnings (PE) ratios are graphed in figure 5–4 on an arithmetic scale. We shall examine the PE ratio, and the role it may have played, just below.

While it is evident that the stock market regarded conglomerates in a special way, averages conceal much diversity. I mean here more

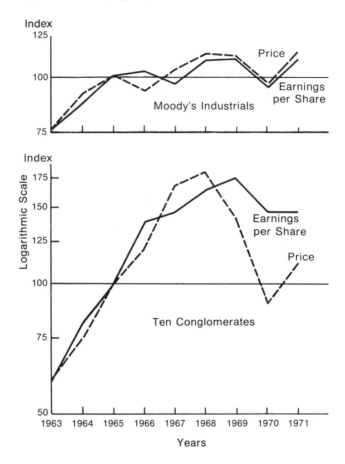

Fig. 5–3.   Differing price-earnings patterns (index 1965 = 100).

than the ever present variance around a central value; I mean instead differences of kind. This is dramatically illustrated in figure 5–5.[4]

In contemplating the conglomerate merger phenomenon—and trying to explain its rise and fall—it is essential to recognize that the conglomerate merger itself is not a homogeneous phenomenon. Conglomeration has occurred for various motives, and with varying effect. The world of Jimmy Ling was vastly different from that of Harold

---

4. Lest one is too impressed with ITT's steady pattern of growth in earnings per share, it should be noted that achieving precisely that pattern was the stated objective of Harold Geneen. As we shall see, the ability to manipulate earnings per share is not overly limited, and can be affected by who is acquired, and when.

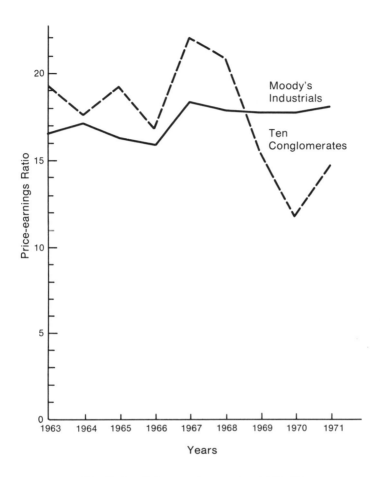

Fig. 5–4.   Price-earnings ratios 1963–71.

Geneen, and the history of LTV and its acquisitions is very different from that of ITT. Ling is (or was) a promoter, a speculator—perhaps even a manipulator of corporate securities. His empire collapsed with the downturn in the stock market. Geneen on the other hand—no less ambitious, no less aggressive— is closer to being a Schumpeterian entrepreneur, relentlessly (and amorally) seeking operating profits by increasing the efficiency of companies acquired, by finding high profit outlets for cash flow, as well as in other, perhaps less salutory ways.

This heterogeneity, reflected in stock market behavior, has a more profound significance. If the category being explained is

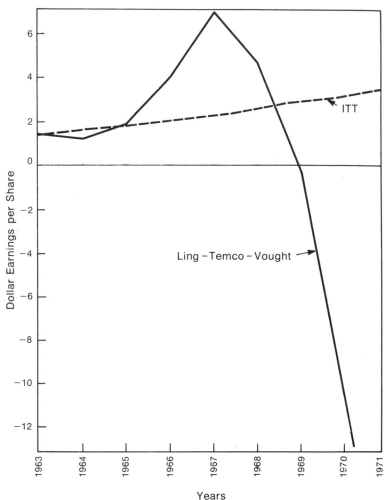

Fig. 5–5.   Earnings per share for two leading conglomerates.

heterogeneous, a variety of explanations may be required, and a general theory will have to discriminate among different types of acquisitions. While there may be some substantial similarity between ITT's acquisition of Hartford Life Insurance and Consolidated Food's acquisition of Gentry, it seems to me that the differences are more important than the similarities. Indeed even two acquisitions by the same company may be so unlike as to require separate analysis. General Dynamics's acquisition of Liquid Carbonic was arguably a straightforward attempt to use General Dynamics's purchasing power to make money via reciprocal dealing. General Dynamics's acquisition of the United Electric Coal Companies was arguably primarily an attempt to acquire and divert the large cash flow of a company that was liquidating its fixed assets (its strip coal reserves) and lacked good replacement investments. High dividends paid to a parent corporation provided a before-tax source of capital for investment. And so on.

The PE Ratio, the PE Game, and the Incentive to Merge

THE PRICE-EARNINGS RELATIONSHIP

The price of a corporate security is, of course, a function of many things, but importantly it is a function of the expected value of the present value of future earnings of the company. Because it is also a function of the expected future price of the security itself there is also a purely speculative element in the prices of stocks. Leaving this aside for the moment, one might expect a dollar's worth of present expected value of an annual earnings stream to command a value that is some well-defined multiple of the annual expected earnings, just as the present value of an annuity is some multiple of the annual payment. In a world of perfect knowledge of the future one might expect the price of every security to be the *same* multiple of the annual certainty-equivalent income stream. This multiple would be related to interest rates pertaining. It would be the same for all securities, for if it were not, profitable arbitrage would be undertaken until the various multiples were brought into equality.

Unfortunately a company's future income stream is not known. Suppose instead that what is known are the earnings of the company in the years past, rather than the years ahead. We can still treat today's price as a multiple of present or past earnings. But now quite rationally the multiples (the price-earnings ratios) will not be the same for different companies because a dollar of past or current earnings may not be the same predictor of future earnings for different companies. Thus, in modern stock market discussions, it is common to regard variable future expectations about a company's earnings per share (and thus about its stock price per share) as embodied in an appropriate price-earnings (PE) ratio. Of course, one can add speculative considerations too. If for any reason one expects a particular company's stock to rise rapidly in the future, this justifies a higher price now, and thus a higher PE ratio.

Table 5–2 shows price-earnings ratios for the ten conglomerates in my index. Clearly Litton and Teledyne, on the one hand, were perceived very differently from Glen Alden and Tenneco, on the other

TABLE 5-2

PRICE-EARNINGS RATIO, SELECTED CONGLOMERATES

	1963	1964	1965	1966	1967	1968	1969	1970	1971
FMC	20.3	19.2	18.6	17.7	18.7	16.6	14.6	11.7	17.8
Glen Alden	9.1	11.2	9.2	9.4	24.0	15.4	16.1	7.0	7.8
Gulf & Western	17.2	14.8	25.3	12.5	13.3	16.2	10.8	7.6	9.5
ITT	18.0	18.0	16.6	16.9	21.6	20.8	18.4	14.3	16.4
Litton	32.0	25.1	33.1	32.0	38.9	45.5	22.7	14.1	21.5
RCA	22.0	22.8	23.7	22.2	23.9	20.9	17.6	21.1	28.0
Teledyne	33.8	28.9	28.6	25.6	41.6	33.6	20.7	13.3	14.7
Tenneco	15.1	14.7	13.7	11.6	14.0	13.2	11.7	11.3	11.3
Textron	10.3	11.4	14.0	13.1	19.5	21.7	14.8	10.5	12.7
White Consolidated	21.2	13.0	15.6	7.8	16.0	13.5	10.1	6.8	13.0

SOURCE: Computed from *Moody's Handbook of Common Stock*, Quarterly Survey of Current Business, Issues 1963–71. (Prices are means of annual highs and lows.)

hand. Clearly too, Teledyne was viewed very differently in 1963–68 than in 1970–71.

The PE ratio embodies all of the "market's" subjective feelings about a company's future, and how investors generally will assess its future. But certain objective indicia are thought to shed light on it. A company whose earnings per share have been rising tends to be valued more highly than one which has not, presumably because the market extrapolates past trends. Similarly, rising stock market prices, high or rising earnings per dollar of tangible assets, high or rising rates of return on equity, all are taken as "good" indicators. Thus, for an important example, a company that pays no (or small) dividends to its stockholders can have a higher PE ratio than one which pays much of its earnings as dividends if it reinvests its earnings in ways that increase one or more of the determinants of the PE ratio.

All of the above is an elementary, and perhaps unnecessary, recital of why the PE ratio plays a role. The PE ratio is a perfectly reasonable summary concept for the whole congeries of things that lead to variable expectations of future events. The price of a company's stock at time *t* is by definition the product of its PE ratio at time *t,* and its earnings per share at time *t.*

BEHAVIORAL ASSUMPTIONS UNDERLYING THE PE THEORY
OF INCENTIVES TO MERGE

The definitional identity just stated can be transformed into a *theory* of behavior that plays an important role in conglomerate acquisitions by the following assumptions:

1. The PE ratio of a particular company tends to become an established parameter and to change but slowly over time. Because of this, anything that increases earnings per share of the company tends to increase the price of its stock.

2. When a Company B acquires a Company S with a different historic PE ratio from its own, Company B's PE ratio becomes applicable to Company S's earnings per share.

3. The PE ratio tends to increase secularly if the rate of growth of earnings increases and if the profits per dollar of net assets increase.

These assumptions may make it possible and profitable to transfer by merger one company's PE ratio to another company's earnings, and thus create an incentive to merge.

A fourth assumption—that the relevant "earnings" to which the PE ratio applies are those as reported in the accounting statements of the firm—creates the role for accounting conventions and changes therein in affecting behavior.

THE PURE PE GAME

It may be intuitively obvious that otherwise unattractive mergers may be eagerly sought if a company with a high PE rating can by merger transfer this ratio to the earnings of a company with a lower one.[5] Table 5–3 illustrates this possibility by an example that provides a useful benchmark for less obvious matters that follow. The example concerns two Companies B and S whose basic financial data is recorded in columns (1) and (2), respectively. Company B is assumed to have a price per share of $1 and earnings per share of .05; its PE ratio is thus 20. Company S's stock also sells for $1 per share, but it has earnings per share of .10 and a PE ratio of 10. A simple combination of these companies into $B + S$, column (3), would show earnings per share of .0667. One might expect its stock, absent any synergy, to have a price per share of $1, and a PE ratio of 15. In every way $B + S$ is the weighted average of Company B and Company S.

Now, however, assume Company B acquires Company S on a share for share exchange ($k = 1$) as shown in column (4). Earnings per share are .0667, as just above, but now these earnings are converted by the stock market into a price per share *using B's PE ratio of 20:1*. The price of C's stock is $1.33 per share instead of $1.00 and everyone is a winner! The same 3,000 shares of stock as in $(A + B)$ now command a third more on the market.[6]

---

5. It is, in any event, proved in the appendix to this chapter that such circumstances create the possibility for profitable mergers.

6. All of the above assumed $k = 1$, and thus avoided any problem of accounting for payments to S in excess of book value, a problem—indeed an opportunity—that will concern us below. Column (5) shows how the example works out if the exchange of stock occurred at a 20 percent premium to S's stockholders. Because there are more shares (3,200) the earnings per share rises only to .0625 and price per share (at a PE of 20:1)

But the advantages are not yet exhausted. Regarding C as the successor to B, B's earnings per share have risen from .050 before the merger to .0667 after it; moreover, its stock price has risen, and so have its earnings per dollar of net assets. Each of these changes is viewed as "favorable" by the market and may lead to an upward revision of B's PE ratio. If it rises to 25 (after all, investors may reason, this is a company showing good growth in profits and in stock prices), its price per share rises to $25 \times .0667 = \$1.67$. This rise is of a different kind from that of the previous paragraph. The earlier one (the rise in earnings per share of B due to the acquisition) is real enough and will continue as long as the two companies' earnings continue at the levels pertaining at the time of acquisition. In contrast, the rate of increase in earnings per share (that may lead to an inflation of the PE ratio) will not be maintained into the following years (absent a real gain somewhere) unless the company makes subsequent acquisitions of companies with positive earnings but relatively low PE's. Thus arises one source of the alleged inexorable search by so-called go-go firms for more and more merger partners: to maintain an upward rate of growth in earnings per share. This would work (by assumption) as long as the investing public continued to assign an appropriate PE ratio by the identity of the acquiring firm, not the source of the earnings.

Obviously, the above mechanism becomes more difficult over time: more or bigger acquisitions are required and as likely targets get acquired, competition for remaining targets would bid up their price relative to their earnings, and—just possibly—the market might begin to reevaluate its rules of thumb. But then an eventual using up of merger targets is consistent both with a merger wave lasting for several years, and with a sharp decline in PE ratios after earnings–enriching mergers cease.

Does this example have any relevance for the reality of actual mergers? The facts are at least superficially consistent with an affirmative answer. In particular, during the great merger wave of 1965–68, acquiring companies tended to have significantly higher PE ratios than acquired companies, and at least in the short run the PE ratios did not fall after the acquisition.

---

to $1.25 instead of to $1.33. The pie is divided somewhat differently. S's shareholders now get half (rather than one-third) of the gain from applying B's PE ratio to S's earnings.

TABLE 5-3

EXAMPLE 1: THE PE GAME

	Company B (1)	Company S (2)	Company B + S simple combination k = 1 (3)	Company C (new B) B acquires S k = 1 (4)	Company C (new B) B acquires S k = 1.20 (5)
Net assets	$2,000	$1,000	$3,000	$3,000	$3,000
Net equity	$2,000	$1,000	$3,000	$3,000	$3,000
[Number of shares]	[2,000]	[1,000]	[3,000]	[3,000]	[3,200]
Earnings	$ 100	$ 100	$ 200	$ 200	$ 200
Earnings per share (e)	$ .05	$ .10	$ .0667	$ .0667	$ .0625
Price per share (p)	$ 1.00	$ 1.00	$ 1.00	$ 1.333*	$ 1.250*
PE ratio (PE)	20:1	10:1	15:1	20:1	20:1
Market value	$2,000	$1,000	$3,000	$4,000	$4,000
Earnings/Net assets	.05	.10	.0667	.0667	.0667
Earnings/Equity	.05	.10	.0667	.0667	.0667

* $p_C = PE_B \cdot e_C$, where the subscripts refer to the company.

This example depended primarily on the willingness of investors to transfer an acquiring company's PE ratio to acquired earnings. To the incentives for merger so created, additional incentives existed in the opportunities to manipulate nominal earnings and the other determinants of PE ratios. Here was the role of imaginative accounting.

Merger Accounting and Incentives to Merge[7]

THE ROLE OF ACCOUNTING

To the economist, although not to the businessman, the first question requiring an answer is why accounting conventions matter. After all, financial reports are supposed to reflect reality, not determine it. I confess that I did not take these matters seriously until I came upon the following headline in the *Wall Street Journal* (March 1, 1970):

> Proposed Measurement
> Of Corporate Goodwill
> May Curb Acquisitions
>
> ───────────
>
> Profits of Surviving Firms
> Would Be Cut by Changes
> Suggested by CPA Group
>
> ───────────
>
> ITT Threatens to Do Battle

The long story that followed said in its opening paragraphs:

> The merger movement that has swept the U.S. in recent years may soon be sharply curtailed.
> That, at least, is the prediction of many investment bankers and corporate financial officers in assessing the likely impact of proposed merger-accounting rules to be unveiled next week by the Accounting

---

7. A convenient introduction to this topic is A. J. Briloff, "Accounting Practices and the Merger Movement," 45 NOTRE DAME LAWYER, no. 4, 604–628 (Summer 1970). The 44 ST. JOHN'S LAW REVIEW, Special Edition, 789–904 (Spring 1970), contains a number of articles on this topic, among them: Homer Kripke, "Conglomerates and the Moment of Truth in Accounting," p. 791; A. R. Wyatt and L. Spacek, "Accounting Principles and Conglomerate Growth," p. 805; L. J. Seidler, "Mergers—The Accountant as a Creative Artist," p. 828; H. P. Hill, "Accounting Options and Conglomerate Growth," p. 855; A. M. Stanger, "Accounting for Business Combinations: Choice or Dilemma," p. 864; H. B. Reiling, "EPS Growth from Financial Packaging: An Accounting Incentive in Acquisitions," p. 880; M. Mellman and N. Prisand, "That Complex Earnings Per Share Figure (A Product of the Merger Movement)," p. 894.

Principles Board (APB) of the American Institute of Certified Public Accountants.

The reason: In the case of most mergers, the rules—involving treatment of such intangible assets as goodwill—would cut sharply into the per-share earnings reported by surviving corporations for as long as 40 years. That would, of course, tend to dampen the enthusiasm of the most merger-minded company.

The broad outlines of the proposals, already disclosed by the board, have created a furor among corporate executives—and among some accountants who disagree with the board's ideas. "We have no intention of allowing (the board's position) to stand," vows Herbert C. Knortz, senior vice president and controller of International Telephone & Telegraph Co., one of the nation's most active acquisitors in recent years.

The explanation for the fact that mere reporting could change behavior in the sophisticated world of high finance lies in the multiplicity and complexity of the measures of performance of huge corporations. Investors, potentially overwhelmed by a flood of measures of corporate performance, have come to rely upon accounting measures sanctioned by the APB and condoned by the Securities and Exchange Commission (SEC). This reliance creates the incentive and the opportunity to creative accountants to operate within the existing rules to achieve unintended ends. Such behavior in turn generates changes in the rules, but often with a sizable lag. Precisely such a period of discovered opportunities and lagged response occurred during the merger wave.

POOLING VERSUS PURCHASE ACCOUNTING

There are two main kinds of merger accounting: pooling and purchase accounting. In pooling the balance sheets and income statements of the two companies are simply added together, as was done in the example of table 5–3 columns (3) and (4). In purchase accounting the assets of S are regarded as purchased by B and enter the acquirer's balance sheet at their acquisition value rather than their book value. This, in turn, often generates intangible assets ("goodwill"), and problems of accounting for it. (When, as in the example of table 5–3, market value and book value are the same, there is no difference in effect between the two methods.)

Pooling is usually more favorable to the merging firms, so I shall consider it first; later I consider the possible limits purchase accounting would impose.

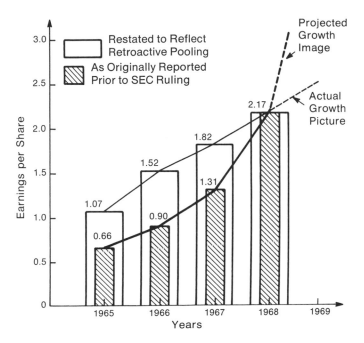

Source: Reinhardt, "Conglomerate Earnings per Share," *The Accounting Review* 47, no. 2 (April 1972): 365.

Fig. 5–6.   The effect of retroactive pooling on the growth image of U.S. Industries, Inc.

Pooling where book value = market value.   Where book value equals market value, the basic mechanism for using mergers to increase earnings per share has already been described, in the example of table 5–3. The *cumulative* effect on a company's growth image can be substantial if acquisitions occur year by year. This is nicely illustrated by figure 5–6, a figure developed by U. E. Reinhardt,[8] about an active conglomerate acquirer. The heavier line reflects the reported earnings per share of the acquiring company year by year. The lighter line reflects the growth in pooled earnings for the identical group of companies over the entire period. Failure to pool retroactively converts an impressive growth record into a spectacular one, and if investors are unwary may provide an artificial stimulus to the acquiring

---

8. U. E. Reinhardt, "Conglomerate Earnings per Share," *The Accounting Review* 47, no. 2 (April 1972): 365.

company's stock, and thus to merger.[9] The SEC now requires such retroactive pooling.

A further artificial boost to earnings under pooling accounting arose through the use of preferred stock or convertible debentures in the takeover. The accounting rules in effect prior to 1968 permitted reporting of earnings per share of common stock only. Consider an acquisition achieved via issuance of convertible debentures. Under these rules, the earnings per share of *common* stock will rise whenever the debenture rate is less than the earnings per share of the company on a fully diluted basis. (Because the owners of the debentures will share in any appreciation of stock prices—but without the risk of a fall in prices—they may be willing to accept very low rates of interest on their debentures—often below the prime rate of interest.) This leverage effect is illustrated in table 5–4, which continues the example of table 5–3. The price per share of $1.33 (based upon fully diluted earnings of .0667 per share) shown in column (3) is the one discussed above. That price rises to $1.40 and $1.60 per share if convertible debentures are used bearing 6 percent and 4 percent, respectively.[10]

The most extreme forms of this particular device for inflating reported earnings per share were eliminated in May 1969, by Opinion 15 of the Accounting Principles Board (APB). A convertible preferred stock or convertible debenture, yielding at time of issue less than two-thirds of the prime rate, is deemed to be a common-stock equivalent for purposes of calculating earnings per share. Since the usual interest rate on corporate debentures is likely to be well above the prime rate, this still leaves a lot of leeway for raising the ratio of earnings per share by decreasing the denominator.

Pooling: market value above book value.   In most acquisitions, the effective purchase price for assets is well above their *book* value, both

9. There are a variety of simple tricks for raising earnings abruptly, that I will ignore in the discussion. For example, a company can complete a merger in the last three months of its fiscal year and pool retroactively over the whole year. The sharp increase in earnings per share in the fourth quarter may trigger an upward spurt in stock values, and appear to validate the wisdom of the merger.

10. Notice however that the effect on earnings rates on assets and equity is somewhat adverse (compared to col. [4]). Not only is this likely to be second-order in effect, but it is remediable in many cases because many assets can be carried at below market values.

TABLE 5-4
EXAMPLE 2: USING LEVERAGE TO INCREASE EARNINGS PER SHARE

	Company B (from table 5-3) (1)	Company S (from table 5-3) (2)	Company C (new B) B acquires S k = 1 (from table 5-3) (4)	Company C B acquires S by use of convertible debentures (6%) (6)	Company C B acquires S by use of convertible debentures (4%) (7)
Net assets	$2,000	$1,000	$3,000	$3,000	$3,000
Net equity	$2,000	$1,000	$3,000	$3,000	$3,000
[Number of shares]	[2,000]	[1,000]	[3,000]	[2,000*]	[2,000*]
Earnings	$ 100	$ 100	$ 200	$ 140†	$ 160†
Earnings per share	$ .05	$ .10	$ .0667	$ .70	$ .80
Price per share	$ 1.00	$ 1.00	$ 1.333	$ 1.40	$ 1.60
PE ratio	20:1	10:1	20:1	20:1	20:1
Market value	$2,000	$1,000	$4,000	$2,800	$3,200
Earnings/Net assets	.05	.10	.0667	.047	.053
Earnings/Equity	.05	.10	.0667	.047	.053

* Common stock only, not adjusting for possible dilution.
† After payment of debenture interest.

113

because of the premium characteristically paid for stock and because in our economy average book values tend to be well below market values of assets. This is partly due to inflation and the use of original cost, and partly to various forms of accelerated depreciation in use. For present purposes the two sources have the same effect, and I will thus continue to assume the acquisition occurs without a premium being paid.[11]

Suppose, with no real changes, Company S in our example carries its assets (which are "worth" $1,000) at only $200 in its balance sheet. Table 5–5, column (4'), recomputes the pooled balance sheet.

TABLE 5–5

EXAMPLE 3: POOLING, MARKET VALUE ABOVE BOOK VALUE

	Company B (from table 5–3) (1)	Company C (new B) B acquires S k = 1 (from table 5–3) (4)	Company S understated book values (2')	Company C B acquires S k = 1 (4')
Net assets	$2,000	$3,000	$ 200	$2,200
Net equity	$2,000	$3,000	$ 200	$2,200
[Number of shares]	[2,000]	[3,000]	[1,000]	[3,000]
Earnings	$ 100	$ 200	$ 100	$ 200
Earnings per share	$ .05	$ .0667	$ .10	$ .0667
Price per share	$ 1.00	$ 1.333	$ 1.00	$ 1.333
PE ratio	20:1	20:1	10:1	20:1
Market value	$2,000	$4,000	$1,000	$4,000
Earnings/ Net assets	.05	.0667	.50	.091
Earnings/ Equity	.05	.0667	.50	.091

Comparison with column (4) (repeated from table 5–4) shows that this has no effect on earnings per share or price but does inflate the rate of earnings on assets and equity. This may result in a small ad-

---

11. Thus we continue to assume $k = 1$, and stay with our example.

vantage to the merging companies' stockholders if it persuades the market to raise the PE ratio appropriate to the company.

The main advantage of pooling undervalued assets is that it creates the opportunity for "instant earnings" in any year that they are required. Suppose Company C now sells all the assets of Company S (worth $1,000, but carried at $200) to another party for $500. It foregoes thereby the $100 per year that those assets earn. *But on the books of Company C this transaction will appear to realize a gain of $300 not a loss of $500.*

The effect on Company C's earnings per share *in the year of the sale* may be spectacular as is illustrated in column (8) of table 5–6,

TABLE 5–6

EXAMPLE 4: SALE OF UNDERVALUED ASSETS TO CREATE
"INSTANT INCOME" POOLING ACCOUNTING

	Company C *B acquires S* *k = 1* *(from table* *5–5)* *(4')*	*Company C* *after sale of S's* *assets for $500* *(8)*	*Company C* *next year* *after sale* *(9)*
Net assets	$2,200	$2,500*	$2,500
Net equity	$2,200	$2,500	$2,500
[Number of shares]	[3,000]	[3,000]	[3,000]
Earnings	$ 200	$ 400†	$ 100
Earnings per share	$ .0667	$ .1333	$ .0333
Price per share	$ 1.333	$ 2.667	$ .667
PE ratio	20:1	20:1	20:1
Market value	$4,000	$8,000	$2,000
Earnings/Net assets	.091	.16	.04
Earnings/Equity	.091	.16	.04

  * $2,200 + $500 receipts — $200 book value of assets sold.
  † $100 income from B's assets + $300 "gain on exchange." I here neglect capital gains taxes payable on this gain. Assume this is the net gain after such taxes.

and if the market continues to play the PE game the price of the stock can shoot up. Of course, the following year, things become less attractive: the company has lost the income stream the assets produced yet still has S's former shareholders among its owners, see column (9). But if another acquisition and another sale can be concluded, the effect on Company C's earnings per share may be counteracted, at least for another year.[12] Once started on this track, the company must continue to acquire companies at an increasing rate if it is not to have its past conversion of future earnings into instant income catch up to it. The best analogy is to the chain letter.

A similar, more realistic, and less extreme form of this conversion of undervalued assets into instant earnings is reported by Briloff.[13] Gulf & Western Industries (G & W) in 1966 acquired Paramount Pictures by giving Paramount's stockholders securities appraised at $185 million at time of issue. The *book* value of Paramount's net assets (largely feature films from its glorious past) was only $100 million and they entered G & W's books at that figure. In 1966, before the acquisition, Paramount had reported a net income of only $3 million. During 1967, G & W sold thirty-two films to the ABC Television Network for $20 million, treated the sale value as income, and showed a "profit" in 1967 of $22 million in its Paramount subsidiary. In 1967, G & W was a leading "glamor" stock, partly for this reason, yet the film sale had been available to Paramount the year before. Paramount's stockholders found it more profitable to sell their company than to sell its films. The evident reason was that G & W could get more mileage than Paramount out of the sale of films as long as the market assigned G & W a higher PE ratio than it assigned Paramount.

I offer the hypothesis that the particular attractiveness of fire and casualty insurance companies for acquisition by conglomerate firms is due to the large portfolio of undervalued investments that insurance companies carry on their books at historical cost. Carefully scheduled realization of book profits on their subsequent sale permits subsequent earnings per share to reflect impressive stability and growth. Briloff cites, and discusses at some length, Leasco's acquisition of Reliance Insurance, City Investing's acquisition of Home Insurance, and National General's acquisition of Great American Insurance Company.[14] These were relatively small insurance companies but each had "instant earnings" potentials of the order of magnitude of $100 million. The Hartford Insurance Company (acquired by ITT) was much larger: the book value of Hartford's assets at the time of

---

12. This example mirrors the one given in FTC, *Economic Report on Corporate Mergers,* p. 123.

13. Briloff, "Accounting Practices," pp. 610–11.

14. See Briloff, "Accounting Practices," pp. 615–20.

acquisition in 1968 was nearly $2 billion. This understated by a substantial (though unreported) amount, the market value of its investments.

Purchase accounting. Pooling accounting *as such* does not motivate mergers when common stock is exchanged for common stock and book values of assets of each company approximate their market values. Such incentives to merge as are created (see table 5–3) are the result not of the pooling of their accounts but of the willingness of investors to apply uncritically one company's PE ratio to another company's earnings.

Pooling accounting may however be deceptive when S's assets are acquired for amounts far in excess of their book value. As we have seen, this creates the opportunities for instant earnings, and potential deception of those who rely on the accounting records. Any premium paid to S's owners over book value is a real cost to B's stockholders, but the amounts of such premiums get lost in pooling accounting. They show up, ultimately, in the diluted ownership which B's stockholders have of the new company's earning assets. This is the problem that purchase accounting is supposed to solve: it requires the new company to recognize assets of an acquired corporation on its books at acquisition value rather than book value.

Table 5–7, column (10), shows how things are supposed to work out at acquisition. The excess of purchase price over book values ($800) is added to total assets. Although it is treated in a separate "goodwill" account,[15] it is assumed to reflect an expenditure by the acquiring company that must be recovered (via amortization) and charged against future earned income. The effect of such amortization is drastically to reduce earnings per share, and remove the inflation of stock prices based upon it. Compare columns (4') and (10) of table 5–7.

Under this kind of purchase accounting, the "instant earnings" opportunity vanishes as well, as columns (8) and (11) show. For, selling S's assets at $500 reduces C's assets by $1,000 ($800 of goodwill, $200 of tangible assets) and adds only $500. The resulting loss of $500 decreases equity and reported income. The transaction, under

---

15. "Goodwill" appears under many names in corporate balance sheets including "intangible assets," "excess of cost," "excess of cost of investments over net assets at date of acquisition."

TABLE 5-7

EXAMPLE 5: POOLING VERSUS PURCHASE ACCOUNTING: "THEORY"

	COMPANY C's BOOKS UPON ACQUISITION OF S		COMPANY C's BOOKS UPON SUBSEQUENT SALE OF S's ASSETS FOR $500	
	Pooling (*from table 5–5*) (*4'*)	*Purchase Accounting* (*10*)	*Pooling* (*from table 5–6*) (*8*)	*Purchase Accounting* (*11*)
Total Assets	$2,200	$3,000	$2,500	$2,500
Tangible	$2,200	$2,200	$2,500	$2,500
Goodwill	—	800	—	0
Net equity	$2,200	$3,000	$2,500	$2,500*
[Number of shares]	[3,000]	[3,000]	[3,000]	[3,000]
Earnings (loss)	$ 200	$ 120†	$ 400‡	$ (400)§
Earnings per share (loss)	$ .0667	$ .04	$ .1333	$ (.1333)
Price	$ 1.333	$ .80	$ 2.667	?
PE ratio	20:1	20:1	20:1	?
Market value	$4,000	$2,400	$8,000	?
Earnings/Total assets	.091	.04	.16	−.16
Earnings/Equity	.091	.04	.16	−.16

* $3,000 before the transaction, less capital loss of $500.
† Assumes goodwill is amortized over ten years on a straightline basis.
‡ See table 5–6, footnote †.
§ $100 income from B's assets, less $500 realized capital loss.

118

the theoretical ideal of purchase accounting, is made to look like the disaster it is.

This sort of consideration led many security analysts and some accountants to press for purchase accounting as the "sound" way of handling mergers. The case for it is, basically, that a merger is a real market transaction with arms-length negotiation of prices, and these realized market values belong in the balance sheet of the acquiring company.

But, in practice, purchase accounting can accomplish almost as much as pooling in providing instant earnings and inflated profits rates. Suppose the company *does* recognize the excess of purchase value over book value, but instead of amortizing this goodwill chooses to regard it as an unamortizable asset—perhaps on the ground that the value of the acquired company's name may last forever. As table 5–8 shows, this leads back to virtually the same results as pooling. "Goodwill" is retained even when the assets of S are sold. If the rate of earnings on assets is calculated using net tangible assets (i.e., excluding goodwill) the only change from pooling accounting occurs in the rate of profits on equity. But this is only a small handicap.

CONSISTENCY VERSUS ACCURACY: THE POLICY DILEMMA OF THE APB

The basic problem with merger accounting is that ordinary accounting principles utilize often unrealistic historical costs (instead of market values). Accounting principles depend on *consistent* accounting rather than on *accurate* accounting to avoid misleading outsiders. Pooling has the advantage of being consistent with the old books of the two companies (however inaccurate those books may have become). It has the disadvantage of not using the acquisition as an opportunity to introduce the evidence provided by the merger to update values on the acquired company's assets. Some regard a stock-for-stock transfer as an internal (not market-tested) transaction with the real value of any consideration paid hard to determine; for this reason, they regard continuation of the use of historical cost as the consistent path to follow. They argue, that if two equally large firms merge and B gives S's stockholders 1.2 newly created securities for each share of old stock, this is not really a purchase at a 20 percent premium, for the value of the new securities is not known until the market responds. To use purchase accounting would be to impute real values to what may be

TABLE 5-8

EXAMPLE 6: POOLING VERSUS PURCHASE: PRACTICE
(NON-AMORTIZATION OF GOODWILL)

	COMPANY C's BOOKS UPON ACQUISITION OF S		COMPANY C's BOOKS UPON SUBSEQUENT SALE OF S's ASSETS FOR $500	
	Pooling (from table 5–5) (4')	Purchase Accounting (12)	Pooling (from table 5–6) (8)	Purchase Accounting (13)
Total Assets	$2,200	$3,000	$2,500	$3,300
Tangible	$2,200	$2,200	$2,500	$2,500
Goodwill	—	$ 800	—	$ 800*
Net equity	$2,200	$3,000	$2,500	$3,300
[Number of shares]	[3,000]	[3,000]	[3,000]	[3,000]
Earnings	$ 200	$ 200†	$ 400	$ 400‡
Earnings per share	$ .0667	$ .0667	$ .1333	$ .1333
Price	$ 1.333	$ 1.333	$ 2.667	$ 2.667
PE ratio	20:1	20:1	20:1	20:1
Market value	$4,000	$4,000	$8,000	$8,000
Earnings/Tangible assets	.091	.091	.16	.16
Earnings/Equity	.091	.067	.16	.12

* Goodwill retained despite sale of assets of Company S.
† Goodwill not amortized.
‡ $100 from B's assets, plus nominal gain of $300 excess of sale price over book value of assets sold.

unjustified "payments" of paper whose real value is doubtful. All it does is create a new kind of "asset" that is vague and misleading. Consider the following attack on purchase accounting by two leading CPA's:

> Simply stated, goodwill is an asset basically different in nature from other assets. For many businesses it may be the most valuable asset to the investor, but the balance sheet cannot be expected to inform the investor about the goodwill. Investors in the aggregate determine the goodwill of a company, and such determination does not rely on the balance sheet reporting of goodwill. The cost of purchased goodwill has no continuing and reliable relationship to its value. Goodwill is not the type of asset that belongs on the balance sheet.
>
> Another common "hang-up" in the accounting profession on goodwill concerns the demand that purchased goodwill be amortized by charges to the income statement. This conclusion fails to recognize that goodwill is not utilized or consumed in the production of earnings. It has no discernible or predictable life. It may live in virtual perpetuity, it may disappear overnight, or it may multiply manifold as time goes by, rather than be diminished. A conclusion to amortize goodwill by charges to income must be based on establishing an arbitrary time period. In many cases the result would be amortization by a charge to income while goodwill actually increased in value during the period.
>
> Amortization of goodwill to income distorts income, misleads users and should be prohibited by the accounting profession and the Securities and Exchange Commission.[16]

Wyatt and Spacek opt for consistent (albeit inaccurate) pooling accounting, which preserves the traditional values of historical cost.

It is these issues with which the APB struggled in February and March of 1970. Wishing to curb abuses and deception in merger accounting while retaining the consistency associated with historical cost, the APB proposed "exposure drafts"[17] of APB Opinion No. 16

---

16. Wyatt and Spacek, "Accounting Principles and Conglomerate Growth," p. 827.

17. J. F. Fotenos, "Accounting for Business Combinations: A Critique of APB Opinion Number 16," 23 STANFORD LAW REVIEW 336, fn. 28 (1971), summarizes APB procedures: "Issues to be decided by the Board are first studied by AICPA's Division of Accounting Research. The report of this research is published for comment and discussion among the members of the profession and interested parties. After deliberation, the Board prepares an 'exposure' draft of its tentative decision. After considering comments received concerning the exposure draft, an affirmative vote of two-thirds of the members of the Board is required to authorize formal publication of an opinion."

and No. 17. The drafts would have required purchase accounting and amortization of goodwill arising from the excess of acquisition value over book value. Such goodwill was to be amortized over not more than forty years, and to be written off if the assets were sold off. Excepted from this ruling were mergers in which each combining firm was as large as one-third of the size of the other, size to be judged by the shares of common stock involved in the exchange.[18] This would have required purchase accounting and the amortization of goodwill in the great majority of acquisitions. This draft triggered the story in the *Wall Street Journal* quoted on page 109. The response to APB was heavy and adverse.[19] The APB bowed to the pressure first by extending the exception (to mergers where the smaller company was at least one-ninth instead of one-third the size of the larger one) and finally making it generally available.

The final forms of APB Opinion No. 16 and No. 17, issued in August 1970,[20] nominally leave no choice as to whether to use pooling or purchase accounting. By specifying the conditions under which pooling is to be used, however, they leave the choice to the acquirer. The key provisions that "require" (i.e., make the firm eligible to use) pooling accounting are:

(1) The acquiring firm must acquire at least 90% of the voting stock of the acquired firm. (2) The exchange is made for voting stock in the new firm. (3) The combined firm does not intend or plan to dispose of a significant part of the assets of the combining companies within two years after the combination.

The absence of a size restriction means this method is available whenever the acquisition involves a stock for stock acquisition. With the tax law reforms mentioned in chapter 4 (see p. 87), this adds to the disincentive to use convertible debentures. Perhaps the most important restriction is the one that prevents "planned" instant earnings realization for two years.

---

18. The notion was that when nearly equal size firms make exchanges, such exchanges were not really market transactions.

19. Cf. Fotenos, "Accounting for Business Combinations," p. 347.

20. Accounting Principles Board of the American Institute of Certified Public Accountants, Opinion No. 16 "Business Combinations" (August 1970); Accounting Principles Board of the American Institute of Certified Public Accountants, Opinion No. 17 "Intangible Assets" (August 1970).

When purchase accounting is used, goodwill is to be recognized and amortized. The opinion recognizes there is no easy answer to the amortization question. It does require an upper limit of forty years for amortization and presumes use of straight-line amortization. Importantly, it indicates that if all or a sizable portion of separable assets of an acquired company are subsequently sold, all or a portion of the unamortized goodwill recognized in the acquisition should be written off. While a forty-year horizon is a long one, one can sympathize with the APB, for the policy issue implicit in the treatment of goodwill is not routine. Excess of purchase price over book value may partly reflect unrealistically low book values. If so, accurate accounting should take the form of a write-up (and subsequent depreciation) of *tangible* assets.[21] A premium paid over market value for the purpose of gaining control is very different. It may be valueless and thus no asset at all, or it may give the purchaser an economic rent that is independent of the assets acquired. There is no single rule that correctly handles all of the possible situations. Yet to give corporations a choice invites self-serving classification and potentially inconsistent accounting.

IS THERE NEED FOR STRICTER ACCOUNTING RULES?[22]

It is clear that, given the behavioral assumptions listed on page 105, accounting rules and changes therein can provide motives for mergers.

---

21. Whether, and if so how, to allocate to previous years the profits created by the sort of write-up is an important and difficult issue for both accounting and tax purposes. But I do not believe this alone makes the suggestions unworkable. From the viewpoint of full disclosure there are a variety of ways of requiring reporting on a retroactive basis for several years prior to the acquisition. Another possibility is to require that all long term capital gains be excluded from ordinary income and be reported as special items.

22. While the issues discussed above represent the main ways in which accounting may motivate mergers, there are others. To mention one, choices among depreciation methods (e.g., straight line, double-declining balance, etc.) can affect the timing of taxes (and thus of cash flows) and the timing of earnings. For example, a switch to straight line depreciation from an accelerated method will increase reported profits before taxes during the current year, and thus provide another source of instant earnings. A merger, or a merger fight, may provide the incentive to change accounting rules to manipulate earnings. Cases of this are often hinted at in the financial press. Piper Aircraft reported an 81 percent increase in

It is tempting to put much of the onus on the arbitrary and mechanical rules of the accountants, or on the laxity of auditors in certifying income statements as acceptable.[23] But the fact is that the manipulation and deception would not be possible without the mechanical behavior of investors. Clearly, demands for honest and consistent reporting justify requiring retroactive pooling if pooling is used, and ample disclosure ought to be required of those who have information that is not otherwise available. This is indeed an outcome of the Williams Act of 1968.[24] Further, insisting on a separation of capital gains from ordinary income in reporting may help the outsider find his way more easily.

I am reluctant to go further with respect to merger accounting because so much of modern accounting, if accepted at face value, is inherently deceptive. Historical costs, allocated overheads, conventional depreciation, all are measures that would lead to uneconomical decisions if accepted uncritically. The case for accounting conventions is that they can be readily understood and consistently applied, whereas such intellectually preferable concepts as opportunity costs, marginal costs, and losses in market value owing to use, are so difficult to measure as to invite fraud.

The SEC has a legitimate interest and legal authority to insist on sufficient disclosure to avoid deliberate deception.[25] Must (or can) it

---

quarterly earnings on a 21.3 percent rise in sales when fighting a merger attempt by Chris-Craft. The earnings rise was partially caused by a change in depreciation methods. (*Wall Street Journal,* February 20, 1969, p. 6, col. 2.) After Youngstown Sheet & Tube and Jones & Laughlin succumbed to outsiders in tender offers many steel companies changed their depreciation methods in an attempt to increase earnings, and thus the market price of their securities. ("How to Fend Off a Takeover," *Fortune* 99, no. 2 [February 1969]: 83–162.)

23. Briloff, "Accounting Practices," pp. 604–28, implies that auditors are virtual coconspirators in the conspiracy to mislead investors.

24. The law entitled "An Act Providing for Full Disclosure of Corporate Equity Ownership of Securities Under the Securities Exchange Act" was originally passed in 1968, and was expanded by Amendments in 1970. See Public Law No. 91–567 (1970). It is discussed more fully in chapter 7.

25. Section 13(b) of the Exchange Act authorizes the Commission to "prescribe, in regard to reports made pursuant to this chapter, the form or forms in which the required information shall be set forth, the items or details to be shown in the balance sheet and the earning statement, and the methods to be followed in the preparation of reports, in the appraisal or valuation of assets and liabilities, in the determination of depreciation

go further and insist that the data made available be, in some sense, foolproof? In attempts to propose a solution to the earnings-per-share growth game, Curley[26] and Reinhardt[27] propose formulae for separating growth by acquisition from real growth. If companies were forced to report such growth separately, they believe, the misleading dynamic effects of the PE game would be impeded.

But this view implies that growth by merger is somehow less valuable (to investors) than growth of other kinds. This need not be so. Lorie and Halpern[28] report on their study of 139 large acquisitions between 1955 and 1967 in which

. . . shareholders received relatively complicated assets such as convertible preferred stock, convertible debentures, warrants, and other species in the genus "funny money."

They conclude:

Despite unquestioned departures from the optimum in financial reporting, the evidence . . . indicates that investors have on the average been able to pierce the accountant's veil of illusion and have made rewarding investments.

Their study is hardly decisive—indeed the subsequent stock market slump, in which many conglomerate issues suffered very badly, appears to reverse their benign finding even about their own sample. But the point is clear that no set of accounting rules will necessarily protect investors who come into market without real interest in discover-

---

and depletion, in the differentiation of recurring and nonrecurring income, in the differentiation of investment and operating income, and in the preparation, where the Commission deems it necessary or desirable, of separate and/or consolidated balance sheets or income accounts of any person directly or indirectly controlling or controlled by the issuer, or any person under direct or indirect common control with the issuer." Securities Exchange Act of 1934, [§13(b)], 15 U.S.C. § 78m(b) (1964).

26. Anthony J. Curley, "Conglomerate Earnings per Share: Real and Transitory Growth," *The Accounting Review* 46, no. 3 (July 1971): 519–28.

27. U. E. Reinhardt, "Conglomerate Earnings per Share: Immediate and Post-Merger Effects," *The Accounting Review* 47, no. 2 (April 1972): 360.

28. J. H. Lorie and Paul Halpern, "Conglomerates: The Rhetoric and the Evidence," 13 Journal of Law and Economics, no. 1, 149–66 (1970).

ing the underlying health of the companies whose securities they hold, buy, sell, or tender. Yet the basic evidence suggests that there are enough such investors to make manipulating the market possible, and for the manipulators, profitable.

Appendix to Chapter 5: The PE Game and Accounting Rules as an Incentive to Merge

DEFINITIONS AND ASSUMPTIONS

Consider further a merger of Company B and Company S into a new Company C, where the number of shares of stock in C is $n_C = n_B + kn_S$ as before. Suppose E_B and E_S are the annual earnings of Company B and Company S, and suppose (for the moment) that the merger brings no synergies that increase E_C above $E_B + E_S$.

Define:

$$\left.\begin{aligned} e_B &= \frac{E_B}{n_B} \\ e_S &= \frac{E_S}{n_S} \\ e_C &= \frac{E_C}{n_C} = \frac{E_B + E_S}{n_B + kn_S} \end{aligned}\right\} \text{earnings per share}$$

$$PE_j = \frac{p_j}{e_j}, \text{ all j.} \qquad \text{price-earnings ratios}$$

Assume:

$$p_B = p_S = 1,$$
$$p_C = PE_B \cdot e_C = \frac{e_C}{e_B} = \frac{1}{e_B}\left(\frac{E_B + E_S}{n_B + kn_S}\right).$$

MERGER MOTIVATION IF $e_S > e_B$

I will treat the motivation of stockholders toward the merger as a function of the market prices of the stocks, and the size of their holdings.

Buyers are assumed to favor the merger if:

(1) $$p_C n_B > p_B n_B,$$

which, given the definitions and assumptions above, simplifies to:

(2) $$\frac{e_S}{e_B} > k.$$

Sellers are assumed to favor the merger if:

(3) $$p_C k n_S > p_S n_S,$$

which, given the definitions and assumptions above, simplifies to:

(4) $$k > \frac{1}{p_C}, \text{ or:}$$

(5) $$k > \frac{1}{1 + \frac{n_S}{n_B}\left(\frac{e_S}{e_B} - 1\right)}.$$

The condition for the merger to be mutually attractive is thus that there exists a k such that:

(6) $$\frac{e_S}{e_B} > k > \frac{1}{1 + \frac{n_S}{n_B}\left(\frac{e_S}{e_B} - 1\right)}.$$

Since n_S and n_B are necessarily positive, it is clear that $(e_S/e_B) > 1$, which is necessary to satisfy the left-hand inequation of (6) for a k value greater than 1, is sufficient to assure that the right-hand term is less than unity. That is, $(e_S/e_B) > 1$ is necessary and sufficient for a value of $k > 1$ to exist that will satisfy (6).

Given $p_S = p_B$, $e_S > e_B$ implies $PE_B > PE_S$. Obviously, the key assumption is the behavioral one that investors will assign $PE_C = PE_B$.

ROLE OF ACCOUNTING

Because p_C figures symmetrically in (1) and (3) anything that raises p_C, *ceteris paribus* raises the incentive to merge. Let us hypothesize:

(7) $$p_C = PE_B \hat{e}_C$$
(8) $$PE_B = f(\hat{e}_C, \hat{e}_B, \hat{e}_C/\hat{A}_C, \ldots .)$$

where the hats indicate *reported* data as approved by accountants, where $\dot{e}$ represents the change in earnings per share, and $\hat{A}_C$ is a measure of the tangible assets of Company C. Further assume that the first partial derivatives of (8) are nonnegative with respect to each of the arguments shown. Now, because p_C varies directly with both $\hat{e}_C$ and PE_B, anything that raises $\hat{e}_C$ above e_C, or that raises $\hat{e}_C$ or $\hat{e}_C/\hat{A}_C$ will tend to increase p_C and provide an additional motive to merge. The text discussed several accounting rules that produced those results, and thus provided a purely accounting-rule incentive to merge.

CHAPTER SIX

Insider Evaluations and
Conflicts of Interest

THE THREE preceding chapters have considered a series of external synergies that might lead the stock market value of a merger to exceed the weighted average of the values of the two companies separately and thus to motivate the merger. Such considerations, and theories based upon them, are sufficient to show the advantage to stockholders of the merger over an appropriate portfolio of stock of the two companies.

A wholly different set of insider evaluations may also create the motivations to support or oppose a particular merger. These gains and deterrents accrue to or are borne by "insiders" rather than, in some proportional sense, the ordinary stockholders of the new company.

Insider evaluations play a primary role in a number of theories of merger activity. Perhaps the clearest example is the "managerial" hypothesis advanced by Dennis C. Mueller, Ajit Singh, and others.[1] They argue that differences in objectives of managers and stockholders can suffice to explain merger activity whereas real synergies are insufficient, particularly where conglomerate mergers are involved. Mueller states:

While . . . "synergistic" effects and managerial insights are often said to be present in various merger situations, their existence in sufficient strength to warrant the high premiums paid for other firms, often appears implausible when the merger is between firms in seemingly unrelated or loosely related industries. This is especially true when, as frequently happens, the acquired firm is left to operate as an autonomous division of the larger unit, operated by the same management team that controlled it before the merger.

Michael Gort focuses on sets of influences that affect buying companies' perceptions of profitability very differently from the way

---

1. Dennis C. Mueller, "A Theory of Conglomerate Mergers," *Quarterly Journal of Economics* 83, no. 4 (November 1969): 643; Ajit Singh, *Takeovers: Their Relevance to the Stock Market and the Theory of the Firm* (Cambridge, 1971). These writers are following in the tradition of Baumol, Robin Marris, and many others.

they affect present owners. He hypothesizes that these influences, which seem to me classifiable as insider influences,

. . . generate discrepancies in valuation [that] are decisive in determining variations in merger rates both among industries and over time. . . . To be sure, particular mergers may still result from the pursuit of monopoly power, economies of scale, or yet other sources of gain, but the question I raise is whether these variables are necessary to explain the general phenomenon of fluctuations in merger rates.[2]

These and related primary-cause theories are reviewed in the latter part of this chapter. Because of them, and because in the theoretical framework I have developed, insider evaluations may play a complementary (rather than a competitive) role to such things as real economies, or the search for market or monopoly power, it is worth considering them in enough detail to see when they are likely to play a significant role in motivating mergers. I am concerned in this chapter with *theories*—such empirical evidence as is available is considered in chapter 8.

A Short Catalog of Insider Motivations

In chapter 2 we noted that many groups might have definably different perceptions of a proposed merger. Among these parties are large and small stockholders of each company involved, managers, and the surrounding financial community. In the subsequent discussion I shall focus on four groups:[3] (1) The large stockholder bloc of the selling company (S); (2) The managerial group of the selling company; (3) The large stockholder bloc of the buying company (B); and (4) The managerial group of the buying company.

In the subsequent discussion I shall appear to neglect the small stockholders and financial institutions. The small stockholders are not really neglected. They may well hold the balance of power, and they are assumed to participate in the final decision. Small stockholders play their role indirectly by choosing which group to follow when there is a disagreement within their company. Small stockholders are never assumed to be decisive as a separate group against

---

2. Michael Gort, "An Economic Disturbance Theory of Mergers," *Quarterly Journal of Economics* 83, no. 4 (November 1969): 624–42.

3. In principle there might be several splinters in each such group. I will, however, assume them to be singular.

the joint view of their co-owners and their managers because they lack a lever with which to exercise their latent power. If disaffected, they are assumed to sell out their holdings. The virtual neglect of brokers, mutual funds, banks, and other financial institutions is real enough, and is perhaps regrettable. I regard this as a major area for further research.

LARGE STOCKHOLDER BLOC OF THE SELLING COMPANY

The members of this group, who will be designated for convenience as "owners" (to distinguish them from "managers"), are expected to value their holdings differently from the way the market values them, partly because their holdings are large and not readily marketed at the market price, partly because the group has potential if not actual control of the company's affairs, and partly because members of the group may have insights into "their" company's prospects and problems not shared by outsiders. These things, which may lead them to be more—or less—receptive to a tender offer than either the small stockholders or the managerial group, include the following:

Good fit. The large owners of Company S may recognize a particularly good fit between Company B's resources and Company S's problems. Things like perceived real economies, pecuniary economies, opportunities for creating or exploiting monopoly power, or creating opportunities for manipulating stock market values, were all included in α. But owners of S may see yet greater advantages than the market sees either because they have a special awareness of their company's inchoate strengths, or its emerging weaknesses.

Desire to liquidate or diversify. Many closely held companies, particularly family-held ones in which the family head is aging, seek to exchange their holdings in a stock with a thin market for securities with a broader market, in order that large blocs can subsequently be liquidated without spoiling the market. If the company is large enough, or highly prosperous, it may be able to "go public," but often these conditions are not met. The underlying motivation may result from an impending need to pay inheritance duties or it may be simply a desire to diversify and spread risks. But in either case it can make being acquired especially attractive to owners of dominant blocs of stock.

Need for new opportunities for reinvestment. If Company S is generating substantial cash flow, but declining opportunities for reinvestment in its traditional activities, its owners may seek alternative investments. Reinvesting via dividend payouts or sale of stock has tax disadvantages that may be particularly large for the ownership group. One alternative that may appeal to the owners is to be acquired by a company whose investment opportunities seem attractive to owners of Company S.

Inadequate management. Owners of a company may come to recognize that the management of their company is failing to "get the job done," because of age, because heirs of past owners occupy, ineffectively, key positions, or because of inability to adapt to changing demands upon it. Gradually to replace an existing management may be difficult (because senior managers tend to recruit young men in their own image), or very slow, and thus potentially expensive. To replace the management suddenly may be difficult, for all of the reasons that give managerial groups a great deal of control. Thus the owners, or a significant subset of them, may be motivated to accept or invite a tender offer as the most effective means of displacing or circumventing an existing managerial group.

Disagreements with management. Sharp disagreements sometimes develop between owners and management with respect (for example) to an appropriate dividend policy, to diversification, to an attitude toward risk. Such disagreements if allowed to simmer may result in a proxy fight, or a deterioration of morale and performance. These can lead to search by the owners of S for an appropriate merger partner. Many contested tender offers involve mergers that promise benefits to buyers and to the owners but not to the managers of the selling company.

Loss of control. Not all of the "insider" influences work in the direction of motivating toward merger. The dominant ownership group in the acquired company will recognize that its ability to control the destiny of its investment is diminished by being acquired. It is unlikely to have as much influence in the new company as in the old, and this involves some risk that a disagreement over policies it feels strongly about will develop. If this risk seems large, it will deter an otherwise attractive merger.

Costs and risks attendant upon an unsuccessful contested merger.
The dominant ownership group may recognize the possibility that the
company's present managerial group will oppose the merger and will
initiate appeals to the small stockholders urging them to reject the
tender. If such a challenge occurs there will be nonnegligible costs of
fighting it. The costs are enhanced by the fact that if the merger is
contested the managerial group may succeed in defeating the merger,
either by a "defensive merger" with another firm, less acceptable to
the large ownership group, or by welding the small stockholders into a
cohesive group. In either event the ownership group may find its subsequent influence and affluence diminished.

MANAGERS OF THE SELLING COMPANY

Managers of the selling company may be in full accord with the
dominant ownership group, either because their economic interests are
determined by the same things generally, or because they perceive
agreement as less dangerous to them than any other course. Each of
the first three motivations listed above as insider motivations may
apply to managers as well as to owners. The great majority of mergers,
conglomerates and others, are not contested.

In addition to these, however, several considerations apply to
management but not to owners.

Managerially perceived weakness. Management may perceive an
impending deterioration of its company's position for a dozen reasons:
It may see the demand for its product declining, its costs rising more
than its competitors', its inability to maintain an efficient scale of
production, its difficulties in acquiring key resources, the aging of its
management. In any of these circumstances, it may well desire to be
acquired *now* before the troubles become widespread. Managers may
be concerned to save or enhance their own managerial reputations by
getting out before the impending troubles are blamed upon them.
Perhaps the easiest way of doing this is to negotiate an advantageous
merger.

Managerial status. Managers may support a merger even if they see
no particular gains to their stockholders if they prefer to be actively
employed in a larger or more rapidly growing, or more prestigious

company. In such a situation, management may utilize its influence to effect a merger, presumably on the condition that its members will be given responsible jobs in the new company.

Loss of status or employment.   Clearly being acquired entails risks for managers of the acquired company. To the extent that inadequacies of the management group motivate the merger, the managers of the acquired firm are likely to be discharged or downgraded. But even if perfectly competent, they may be redundant if there is an economy of scale in the use of management and they are likely to be less favored than their counterparts in the acquiring company. Ill-treatment of acquired managements is frequent enough to have spawned the mushroom analogy: "first they put you in a damp, dark room in the basement, next they shovel manure on you, finally they can you." In any event this possibility must be weighed against the advantages of being an executive of a larger, more prestigious institution.

Management versus owners.   Managers may recognize a divergence of views with the principal stockholders and thus seek a merger with a group that shares *their* views. This will tend to lead to a search for a different merger partner than the one owners may seek.

LARGE STOCKHOLDER BLOC OF THE BUYING COMPANY

Several perceptions may lead the dominant stockholder group to favor (or resist) an acquisition on "insider" grounds that was just a break-even proposition when viewed externally. Each of them is also potentially an influence (in the same direction) on the managerial group.[4]

Good fit.   The actual dimensions of the good fit as perceived by the buying company may well be different from those perceived by sellers. For example, belief in their company's superior managerial ability, and in underutilized managerial talents tends to lead the buying company to expand its scope. Similarly, a feeling that cash flow and venture capital

---

4. For reasons discussed below, conflicts between managers and owners of a buying company are not likely to take the form of a merger attempt.

are the critical things holding the company back from yet greater triumphs may lead managers or stockholders groups to seek to acquire
companies that (in any of a number of ways) can give them control
over cash flows. As one conglomerator told me, he hated to see large
sums of cash "lying idle or being paid out in unnecessary dividends to
strangers."

Critical bottlenecks.   Some companies may face, and their owners or
managers perceive, an emerging critical bottleneck that can be solved
by acquisition. Such bottlenecks may result from a shortage of vital
raw materials or specialized talent, or shortage of cash flows in
sufficient volume to pursue an optimal rate of expansion. This point
differs only in degree from the "good fit" just above; here it is not the
mere opportunity to make a profit, but the need to avert an impending
worsening of one's situation that may lead to a great willingness to
consummate a merger that will solve a particular kind of problem.

Growth as a necessity.   For some companies growth is an essential
ingredient of health, at least for a period of time. This may be because
the company is essentially a managerial team whose forte is renovat-
ing old companies. It may be because the company in its basic operations is generating a heavy cash flow which it lacks internal ways to
invest and which its dominant stockholders do not wish to have
distributed as taxable income. In either of these circumstances growth
by acquisition may seem the easiest and most successful way to solve
the problems of the company. Similar, though less salutary motives
for growth by acquisition may be to create a growth rate that will
justify an abnormally high price-earnings ratio for the company's
stock. Insider perceptions of the opportunities for doing this will provide a motive for merger if the stock market responds to such accounting indicia as apparent increases in profits per share, or if stockholders
prefer to own an active, growing company. An even less salutary insider motive for growth may be that in a company whose assets and
earnings are rapidly changing, it is harder for outsiders to discern
signs of emerging weakness.

Risk of an unsuccessful tender.   A significant fraction of tender offers
end up provoking a contest, and a significant fraction of these result
in failure of the tender attempts. A study by Denis Binder uncovered

114 contested tender offers in the period 1965–69 of which only 35 (31 percent) resulted in the bidder actually gaining control.[5] In 43 (38 percent) cases the target successfully retained its independence, and in the remainder it merged elsewhere. Thus failure of a tender offer must be considered a nonnegligible risk. The costs of that failure are borne largely by the stockholders of the buying company, who have paid a premium to acquire shares of stock in the expectation of gaining control, and must now liquidate large blocs of stocks at market prices. Since the average premium is 15 percent to 20 percent above market price, this may amount to a substantial sum, in addition to the resources spent on the acquisition campaign.

Risk of an unprofitable merger. If the expected values of the merger were correctly included in the basic calculations there would be no *average* loss here to owners of the buying company in having some acquisitions prove unprofitable. The unexpectedly profitable acquisition would offset the unexpectedly unprofitable. But the mere fact of failure may lead the market to reevaluate downward its opinion of the company's stock, and thus reduce (or eliminate) the rising stock prices that owners had sought as one of their objectives. If the market overreacts to failure, the large stockholder group will suffer a loss in liquidity until the market evaluation is straightened out. This may take a long time—as the stockholders of Ling-Temco-Vought have discovered.

MANAGERS OF THE BUYING COMPANY

Managers may be more (or less) eager than their owners to pursue mergers as a policy for their company. Managers may be more interested in growth (and the salary and perquisites it brings) than in achieving high profits and rapidly rising prices of the company's common stock. But they may be less willing to take large risks to achieve windfalls that have some probability of generating large capital gains if things work out, and losses that can be used as tax offsets against other income if they do not work out. To managers a calamitous year can cost them their jobs or their reputations.

5. Denis Binder, "An Empirical Analysis of Contested Tender Offers: 1960–1969, Part II," (S.J.D. thesis, Law School, University of Michigan, 1973).

The following additional considerations seem of some relevance:

Managerial self-confidence.   Managers in their regular contacts see a great many managers of other companies. If the buying company's managers become convinced that another company's managers are sufficiently ineffective, they may wish to acquire that company and reap the gains available to proper management. This differs slightly from the good fit considerations in which a fit may arise due to a merging of strengths and weaknesses: here there is an assumption of managerial rewards to be had without any necessary close integration of operations.

Bigness or growth as a corporate goal.   The "growth maximization" literature gives great emphasis to this managerial objective in explaining corporate behavior generally, and mergers specifically. The emphasis is on power, prestige, or influence rather than profits.[6] The advantages to the managers of being top executives in large corporations is that salaries and perquisites tend to be a function of number of employees supervised and the rate of growth, as well as profit rates.[7] Managerial status considerations may well operate with greater force on the buying side than on the acquired firm side since the top managements of acquiring firms are likely to hold the upper hand and thus the better jobs in the combined company.

Managerial risks of unsuccessful acquisitions.   Although managers can be displaced for too sluggish an attitude toward growth, retribution is likely to be swift if an expensive acquisition proves disappointing. The risks of job and reputation loss to the very top management group may be both large and unshiftable. Thus they may affect that group's decision to seek a particular merger.

Constellations of Attitudes and Predicted Effects

It proves important in discussing mergers to distinguish among different groups within the corporation for the reason that different per-

---

6. Profit advantages from rapid growth—say due to stock market appreciation—are included in the "external influences" discussed in chapter 5. We here talk about size or growth in excess of that optimal to a sophisticated profit maximizing objective.

7. See Robin Marris, *The Economic Theory of Managerial Capitalism* (Glencoe, Ill., 1964), chap. 2.

ceptions among them can play critical roles in inviting or accepting a merger. Presumably if all four of the groups discussed above want the merger, or all do not want it, the outcome is unambiguous. But there are many intermediate cases and once a contest develops other groups may play a major role.

For a merger to occur it must be proposed and accepted. Superficially this suggests that the views of whoever controls the buying company are critical in making the offer, and the views of the owners of the selling company will determine its acceptance. But the formal offer and acceptance (or rejection) is often partly facade. The discussions leading to the offer may be initiated by any party and the nature of a tender offer (or a decision not to tender) may reflect infighting, compromise, or compensated acquiescence of an otherwise dissident group. A group that is not nominally or legally a party to the transaction (e.g., the managers of the selling company or a brokerage house or mutual fund with large stockholdings) may actually be the decisive force if it holds proxies for shareholders or if its advice is sought and accepted.[8]

There is an important nonsymmetry between buyers and sellers in my subsequent treatment. Conflicts of interest within the selling company seem to me to be of much greater importance than in the buying company, and thus small stockholders of the sellers (who are, after all, among the targets of the tender offer) play a much larger role. I do not mean by this remark to neglect differences between owners and managers of acquiring companies. But, by and large, when owners and managers come into sharp policy conflict, they are not likely to be making tender offers to another company. Their disagreement is more likely to take the form of a proxy fight, or a search for a firm to *acquire them*. Differences within the buying company as to whether to seek a merger will usually have been settled by

---

8. Denis Binder, "An Empirical Analysis of Contested Tender Offers: 1960–1969, Part IV," (S.J.D. thesis, Law School, University of Michigan, 1973), finds the neglect of institutional holders of corporate securities a major defect in most analyses. After a detailed look at over 100 tenders he concludes: ". . . It is only when the veil of secrecy is lifted, and we can look behind-the-scenes that many cases come into focus. A discussion of the role played by institutional holders is essential to a full understanding of contested tender offers. Institutions with large holdings or the economic power to acquire such holdings were often decisive in the outcome of takeover bids."

dominance of one group or the other, or by a compromise, before the takeover offer is planned. Of course, to the extent that the views of the two groups differ, a shift in control can change the company's motive to merge.

A further nonsymmetry is that managements make tender *offers,* and owners make the ultimate critical decisions as to whether to accept the offer. Thus managers of the buying company and owners (large and small) of the selling company may be somewhat more immediately influential than their counterparts in the other company. Perhaps because of overattention to form, virtually every discussion of merger motivations that I know about places the emphasis on the *buyers'* side. In the literature it is *buyers* who are supposed to want to get or exercise monopoly power, *buyers* who perceive economies of joint operations, *buyers* who see promotional or speculative gain, *buyers* who perceive insider possibilities, *buyers'* managements which seek growth or status, or power, etc. The differences among theories concern whether it is insider or outsider influences (and which specific influences) that motivate buyers, and which buyers group (e.g., owners or managers) that are the motivating forces. I shall argue below that this is an important oversight.

Because of the diversities of interests and the nonsymmetries, there is a rich set of possibilities to explore. Figure 6–1 schematically identifies what I believe to be an interesting diversity of cases, and they will be discussed below.[9] (The multiplicity may be more important than anything else. My major objection to most merger theories is that they seek or postulate a single scenario to represent multiple phenomena.)

Nominally figure 6–1 merely provides a theoretical framework with which to address the question: "Will a particular merger be consummated." But it also may be suggestive in shedding light on the more interesting questions as to when and why merger rates are high,

---

9. Once again I wish to abstract from the dynamics of merger negotiation. The attitudes represented in the schema are the attitudes after various attempts at compromise or negotiation have taken place. For example, suppose a buying company wishes to acquire the selling company on terms that seem favorable to S's owners, but inquiry reveals that S's managers are slightly reticent because of fears for their status. The actual tender offer may well be preceded by giving the worried managers anything from promises of particular jobs to generous stock options to offset their latent hostility.

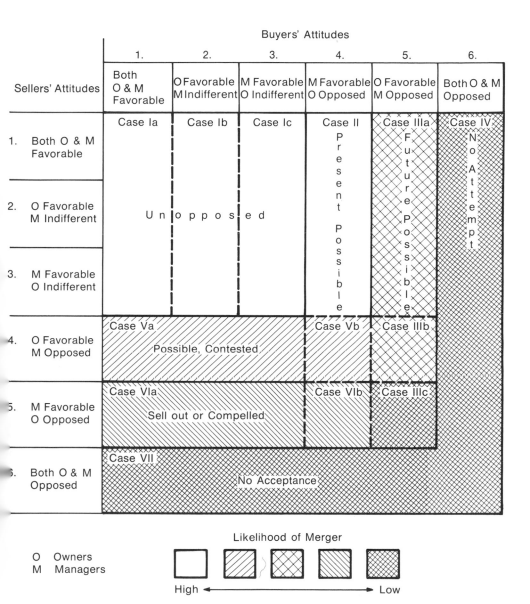

Buyers' Attitudes

Sellers' Attitudes	1. Both O & M Favorable	2. O Favorable M Indifferent	3. M Favorable O Indifferent	4. M Favorable O Opposed	5. O Favorable M Opposed	6. Both O & M Opposed
1. Both O & M Favorable	Case Ia	Case Ib	Case Ic	Case II	Case IIIa	Case IV
2. O Favorable M Indifferent	Un	oppos	ed	Present Possible	Future Possible	No Attempt
3. M Favorable O Indifferent						
4. O Favorable M Opposed	Case Va — Possible, Contested			Case Vb	Case IIIb	
5. M Favorable O Opposed	Case VIa — Sell out or Compelled			Case VIb	Case IIIc	
6. Both O & M Opposed	Case VII — No Acceptance					

Likelihood of Merger

O Owners
M Managers

High ◄────────────────► Low

Fig. 6–1.   Constellations of attitudes and likelihood of merger.

and why they change over time. Merger rates will be high when the conditions conducive to mergers are readily generated by the workings of the economy. It is conceivable that a dynamic economy might make mergers highly attractive at all times. But it is also possible that changing circumstances might motivate mergers at one period of time, but dismotivate one or more critical groups at other times. These are the things of which merger theories are made.

BUYERS' MOTIVATIONS, ASSUMING SELLERS' WILLINGNESS
TO MERGE (TOP HALF OF FIGURE 6-1)

Obviously, given the assumed willingness of sellers, if both owners and managers of the buying company are eager to merge, the merger is predicted to occur, and as long as such conditions pertain, mergers will be expected to occur at a high rate. Is it necessary that both groups be enthusiastic, or at least not opposed? Most commentators tend to neglect this issue. Gort, for example, is concerned with owners' valuations and does not mention any conflict with managerial views. Mueller, contrariwise, treats managerial values as decisive because he believes managers are more merger prone than are owners. My own view is that both groups must be reckoned with, albeit somewhat nonsymmetrically.

Managers favorable, owners indifferent or hostile (cases Ic, II). This is the domain of the managerial theories. It seems to me possible, at least in the short run, for eager managers to foist "unsound" mergers on reluctant owners because (assuming managerial control) the disadvantage of the merger to owners may be less than the costs and risks of attempting to dislodge the management group. Thus cases Ic and II seem to me to be perfectly possible ones as long as owners are not *too* opposed. It is the essence of the managerial theories (e.g., Marris, Mueller, Singh) that managerial desires to grow often take the form of desiring to manage more and bigger companies. This leads them to seek mergers that take the company past the point that maximizes owners' welfare. Mueller, who explicitly deals with the conglomerate merger phenomenon, argues that managerial growth-maximization objectives lead managers (via too low a discount rate) to seek mergers even when there are no external synergies to exploit. In Mueller's view the conglomerate form of merger is explained chiefly because it serves managers' aims even though synergies are hard to come by.[10]

On purely theoretical grounds this theory is insufficient. Without constraints it explains too much. If it is valid, why are there any limits to the mergers growth-prone managers will seek?[11] Clearly managers *are* constrained by their stockholders' tolerance and sensibilities. If owners get too unhappy they will be moved to upset the managerial group. An implicit limit to mergers, in this kind of theory, comes when owners are pushed to (case Ic) or somewhat past (case II) the point of their indifference and will no longer acquiesce in managers' serving themselves at the expense of the owners. At this point owners may try a proxy fight, or indeed, they may seek another company to *take them over.*

The chief virtue of this kind of managerial hypothesis is that it suggests reasons why mergers might occur even in the absence of any synergies. Its chief defect is that it is not readily expanded into a theory of merger movements, since it does not readily explain why merger rates vary over time.[12]

One might convert the managerial hypothesis into a genuine merger theory in a variety of ways—none of them terribly satisfactory. (1) One might show that the opportunities for growth are cyclical and a function of such underlying phenomena as stock market prices, interest rates, and so on. But if this is so then managerial attitudes are merely an important permissive aspect of the merger movement rather than its dominant propelling force. (2) Perhaps managerial incentives

---

10. That there are potential external synergies even in conglomerate acquisitions, was expounded in chapter 3. D. E. Logue and P. A. Naert make this same point as a criticism of Mueller in "A Theory of Conglomerate Mergers: Comment and Extension," *Quarterly Journal of Economics* 84, no. 4 (November 1970): 663–66.

11. Michael Gort and Thomas F. Hogarty, "New Evidence on Mergers," 13 JOURNAL OF LAW AND ECONOMICS, no. 1, 167 (April 1970), attempt to refute the managerial theories using (in part) this kind of argument.

12. Mueller does view the *conglomerate* aspect of the 1960s merger movement as a response to the progressive closing of the door to horizontal and vertical acquisitions. This explanation could account for the failure of merger rates to fall after the legal changes of the 1950s but it does not account for the sharp rise and subsequent fall in the total number of mergers during the 1960s.

to grow are a newfound or variable phenomenon, rising and falling in response to some hidden tides of human aspiration. No one has so argued. (3) Another possibility is that the motivation is always there, but the force of the ownership constraint changes. If so it is the latter (the ownership attitudes) that explains variations in merger rates. (This is Gort's view. See below.) (4) It is possible that managerial considerations come into play because managerial influence is substantially different from ownership influence *and* managers are increasingly getting control. Neither proposition seems established. Certainly the pattern of dispersed ownership that is taken to be a requisite for managerial control is hardly a new phenomenon, nor a suddenly changing one.[13] Moreover Larner, Kamerschen, and others cast doubt on the extent to which performance does differ between what they identify as ownership- and management-controlled firms, but their findings have been challenged.[14]

For these reasons the managerial-goal view does not seem to me to provide a satisfactory theory of mergers and of variations in merger rates. It does, however, provide a potentially important conditioning influence if other conditions for mergers are ripe.

Ownership dominance in buyers' decision making (cases Ia, Ib). Those who articulate merger theories in terms of owners' insider attitudes tend to suppress the possibility of conflicts of interest either by assuming managerial influences are not consequential elements in the decision process (case Ib) or by supposing them to be sufficiently similar to owners' that it is unnecessary to distinguish them (case Ia). Michael Gort's theory is that certain kinds of economic circumstances, particularly rapid technological change and rapidly changing (rising) stock market prices, make it hard to predict the future accurately, and

---

13. Cf. Robert J. Larner, "Ownership and Control in the 200 Largest Non-Financial Corporations, 1929 and 1963," *American Economic Review* 56, no. 4 (September 1966): 777–87. It is worth noting that "control," as defined in this study and in those cited in footnote 14, is not necessarily the same thing as the control of the merger decision that Mueller supposes.

14. Cf. Robert J. Larner, *Management Control and the Large Corporation* (Cambridge, Mass., 1970); David R. Kamerschen, "The Influence of Ownership and Control on Profit Rates," *American Economic Review* 58 (June 1968): 432–47; Monsen, Chiu, and Cooley, "The Effect of Separation and Ownership and Control on the Performance of the Large Firm," *Quarterly Journal of Economics* 82, no. 3 (August 1968): 435–51.

thus lead to the possibility of discrepancies between insider and out-sider valuations. By definition the owners of the acquiring firm are revealed to place a higher value on the stock of an acquired firm than those who sell out to them. This might be due to all sorts of shrewd insider perceptions about opportunities for making more money, or it might be simply a bias toward overoptimistic evaluation. Gort's theory is quite eclectic here. Anything, from a systematic occurrence to a random shock, that disturbs the preexisting patterns of evalua-tion of the target company's stock will tend to increase some evalua-tions of the stock, and reduce others. Those for whom the valuations were reduced continue not to be interested in acquiring the stock, but those whose valuations were increased become potential acquirers.

Gort's analysis is useful in suggesting that expectations—and hence motivations for mergers based upon them—may be a function of certain sets of economic conditions. He thus avoids the problem that mars the managerial theories—failure to explain fluctuations in the merger rate over time.

I am, so far, unpersuaded that this is the most important set of cases on both theoretical and empirical grounds. (I shall explore the empirical data Gort provides in support of his hypothesis in chapter 8. I do not find it compelling.) My first concern is with Gort's over-zealousness in seeking a *single* explanation of merger variations. He postulates that it is the buying company's owners' motivations that are decisive and purports to show that these "insider" motivations pro-duced by discrepant valuations are more satisfactory as explanatory variables than either the search for monopoly or economies of scale. But there is no reason why one must regard *one* set of valuations as logically decisive. Why can not external and insider motives be com-plementary with one another?

My second concern is of a different character. Suppose the Gort theory is able to explain the merger activity of a particular period. The Gort theory is silent as to whether the perceptions leading owners of the acquiring company to the merger are justified or are mistaken. However, if the merger-inducing expectations prove unconfirmed the explanatory power of the theory will survive only if owners fail to learn that their expectations are erroneous. Behavioral theories based upon errors are not unknown, but they seem inappropriate (or at least questionable) for explaining investment behavior in the long run. Suppose we accept Gort's finding that rising stock market prices and changing technology in the 1960s led buyers to overestimate the advantage of acquisitions and thus to consummate enough mergers to create a merger boom. Would we anticipate that if these conditions (rapid stock market rise and changing technology) reemerged in the mid-seventies we would have another similar burst of mergers? We might do so if we assume owners do not learn, and are perennially overoptimistic. We would not if we assumed that the lessons of the sixties were even partly learned. Without knowing which, the theory lacks predictive value. Nor is this a red herring. A subsequent Gort and Hogarty study concludes that the divergent valuations that motivate these mergers tend to be unjustified in the subsequent profit experience of merged companies.[15]

In sum, Gort's theory of discrepant valuations is that some potential acquirers overestimate the attractiveness of the target's securities during certain economic conditions, particularly during periods of rapid technological change and rising stock market prices. It is much easier to accept this as *one* consideration rather than as *the* consideration explaining merger activity. Fortunately this is possible: the role of the buying company's owners' rising evaluations will be to increase the motivation for mergers along with other motivations, and the relative strength of various insider or external motives may rise and fall in response to economic and institutional considerations.

Favorable owners, hostile managers (case IIIa).   This division of views within the buying company can arise if the owners feel their managers are too unaggressive, or too risk averse, or if the major perceived gains by stockholders are insider speculative gains in which their managers will not participate. Suppose, for example, the motivating force is a belief that the merger, although basically uneconomical, will lead to a temporary spurt in the price of the company's stock. The ownership group might profitably plan to complete the merger and then sell their stock. The owners reap the gains but the managers will have to cope with and serve the disappointed subsequent owners.

Could owners *make* a tender offer over the active opposition of managers? I do not really see how. Sharp disagreements between the two groups on such a matter is, of course, possible but will be expected to take the form of a fight for control—perhaps via a proxy fight—rather than a takeover attempt. Thus I am disposed to consider

---

15. Gort and Hogarty, "New Evidence on Mergers." Other studies come to a different conclusion. See chapter 8.

such circumstances as presaging a possible future merger attempt, not a current one. That is, while this constellation of attitudes may well occur, it is not likely to be the observed set of attitudes at the time of a tender offer.

SELLERS' MOTIVATIONS, BUYERS ASSUMED WILLING
(LEFT-HAND HALF OF FIGURE 6–1)

Sellers' motivations have received less attention than buyers' motivations, despite the significant number of contested and defensive mergers.[16] Conglomerate takeovers tend often to be concerned with managerial economies or to be motivated by opportunities to improve on management performance in the acquired firm. For this reason, and because most tender offers provide an immediate premium over stock market prices to stockholders of the selling company, owners of a selling company may well be more disposed to accept a tender offer than their managers: owners often have more to gain *and* less to lose. But the opposite case—managers more avid than owners—is not impossible.

The managerially opposed merger (case Va). This is perhaps the most common source of contested mergers. Suppose first that the selling company's large owners favor a merger but managers are somewhat reluctant and hold a credible threat of being able to persuade small stockholders to frustrate the merger by refusing to tender. If their reluctance is small enough, managers can conceivably be induced to go along (say by being given stock options, or by promises of good and secure jobs in the merged company, or by generous severance pay) or threatened as to what will happen after the fight is over.

Suppose, however, that the selling company's managers cannot be bought off because they are truly and severely threatened. Can these managers prevent the merger, which is an offer from the buying company to the stockholders of the target company? They may be able to, even if they are unable to persuade their stockholders groups that

---

16. I define a contested merger as one in which the management of the company advises its stockholders against accepting the tender and takes such steps in opposition to the merger as it deems appropriate, including possible court action. In a subset of these cases, the management seeks an alternative merger partner as a defensive tactic against the takeover attempt.

their original evaluations were incorrect. By mounting a contest internally or in the courts they can raise the costs to all parties by increasing the transaction costs of merging and by affecting the probability of success of the tender offer. Sufficient increases in these costs can make unattractive an otherwise attractive merger. Nor is the alternative (to the owners of the target company and the buyers) of a proxy fight to upset the existing management necessarily preferable to abandoning the attempt, for it may well impair the earning capacity of their company and thus make its acquisition unattractive even to the former potential acquirer.

Use of the sudden and carefully kept secret tender offer is perhaps best understood as an attempt to catch a potentially hostile management unaware and assure success of the takeover bid before the target's management can organize to resist it. If the hostile management cannot get an injunction to stop the tender offer, its ability to defeat it may be critically impaired. The other parties' hope in the blitzkrieg strategy is that once a merger is virtually assured by the surprise action, reluctant managers will recognize that to oppose it vigorously would be suicidal. Thus, although opposed, managers can cut their losses by holding their fire. Indeed individual managers may seek to make peace with the managers of the buying company in an effort to disassociate themselves from the losing group, and in so doing break the back of managerial opposition.

Selling managers want the merger, larger owners opposed (case VIa). Suppose the merger is attractive to the target's managers but is not particularly attractive to its major stockholders. If the latter are largely indifferent it seems likely that the managers can effect the merger by advising stockholders to tender their stock. Can managers effect a merger that large stockholders oppose? Perhaps. If, for example, a somewhat higher premium would offset the resistance of the target's owners, the managers of the target company might themselves agree to absorb some of the cost of sweetening the offer to owners by agreeing to postmerger employment conditions that would not be possible without their cooperation.

If no system of side payments will satisfy large stockholder groups, the probable success of a *stock acquisition* merger depends upon which group is most credible to the small stockholders, or whether managers can cajole or deceive their stockholders into tendering their shares against their preconceived wishes. The probability of success seems relatively small. But other forms of merger may succeed. Managerial discretion may extend to offering to sell to an acquirer so many of the *assets* of the potential target, that the latter will become heavily dependent on the former, perhaps to the point of being a de facto subsidiary. By the time the sold-out owners discover what is going on, the costs of a proxy fight to upset their managers or prevent the continuing sale of their firm's earning assets may be so high as to persuade the owners to acquiesce in a complete takeover that they would have rejected at the outset. It is this sort of sellout that Senator Harrison Williams had in mind when he decried the practices whereby "proud old companies [are] reduced to corporate shells after white-collar pirates have seized control."[17]

This kind of case, although surely not typical, is not impossible. The problem is to identify it empirically from the information available at time of merger. If the groundwork was properly done, it would look to be a merger to which the selling owners acquiesce. Many of the mergers where a "good fit" between companies seems so evident, may be the result of years of managerial contriving to place the two companies in a complementary position. This is particularly apt to be the case where, in family-controlled companies, nepotism has placed relatively incompetent relatives of founding owners in positions that impede the company or block the promotions of the nonowning managers. These managers may have no better hope than to create critical lacks which only a merger with an outsider can remedy.

Because this is a risky strategy for managers—who must worry about being swallowed up after being taken over—the kind of managerial antipathy that this case supposes must be great. It is perhaps most likely if the ownership group has already made it plain, perhaps by seeking a merger partner, that it intends to displace the management. Here a sellout may be a defensive measure by the managers, who may barter their company for assurances of adequate personal treatment.

MERGERS OPPOSED BY TWO MAJOR GROUPS (LOWER RIGHT QUARTER OF FIGURE 6–1)

Can a merger succeed if two or more major parties oppose it? Obviously, if both buying groups oppose (case IV) there will be no tender offer and if both seller groups oppose (case VII) there will be

---

17. 111 *Congressional Record* 28, 258 (1965), remarks of Senator Williams.

no acceptance. The other cases—where one party on either side is favorable—have some chance of producing a merger.

Managers of B and owners of S favorable (case Vb).   This is perhaps the most likely of the cases where two groups are opposed. As we have suggested, it is quite possible for a controlling management to make a tender offer that is opposed by its owners (case II), and if done suddenly it may reach the selling company's owners before S's managers can organize to oppose. There seems no broad community of interest between B's owners and S's managers that would lead them to be able to stop the merger—indeed it may well be antipathy to one another that leads them to their common opposition to a union of the two companies.

Owners of B and managers of S favorable (case IIIc).   Since a tender offer comes (in form at least) from the managers of B to the stockholders of S, this is a difficult merger to visualize being consummated unless or until B's owners gain control of the management of their company. Even if they do, S's managers will have a major job of persuasion to convince enough small stockholders to accept the merger to offset the hostility of the controlling group. This type of merger seems to me to be all but impossible.

Both ownership groups favorable (case IIIb).   This kind of merger seems quite difficult to visualize without first persuading or displacing the buying company's management. The mere hostility of both managements (quite possibly to one another) would seem to presage negative synergies if the merger were somehow consummated. Thus merger probabilities here seem exceedingly low, until one or the other management is displaced.

Both managements favorable (case VIb).   This case is unlikely to lead to a stock acquisition merger, but if both management groups exercise effective day to day control it is the kind of merger that can be made inevitable by imperceptible steps. Managers, however, play a dangerous game here in that they are inviting a continuing disagreement with their ownership groups of the kind that may lead to their displacement one way or another. In contrast to case VIa in which the managers who sell out subsequently work for owners who approved of their actions, or case II where the opposing stockholders have their control diluted by the acquisition, this case is strictly a managerial power play which, unless it ultimately proves wise to owners, will foreshadow continuing tension between owners and managers. Thus while not impossible (in a form other than a tender offer made and accepted) such mergers seem likely only between companies with tremendously well-entrenched managerial groups.

The Role of Insider Attitudes: Summary

The discussion of this chapter has been concerned first to define various sorts of insider influences as they bear on each of the four principal parties, and second to examine how constellations of attitudes might affect the merger rate, assuming all else was neutral. This framework proves useful not only in placing certain theories of merger motivation such as the "managerial" and "discrepant valuation" hypotheses in perspective, but also in suggesting the conditions that may lead to contested mergers, to defensive mergers, or to mergers made inevitable by the premerger activity of the target company.

Can the usefulness of the framework be tested by objective evidence? Parts of it can. It is easy in principle, though painstaking in practice, to study the motivations as reported in the trade press behind mergers that have been consummated; it is not hard, further, to identify merger proposals that generated major contests, and to attempt to analyze the considerations at work that generate the contest—or affected its outcome. The study by Denis Binder is an impressive start in that direction, but it serves to illustrate why this is a difficult area in which to do research. The moment of a tender offer is the climax to dynamic developments that in some cases have their origins much earlier. One merger reflects a successful (or unsuccessful) proxy fight of three years previous; another is a defensive response to a tender offer by an acquirer that is unsatisfactory to the managers of the target company; yet another may be regarded by the acquirer as a mere tactic to give it something to bargain about with the Department of Justice, and so on.

In saying that every case is complex, and many are unique, I do not intend the conclusion that search for generalization is fruitless. But even to test simple hypotheses about motivation will require a substantial amount of case-by-case analysis to see what the facts really are. In table 6–1 I offer a hypothesis based upon the analysis of this chapter. How well these predictions will stand up—and indeed, how best to test them—is the subject for a major empirical study. I urge some attention to it.

TABLE 6–1

SUBJECTIVE ORDERING OF LIKELIHOOD OF MERGERS FOR
CASES OF FIGURE 6–1

	Cases	*Group(s) Opposed*
Merger probable now	Ia,b,c	none
	II	OB
Merger attempt probable, contest possible	Va	MS
	Vb	OB, MS
Attempt not likely now, but possible later	IIIa	MB
	IIIb	MB, MS
Merger possible but not by tender offer or stock acquisition	VIa	OS
	VIb	OB, OS
Merger not likely	IIIc	MB, OS
	IV	OB, MB
	VII	OS, MS

NOTE:
  OB: Ownership group, Buying company.
  MB: Managerial group, Buying company.
  OS: Ownership group, Selling company.
  MS: Managerial group, Selling company.

CHAPTER SEVEN

Inhibitions (Deterrents) to Mergers

THERE ARE negative as well as positive inducements to mergers, and their force may change over time in such a way as to affect the likelihood of merger.[1] Certain of these—those that operate with particular force on insiders, such as the threats to managerial status— were discussed in chapter 6.[2] I shall be concerned in this chapter with three potentially important sources of deterrents: (1) the antitrust laws; (2) the laws regulating the issuance and exchange of securities; and (3) the costs of making and effecting a tender offer. Of particular concern in explaining the merger wave is whether these deterrents may have been relatively ineffective as of 1965 and relatively more effective after 1968.

Antitrust as a Deterrent

Antitrust aspects of mergers in general and conglomerate mergers in particular have been given repeated and extensive discussion. I wish neither to summarize nor extend that literature at this point. But a brief, and perhaps idiosyncratic sketch is useful in understanding the forces operative in the late sixties, and in laying the foundation for the more detailed discussion of recent and future policies that will concern us in chapters 9 through 12.

There is no doubt that *if* a merger is held to be violative of the antitrust laws there is an impressive arsenal that may be used against it. Criminal and civil sanctions are available to the government under

---

1. In the formal model developed in chapter 2 these are incorporated in the γ coefficients.

2. While insider motivations were discussed in the previous chapter, those motivations cannot truly be divorced from the kinds of costs or inhibitions discussed here. For example, a disgruntled or fearful management of a target company might, because of these insider motivations, initiate private legal activity against the merger under either the antitrust or securities laws, it might persuade the Justice Department, the FTC, or the Securities Exchange Commission to intervene in opposition to the merger, or it might in a variety of ways undertake activities that raise the direct or indirect costs of merging. The emphasis in this chapter on external (rather than "insider") costs concerns who bears the costs, not who initiates the activity that leads to them.

151

the Sherman Act, and Section 7 of the Clayton Act provides for temporary or permanent injunctive relief or divestiture to the Department of Justice, the FTC, and private plaintiffs. Moreover, treble damages are available to private plaintiffs. The general view, however, is that at least until 1968, the antitrust laws did more to encourage than to deter conglomerate acquisitions, and may well have played a motivating role in the great merger spurt of 1965 to 1968. Important changes in and around 1968 may further have contributed to the end of the boom. It is this view that I wish to sketch here. This latter view may be expanded into a regulatory theory of merger motivation, with clear implications for policy.

THE PREHISTORY: 1890-1950

Antitrust is usually said to start in this country with the passage in 1890 of the Sherman Antitrust Act; a date that preceded the first great merger movement.

The Sherman Act, though clearly not passed with mergers in mind, was not *inherently* unable to deal with them. After all, a merger was a combination, and Section 1 prohibited "*every combination in the form of trust or otherwise* . . . in restraint of trade." The famous Northern Securities case (1904) held the unification of the Great Northern and Northern Pacific Railroads a violation of Section 1.[3] The Court felt it had no choice in view of the word "every" in the statute. This extreme interpretation of the statute was clearly not a viable one and had the effect of generating its own rejection, which took the form of the famous Rule of Reason, usually cited to the 1911 decision in Standard Oil.[4]

Under the rule of reason only *unreasonable* restraints were to be held illegal under Section 1; restraints that were merely ancillary to normal and efficiency-producing business practices were exempt. There is little doubt that, had the issue been so raised, a merger to achieve an economy would have been deemed reasonable.

While the Sherman Act *was* effectively used in a number of railroad cases, even after 1911,[5] it was not used widely and left the

---

3. *Northern Securities Company v. United States,* 193 U.S. 197 (1904).

4. *Standard Oil Co. v. United States,* 221 U.S. 1 (1911).

5. See e.g., *United States v. Union Pacific RR,* 226 U.S. 61 (1912), and *United States v. Southern Pacific Co.,* 259 U.S. 214 (1922).

great mergers in mining and manufacturing all but untouched. In a symbolic if not literal sense the ultimate case, decided by the Supreme Court in 1920, was U.S. Steel.[6] U.S. Steel had been formed in 1901— the ultimate outcome of a series of mergers involving 180 former competitors, and it had achieved overnight a dominant position in the steel industry. The Court however found that these acquisitions had not violated Section 1 of the Sherman Act because U.S. Steel had not achieved its purpose of a monopoly. If such a merger was immune, the Sherman Act would prove toothless in the merger area.[7]

The Clayton Act, passed in 1914, was in part at least a product of the merger movement, and a reaction to the Rule of Reason. Congress attempted, ineffectively it turned out, to provide a basis for attacking the merger, *qua merger* and at the time of merger. The original Section 7 read, in relevant parts:

That no corporation engaged in commerce shall acquire . . . the whole or any part of *the stock* . . . of another corporation . . . where the effect of such acquisition may be to substantially lessen competition *between the corporation whose stock is so acquired and the corporation making the acquisition,* or to restrain such commerce in any section or community, or tend to create a monopoly of any line of commerce. [Emphasis supplied.]

The primary defects in the original Section 7 were in the italicized language. Most importantly while prohibiting *stock* acquisitions, Section 7 neglected *asset* acquisitions. This loophole was quickly recognized and widely utilized. It was not to be removed until the 1950 Cellar-Kefauver Amendment to the Clayton Act. A further deficiency, in the eyes of many, was that the language limiting the attention to

---

6. *United States v. United States Steel Corp.,* 251 U.S. 417 (1920).

7. Of course the Sherman Act today may be useful in reaching some mergers not reachable by other means. See for example, *United States v. First National Bank & Trust Company of Lexington,* 376 U.S. 665 (1964). Bank mergers are something of a special case. Before the Philadelphia Bank case, *United States v. Philadelphia National Bank,* 374 U.S. 321 (1963), bank mergers had been thought to be excluded from Section 7 prosecution, but subject to the Sherman Act, Sections 1 and 2. The Bank Merger Act of 1966, 80 Stat. 10, was a Congressional response to Philadelphia and said in pertinent part: "Any merger . . . which was consummated prior to June 17, 1963 . . . shall be conclusively presumed to have not been in violation of any antitrust laws other than [section 2 of the Sherman Act]." Because of Section 2, Lexington Bank was not legislatively reversed as were other prominent cases, including *United States v. Manufacturers Hanover Trust Co.,* 240 F.Supp. 867 (S.D. N.Y. 1965).

competition between the acquiring and acquired companies, arguably limited the Act to horizontal acquisitions. (But see duPont-GM for a contrary view.)[8] This too was to be modified in 1950.

While the late thirties witnessed a major revival in antitrust activity spurred by the TNEC investigations and pushed by the appointment in 1937 of Thurman Arnold as head of the antitrust division, it was not until the aftermath of World War II that a major merger case came up again. This was the so-called Columbia Steel case.[9] Columbia Steel, a wholly owned subsidiary of U.S. Steel, acquired the assets of Consolidated Steel, and was sued under Sections 1 and 2 of the Sherman Act. Because it was an asset acquisition, Section 7 was not available. The difficult burden of proof via monopolization, or as an unreasonable restraint of trade, that the government faced led first the district court and later a Supreme Court divided 5 to 4 to uphold the merger. The frustration that ensued provided a dominant push for new and tougher legislation.

The Cellar-Kefauver Act of 1950 amended Section 7 to read as follows:

That no corporation . . . shall acquire . . . the whole or any part of the stock . . . [or] any part of the assets of another corporation . . . where in any line of commerce in any section of the country, the effect of such acquisition may be substantially to lessen competition, or to tend to create a monopoly.

With this Act, modern merger policy may be said to begin; asset acquisitions were included, and adverse effects on competition whether between the acquiring and acquired companies, *or elsewhere,* were within the scope of the Act.

THE STIFFENING OPPOSITION TO HORIZONTAL AND
VERTICAL MERGERS

The Cellar-Kefauver Amendments to the Clayton Act were followed by a long series of progovernmental Supreme Court decisions—of these Brown Shoe, Philadelphia Bank, Von's Grocery, and Pabst are

---

8. *United States v. E. I. duPont de Nemours & Co.,* 353 U.S. 586 (1957).

9. *United States v. Columbia Steel Co.,* 74 F.Supp. 671 (D. Del. 1947); 334 U.S. 495 (1948).

particularly vital.[10] These and other decisions increasingly closed the door to horizontal and vertical acquisitions by large firms. To the extent that the incentives to merger for large firms were due to any of the large number of non-product-market-oriented factors, this tended to redirect acquisitive interest from barred acquisitions to acceptable ones at least as much as to encourage internal growth or *de novo* entry into new industries. In the first instance, one witnessed a surge of acquisitions of companies which, despite many differences, had in common that they produced "related" products—the kinds of merger that, although labeled conglomerate in the FTC statistics, were subtitled market-extension or product-extension mergers. A series of 1964 Supreme Court decisions served to bring such acquisitions under the horizontal or vertical rules being hammered out. El Paso Natural Gas Co.'s acquisition of Pacific Northwest Pipeline Company, ALCOA's acquisition of Rome Cable, primarily a manufacturer of copper cable, and Continental Can's acquisition of Hazel-Atlas Glass, a manufacturer of glass bottles, were each held by the Court to violate Section 7.[11] These cases are themselves diverse and are complex internally but in each case the Court buttressed such actual competition as already existed by the potential competition that might develop, in defining relevant markets and the potential of injury.[12]

By the mid-1960s, any reasonably observant large company seeking growth by acquisition had to be aware of the mounting antitrust hazards it faced if it expanded by acquisition into lines that were even loosely horizontal or vertical. For many companies without a

---

10. *Brown Shoe Co. v. United States,* 370 U.S. 294 (1962); *United States v. Philadelphia National Bank,* 374 U.S. 321 (1963); *United States v. Von's Grocery Co.,* 384 U.S. 270 (1966); *United States v. Pabst Brewing Co.,* 384 U.S. 546 (1966).

11. *United States v. El Paso Natural Gas Co.,* 376 U.S. 651 (1964); *United States v. Aluminum Co. of America,* 377 U.S. 271 (1964); *United States v. Continental Can Co.,* 378 U.S. 441 (1964).

12. This is not the place to explore the somewhat tortuous inclusions and exclusions that were involved in the market definitions. The evident fact is that the Supreme Court was seeking a way to broaden the ambit of the Clayton Act and it did so through market redefinition. That same tendency to widen the net seems to me to recur in the modern use of the concept of potential competition. Another case of the period, *United States v. Penn-Olin Chemical Co.,* 378 U.S. 158 (1964), is now regarded as the first of the important potential competition cases. It is discussed at length in chapter 10.

conglomerate outlook this no doubt deterred their acquisition activities; others took the risks and a very large number of complaints were filed by both the Justice Department and the FTC. But for the new breed of conglomerators, emerging antitrust law suggested a new and different kind of target—the truly unrelated company. Well into the 1960s both the courts and the Justice Department appeared to accept the absence of a basis for a direct attack on such conglomerate acquisitions. This is nicely illustrated in an otherwise unimportant case.[13] In seeking a temporary injunction to block the (conglomerate) acquisition by Food Machinery Corporation (FMC) of American Viscose Co. (Avisco) the government strained to find horizontal and vertical aspects of the acquisition in presenting its case. The district court would have none of it. It found that:

FMC and Avisco are not and never have been competitors in the manufacture and sale of any product,—Avisco has sold no products to FMC and manufactures none needed by it. FMC has sold only two products of any value to Avisco. These products are essentially incidental and de minimis in relation to the entire transaction.

Once the court had decided that the merger was neither horizontal nor vertical, it regarded the burden of proof as falling heavily on the government. Stating that "[t]he government has not cited a single case in which a preliminary injunction has been issued or granted to prevent the consummation of a conglomerate merger," the court decided against the government.

Expected judicial tolerance with respect to the purely conglomerate merger, combined with vigorous striking down of horizontal and vertical acquisitions, is at least consistent with the hypothesis that the merger wave of the sixties was turned into a predominantly conglomerate merger movement by progressively making other forms of acquisition illegal. Donald Turner, who was to serve as head of the Antitrust Division from 1965 to 1968, made it clear both before he took office and after, that in his view the conglomerate merger (except in well-defined situations) did not (and should not) come under the general antitrust deterrents of Section 7.[14] If one believed this to be

---

13. *United States v. FMC Corporation*, 218 F.Supp. 817 (S.D. Colo. 1963); appeal dismissed, 321 F.2d 534 (9th Cir. 1963); affirmed by the Supreme Court on procedural grounds, 845 Ct. 4 (1963).

14. Donald Turner, "Conglomerate Mergers and Section 7 of the Clayton Act," 78 HARVARD LAW REVIEW 1313–95 (May 1965).

unfortunate, the remedy, Turner felt, lay in having Congress enact new legislation.

Despite Turner's somewhat skeptical view of the ability to deal with conglomerate mergers under the rubric of Section 7, several of the cases brought and tried in the mid-sixties began to erode the distinction between conglomerate acquisitions and those with direct market effects.

As early as 1966 Mr. Justice Stewart was to complain that the sole consistency he could find in the Supreme Court's decisions under Section 7 was "that the government always wins."[15] Between 1964 and mid-1968, as part of the general attack on mergers, a series of conglomerate cases had reached the courts. By one device or another some judges were finding ways to include the conglomerate acquisitions within an antitrust net that reflected the Warren Court's general disposition to back the government in its attacks on mergers.

Key cases of this period included Consolidated Foods's acquisition of Gentry, Procter & Gamble's acquisition of Clorox, General Foods's acquisition of SOS, and General Dynamics's acquisition of Liquid Carbonic.[16] While only the last was a pure conglomerate acquisition untainted by any horizontal or vertical aspects, they all have an important common aspect. In each case the court found against the acquisition, at least in part on new and unconventional grounds that appeared (to some) to provide a basis for a general attack on conglomerate acquisitions. The new bases were reciprocity and potential competition.[17] There seems to me little doubt that it is these decisions

---

15. Dissenting opinion *United States v. Von's Grocery*, 384 U.S. 270 (1966).

16. *FTC v. Consolidated Foods Corp.*, 380 U.S. 592 (1965); *United States v. General Dynamics*, 258 F.Supp. 36 (S.D. N.Y. 1966); *FTC v. Procter & Gamble Co.*, 386 U.S. 568 (1967); *General Foods Corp. v. FTC*, 386 F.2d 936 (3d Cir. 1967), cert. denied 391 U.S. 919 (1968). These cases are discussed in greater detail in chapters 10 and 11.

17. Potential competition as I use it here embraces at least two distinguishable legal notions: (*a*) elimination of the acquiring firm from a status of potential *de novo* entrant into the industry, and (*b*) entrenchment of the acquirer into the industry in such a way as to discourage further entry by other potential entrants. These matters are discussed fully in chapter 10.

that led both to the conglomerate merger guidelines, and to the new posture toward conglomerates that the Nixon appointees to the Department of Justice were to take.

THE EVENTS OF 1968 AND 1969

The explosion in the number and size of conglomerate acquisitions during 1967 and 1968 has already been noted, and was widely observed with alarm in antitrust and congressional circles. The period 1968–69 was notable for conglomerate mergers in ways that were a direct response to this explosion. It witnessed the issuance of the merger guidelines (including conglomerate guidelines) by the Department of Justice, and the selection and confirmation of Richard McLaren as the incoming head of the Antitrust Division. It also, less notably, saw the formation and reporting of two task forces on antitrust policy whose recommendations, including recommendations with respect to conglomerate policies, were made public in the summer of 1969. In retrospect the reaction and attention given to conglomerate mergers in 1968 seems overblown, for this year was to prove to be the turning point in a merger movement that seems to have been likely to lose its momentum with or without any change in antitrust policy. But that is hindsight—at the time the rising trend in acquisitions was visible and alarming.

The guidelines. On May 30, 1968, the Department of Justice issued its heralded merger guidelines, which opened as follows:

. . . The purpose of these guidelines is to acquaint the business community, the legal profession, and other interested groups and individuals with the standards currently being applied by the Department of Justice in determining whether to challenge corporate acquisitions and mergers under Section 7 of the Clayton Act.

The guidelines aroused more than routine interest because they came at a time when it appeared the Supreme Court was disposed to back the government in every case, and thus in effect to delegate antitrust policy to the Justice Department; Department decisions as to what cases to bring would tend to be decisive if it always (or nearly always) won. Thus, although the guidelines nominally merely codified the Department's understanding of the law, they actually were regarded as making the law.

Guidelines are presented separately for horizontal, vertical, and conglomerate mergers. Not only did they codify (and arguably extend) the hard line of the recent court decisions with respect to horizontal and vertical mergers, but they also attempted to extend it to conglomerate mergers using the potential competition, reciprocity, and entrenchment arguments developed in the cases cited in footnote 16.

The specifics of the guidelines will concern us in chapter 12; for the moment it is sufficient to note that they came close to being per se rules against conglomerate mergers that met certain structural standards. As a slight overstatement, the guidelines seemed to identify for attack any acquisition of a significant-sized firm by an already large diversified firm under one or more of the bases—potential competition, reciprocity, or entrenchment—that were regarded as predicting probable competitive harm. At the same time the guidelines rejected efficiency defenses.

The guidelines were the final product of Turner's tenancy in charge of the Antitrust Division, reflecting both his theoretical and administrative views of the problem and his way of stretching Section 7 to include the most arguably anticompetitive conglomerate mergers. There is little doubt that if conglomerate mergers had once appeared immune from attack, that immunity was gone.

The task force reports. Neither of the two 1968 task forces were comfortable with the implicit view described above though for somewhat different reasons. The Neal Task Force, appointed by President Johnson in anticipation of the 1968 campaign, was concerned about their sufficiency:

> Potentially anticompetitive mergers may be allowed to proceed because economic theory and analytical foresight are inadequate to predict anticompetitive effects in specific cases, even though there may be good reason for believing that some classes of mergers, considered in the aggregate, are harmful to competition.
>
> Because of these difficulties, and because the incentives that have produced the current conglomerate merger movement can and should be directed to increase competition, we propose a statutory prohibition to supplement the merger prohibition of Section 7 of the Clayton Act.[18]

The proposed legislation would have forbidden mergers between "large firms" (sales in excess of $500 million or assets in excess of

---

18. "White House Task Force Report on Antitrust Policy" (Neal Report), submitted July 5, 1968, reprinted in BNA, *Antitrust and Trade Regulation Report,* no. 411 (May 27, 1969): pt. II.

$250 million) and "leading firms" (market share 10 percent or more in an industry with four-firm concentration in excess of 50 percent).

The Stigler Task Force, appointed by President-elect Nixon to provide him with preinaugural policy position papers, was largely unconcerned about the conglomerate mergers, and feared the guidelines view would prove effective in disrupting economic activities by being indiscriminately applied:

> We seriously doubt that the Antitrust Division should embark upon an active program of challenging conglomerate enterprises on the basis of nebulous fears about size and economic power. These fears should be either confirmed or dissipated, and an important contribution would be made to this resolution by an early conference on the subject. . . . If there is a real political threat in giant mergers, then the critical dimension should be estimated. If there is no threat, the fears entertained by critics of the conglomerate enterprises should be allayed. Vigorous action on the basis of our present knowledge is not defensible.[19]

If there was need for legislation (which the Stigler Task Force doubted) it probably lay in the areas of securities regulation rather than antitrust.

Whether the task forces produced either lasting effects or sufficiently interesting documents to have justified the efforts that went into them seems to me an open question. On two points at least their suggestions have been followed: both task forces urged an end to use of the Robinson-Patman Act as a government antitrust device and its use has all but ceased. The Stigler Task Force stressed increased attention to anticompetitive practices in regulated industries, and it has occurred. Beyond this the recommendations seem to have misjudged the mood of the country. The major recommendation of the Neal Task Force, the giant merger bill, aroused no substantial legislative interest, although arguably if the election of 1968 had turned out differently it would have. The Stigler report failed to recognize the desire of the Division under McLaren not to be labeled a "pawn of the reactionary establishment" and also failed to recognize the hostility of the old industrial establishment to the new style corporate raiders. Whether task force reports ought to be responsive to political realities is another matter; my own view is that they should.

---

19. "Task Force Report on Productivity and Competition" (Stigler Report), submitted January, 1969, reprinted in BNA, *Antitrust and Trade Regulation Report,* no. 413 (June 10, 1969): X1–X8. I was a member of this task force.

Mr. McLaren's attempt. Whatever Richard McLaren's preappointment views as an antitrust lawyer for a leading Chicago firm, by the time of his confirmation hearing before the Senate he exhibited a genuine sense of urgency in dealing with the conglomerate problem. His early speeches have a messianic quality that must have astounded his former colleagues of the defense bar. They began to reflect a very different implicit view from that which I have attributed to the guidelines. Mr. McLaren was to argue that Section 7 was broad enough to cover conglomerate mergers even without any well-defined anti-competitive consequences in the usual economic sense of competition in a well-defined market. The *possibility* of reciprocity, or of "reciprocity effect," or an increase in overall concentration in the economy were suggested bases of attack.

Five testing cases were initiated in the early months of the Nixon Administration, and each involved acquisition attempts by "real" conglomerates: Ling-Temco-Vought's bid for Jones & Laughlin Steel, Northwest Industries (contested) attempt to acquire B. F. Goodrich, and three uncontested mergers undertaken by ITT involving Grinnell Corporation, Canteen, and Hartford Life Insurance. To those who had long argued that the Antitrust Division ought to bring key test cases, this was exciting news: it seemed to promise an early resolution of the central issue as to whether the conglomerate merger was "in" or "out" under the antitrust laws. They were to be disappointed. The LTV case was settled by a consent decree on the eve of the subsequent collapse of the LTV empire—a collapse no little aided by LTV's inability to make Jones & Laughlin a profitable operation.[20]

The government's attempt to get an injunction against the Northwest-Goodrich merger was rejected by Judge Will in the Northern District of Illinois who was unimpressed by the reciprocity and potential competition arguments presented to him.[21]

---

20. *United States v. Ling-Temco-Vought,* 315 F.Supp. 1301 (W.D. Penn. 1970) 1970 *CCH Trade Cases* ¶ 73,105, 73,227, 73,228. The principal terms of the decree required that LTV divest itself of Braniff Airlines and the Okonite Co. *or* of J & L.

21. *United States v. Northwest Industries, Inc.,* 301 F.Supp. 1066 (N.D. Ill. 1969). The merger attempt failed after one of the most bloody and well-publicized corporate contests of recent decades. It is clear that the government antitrust suit added to Northwest Industries's costs and its woes, but how significant a role the suit played in the outcome is not known to me.

In the three ITT cases the government fared uniformly badly in the district courts—and none of the interesting decisions of those courts reached the Supreme Court. Chief Judge Timbers of the Connecticut District rejected the government request for preliminary injunctions against both the Grinnell and Hartford acquisitions, and found ringingly against the government in the Grinnell case after a full trial.[22] Judge Austin in the Northern District of Illinois accepted fully defendant's arguments in finding against the government in the Canteen case.[23] All three ITT cases were part of the to-become-famous "Dita Beard" settlement in which ITT consented to give up Grinnell and Canteen, but kept Hartford.[24] Whatever the merits of that settlement, the chance of establishing legal precedent was lost.

THE IMPACT OF 1968–69

In the end the McLaren attempt to embrace conglomerates within the general antimerger net proved a brave failure. McLaren himself had tired of the fray, and by the end of 1971 had sought and received appointment as a District Court Judge in the Northern District of Illinois. (One wonders at his early conversations with his colleagues, Will and Austin.) The legal stance of conglomerate mergers was hardly clearer when he left than when he started.

But that is not the main point in evaluating the effect of all the activity on the propensity to merge. If in 1965 the conglomerate merger had seemed largely immune to antitrust attack, first the guidelines and second the even broader McLaren approach surely removed that assurance. The fear of a costly and potentially successful antitrust attack on a purely conglomerate acquisition could not be overlooked from May of 1968 on, and may well have added to the inhibitions to merge, at that critical date in the merger wave.

---

22. 1969 *CCH Trade Cases* ¶72,943 (D. Conn. 1969), for denial of injunction; *United States v. ITT,* 324 F.Supp. 19 (D. Conn. 1970); appeal dismissed 404 U.S. 801 (1971). The court explicitly rejected the macro-concentration argument here.

23. *United States v. ITT (Canteen),* 1971 *CCH Trade Cases* ¶ 73,-619 (N.D. Ill. 1971). For the record, let me note that I appeared as an expert witness for the defense in this case.

24. See *United States v. ITT (Grinnell),* 1971 *CCH Trade Cases* ¶ 73,665 (D. Conn. 1971); *United States v. ITT (Hartford),* 1971 *CCH Trade Cases* ¶ 73,666 (D. Conn. 1971); *United States v. ITT (Canteen),* 1971 *CCH Trade Cases* ¶ 73,667 (N.D. Ill. 1971), for the consent decrees.

It may well be that the government's reverses in the tried cases, together with an apparent shift to a more conservative court have meant that the inhibitions that appeared to be developing in 1968–69 were never really there. But uncertainty is itself a deterrent, and it seems likely that the fear of a costly and potentially successful anti-trust attack was, and indeed remains, a significant net inhibition to a conglomerate merger.[25]

Security Laws as a Deterrent[26]

Virtually every conglomerate acquisition involves some exchanges of securities. Because of this, the regulation of exchanges of securities by legislation (from the Securities Exchange Act of 1934 to the 1970 Amendments to the Williams Act) and by administrative agencies (especially the SEC) plays a significant role in the merger picture. Ideally, securities regulation as it affects mergers would not add to the incentives for "undesirable" mergers, but would not unduly impede "desirable" ones. Because there is no simple rule for distinguishing between desirable and undesirable mergers it is likely that the greater the force with which security regulations are applied to acquisitions, the greater are the impediments to all mergers. Has securities regulation, for good or for ill, been a significant deterrent? Did the force of such deterrents as existed change over the period of the late 1960s?

The principal thrusts of securities regulation have been toward compelling disclosure and prohibiting fraud. These are surely laudable objectives since they contribute to letting stockholders faced with choices make those choices intelligently, and to eliminating such unworthy bases for merger as redistributions of wealth resulting from

---

25. As we shall see in chapter 10, a current legal basis for attacking conglomerate acquisitions does seem to be developing in the potential competition area. In any event the merger wave of the late 1960s is not likely to be soon forgotten, and new legislation such as the Hart Bill against large firms is regularly introduced. The political climate is stormy if unclear, with a significant populist undertone. Thomas Kauper, McLaren's successor, has not indicated any disposition to retreat from the McLaren public stand on conglomerates although one doubts that he has failed to note the lack of success it has achieved.

26. The debt this whole section owes to my former student Denis Binder is enormous. His research on contested tender offers both educated and informed me. I cite him repeatedly, but that fails adequately to convey my thanks for his help.

fraud by informed groups against less informed ones. But the devices used to achieve these objectives—particularly the granting of injunctive relief against tender offers, and the requirements for early and detailed disclosure of interests and intentions may be two-edged swords.

INJUNCTIVE RELIEF AGAINST FRAUD

The basic antifraud provision is given in Rule 10b–5 of the Securities Exchange Act. It provides:

> It shall be unlawful for any person, directly or indirectly, by the use of any means or instrumentality of interstate commerce, or of the mails or of any facility of any national securities exchange,
>
> (*a*) To employ any device, scheme, or artifice to defraud,
>
> (*b*) To make any untrue statement of a material fact or to omit to state a material fact necessary in order to make the statements made, in the light of the circumstances under which they were made, not misleading, or
>
> (*c*) To engage in any act, practice, or course of business which operates or would operate as a fraud or deceit upon any person, in connection with the purchase or sale of any security.

As a practical matter protection against fraud in the context of a tender offer virtually requires use of a preliminary injunction to stop the fraudulent offer, for reestablishing the status quo ante after a series of exchanges has been made is all but impossible. Moreover, accurately awarding damages based on what particular traded securities would have been worth absent the fraud is not possible, and protecting investors against any loss whatever is not appropriate—the security laws are not designed to protect investors or speculators against losses from poor investments.

A major deficiency of the preliminary injunction is that its use will usually have the effect of stopping permanently the tender offer. Thus "buying time," which the preliminary injunction is designed to do, will also prejudge the merits of the allegations, which the preliminary injunction is not designed to do. As a result, the courts have moved with great care in this area. There are, of course, some easy cases. In the most recent case of this kind to reach the Supreme Court, the purchaser of an insurance company paid for his purchase by selling the United States Treasury bonds of the acquired corporation. In *Sup't of Insurance v. Bankers Life & Casualty Co.*[27] the Court held

---

27. 404 U.S. 6 (1971).

this was unmistakably fraud within the meaning of Rule 10b–5 and the corporation was entitled to be protected against it.[28] Another straightforward fraud situation was disclosed in *Butler Aviation Inc. v. Comprehensive Designers, Inc.*[29] Comprehensive Designers, as part of a plan to tender for Butler Aviation, released false statements and estimates of its earnings. In the key year it predicted earnings per share of $.60, when actual earnings proved to be $.33 and could not reasonably have been expected to reach $.60. It subsequently changed accounting practices with the primary purpose of boosting nominal fourth quarter earnings. The effect of these acts was (via the PE game) to push its stock prices up from $15 to $35 and to potentially defraud all stockholders of Butler Aviation who accepted overvalued Comprehensive Designers securities for their stock. The court found clear fraud and enjoined the tender offer.

While each of these cases is a clear example of courts' willingness to inhibit a merger that might otherwise occur, what is surprising is how few such cases there have been and how seldom courts have been willing to enjoin tender offers on the basis of alleged violations of the securities laws. Before the 1968 Amendments, this reluctance took the forms of denying standing to sue to all but the most directly involved in a tender offer—those tendering—and demanding a high standard of proof of fraud which was difficult to meet because of the limited disclosure required of those making tender offers. These matters are covered at length and with insight by Binder, and need no review here.[30]

This inability of targets of takeovers to succeed under 10b–5 led Senator Williams to introduce legislation to strengthen their hands as early as 1965, and led Congress to pass a strong Act (the

---

28. The reason such an apparently straightforward case got to the Supreme Court was that the sole stockholder was a party to the uncontested transaction. Thus, the lower courts found no injured person.

29. 307 F.Supp. 910 (S.D. N.Y. 1969); affirmed, 425 F.2d 842 (2d Cir. 1970).

30. Denis Binder, "Securities Law of Contested Tender Offers," 18 NEW YORK LAW FORUM, no. 3, 569 (Winter 1973). The germinal case is *Birnbaum v. Newport Steel*, 98 F.Supp. 506 (S.D. N.Y. 1951); 193 F.2d 461 (2d Cir. 1952); cert. denied 343 U.S. 956 (1952). The court rejected the complaint of Birnbaum's stockholders that the controlling shareholder had rejected an advantageous (to them) merger offer in order to sell his interest to Newport at a substantial premium, and that misrepresentations played a large part in the transactions.

Williams Act) in 1968, and to further strengthen it in 1970 Amendments both with respect to standing and to disclosure. The effect was
to cause the courts to deny injunctions on different bases than before.
It is empirically demonstrable that the courts have not reversed their
reluctance.[31] The courts have been notably and deliberately less willing than Congress intended to issue injunctions penalizing incomplete
or inaccurate disclosure. Two important cases of 1968 and 1970
illustrate the courts' reluctance to act even in the face of what appears
to have been deliberate misleading in the context of a contested tender
offer.

The basic facts in *Electronic Specialty Co. v. International Controls Corp.* are these.[32] A small conglomerate, International Controls
(ICC), was attempting to take over Electronic Specialty (ELS) despite the vigorous opposition of ELS management. Robert Vesco, later
to become a central figure in both securities and political contribution
scandals, but then merely ICC's president, engaged in arguably misleading statements, both to the *Wall Street Journal* and to the management of ELS. The statements were misleading both in exaggerating
how much stock ICC already owned of ELS (thus suggesting it would
be futile to resist ICC attempts to gain control, if ICC chose to seek
control) and denying merger intent (thus disarming concerted efforts
to oppose the merger or expose the errors in Vesco's statements). For
example, on August 13, 1968, Vesco gave an interview to the *Wall
Street Journal* admitting prior interest by ICC in a tender but suggesting that that interest was past, and that ICC wanted to sell its (close to
5 percent) holding of ELS stock. In fact, the actual holding was less
than 2½ percent and that *same* evening Vesco urged his board to
make the tender offer. Less than a week later the offer was made, and
succeeded. The district court, impressed, granted a temporary injunction enjoining ICC from voting its stock in ELS. But the Second Circuit disagreed.

The second case is almost equally straightforward. Susquehanna
Corporation in tendering successfully for the shares of Pan American
Sulphur Co. (Pasco) stated as part of its forms filed with the SEC,
"Susquehanna does not plan or propose to liquidate Pan American,
to sell its assets to, or merge it with, any other person, or to make any
major change in its business or corporate structure." This statement

---

31. Binder, "Securities Law," p. 569.
32. 295 F.Supp. 1063 (S.D. N.Y. 1968); affirmed in part and reversed in part, 409 F.2d 937 (2d Cir. 1969).

originally filed on November 25, 1968, was left unchanged in a modified statement filed on December 9, 1968. On December 10, Susquehanna sent a telegram to American Smelting and Refining proposing it merge with Pasco. Pasco's management shrieked "fraud" and sought to force Susquehanna to divest its holdings in Pasco or to be permanently enjoined from voting its stock. The Fifth Circuit denied the request.[33]

What explains the judicial reluctance in the face of evident fraud? Is it, as some have charged, a callous emasculation of laws passed with unmistakable legislative intent to ease the burdens on plaintiffs? The courts themselves have been at some pains to defend their caution as a recognition of competing interests. It is widely held that securities laws are primarily aimed at protecting the investing public from the shenanigans and manipulations of insiders. When fraud occurs in such forms (as in the Bankers Life and Butler Aviation cases cited above) courts have not hesitated to enjoin it. But frequently the suit against a tender offer is brought by the *management* of the target company, nominally on behalf of their stockholders but really in management's own interest. Since the target company's managers and stockholders may have different interests, the courts must guard against protecting insiders (management) and injuring outsiders (stockholders).

These judicial concerns seem to me to be well merited. One may argue that the management of a target company already has enormous (perhaps undue) natural advantages in communicating with its stockholders, including access to the company's stockholder lists, its treasury, and its counsel; to say nothing of being the inertial recipient of proxies from a great many stockholders. One fear in granting an injunction is that management of the target company is using the courts to help it stop a merger that its stockholders would benefit from. Another is that it is a device to favor an alternative merger partner more favorable to management but less favorable to its stockholders. The courts have held that public stockholders deserve to have the genuine and uncommon opportunity to sell their shares at a premium which the tender offer provides. Even a preliminary injunction against the tender may well deprive them of it.

An actual example based on a litigated case may serve to illustrate the problems.[34] In 1969, Armour and Company was the target

33. *Susquehanna Corp. v. Pan American Sulphur Co.,* 423 F.2d 1075 (5th Cir. 1970).

34. *Armour and Co. v. General Host,* 296 F.Supp. 470 (S.D. N.Y. 1969).

of a tender offer by General Host in which the stockholders of Armour were offered a complex bundle of Host securities for their Armour shares. A major motive for the tender offer by Host was thought to have been Host's belief that a generally sluggish performance of Armour's management, and its inability to respond to the changes that were transforming the meat-packing industry, offered Host's aggressive management an opportunity for quick profits. Armour's management, recognizing that *it* was threatened with replacement, bitterly fought the tender, not only sending letters and telegrams to stockholders but also stating its claims in full-page ads in the *Wall Street Journal, New York Times,* and other places. All of this was at company expense. Armour's management next sought and got a competing tender offer (from Greyhound) and then moved into court to seek an injunction against Host under the securities laws. The basis of its suit was alleged misstatements and omissions in the Host tender offer about the subordinated and long-term nature of the securities and the lack of protective covenants restricting loans to others and investments elsewhere. In addition, Armour claimed that if the tender offer succeeded, General Host would have such a shortage of working capital as to be unable to meet principal and interest payments on its debentures.

The court rejected the claims and denied relief on the ground that "the stockholders are entitled to exercise their own judgment as to these matters." Most importantly, it noted that an injunction against General Host would leave open the competing tender offer for Armour by Greyhound, which had the support of Armour's management. An injunction would thus have the effect of reducing the choices open to Armour's shareholders. They would either have to tender to Greyhound, or let that offer expire and run the risk that no other desirable offer would come along. The court concluded that the issuance of a preliminary injunction would in effect grant Armour's management the full relief sought at trial, and that even if Host subsequently prevailed on the merits, it would have lost. Thus, preserving the choices of investors took precedence over protecting them from making an unwise choice.

Looking merely at the decided cases both before and after 1968, one would conclude that successful injunctive relief to deter mergers has not been a powerful deterrent. Such injunctions are few in number. But after 1968 the number of cases *tried* increased substantially. Binder sums up as follows:

One gets the impression that [target companies' managements] examine [the acquiring company's] statements with an electron microscope and then cry "foul" upon discovering the slightest error. They proceed to rush into court seeking injunctive relief, knowing that if they succeed, the tender offer will be all but over. On the other hand, the courts, being well aware of what is happening, refuse to play management's game. They are unwilling to destroy the tender offer because of minor mistakes uttered in the heat of battle. They will grant relief . . . only if the target can show manipulative practices or flagrant misrepresentations and omissions that go to the heart of the market mechanism. These conditions are generally not met by plaintiffs because the contenders are well aware of the threat of litigation so they try structuring their operations to avoid material transgressions.[35]

The increased use of the courts, despite the lack of success, may simply reflect the lag in the learning process. If so the fraction of litigated cases may be expected to decline to the pre-1968 levels. An alternative hypothesis which seems to me a priori at least as likely is the fact that even a losing battle may be an effective deterrent. The Armour case is an example in point; in the end Armour's management was to win the war despite the court's refusal to grant its request for an injunction. Although Host acquired a majority of Armour's shares in its tender, management's opposition and development of the competing offer gave a large minority interest to Greyhound. Because of the staggered terms of Armour's directors and cumulative voting rules, Host was able to elect only four of the six directors up for reelection and thus to control only four of seventeen directors. It would have taken two more years to achieve a majority of the Board, even if the Board did not meanwhile modify its rules. This prevented Host's having sufficient control for its purposes, and a negotiated sale of the Host holdings to Greyhound was ultimately consummated.

More generally, litigation surely raises the costs of the tender offer, and the ease of getting before the courts on Rule 10b–5 matter under the Williams Act invites the use of this tactic in contested mergers.

DISCLOSURE PROVISIONS AND THEIR EFFECTS

The Williams Act and its Amendments greatly expanded the disclosure required by parties to a tender offer. These new requirements

---

35. Binder, "Securities Law," p. 603.

of course expanded the scope for fraudulent statements (or assertions thereof) but they are important in their own right as well. The most important requirements now imposed are these:

1.   Disclosure of detailed information *before* the tender offer is made by a group making a tender offer, if as a result of a successful tender the group would achieve control of 5 percent or more of a class of the target's securities.[36] Among the information required is:

    a) the identities and backgrounds of the purchasers;

    b) the source and amount of funds to be used to finance the purchase;

    c) the bidder's plans for the company if the tender is successful;

    d) the number of shares presently owned by the bidder and its associates;

    e) the details of any agreements with other persons concerning the affairs of the target company, including the giving or withholding of proxies, divisions of profits, existing or proposed joint ventures, and any agreements concerning willingness or intentions to tender previously reached with large holders including mutual funds and other institutional investors.

2.   Disclosure of essentially similar information by any group that *achieves* a 5 percent stock holding, whether or not they have any present plans to seek control of the corporation.[37] The purpose of this disclosure is to identify potential takeover positions.

3.   Disclosure of essentially similar information by the management of the target company *if* it recommends to its stockholders as to how they should respond with respect to any tender offer. Importantly management is required to reveal any agreement or arrangement that it has made with the bidders with respect to future employment, or stock ownership.

---

36. Before the 1970 Amendments to the Act the amount was 10 percent. There are, of course, exceptions—if for example the amount acquired in the tender offer and in the previous twelve months does not exceed 2 percent. For a detailed discussion, see Binder, "Securities Law," p. 611.

37. I neglect a number of exceptions here as well.

4. A de facto rule that requires tender offers to remain open for a minimum of seven days and a maximum of sixty days.[38]

The beneficial aspects of these disclosure and timing regulations hardly require explication: all of the information required is relevant to stockholders in judging the motives, capacities, and prospects of success of those involved in the proposed takeover. Moreover, the provisions requiring disclosure of private arrangements seem particularly important in preventing stockholders being victimized by others' self-serving statements, and may make more difficult the "sellout" of the target company. The setting of a minimum time is designed to give stockholders time to seek advice, to evaluate tender offers, and not to be stampeded into a premature acceptance. The effective outer limit prevents the acquiring company from holding the target company and its stockholders in a state of uncertainty for too long.

Considering these provisions as they may have affected the propensity to merger brings other considerations into play as well. The same provisions that protect stockholders serve to warn and arm those who would oppose an acquisition. A predecessor of the Williams Act introduced in 1965 contained a provision that (in effect) required advance warning to management of a tender offer. When the bill was reintroduced in 1966 this section was deleted because it was felt that it gave too strong a weapon to management.[39] Binder cogently states the hazard:

Early disclosure can also be extremely inconvenient for the "group," since aside from the initial objective of obtaining control, its plans may still be at a preliminary stage. Yet a 13D statement must be filed detailing these plans—no matter how sketchy they might be. Either the group files a false 13D for which they will justifiably invite a lawsuit, or it files a sketchy one which would portray its position as being hasty and precipitous. If they subsequently amend the earlier filing, they always face the danger of being sued for "knowingly filing an earlier, deceptive 13D." The Congressional objective is full disclosure, but a requirement of premature disclosure hardly achieves this end. And once the preliminary 13D is filed, the insurgent group may find itself spending much of its time defending itself

---

38. The rule provides that outside of these limits a stockholder can withdraw shares already tendered; obviously this means that the offering company will have to operate within the time limits if it is to know its position with certainty.

39. See *Memorandum of the SEC to the Committee on Banking and Currency,* U.S. Senate on S 2731 (1966).

in lawsuits brought by management to delay or disrupt their plans. They may not have time to prepare a viable alternative to existing management. Many erstwhile members of the group may be unwilling to assume these burdens.[40]

Because disclosure provisions apply not only to tender offers but to accumulations of stock in amount of 5 percent or more, they may also serve to protect an entrenched management from the formation of an insurgent group of its own stockholders. While disclosure of accumulation of substantial holdings seems reasonable in alerting other stockholders to potential takeovers of their company, such disclosures may less desirably arm management against the insurgents who would challenge its control.[41]

A second and perhaps more subtle probable effect of the specific disclosure provisions is that such disclosure may weaken the "insider" motivations for mergers. As we have seen, such motivations may be socially beneficial as well as adverse, and weakening them may eliminate beneficial motives for merging. For example, the disclosure of postmerger plans can jeopardize the fulfillment of those plans in a cash tender offer. If the plans promise a profitable reorganization of the target company it may pay stockholders to hold their shares rather than accept a tender offer in order to participate pro rata in the increased profits. But if many hold out, the tender will fail. A stock tender could meet this problem, but may greatly increase both the costs of the transaction and the speed with which it can be accomplished.

More basically the incentive to find new ways of improving performance may lie in the "finders' fee" that innovative acquirers earn. By forcing disclosure, the potential benefits become available at least in part to outsiders at the expense of the innovators and thus the innovative increment is dissipated. There are other deterrents: the provisions requiring disclosure of sources of funds may dry up those

---

40. Denis Binder, "Securities Law," pp. 618–19.

41. A case in point: The management of GAF Corporation attempted to stop the Milstein family which owned 10 percent of its preferred stock from acquiring more shares or voting the shares they had in a proxy fight on the grounds that they had not fully disclosed their holdings when they reached the critical levels. The district court dismissed, but the Second Circuit reversed and remanded for trial on the merits. See *GAF v. Milstein,* 324 F.Supp. 1062 (S.D. N.Y. 1971); 453 F.2d 709 (2d Cir. 1971), affirmed in part, reversed in part.

sources because, e.g., banks are reluctant to be involved in a contro-versial matter; and requirements to disclose agreements may make agreements that reasonably quell unreasonable fears seem sinister and suspicious.

In overview, the problem is that, because much of the time a tender offer occurs in an adversary setting, the desire to protect the investor must be balanced by the sure knowledge that the more the disclosure, the greater the scope for harassing actions by those op-posed to the merger. Even though courts have proven unsympathetic to flimsy assertions of improper conduct, the mere bringing of a law suit may serve to create conditions that lead the merger to fail. For, while all mergers are costly, the cost of a contest can greatly expand the total cost. Thus, while disclosure and antifraud provisions con-tribute to making intelligent choices possible, to weakening some il-legitimate motives for merger, and to making more difficult the self-serving behavior of one group at the expense of another, they also weaken some legitimate incentives to merge, and warn and arm some of those who would delay, stop, or subvert the merger for self-serving (and socially unworthy) reasons.

Whether, in total, securities regulation has been a significant deterrent to many acquisitions that did not occur is not known. It seems clear that the force of whatever deterrent existed has been increased by the 1968 and 1970 Amendments. Clearly the deterrent effect after 1968 was greater than the few injunction cases suggest, but whether the securities laws resulted in only minor harassment or major inhibitions to merger attempts is not clear to me. Perhaps the major effect came via the raising of transaction costs. This is not be-yond researching, but the statistical problems are formidable since the data now available are dominated by the coincidence of the passage of the Williams Act and the collapse of the merger wave. Within a few years a determinative study should be possible.

Transactions Costs as a Deterrent

Because only fragmentary cost data are available, the discussion here will not resolve the question of whether acquisition costs and changes therein play a vital role in explaining merger activity. It too is a ques-tion that is capable of, and merits, systematic study. What *is* clear is that there are costs of various kinds, that they are absolutely large enough that they might well be significant, that the costs are in fact manipulable by those who would prevent a proposed merger, and that the burden of those costs need not be shared equally by all parties.

But none of this is decisive: one man's cost is another man's income. It is possible to argue that to the extent one kind of cost (e.g., brokerage fees) may deter some groups from initiating takeover attempts, it may motivate another group (e.g., brokers) to encourage or arrange a merger.

COSTS OF AN UNCONTESTED ACQUISITION

A principal cost to the buying company is the commissions and fees paid to brokers to solicit tenders and accept tendered securities. By New York Stock Exchange regulations, purchasers must pay at least a double brokerage fee, and brokers may not charge a fee to sellers.[42] But this double fee is a minimum and the role of the brokers in both contacting and persuading the stockholders of the target company is so crucial to the success of a tender offer that negotiated commission rates at levels above the required minimum are common. Brokerage fees to the buyers of 3 or 4 percent of the market value of the acquired stock are above average but not uncommon. Leasco paid approximately $9 million in various fees to acquire its controlling interest in Reliance. It is hard to evaluate the significance of this figure. The Leasco-Reliance merger was initiated by the brokerage house of Carter, Berlind, and Weill (CBW) which saw an opportunity to promote a profitable conglomerate merger and earn a major finder's fee for itself, and thus approached Leasco with a well-documented proposal. CBW is said to have earned $1.3 million in fees and payments from Reliance, even though, in the end, it did not act as the managing broker in the tender offer. In this case, the enormous potential gains to Leasco of acquiring an insurance company which had both a portfolio of undervalued assets and a substantial surplus of reserves made the overall fee of $9 million (roughly 4 percent of the value of stocks acquired) a reasonable cost for the large benefits that were to accrue to Leasco. But, more generally, as extraordinary merger opportunities are exhausted, every additional percentage point in cost must have an

---

42. Of course, if sellers choose to reinvest cash proceeds, or subsequently to sell or convert securities received in an exchange, they will normally be charged a brokerage fee.

effect on the ability of the parties to reach a satisfactory merger agreement.

In contrast to brokerage fees, basic filing and registration fees are modest. More importantly, use of inhouse legal, management, and accounting talent involved in providing the required information is likely to be substantial, even though not readily computed.

The levels of relatively routine costs incurred in a merger attempt are rarely revealed, but in a handful of cases, for example those in which an unsuccessful bidder is reimbursed by a competing bidder, some estimate of out-of-pocket costs is possible.[43]

As the roughest of estimates, the combination of brokerage fees, registration, advertising, mailings, and other out-of-pocket costs in routine acquisitions results in a cost of acquisitions of at least 3 percent of the market value of shares acquired and more usually 4 or 5 percent. In addition, there are the indirect costs of the absorption of corporate and managerial energies in the acquisition process. For those companies with managerial excess capacity, this latter may be a minor matter, and indeed the absorption of that talent is the opposite side of the coin of managerial synergies. I emphasize these indirect costs now because their contribution to costliness (and thus their deterrent effect) can become vital in the contested merger.

COSTS IMPOSED BY A CONTESTED MERGER

I am aware of no systematic study of (even) the direct costs imposed on the parties by a major contested merger fight. Denis Binder, who spent two years studying the contested mergers of the 1960s, estimates the direct outlays in contested mergers to have been at least twice as high as the cost of a routine uncontested merger, and in major contests, the costs may double again.

One source of the higher costs of contested mergers arises from the fact that once the management of a target company begins seriously to contest a tender offer, the help of the financial community becomes decisive and the concessions offered to financial institutions by each side to enlist their support may escalate. Because the bidding company is likely to be denied access to stockholder lists by the contesting management, it must usually rely on brokers to help it find large blocs of

---

43. Cf. Denis Binder, "Securities Law."

the stock being sought, and to give favorable publicity to the tender offer. This often means agreeing to pay significant fees to brokers, particularly those who may hold large blocs of the target's stock in street names for their customers. Mutual funds, too, play vital roles, for their tendering decisions can be decisive. One way that an acquiring company can enlist the loyalty of a mutual fund and arm itself to win a contested merger is known as "warehousing." The practice is simple enough: a mutual fund is given ample but secret advance warning of an impending tender offer in return for an implicit commitment to tender shares subsequently acquired. The fund can gradually accumulate a substantial position in the target company's stock at prices below the price that will be offered in the tender. The mutual fund, from the viewpoint of the potential acquirer, serves as a friendly warehouse for the target company's stock between the conception and the execution of the tender offer.[44] This profitable (to the mutual fund) maneuver is, of course, not costless to the acquiring company, for it serves to bid up the price of the target company's stock, and thus increase the price that will have to be offered in the tender offer. Banks, particularly those with large trust departments, are also solicited, and may be induced to tender their holdings on the basis of traditional or newly established banking connections.

A second source of rising costs is the competition among potential acquirers. Defensive or competing merger attempts occurred in roughly half of the contested tenders studied by Binder. Regardless of who wins these struggles, they serve to bid up the price of the target stock, and often lead to upward revisions of tender offers in the course of battle. How much all of this ultimately deters acquisition is not known. If the merger attempt succeeds, this price rise simply changes the division of the probable gains among the victorious buyers, the sellers, and the defeated alternative bidder. (It is sometimes highly profitable to *lose* a tender fight, for the winning company is likely to end up purchasing the losing bidder's holdings at a negotiated price above its costs of acquisition.)[45] But, by dispersing widely the potential gains of the merger, this sort of competition for a likely target may

---

44. The practice of warehousing is frowned upon by the SEC but it is all but impossible to stop.

45. The *Wall Street Journal* of January 27, 1969 (p. 1, col. 6), details a number of spectacular gains made by losers in takeover bids. Gulf and Western is estimated to have netted $75 million in losing battles for Sinclair Oil, Pan American World Airways, and Armour.

destroy the incentive for the merger to occur. Bidding the price of the company's stock up above the tender price is a defensive technique that the management of the target company (and its allies) often use.

The largest costs of major contests may be the diversion of all participants from productive activities to combat, and the resulting damage to the smooth operation of the company. Only a series of case studies could shed light on the quantitative importance of this.

RISKS OF FAILURE

A merger attempt, no matter what the level of costs expended, has some probability of turning out unsatisfactorily. Indeed in a contested merger this is almost definitionally going to happen to some group. But even for the winners in a contest, a short-run success may end up in long-run failure for a number of reasons: an acquiring company may fail to consolidate its control; the combined operations may prove unprofitable; or the merger may trigger antitrust actions that lead to divestiture, or limits on the company's future activities.

The principal short-run costs of an unsuccessful merger are the expenses incurred in the attempt and the diversion of activity into what has proven an unproductive venture. For the "go-go" company there are additional risks in a well-publicized failure: its image as an effective aggressive acquirer will suffer in the public eye and the whole mystique that surrounds it and creates the conditions that give it a very high PE ratio may erode. Further, other later targets may be emboldened to fight it. Moreover, a losing contest may leave the company with significant holdings of unwanted securities, which it may have to dispose of at a loss,[46] or suffer a loss of liquidity; at the very least it will have lost time, and its growth rate may suffer directly.

From the point of view of managers of target companies the costs of unsuccessfully contesting a merger attempt are likely to be severe—both in hastening their departure from the company, and possibly in their ability to find employment elsewhere.

---

46. But see footnote 45. The possibility of costless liquidation of substantial holdings of the target's stock that leave the bidder short of control is very much greater when the target company ends up being acquired by another firm, than when it retains its independence. It is also much affected by the general stock market conditions. The *Wall Street Journal* story cited above focuses on the lucky (or perhaps skillful) examples. It does not seem likely that one can make a long-term profitable practice out of losing tender offers.

Some clue as to how large is the risk of failure is suggested by the following statistics. The FTC reports roughly 1,100 large acquisitions during the 1960s. Against that backdrop, Binder found 145 contested tender offers over the decade.[47] In 92 of these the tender offer failed in the short-run, and in 7 more (e.g., Host's takeover of Armour, see p. 169) it appeared to succeed but ended up in failure to gain control. Of these 99 failures, 56 ended with the target company remaining independent, under its original management, and in 43 the company ended up merged with a different company. Clearly to both acquiring companies and defending managements, the decision to fight imposes real risks of failure.

The Overall Importance of Inhibitions

Taken together, antitrust risks and security regulations both independently and as sources of increasing transactions costs, combine with the routine costs of effecting major security transactions to make actual mergers far from the risk-free, zero-transactions-cost ventures that economists are fond of considering.

How important are these "imperfections" or "frictions" in the market for companies? I do not know for sure, and I suspect my ignorance is shared. It is my impression after reviewing the major merger contests of the 1960s that they imposed very great costs on the potential merger partners. During the heyday of the movement, particularly in 1966–68, high costs were dominated by even higher benefits, both insider and outsider, both speculative and real. Even rising costs seemed of secondary concern. Indeed, during this period the merger-created opportunities for high brokerage fees, for banks and mutual funds to make quick profits, and for lawyers and promoters to earn large fees probably did more to stimulate mergers by creating

---

47. The figures are not directly comparable because Binder looked at major contests whether or not the target was large. Moreover, Binder excluded "abortive" tender offers, where an offer was made and then withdrawn before it became effective, in order to avoid the difficulty of determining how sincere a bidder may be in announcing an offer. Sometimes, it seemed that the announcement of a tender offer was really a test of the wind. If the market reacted favorably, the tender would be made. If not, the bid would be quietly dropped. Because of this, it would be a mistake to think that contests occurred in 13 percent of mergers attempted. It is clear however that the contest is a frequent if not regular occurrence.

a positive attitude toward them in the legal and financial community than to deter them.

Whether the heightened risks after 1968, caused by increasing possibilities of antitrust and securities prosecutions, and the added costs of complying with new securities regulations would have had an important effect if nothing else had changed is not known. Other things did not remain equal. When the stock market slumped in 1969, many of the potential gains vanished, but the deterrents remained. When the costs of a transaction plus premium paid to induce tendering reached 25 percent or 30 percent, and when there was no instant reward in the stock market, many acquirers took a closer look at the benefits of an acquisition, as did the banks and other institutions that helped to underwrite the acquisition.

Once the notion of failure was seriously considered—once the bubble was slightly deflated if not yet burst—a merger had to promise real economies rather than speculative ones. If the transaction costs required to consummate the merger amounted to 4 or 5 or 8 percent of the combined net assets of the merging companies, it was not so easy to find a merger that benefited both groups of stockholders. Moreover, the ability of unwilling managers (or the antitrust authorities) to raise those costs was now well understood and meant that transaction costs might readily double. The situation of 1969–71 was one of high and rising costs and falling benefits; together they surely contributed to the damping of the merger fever. We must await further research to tell us which blade of the scissors was doing the most effective cutting.

CHAPTER EIGHT

Empirical Studies: Problems and Findings with Respect to Motivation

Introduction

CHAPTERS 2 through 7 developed a multivariate theory of motives for mergers and explored a variety of possible forces conducing toward or away from mergers. Taken together they might be characterized as providing an eclectic framework for considering mergers. One of the functions of empirical analyses, from simple tabulations to sophisticated multivariate analyses, is to define which subsets of the theoretically possible cases merit particular attention; to determine which of many possible linkages among variables receive sufficient confirmation by the facts to warrant being held as theories, and which may be regarded as effectively (albeit perhaps temporarily) refuted.

One of my purposes in this chapter is to see the extent to which such a sifting and winnowing is possible. The second purpose is to see why an impressive quantity of empirical work into the postwar merger movement by a wide range of scholars has proven so disappointing;[1] why, in the words of one contributor, "[t]he stock of literature on

---

1. The subsequent citations will make clear what I have reviewed. While I have not managed an exhaustive survey, I believe I have caught the range and the flavor of the recent empirical work. A distinguished paper by Jesse W. Markham written in 1952, "Survey of the Evidence and Finding on Mergers," National Bureau of Economic Research, *Business Concentration and Public Policy* (New York, 1955), surveys a surprisingly large prewar literature. I incorporate it by reference. One of the most thought-provoking studies of the period is Ansoff, Brandenburg, Portner, and Radosevich, *Acquisition Behavior of U.S. Manufacturing Firms, 1946–1965* (Nashville, Tenn., 1971). It is deficient for my purposes because it consciously and systematically undersampled (1) conglomerate acquirers, (2) firms whose acquisitions invited antitrust inquiries, as well as being limited to acquisitions before 1965, and for most purposes before 1963. It, nevertheless, provides some background material.

mergers has in recent years grown even faster than the number of mergers, though the stock of knowledge on this subject reveals little growth,"[2] and in the words of another, the empirical evidence seems "scanty, desultory, and unrefined."[3]

Three possible reasons for the overall inadequacy may be noted at the outset. First different investigations were addressed to many different questions, of which understanding merger motivations and testing theories about motivations was but one. Some have been chiefly concerned accurately to forecast the level of merger activity, and while forecasters would obviously not be averse to forecasting on the basis of a fully specified model, it is the adequacy of the forecast, not of the theory, that concerns them. Others have been concerned primarily with identifying who gains and who loses in merger transactions, in order to determine whether our laws provide sufficient protection to those who merit protecting. Still others have had as their primary concern evaluating the effects on competition of the mergers that have occurred, and so on. In this chapter I shall review the existing studies from the point of view of what they tell us about theories of motivations, whether or not that was their own frame of reference. In chapter 12 I will be concerned with what they may tell us about effects of mergers on competition and the implications for policy.

The second reason for the somewhat unsatisfactory state of our empirical knowledge is that regardless of the number of individual studies, we have too few data and too many variables to make a definitive reduction in the theoretical possibilities. Mergers result (or fail to result) from the interactions of many actors who perform upon a changing stage. One can of course abstract from "noise" and seek underlying truth in a multivariate world in a variety of ways, but this requires both a large number of observations and some agreement on a manageable number of relevant variables. We have neither. The motivations of the actors and the climate in which they make decisions are affected by a great many variables. Cross-sectionally at a moment in time there are a great many pairs of relationships which might be

---

2. Michael Gort and Thomas F. Hogarty, "New Evidence on Mergers," 13 JOURNAL OF LAW AND ECONOMICS, no. 1, 167–84 (April 1970).

3. D. R. Kamerschen, "A Theory of Conglomerate Mergers: Comment," *Quarterly Journal of Economics* 84, no. 4 (November 1970): 668–73.

estimated, but our data are highly limited. Pooling data over several years adds to the data but runs the evident risk of assuming stable relationships when the actual relationships are themselves rapidly

TABLE 8–1

THE MULTIVARIATE NATURE OF MERGER MOTIVATION

I.   *Actors*
        Stockholders of affected companies
        Managers of affected companies
        Investors generally
        Speculators
        Financial community
        Antitrust authorities
        SEC
        Congress
        Courts
        President and Executive branch
        Lobbyists
        Political parties
        Public interest groups
        Press
II.   *Climates*
        State of economy
        Stock market
        Legal
        Regulatory
        Tax
        Accounting
III. *Types of Motivation for and against Mergers*
    A.   Profit increasing for the firm:
        Achieving real efficiencies
        Increasing market power
        Tax and accounting opportunities
    B.   Growth as a goal
    C.   General (external) speculative
    D.   Insider opportunities:
        To stockholders
        To acquiring managements
        To acquired managements
        To financial groups
    E.   Deterrents:
        Antitrust law enforcement
        Securities law and enforcement
        Transactions cost
        Public and Congressional opinion

IV. *Participants in Individual Mergers*
   A. Bidders—classified by
       Type
       Success in attempt } versus nonbidders
          —with respect to
          Industry, extent of diversification, size, managerial or owner-
             ship control, growth, profitability, liquidity, stock market
             performance, etc.
   B. Targets—classified by
       Resistance
       Outcome } versus nontargets
          —with respect to
          Industry, extent of diversification, size, managerial or owner-
             ship control, growth, profitability, liquidity, stock market
             performance, etc.
   C. Financial institutions:
       Brokers
       Banks
       Mutual funds
       Others

---

changing. Limited data points illuminate multivariate hypotheses when the structural interrelationships among the variables are well understood. Variations in merger rates, unfortunately, do not meet this test.

This relative paucity of data to confront a multivariate problem head-on invites ingenious pushing of competing hypotheses to yield conflicting predictions about specific measures of economic activity, and testing these predictions with appropriate bits of data. As we shall see below such contrived "tests" create their own polemic: one scholar's showing that growth is more important than profits leads to another's showing the reverse. This is of course the way progress is ultimately achieved, but early in the process (as we are) there may be more chaff than grain.

The general complexity of the problem need not be labored, but it must be recognized. Table 8–1 suggests why there are a vast number of links between actors and actions that might be explored. Beyond table 8–1, moreover, there are the potentially dozens of dimensions in which mergers can be evaluated ex post, from the points of view of the parties involved, and the general welfare.

But the lack of definitive findings is not entirely a matter of quantity of data relative to questions to be asked. The third and final source of trouble I want to mention is more methodological in character and centers around the difficulty in debating whether principal-cause or multiple-cause hypotheses are required.

The essence of the problem can be stated simply. With a small amount of data it may well be possible to choose between which of two hypotheses is correct, if it is known that they cannot both be correct. But showing that one explains more than the other (or that one has significant explanatory value and the other does not) on some data sample, can never show that the two are competing rather than complementary explanations.

I have developed earlier a multiple-cause hypothesis. It is, of course, possible to reject one or more elements of it if the evidence repeatedly shows either that while a measure of this element varied, the dependent variable did not, or that the variations in the dependent variable were uninterestingly small. If, however, the element in question is important in some situations (or on some data sets), but not others, it means the theory is underspecified (in not yet identifying the realm of relevant cases in which that element is important) not that the element is shown to be defective as an explanatory variable.

Suppose that the weight of evidence does not lead to a rejection of a multiple-cause hypothesis. What then is shown by the study of an investigator who holds to a primary-cause hypothesis and demonstrates that his candidate for primary cause is more satisfactory than someone else's? This is a central problem in what follows because a large number of empirical studies either purport directly to choose among alternative motivational forces, or indirectly to bear on such a choice. My view is that their findings become data points for a future study that explains what underlying circumstances made the variable in question seem decisive in that sample of data.[4]

Before summarizing what the studies undertaken do suggest as to motivations, it is helpful to look at certain of the findings simply on their own terms.

The Characteristics of Firms that Merge

A first approach to evaluating either the motivations for or the consequences of mergers is to distinguish firms that merged from firms that did not merge.

---

4. The problem, and particularly its relevance to multiple regression analysis, is considered more formally in the appendix to this chapter.

THE CHARACTERISTICS OF ACQUIRED FIRMS

Studies of mergers occurring in the period from 1955 to 1965 tended to produce a uniform picture of merger targets as relatively unprofitable, sluggish, over-liquid firms, often with a history of static or declining earnings and dividends. In general these were the findings of Hayes and Taussig with respect to cash takeover bids in the United States for 1957–66[5] and of Ajit Singh for 1954–60 in the United Kingdom.[6] This kind of finding opened the possibility that many, perhaps most, merger targets were "potentially failing firms," and to the view of mergers as an efficient alternative to bankruptcy.[7] Boyle explored, and largely exploded this possibility.[8] He studied 698 of the 1,275 acquired firms in large acquisitions over the period 1948–68 for which complete financial data were available for the five years preceding acquisition. After satisfying himself that his sample was not greatly biased he showed that few were suffering losses, and that on the average acquired firms were only slightly less profitable than all firms. Moreover the firms acquired by conglomerate acquirers were among the more profitable and were ones for which rates of return were growing. His study effectively refutes the hypothesis of merger as a response to impending bankruptcy.

This finding has received repeated support from other samples. The 1972 FTC Report,[9] studying the 1960–68 acquisitions of nine leading conglomerate acquirers, found that the great majority of target

5. S. Hayes and R. Taussig, "Tactics of Cash Takeover Bids," *Harvard Business Review* 45, no. 2 (March–April 1967): 135–48.

6. Ajit Singh, *Takeovers: Their Relevance to the Stock Market and the Theory of the Firm* (Cambridge, 1971). Singh's study, though recently published, covers a sufficiently remote place and period that it is of more interest for its methodological contributions (an attempt to use discriminant analysis of merger activity) than its substantive ones.

7. Cf. Donald Dewey, "Mergers and Cartels: Some Reservations about Policy," *American Economic Review,* Papers and Proceedings, 51, no. 2 (May 1961): 255–62; and Henry Manne, "Mergers and the Market for Corporate Control," *Journal of Political Economy* 73, no. 2 (April 1965): 110–20.

8. Stanley E. Boyle, "Pre-merger Growth and Profit Characteristics of Large Conglomerate Mergers in the United States 1948–1968," 44 ST. JOHN'S LAW REVIEW, Special Edition, 152–70 (Spring 1970).

9. Federal Trade Commission, *Economic Report on Conglomerate Merger Performance, An Empirical Analysis of Nine Corporations* (Washington, D.C., November 1972). Hereafter FTC II.

companies earned profits in the period before acquisition, even though they were somewhat below average for their industries. Denis Binder,[10] dealing with a sample biased by the self-selection of targets as those that have contested the attempt to acquire them,[11] found the target companies to be generally profitable throughout the decade. Binder's findings are among the few we have that cover the late 1960s as well as the earlier years, and they show a number of ways in which the second half of the decade differed from the first half.[12] Perhaps of particular significance, while targets were of below average profitability during the first half of the decade, the target companies in the period 1965–69 were relatively more profitable. In particular they had relatively high price-earnings ratios (the average was 18). This is within the range that Wall Street analysts of the period regarded as showing respectable prospects of future growth and profitability and thus suggests that during the late 1960s targets were not generally sluggish, unprofitable, unpromising companies.

The relevance of these findings for a "real efficiencies" hypothesis is explored subsequently along with some other data.

Brian Hindley sheds a different, but not contradictory light on this question as a by-product of an attempt to explore the hypothesis that mergers are motivated by the profit opportunities arising from takeovers of inefficiently run firms.[13] His hypothesis led him (like Binder) to focus on mergers where incumbent managements of the targets have opposed the merger. His usable sample concerns 49 contested takeovers in the period 1958 and 1963 which are compared with composite controls, formed by taking the average of firms with similar product mixes. His principal finding, put briefly, is that an index of the "ineffectiveness of the incumbent managements" was very much higher for the targets than for the controls, and thus pro-

---

10. Denis Binder, "An Empirical Study of Contested Tender Offers: 1960–69" (S.J.D. thesis, Law School, University of Michigan, 1973).

11. How serious this bias is is not known; comparison of Binder's data with FTC data suggests that contesting target firms were about 50 percent larger than average acquired firms.

12. A very important aspect of this in interpreting most of the studies available, as they apply to the 1965–68 merger wave, is that Binder's data suggest the merger wave of the late 1960s was different in anatomy, as well as in level of activity, from mergers in the 1955–65 period.

13. Brian Hindley, "Separation of Ownership and Control in the Modern Corporation," 13 JOURNAL OF LAW AND ECONOMICS, no. 1, 185–221 (April 1970).

vided support for the hypothesis that mergers were transactions in the market for corporate control.[14]

Turning from profitability to *size* of acquired companies presents more difficulty because the main body of statistics concerns *large* acquisitions (i.e., $10 million in assets or more). Some of these data are shown in table 1–2, chapter 1. But large acquisitions are not the only acquisitions.

The most useful data on size come from FTC II, which is concerned with all the acquisitions (348) of nine large conglomerates[15] over the period 1960–68. The average size of acquired companies was about $28 million.[16]

This size, however, was very different at the beginning and end of the period. During 1960–65, 194 acquisitions occurred, with an aver-

---

14. Hindley's measure of inefficiency is sufficiently unusual and perhaps controversial that I had best describe it briefly. It is based upon the ratio of book value of a company to the market value of its common stock. His justification for this measure is as follows: The stock market value may be taken as a measure of present and probable future performance under existing management. Book value is a proxy for potential value. Two companies with similar production processes may be expected to have similar book values, but the one that is more successfully managed will tend to earn larger profits and have higher stock prices. Thus, if targets have a consistently higher ratio of book to market value, this suggests either that they have too much book value for their earnings, or too little earnings for their book value. In either case this suggests inefficient management. Of his 49 cases, 35 acquired companies fell unambiguously on the "inefficient" side (high index) relative to the controls, 10 were ambiguous, and 4 were unambiguously more efficient than the controls. On average the ratio was more than 50 percent higher for targets than for controls.

As Hindley recognizes, "Economists are justifiably suspicious of the equation of accounting values with economic concepts." While there may be large amounts of "noise" in book values, due to variations in accounting practices, particularly in connection with past acquisitions, I find persuasive Hindley's arguments that he has *some* basis for drawing real conclusions about efficiency on the basis of these data.

15. The conglomerates, each of which was among the 200 largest manufacturing companies in 1969, were Litton Industries, LTV, Gulf & Western, ITT, Textron, Rapid-American, White Consolidated, FMC, and Norton Simon.

16. The average size of the 695 acquisitions of the 25 most active acquiring firms (shown in table 1–3, chapter 1) was almost identical, $29 million for 1961–68. Seven of the nine FTC II sample were in this group of 25.

age size of $9.6 million; in 1966–67 an additional 85 acquisitions occurred with an average size of $23.7 million; and in 1968, 69 acquisitions occurred with an average size of $84.5 million. Thus the large acquisition was distinctly a feature of the relatively short-lived merger wave.

How significant these sizes were in a competitive sense and thus with respect to market power motivations, relates to the market share of the acquired company in its market, and the share (if any) of the acquirer in those same markets. Obviously, there were a number of leading firm acquisitions, as the antitrust cases discussed below make clear. But on average, it is the conclusion of FTC II that these active acquirers did not acquire substantial market positions in new areas. Indeed, as of 1968 in over 50 percent of the product classes in which they operated, the conglomerates ended up with less than a 1 percent share, and in 82 percent they had less than a 5 percent share. In only 6 product classes, 2.7 percent of the total in which acquisitions were made, did they have 20 percent or more of the market share. Another study of 44 conglomerate acquisitions by Goldberg,[17] picked in an unspecified manner, showed an average market share of acquired companies of under 5 percent, notwithstanding inclusion in the sample of acquisitions of at least three leading firms (Gentry, Clorox, and Minute Maid). What these fragmentary data sources suggest is that, in the large, target firms were apparently not primarily selected for their market positions; a suggestion not contradicted by any data set of which I am aware. Of course this does not show that particular mergers (e.g., Procter & Gamble's acquisition of Clorox) may not have been heavily influenced by Clorox's large market share.

In capsule overview, acquired firms were not all that different from the average firms in their industries: perhaps slightly below average in their premerger profitability but certainly not generally on the brink of financial disaster. Nor were they characteristically dominant firms, nor even industry leaders.

CHARACTERISTICS OF ACQUIRING FIRMS

While the overall size of acquiring firms was seen in chapter 1 to be quite modest in size, a small number of very large companies played

---

17. Lawrence G. Goldberg, "The Effect of Conglomerate Mergers on Competition," 16 JOURNAL OF LAW AND ECONOMICS, no. 1, 137–58 (April 1973).

a major role in the large acquisitions of the decade of the sixties. One clear, but virtually definitional attribute of actively acquiring firms was that they showed exceptionally large growth in assets.

The studies of Hayes and Taussig, Singh, Binder, and others cited above tend to show acquiring firms to be somewhat above average in profitability, with a tradition of retaining and reinvesting profits rather than paying large dividends, and with having less than average liquidity. Binder in particular finds they had lower than average profit margins on sales and higher than average profit margins on assets. One might have expected active acquirers to have well above average PE ratios, but a study I made of PE ratios of all acquirers in the FTC sample of 1,099 large acquisitions during the decade of the 1960s, while not inconsistent with this hypothesis, failed to show a significant consistent pattern.[18]

The FTC II study of nine leading conglomerates found as a major characteristic of its sample the tendency toward great diversification, particularly after 1964, both within manufacturing and out of manufacturing into trade and services. This of course reflects the increasingly conglomerate behavior of these companies. The competitive significance of this finding will concern us subsequently.

Ansoff et al., for their earlier period, found an interesting difference between acquirers who had slow growth rates before they embarked on acquisition behavior and those who had rapid growth. The former appeared to be weaker than average and thus to be responding to poor performance; the latter were at or above average and were judged to be motivated by aggressive managements rather than poor performance.

The major empirical concern with acquiring firms in mergers has been how acquiring firms have fared after mergers. I shall briefly review six attempts to answer this question, attempts which do not lead to a single view.[19] Each of these studies compares a sample of

---

18. This study based on Federal Trade Commission, Bureau of Economics, *Large Mergers in Manufacturing and Mining 1948–1971,* Statistical Report No. 9 (Washington, D.C., May 1972), was undertaken for me by Mr. Kenneth Mayfield, a third-year law student. Some of its preliminary findings are referred to below, but its more complete analysis must wait upon refinement of the PE data derived from Moody's and Standard and Poor's.

19. These are: Eamon M. Kelly, *The Profitability of Growth Through Merger* (University Park, Pa., 1967); Samuel R. Reid, *Mergers, Managers and the Economy* (New York, 1968) pp. 317–27; Thomas F.

acquiring firms with a control group and evaluates, according to some criteria of success, whether acquiring firms performed better than the less acquisitive controls. All of the studies include mergers occurring in subparts of the period 1946–68.

Eamon Kelly's study deals with 21 matched pairs of firms from the population of the 500 largest manufacturing and 50 largest merchandising firms over the period 1946–60. The merging member of the pair had achieved at least a 20 percent increase in sales due to merger; the control was selected according to size and industry and the constraint that it had achieved no more than a 5 percent increase in sales by merger. Kelly studied the profits to stockholders of the two firms as judged by the market performance of the stocks of the companies, comparing the five premerger and five postmerger years. He found no significant clear pattern of differences in the success of the two groups measured by this standard. The intrapair differences in change in stock prices were of variable sign and high variance. In other dimensions there were some significant differences. Merging firms grew faster, and had higher PE ratios than their nonmerging counterparts, but did not translate this into more rapidly increasing stock prices over the period. Kelly concludes that acquiring firms apparently paid too high a premium for the extra sales they acquired. His chief policy conclusion is that corporate investors ought to reevaluate their policies and apply a higher discount to merger-acquired sales.

Kelly's was a small, and somewhat subjective sample, but it was a pioneering effort subject to all the constraints that accompany Ph.D. dissertation research. He was comparing companies with a high propensity to merger with companies of similar size and industry for whom merger had been much less significant over the same period.

Hogarty, "The Profitability of Corporate Mergers," *Journal of Business* 43, no. 3 (July 1970): 317–27; Gort and Hogarty, "New Evidence on Mergers," 13 JOURNAL OF LAW AND ECONOMICS, no. 1, 167–84 (April 1970); J. Fred Weston and Surenda K. Mansinghka, "Tests of the Efficiency Performance of Conglomerate Firms," *Journal of Finance* 26, no. 4 (September 1971): 919–36; and B. Lev and G. Mandelker, "The Microeconomic Consequences of Corporate Mergers," *Journal of Business* 45, no. 1 (January 1972): 85–104. I shall neglect the Ansoff et al. analysis of this problem because their exclusion of the major conglomerate acquirers is so critical. Their general finding comparing 271 acquirers with 82 firms who made no acquisitions for a twenty-year period is that acquirers fared worse in most dimensions of performance *except* in terms of profits to total capital. High growth acquirers did well relative to nonacquirers in price-earnings ratios.

The most serious quarrel with it is in its assumption that market price of the company's stock is the primary or even sole relevant criterion motivating mergers. For one example, he regards achieving a high postmerger PE ratio as evidence of poor performance; but, as we have seen, it may subsequently prove profitable to the managers or promoters of mergers.

Samuel Reid, in a much more ambitious study than Kelly's, looked at 478 of the 500 largest 1961 firms, and classified them according to the intensity of their merger activity over the period 1951–61. Forty-eight engaged in no mergers, 214 had one to five mergers, 142 had six to ten mergers, and 74 had had eleven or more mergers. Comparing these groups, and crossclassifying them by industries, he related intensity of merger activity to two sets of variables: "growth" variables (changes in sales, assets, and employees over the period) and "profit-to-stockholders" variables (changes in market prices, and capital gains as a percentage of base period assets and sales). His major findings are that the more intensive the level of merger activity, the relatively better the performance of the growth variables, and the relatively worse the performance of the profit variables.

Reid's principal interest centered on the significance of managerial control, which he takes to mean valuing growth for its own sake as well as for profits. Because the greater the tendency to merge, the more important the growth variables, he thus concludes that managerial firms have a greater propensity to merger than do nonmanagerial ones. Surprisingly, he does not look at ownership patterns directly, which might have been directly classified against frequency of merger (following Berle and Means, Larner, Kamerschen, and others).

While Reid's conclusions seem to me to support his managerial hypothesis in part by assuming it, the profits and growth findings tend to be consistent with Kelly's much more limited sample.

Thomas Hogarty studied 43 heavily merging firms over the period 1953–64. As a control for each such firm he used (instead of a matched nonacquiring firm) the average of the industry of the acquirer. His performance measures rely both on the prices of stocks and also on dividend policies, thus correcting an unfortunate oversight in Kelly's measures. Heavily merging firms were defined as those that acquired (in aggregate) assets of at least 20 percent of their preacquisition levels. Hogarty found most of these firms did not generate stock market performance for their stockholders that was better than the average firm of their industry, and many performed worse. There was however great variance, and a few were enormously successful. Hogarty concluded by suggesting that despite the poor typical performance of merging firms, the few enormously successful ones may have made the whole pattern justified on an expected value criterion. Merging, like drilling for oil, may be profitable if you are either lucky or do a lot of it.

Gort and Hogarty using the Hogarty sample (and for some purposes a subsample of 26) apparently exploded this last possibility. A closer look at the data suggested to them that buyers as a whole lost, and sellers gained, with the net transaction proving approximately zero-sum. Thus unless managers are risk prone, they concluded, mergers of this period were founded on the unjustified optimism of the acquiring firms.

Weston and Mansinghka compared 63 conglomerate companies with two control groups randomly selected from among the Fortune 500 industrials and 250 nonindustrials. Their data cover the periods 1958–68 and 1960–68 and thus they avoid the disadvantage of the preceding studies, which were limited to data for a period before the great merger wave of the late 1960s. They reach three principal conclusions:

1.   The greater than average relative growth of acquirers reflected merger activity rather than greater internal growth. This greater growth, contrary to earlier studies, extended to stock prices. Earlier studies they believe suffered from a too-early termination date.

2.   To the extent that earnings performance on net worth of conglomerates was somewhat higher than for the control groups, this resulted from increased use of debt financing. But the actual differences in earnings were small.

3.   The earnings of the conglomerates at the start of the period were lower than those of the controls but by 1968 they had become not significantly different. This, Weston and Mansinghka conclude, is of primary importance for it suggests the conglomerates' economic success was in raising the profitability of firms with depressed earnings to the average for industry generally. They regard this as evidence of successful "defensive diversification" of over-specialized companies in industries such as aerospace, textiles, tobacco, etc. This conclusion supports generally the conglomerate-firms-as-a-bundle-of-managerial-efficiencies proposed by Jacoby, whose help is acknowledged.[20]

---

20. Much of the paper, Weston and Mansinghka, "Tests of the Efficiency Performance," pp. 919–36, is a polemic against Reid, the intensity

Baruch Lev and Gershon Mandelker studied 69 matched pairs of firms covering the period 1952–63. Their study is similar in many ways to the Kelly study, although more fully and carefully done. Their focus, however, was on major mergers rather than on heavily merging firms. Each acquiring firm in a major merger was matched with a firm from its own four-digit industry by asset size. Profits and other measures were computed for the five years prior to the merger and for the five subsequent years. Both levels and dispersion of selected measures of performance were studied.

In contrast to the earlier studies, but consistent with Weston and Mansinghka, Lev and Mandelker found that acquiring firms were somewhat *more* profitable than their nonmerging partners, in terms of subsequent stock market performance. Additionally, they found that mergers did not appear to reduce the variance of the combined company's stock relative to the stock of the control, thus arguing against stockholder risk reduction as an important motive. Like Weston and Mansinghka they found that if "growth" is defined to mean acquisition of assets by any means, merging firms tended to grow faster, but that if growth is defined to be postmerger internal growth, they tended to grow more slowly.

Two further findings emerged that Lev and Mandelker did not stress greatly but that seem of particular importance to me. First, in the year of the merger, the acquiring firm's stock tended to do very well, thus providing potentially important short-run or speculative incentives for mergers, whatever the longer-run experience. Second, average earnings per share of acquiring firms tended to increase almost continuously in the postmerger period. Lev and Mandelker attributed this to a tendency of acquiring firms to retain a steadily larger portion of their earnings, not to higher earnings. But its importance for maintaining high PE ratios should not be neglected.

I am not sure what this set of studies adds up to. Despite two important limitations on the applicability to the period since 1966 and despite the possible contradictions in their findings, they do contain information. The first limitation is that the great bulk of the evidence concerns the fifties and early sixties, a period quite different from that of the late sixties in which the great merger wave came to a crest and subsided. The second is that except for Weston and Mansinghka the

of which is surprising. Reid replies in kind (unkind) in S. R. Reid, "A Reply to the Weston/Mansinghka Criticisms Dealing with Conglomerate Mergers," *Journal of Finance* 26, no. 4 (September 1971): 937–45.

matching process assumes the relevant control is in the same industry as the acquirer, a useful assumption for horizontal and vertical mergers, but a questionable one for the conglomerate acquisitions which were to become increasingly important. Moreover, difficulties in finding appropriate controls tended to bias the sample of included companies against conglomerate acquirers. Weston and Mansinghka avoided both of these difficulties to some extent, but the fact that their terminal date (1968) is at the absolute peak of the merger wave creates problems of its own, and the biases in their control groups are not known to me. It would be nice to see their study replicated using 1970 and 1971 data before relying on it too heavily.

Suppose first that we neglect the Lev and Mandelker's and Weston and Mansinghka's findings that acquirers do profit from mergers, and accept instead the findings (of all of the others) that no clear stock market success accompanies the securities of merging firms relative to their nonmerging counterparts. If what this says is that the stock market formula "buy the securities of companies with a high propensity to merge, and simultaneously sell the securities of a control group that differs only in its merger propensity" will not assure success, I am not very surprised, for neither will any other mechanical formula. Indeed, if such a formula worked, a smoothly functioning stock market and arbitrage would tend to quickly wipe out the gains. Thus the finding may tell us that arbitrage works reasonably well.

Perhaps the apparent absence of more evident gains to acquiring companies' stockholders tells us more than that. One possibility is that acquirers are (or were in this period) naïve, overoptimistic or foolish —this is loosely the Kelly, and the Gort and Hogarty, thesis. A second possibility is that the benefits accrue not to stockholders, but to insiders, particularly managers who respond to a different set of motives—this is roughly Reid's interpretation. A third possibility is that benefits will take longer to show than these data permit,[21] and that real and/or speculative advantages lie ahead for the acquiring firm. I find some support for this in the higher PE ratios and higher earnings per share for merging firms. A fourth possibility is that acquiring firms are not a random sample of the firms in their industries, but

---

21. The possible reply to this that present stock market prices reflect a discount of all future effects, proves too much. By that argument premerger stock prices would have reflected the discounting of the best strategy of the firm, which may well have been to merge.

that they are self-selected by virtue of the particular strengths *or weaknesses* of their firms. A fifth possibility is that yet other groups—e.g., members of the financial community—may be gainers enough to motivate mergers. As among these five explanations the only one I regard as uninteresting is the first, partly because I disbelieve it, but also because if it is true, it is not going to tell us much unless one assumes people do not learn (see pp. 143–44).

If Lev and Mandelker (supported by Weston and Mansinghka) are right in saying that acquirers do profit, this may or may not imply a conflict with the other studies. It may not: (1) because Lev and Mandelker focused on particular mergers, not merging propensities, e.g., one big merger in the 1950s would have put a firm in a low-intensity category in Reid's study, but a high one in Lev and Mandelker's, or (2) because Lev and Mandelker took greater pains and different methods in selecting a larger sample of merging firms and of the controls.

My own view, which I can express rather than document, is to be more impressed with the Reid, the Weston and Mansinghka, and the Lev and Mandelker studies than with the other three. The differences among these three in sample selection, in matching, in time periods used, and in techniques used is great enough that I would regard them as providing complementary rather than conflicting evidence.

But unless one is disposed to discard the Lev and Mandelker or the Weston and Mansinghka findings on the grounds that they contradict known truths—which I am not—they do not threaten any of the five interpretations offered above, except the first.[22] They suggest additional possibilities, among them that short-run speculative gains may be available to insiders; that stockholders of the acquiring firm do not suffer by the premiums offered to acquired firms; and that there may, on average, be real gains available to all. This last is particularly comforting since it is a usual precondition of continuing commerce.

Evidence as to Motivation

It is time to confront more explicitly alternative (or complementary) explanations of merger motivations. It is convenient to do so with respect to several frequently postulated motivations.

---

22. The controversy that pits Reid versus Weston and Mansinghka concerns which *one* of these explanations is the best. Within a multiple-cause hypothesis, I find their findings quite compatible.

REAL EFFICIENCIES AS MOTIVATIONS

Despite several studies suggesting that acquiring stockholders did not, on average, profit by their acquisitions, and despite the Gort and Hogarty finding that sellers' gains do no more than offset buyers' losses, I am not persuaded that a prima facie case against the existence of real economies in conglomerate acquisitions has been made. Indeed, Lev and Mandelker persuasively suggest that if one looks at particular mergers with some care, one finds profitability to the acquirers as well as acquirees.

The finding that acquired firms tend to be excessively liquid, both in the sense of having high current ratios, and in the sense of being relatively debt free compared both to their acquirers and to selected controls, suggests an important possible real economy in conglomerate acquisitions. In institutional circumstances where there are tax and capital market impediments to the interindustry flow of corporate funds, such underutilized financial capacity provides an available real economy via merger and subsequent intracorporate (but interindustry) transfers of funds. This incentive is likely to be particularly strong during periods when the opportunity cost of capital is high.

Further fuel to a real synergy theory is provided by data suggesting greater-than-average managerial inefficiency in the premerger conduct of acquired firms. Hindley and FTC II most recently, Hayes and Taussig, and Singh earlier, all suggest that target firms tend to be less profitable than appropriately chosen control firms, or than their acquirers. Binder's data for the early sixties suggest a similar conclusion, particularly in the finding that merger targets tended to have higher profit margins on sales and lower rates of return on assets. Together these findings are consistent with an underutilization of assets by firms that became merger targets.

Chapter 3 of the 1972 FTC survey confronts this possibility head on by looking at the post-merger organizational and management changes. Finding that conglomerate acquirers made only minor changes in the operations of acquired companies, with inconclusive effects on their profitability, they regard as "not proved" a hypothesis of increases in the postmerger efficiency of acquired units. This finding is quite properly qualified by noting the shortness of the time period after acquisition, and implicitly, by the small sample of acquired companies for which detailed postmerger performance can even be calculated due to the frequent use of consolidated income statements with inadequate divisional breakdowns.

Tables 8–2 and 8–3 are taken from this study. What *is* clear from table 8–2 is that most conglomerate acquirers leave the basic structure of the acquired companies unchanged, utilizing a multidivisional or "profit center" form of organization.[23] But this hardly shows that new managements' standards may not, for example, lead an unreorganized purchasing department to strive more vigorously (on the one hand) or to adopt new, anticompetitive practices (on the other hand). A new ownership may shake up existing management without replacing it.

In a similar vein the management turnover shown in table 8–3 seems quite consistent with either normal turnover without much change of duties, or of very great reassignments of duties. This is a promising line of research, but I do not believe the FTC study does more than suggest it.

The most impassioned arguments against the presence of efficiency motivations have come from those seeking a different principal

TABLE 8–2

POSTACQUISITION CHANGES IN ADMINISTRATIVE FUNCTIONS OF FIRMS ACQUIRED BY SAMPLE CONGLOMERATES

	NUMBER OF COMPANIES WHERE ADMINISTRATION OF FUNCTION WAS:			
Function	*Changed*	*Unchanged*	*Partially Changed*	*N.A.**
Accounting	21	56	22	0
Auditing	61	21	17	0
Legal counsel	29	17	53	0
Insurance	74	9	14	2
Employee benefit admin.	25	38	35	1
Charitable contributions	10	56	32	1
Checking accounts	19	52	26	2
Borrowing, credit lines	70	24	4	1
Research & development	7	75	3	14
Advertising & promotion	9	80	8	2
Purchasing	4	77	17	1

SOURCE: FTC II.

* Not applicable or data unavailable.

---

23. Oliver E. Williamson, *Corporate Control and Business Behavior* (New York, 1970), has argued that this is the optimal form of organization of a diversified form.

TABLE 8–3

CHANGE IN STATUS OF THREE TOP MANAGEMENT OFFICIALS AFTER
FIRMS WERE ACQUIRED BY CONGLOMERATES

Status after Acquisition	Number of Officials	Percentage of Total
Stayed indefinitely*	151 } 151	51.4 } 51.4
Remained initially, later left		
a) Retired†	41 ⎫	13.9 ⎫
b) Resigned	55 ⎬ 115	18.7 ⎬ 39.1
c) Moved to another position with conglomerate	19 ⎭	6.5 ⎭
Left immediately after acquisition		
a) Retired	10 ⎫	3.4 ⎫
b) Resigned	16 ⎬ 28	5.4 ⎬ 9.5
c) Moved to another position with conglomerate	2 ⎭	0.7 ⎭
Total	294	100.0

SOURCE: FTC II.

* Stayed until three years after firm was acquired or until 1969–70, after which information was not available.
† Includes six officials who died.

cause, and finding a more promising candidate. Reid's study, in behalf of managerial growth motivations, cited in the previous section is a case in point. Michael Gort used regression analysis in an attempt to explain variations in the merger rate and to choose among competing theories.[24] His is a large-scale cross-sectional study for the period 1951–59 of mergers among manufacturing companies mostly with assets of $500,000 or more. There were 5,534 included acquisitions in his sample (out of a population of over 100,000 firms of the same size classes.) These mergers were classified by the industry of the acquired firm at the three-digit level. Gort attempted to account for the interindustry variation in merger rates by reference to a series of variables, and thus to identify variables which are of underlying importance. His data permitted analysis of either 46 or 101 industries, depending on the variables included.

Formally, Gort attempted to choose between what he regards as three competing explanations of merger frequency: (a) economic

24. Michael Gort, "An Economic Disturbance Theory of Mergers," *Quarterly Journal of Economics* 83, no. 4 (November 1969).

disturbances leading to valuation discrepancies, (*b*) attempts to reduce competition, and (*c*) economies of scale.

He regressed the merger rate (mergers in the industry as a fraction of industry size) against seven variables representing characteristics of the industry of the acquired firm. His independent variables, briefly defined, were:

1. the technical personnel ratio, 1950;
2. the rate of productivity change, 1947–54;
3. growth in an index of production, 1947–54;
4. the four-firm concentration ratio, 1954;
5. the rate of change in the concentration ratio, 1947–54;
6. the rate of change in asset size of the average firm, 1948–54;
7. the rate of change in number of firms and proprietors, 1947–54.

Much of Gort's paper strives to link these variables to the three hypotheses and suggest a priori signs under each hypothesis.

The "efficiencies" hypothesis in Gort's analysis is related only to economies of scale. He hypothesizes that if such motivations are important the average size of firm in the industry should be rising, which is plausible enough; and, more questionably, that merger activity should be inversely related to growth. His argument is that given rapid growth in the industry it is *ceteris paribus* easier to get large by means of internal growth and thus less necessary to merge.[25]

In his findings, the average firm size does increase, but merger rates are positively associated with growth, and Gort thus regards "scale" as a (relatively) discredited hypothesis.

The problem with this mode of analysis is that so much rides on a priori assertion. A theorist whom I shall call Antigort might have argued as follows: "Industry wide growth will create backlogs in key factor markets and attempts to grow by internal expansion will be difficult. It is easy to grow quickly only by acquisition. Scale considerations would impel mergers in periods of rapid growth—partly because a high and growing demand would make any investment in fixed capacity more attractive, and partly because it would generate potential economies of distribution and promotion which are most easily achieved by acquisitions." Antigort would find in Gort's data support for the notion of scale economies being important.

---

25. Gort, "An Economic Disturbance," p. 630.

All in all the data we have, while hardly suggesting real synergies are always present or are the predominant motive, do seem to me consistent with the presence of real efficiencies. Such motivations may well have played a bigger role in the first half of the decade than during the merger wave, not necessarily because they were absolutely less important, but because other motives also came to play important roles.

MARKET POWER MOTIVATIONS

There is nothing in the evidence assembled that suggests that achieving market power was a dominant motivation in the merger wave of the late 1960s. Ansoff et al. in the period 1946–65 had found that maintaining or increasing market penetration was one of the several stated reasons for acquisition in their survey of 93 acquirers, ranking behind "completion of product lines" and just ahead of "to fully utilize existing marketing capabilities," and "to offset unsatisfactory sales growth" as the most commonly stated motivations. But I think this has no market power implication absent knowledge of shares before and after mergers. Indexes of antitrust activity proved poor correlates of mergers over time, and while Gort found some positive correlation across industries between merger rates and levels of concentration, he found none between merger rates and changes in concentration. The small size and market shares of many acquired companies again suggest that achieving dominant market shares was not the typical motivation. Both FTC II and Goldberg found the levels of concentration achieved in the mergers they studied to be relatively low both before and after acquisition.

Those who believe anticompetitive opportunities arise largely through reciprocal dealing or via opportunities for communities of interest to develop among diversified firms, may infer some increase in the opportunities for heightened exercise of market power in the increased diversification that FTC II shows to have occurred.[26] There is no doubt that the largest manufacturing firms were substantially more diversified in 1968 than they were in 1950, and that the leading conglomerate acquirers sought and achieved a very substantial diversification. But, for reasons discussed in detail in subsequent chapters, there is no easy conclusion that such diversification is undertaken in

26. See FTC II, chap. 4.

order to exercise market power, nor that exercise of such power is a probable result.

Having said that the available data give no substantial support to market power as a *primary* objective of mergers generally does not rule it out as a significant motivation in particular cases, nor as a more general secondary objective. The fact is that the frequency of mergers and of large mergers rose steadily over the period 1960–68 despite steadily rising legal barriers. Since antitrust risks were increasingly being taken, may one infer that the potential private gains were rising more than proportionately? While this is a possible argument it does not seem, without more, very persuasive of the argument that the private gains were necessarily related to market power, rather than to other gains from merger.

In this connection it is important to recall that antitrust deterrents may operate effectively to stop mergers that are not motivated by anticompetitive considerations. Thus a conclusion that anticompetitive considerations are of minimal positive importance in motivating mergers does not belie the possibility that a widening antitrust net effectively contributed to the end of the merger wave.

GROWTH MOTIVATIONS

The notion that growth motivations play a significant role in understanding mergers cannot be rejected on the basis of the evidence examined. But the notion that it is growth rather than other motives cannot be accepted on these data. Growth in sales and in assets are, of course, positively correlated with companies' profits and with speculative opportunities for those who correctly anticipate them. Thus the mere fact that merger activity correlates positively with industry and economy-wide growth and with the proxies that perhaps measure opportunities for future growth (such as technical base, rate of productivity increase, size of firms) proves little. Refined tests of whether observed growth is the optimal growth rate consistent with other objectives, or whether it instead is understood only if maximum growth is the objective, subject to constraints, are hard to pose and harder to execute convincingly.[27]

---

27. This is shown by the long and continuing controversy between "profit maximization" and "sales maximization" advocates. Despite a large empirical effort the proponents of neither side regard their theories as

The direct evidence provides no more than straws to either view. During the period from 1966 on, when the merger rate accelerated, the size of acquired firms grew sharply. This is consistent with a view that the acquisitions were an end in themselves to many companies, particularly because many of these acquisitions proved unprofitable (indeed indigestible) as operating entities and were ultimately disgorged. However, the collapse of the merger wave and the decline in both absolute and relative size of acquisitions after 1969 may be taken to suggest that growth was not pursued for its own sake alone, but rather because (in the earlier period) growth was thought by investors to be valuable. The fact that they were wrong part of the time is irrelevant. When investors' expectations changed, all-out growth stopped being a sensible strategy.

The indirect attempts to support or reject the significance of growth motivations seem to me to flounder within a multiple-cause framework. The Reid and the Weston and Mansinghka papers, although intended to be in direct opposition to one another, seem to me fully consistent with both growth and profit motivations being important. One can grant for sake of argument that every particular merger was motivated by either profit *or* growth considerations and still conclude that the aggregate merger movement included both kinds of mergers. After all owner-controlled firms and managerially-controlled firms were in both the groups that were active acquirers and in the group of nonacquiring firms.

Gort does not attack the growth hypothesis explicitly, but his implicit argument would surely be that if the desire to grow is the motivating force behind managerial actions, then one would expect a negative relation between growth of the economy and merger rates for, in a period of rapid growth, it is easier to grow internally, and thus *ceteris paribus* less necessary to engage in mergers in order to achieve the optimal rate of growth. Antigort would surely reply that if growth is management's objective, generally rising demand will create backlogs in capital goods industries and attempts to grow by

---

seriously shaken. For a discussion of this issue in the merger context, see Dennis C. Mueller, "A Theory of Conglomerate Mergers," *Quarterly Journal of Economics* 83, no. 4 (November 1969): 643–59; David R. Kamerschen, "A Theory of Conglomerate Mergers: Comment," *Quarterly Journal of Economics* 84, no. 4 (November 1970): 668–73; and D. C. Mueller, "A Theory of Conglomerate Mergers: Reply," *Quarterly Journal of Economics* 83, no. 4 (November 1969): 675–79.

ordering new capacity will be frustrated. It is easy to grow quickly only by acquisition. Thus, whether or not mergers correlated with growth of an industry or an economy would prove inconclusive.

My own view is that growth per se did play a role during the height of the merger movement, not primarily because the underlying business ethic changed, but because the always present constraints on managerial desires to grow were greatly loosened by opportunities for real and speculative gains. Moreover, some of the accounting miracles that produced growing profits via acquisitions demanded continuing acquisitions to work. But this says that growth motivations reinforced others—the essence of a multiplicative model.

SPECULATIVE MOTIVATIONS

Clearly the stock market's movements, investors' and brokers' prejudices, and rules of thumb can each affect the profitability of mergers. Changes in stock market indexes prove to be an important correlate of merger activity much of the time. The increasing reliance, during the decade of the sixties, on exchange (rather than cash) tender offers certainly adds fuel to the importance of stock market aspects of the merger movement.

Denis Binder's finding that, during the height of the merger movement, the PE ratios of acquiring companies were higher than those of their targets, suggests support for a "PE game" speculative hypothesis. If acquiring firms had significantly higher PE ratios than the firms they acquired, *and* if the combined companies' PE ratio a year or two later was higher than the weighted average of the component companies' ratios (adjusted for changes in overall PE ratios), there might be a presumption that a purely pecuniary synergy was there to be had. I attempted to test this hypothesis, in the study referred to earlier.[28] If the hypothesis is correct, it would imply (1) the PE ratio of the acquiring company was significantly above that of its targets; and/or (2) the combined PE ratio was significantly higher than a mere weighted average of the components would have produced. Preliminary findings suggest that, year by year over the decade, neither implication was satisfied for horizontal, vertical, or market extension mergers. For product extension and purely conglomerate mergers the first implication tended to be satisfied, and during 1966–68 was

---

28. See footnote 18 above.

overwhelmingly satisfied. The second condition was not satisfied before 1965, but was clearly satisfied during 1967 and 1968, and was perhaps satisfied in 1966. Adequate post-acquisition data for mergers consummated in 1969 and later are not yet available. I regard this study as providing a bit, albeit only a bit, of support to a purely speculative dimension to the great merger spurt of 1966–68. But of course this need not be exclusive of other motives.

A number of the studies cited above concerning the profitability of the companies involved in mergers, utilized stock market measures and these may be reinterpreted as saying something about speculative as well as real opportunities. As we noted there is disagreement about whether there were overall gains. Gort and Hogarty[29] compared the dividends and capital gains earned by stockholders of acquired firms from the stock they were given in exchange, with the dividends and capital gains they would have earned if they had kept their old stock, and if their old company's stock had kept pace with the average performance of other firms in their industry. Of 27 cases studied, stockholders of 16 of the acquired firms benefited by this measure, and the average benefit was large enough so that over the whole 27 cases the average gain was large.[30] They found, however, that these gains were matched by losses to the acquirers.

I am not prepared to dismiss the Gort and Hogarty zero-sum finding, but I would prefer to see it replicated with a larger sample over a longer time period before I feel constrained to abandon the view that it was not proved.[31] But whether or not there were net

---

29. Gort and Hogarty, "New Evidence on Mergers."

30. Median gain 33 percent; mean gain 127 percent. Clearly the variance was high.

31. James H. Lorie and Paul Halpern in a paper that is longer on rhetoric than on evidence, "Conglomerate Mergers: The Rhetoric and the Evidence," 13 JOURNAL OF LAW AND ECONOMICS, no. 1, 149–66 (April 1970), present some evidence that might be thought to bear on this question, but that, in my view, does not. They are concerned with whether the "funny money" received by sellers in acquisitions, particularly conglomerate acquisitions, was sufficiently spurious that innocent investors were being deceived. They found that the convertible debentures et al., received, had proved splendid investments. Unfortunately the terminal point of their study of postacquisition stock prices was 1967. A glance at figure 5–3 will suggest why this may have proved to be a biased result. There were large speculative gains to be made by switching from a balanced portfolio to conglomerate stocks in the period 1963–67, but such

gains, there were always some gainers and thus room for speculative motivations. Gort's discrepant valuation hypothesis depends on differing sets of evaluations, which increase during periods of rapid change in stock prices and in periods of growth. A question he leaves unanswered is why (if there are not economies to be achieved by management) the form of speculation is takeover rather than simply stock market speculation. But if one concedes both speculative and efficiency motives play complementary roles, then takeover may be the best way to realize the speculative gains to be had by replacing or reforming an inefficient management.

Finally, the immediate stock market gains found by Lev and Mandelker, and the high brokerage fees in takeovers, support the possibility of significant "insider" gains.

The general agreement that stock prices do play a role supports at least superficially four different merger hypotheses: (*a*) the Gort discrepant valuation hypothesis; (*b*) the hypothesis that a receptive stock market creates a pecuniary synergy to all involved in a merger; (*c*) the hypothesis that corporate insiders could reap a quick speculative profit even if long-run gains were to prove ephemeral; (*d*) the hypothesis that large fees and profits could be earned by the financial community simply by encouraging a rise in the level of merger activity. But, supporting them all, these data do not discriminate among the four hypotheses. Most seriously these hypotheses fail to explain why the stock market played so much less predictable a role after 1969.

Summary

This review of empirical findings has focused on data that bear on the causes or correlates of merger activity. At first glance this diverse literature, this array of fragments, seems unsatisfactory despite its large volume. Indeed, reviewing the empirical literature, my dominant image is of a residue of vapor trails in a cloudless sky. While there has been moderate traffic, there is no pattern of ground control discernible. Once in a while two fragments of trails suggest a parallel path, or a

---

switching could be done in a variety of ways, of which selling one's company was only one. Whatever their findings show about the need to protect investors, they do not tell much about long-run consequences to owners of companies that were acquired, because of the cyclical context in which the findings were generated.

collision course, but in the end they pass on different headings, at different altitudes, on different rates of climb. My image (or perhaps it is the vapor trails) is blurred by a light, cold wind that reminds me that it is now late and that all those planes passed by some time ago.

But a second glance is reassuring. To be sure it does not seem possible to find definitive support for a principal cause of merger activity, but remembering that a merger wave is an aggregate of many mergers, there is substantial support in these data and in the historical experience taken as a whole for a multiple motivation model.

Let me restate the nature of my proposed multiple-cause hypothesis. Suppose that certain motivations are always present with respect to *some* potential mergers. These would include opportunities for real economies, for increased profits via market power, for settling intracorporate fights, for achieving growth objectives, and for earning commissions on the exchanges of securities. Let me postulate that these are important motivations and that while they may become stronger or weaker in response to exogenous influences they are always there to a significant degree. For any level of other variables they would always motivate some mergers. But the more conducive other considerations become the more mergers actually get consummated. It takes mutual benefits to make a merger. If the stock market suddenly becomes bullish toward mergers, a merger that managers always wanted (but owners resisted) may become attractive to the owners of the target company. If credit conditions tighten and interest rates rise, the advantage of acquiring idle liquid assets and transferring them tax free, may be the straw that motivates a merger that previously had latent market power advantages which were, however, not by themselves worth the antitrust risk.

The case *for* a multiple-cause framework of the kind I suggest rests heavily on its consistency with the historical evidence. The mid-sixties provided an amazing constellation of "go" signals, particularly for conglomerate acquisitions. Capital was being rationed and interest rates were high. A bull market was developing with growth stocks the darlings of investors imbued with a market outlook that was prepared to extrapolate growth in earnings per share without looking closely at the source (or the genuineness) of the reported growth. Some found that tax laws and accounting conventions made it easy to play the PE game and realize instant earnings from mergers. Many of those best able to detect the manipulative aspects of the transactions—the corporate insiders, the managers of mutual funds,

and the leading brokerage houses—were in the best positions to benefit and thus were slow to blow the whistle. Courts, which traditionally
have interpreted securities laws to protect stockholders and to pre-
serve their options, were reluctant to let these laws be used to stop
mergers because such use might deprive stockholders of the opportunity to sell out at a premium. At the same time the antitrust laws
were more and more heavily restricting horizontal and vertical acquisitions, but seemed relatively congenial to conglomerate acquisitions. Conglomerates meanwhile were perhaps best suited to exploit
the opportunities for redirecting cash flows from one enterprise to another and to generate rapid growth in reported earnings.

Like many self-reinforcing movements, the early market success
of the conglomerate acquisitions tended to justify the perhaps shaky
assumptions being made about PE ratios, and reinforced a genuinely
favorable speculative climate.

But by 1969 a number of key signals had turned from green
to red. Tax options, although probably never critically important, were
reduced by the changes included in the Tax Reform Act. Changes in
accounting rules limited what was possible, and perhaps even more
importantly, called attention to what had been happily neglected. Once
the bull market showed some weakness, many who had ridden the
glamor stocks up decided to get out. The resulting sharp downturn in
the prices of many conglomerate stocks evidently led to a reevaluation
of the appropriate PE ratios, and when that occurred the attractiveness
of many mergers evaporated. At the regulatory level both Securities
and Antitrust authorities began taking a closer look at the conglomerate phenomenon and announced their intention to cope with the
problems. In so doing they increased the risks of merging companies
and the financial community. By 1970 the credit crunch appeared to
be easing some, and weakened yet another merger motive.

None of these changes eliminated the most attractive merger
opportunities, but they surely changed the margin. Whereas in 1967 a
merger with small (or no) real synergies might well be attractive
enough to justify a merger premium of 20 percent and transactions
costs of another 5 to 10 percent because the stock market promised
to provide a quick gain of 30 percent, by 1970 the costs were there but
the gains were more problematical.

All of the above is only suggestive of course. But I am persuaded
we have enough fragments of data and historical evidence to encourage, if not compel, adherence to a multiple-cause hypothesis.

I am persuaded that many of the empirical attempts have proven un-satisfactory because they have been imbedded in a principal-cause framework that the data we have refute. We have not yet had the data or the ingenuity to develop a satisfactory explanatory and pre-dictive multiple-motive model. This is the frontier of our ignorance. If we breach it we are likely to learn a great deal more than what it is that motivates mergers. It has much more general implications for and about the behavior, and control, of large corporate firms in an econ-omy in which such firms are dominant elements.

Appendix to Chapter 8: Using Regression Analysis to Discriminate between Multiple-Cause and Principal-Cause Hypotheses

If one wishes to test a pluralistic, eclectic, multiplicative theory of merger activity (of the kind I have tried to develop) there are sub-stantial methodological problems in using and interpreting multivariate regression results. This appendix is an econometric digression that explores one that I find troublesome.

Suppose we start with the following hypothesis, which would command almost universal assent:

(1)   *Merger activity is a function of business and economic condi-tions, speculative opportunities, credit conditions, the relevant tax laws, the level and focus of antitrust activity, and other things.*

Purely formally this hypothesis can be expressed

(2) $$M = f(X_1, X_2, \ldots X_i, \ldots X_n),$$

where M is "merger activity" and the X's are the relevant explanatory variables. If we could directly measure these X_i, we could presumably observe them over a sufficient period to find out which of them ap-peared to account for variations in M. Suppose, however, that the X_i are not directly measurable, but that there are a series of more or less imperfect but measurable proxies, Z_j, that may serve for the X_i. Specifically suppose:

(3) $$X_i = \phi_i(Z_1, Z_2, \ldots Z_j, \ldots), \text{ all } i.$$

Let Y be a measure of M and regress it against the Z's:

(4) $$Y = a_0 + a_1Z_1 + \ldots + a_jZ_j + \ldots.$$

Now suppose that a small number of the Z's have significant regression coefficients and explain most of the explainable portion of the variation in Y. How these results are to be interpreted depends upon the hypothesis we hold. Let me pose, and explore, two very different hypotheses:

THE PRINCIPAL-CAUSES HYPOTHESIS (MODEL A)

This hypothesis is that although many things play a role in equation (3), some are of major importance, and some are of minor importance. Imagine we estimate equation (4) on some sample of time series data, cross-sectional data, pooled data, or panel data. With reasonable luck we will find a small set of Z's for which (a) the signs of the coefficients accord with the prior expectations about their effects as proxies, (b) the coefficients are statistically significant and relatively insensitive to the variables ultimately excluded, (c) the R^2 is respectably high, and (d) the Durbin-Watson statistic, if relevant, is in the acceptable range.

Further suppose we can identify the X_i for which the significant Z_j are proxies. These X_i become leading candidates for labeling as "principal-causes." If one believes there is a *primary* cause, the most significant X_i is a candidate for "primary" cause. Caution is required, because what is truly the (or a) principal-cause might not (in the sample period) have varied enough to prove its importance. (Of course, if that is true over a long period or a period when there is a lot of variation in the dependent variable to explain, such a variable's claim to being "principal" tends to fade.)

Importantly, under a principal-cause hypothesis, independent variables whose proxies showed reasonable movement, but played relatively small explanatory roles, can be eliminated from the list of principal-causes. These negative findings are of substantial importance in discovering the truth.

Having identified the principal-causes (say X_1 and X_2 by the proxies Z_1 and Z_2), one might predict future variations in Y by variations of $Y = a_0 + a_1 Z_1 + a_2 Z_2$. If the projections prove poor, one must (a) seek variation in a hitherto stationary variable, (b) argue for a structural shift, or (c) question the principal-cause hypothesis.

A MULTIPLE-CAUSE HYPOTHESIS (MODEL B)

Let me now make an apparently small change in the model. Suppose instead of (2) we hypothesize that

(5) $M = g(W)$, where W is

(6) $W = h(X_1, X_2, \ldots X_i, \ldots X_n)$.

The X_i are assumed unobservable, but once again we suppose that:

(7) $W = W(Z_1, Z_2, \ldots Z_j, \ldots)$

where the Z_j are proxies for the X_i.

We once again estimate (4): $Y = a_0 + a_1 Z_1 + a_2 Z_2, \ldots a_j Z_j$, and find Z_1 and Z_2 to be the significant and important regressors over the period. If we can identify the X's for which they are proxies, we would say that those variables played the important roles in determining the variation in Y in that period. *But we would recognize that the influence of Z_1 and Z_2 was felt through the effect on* W, *and that in a later period* W *might vary because of changes in Z_3 or Z_4.* Suppose we had forecast Y on the basis of Z_1 and Z_2 and the forecasts "went bad." This might have happened, *with no damage to our hypothesis,* if Z_4 (say) had become important and its effect on W (and hence on Y) was not representable by means of Z_1 and Z_2 in the estimated relation

$$Y = a_0 + a_1 Z_1 + a_2 Z_2.$$

Poor predictions in this model suggest that in the subsequent period Z_1 and Z_2 are poor predictors of W, not that W is a poor predictor of Y. We should therefore recognize that the principal correlates of W in some period might not be its principal determinants in other periods.

Because the same equation (4) is used in both hypotheses it cannot discriminate between them. If we *know* we are dealing with model A, the equation tells us a good deal about the theoretical relevance of the X's; if we *know* we are dealing with model B, it tells us much less about the relevance of the X's; if we are debating whether model A or model B is correct, it does not contribute to the debate.

With enough data over many periods and subperiods, it would be relatively easy to distinguish between models A and B. With a small amount of data it is all but impossible. Equation (4) thus tells us very little that we want to know if we believe model B is, or may be, the interesting hypothesis.

I will illustrate this point by reviewing a regression analysis conducted for me by a research assistant, Alan Beckenstein.[32] Although

---

32. Dr. Beckenstein, now teaching at the University of Virginia, shares some but not all of my reservations about his analysis. I have

the study in question was intended to be a relatively naïve forecasting model, it clearly illustrates a problem shared by many more sophisticated analyses.

BECKENSTEIN: TIME SERIES FORECASTING MODEL

Beckenstein started with the general hypothesis shown as (1) above and utilized the FTC time series of large manufacturing and mining mergers. He used four different dependent variables: the number of mergers in year *t*, the dollar value of the assets acquired in year *t*, and the first differences in each of the first two. The first difference models were designed to cope with some collinearities, but for my purposes here, the first two variables are equally serviceable, and I will focus the discussion on them.

Beckenstein used the following explanatory variables:

1. the level of GNP;
2. the change in GNP;
3. the change in Standard and Poor's index of 500 stock prices;
4. the prime rate of interest;
5. a dummy variable to distinguish 1969 and subsequent years, from 1968 and earlier years;
6. an index of antitrust cases commenced in the previous year by the Department of Justice and the FTC;
7. a linear time trend.

The first two were taken as proxies for general business conditions; the third as a measure of speculative and promotional opportunities; the fourth as a proxy for credit conditions; the fifth to represent the change in tax laws resulting from the passage in 1969 of the Tax Reform Act. The sixth, taken as an index of the vigor of antitrust enforcement, never proved significant and was therefore dropped from the analysis.

These variables were used in various combinations in a series of linear regressions on time series data. Originally ("Beckenstein I") they were estimated for the period 1949–70. When 1971 data be-

---

neither reproduced it in full nor do I here attempt to do justice to its positive contributions. I use it instead solely to illustrate my more general worries about regression results in choosing among competing types of hypotheses.

came available, they were reestimated ("Beckenstein II") for 1949–71, and interesting changes occurred.

Beckenstein I.   Part A of table 8–4 reproduces two of the regression equations. While their specifics are of relatively little interest, certain results stand out.

The proxy for credit conditions (prime rate) did not prove helpful, neither did the change in GNP. GNP itself had a positive and highly significant coefficient, the coefficient of the stock market index was positive and significant, and the dummy variable for the Tax Reform Act (which restricted the tax options of acquirers) proved gratifyingly negative and significant. The R^2 were in the neighborhood of 0.9, respectable if not spectacular for time series. There was some collinearity, but not so much as to shatter confidence in the results.

The test of a predictive model is how well it projects. The period from 1966 to 1972 imposed a severe test on a predicting model, because both the sharp rise, and the sudden reversal in merger activity were there to be predicted. Columns 1 and 2 of table 8–5 suggest that the model Beckenstein I, utilizing data through 1970, truncated the 1968 peak, but caught the turning point. It overestimated the 1969 fall, and underestimated the further fall from 1969 to 1970. But all in all *as of 1970* it doesn't look too bad. But 1971 was to prove disastrous. The merger rate, predicted by the model to reverse its fall, to resume sharply its upward thrust, and to approach or exceed the 1968 highs fell sharply and by 1972 had shown no signs of reversing its steady four-year decline.

What went wrong is immediately clear from inspection of the time series plotted on a log scale in figure 8–1. Two versions of the dependent variable (number of large mergers and dollars of assets acquired) are plotted, along with four of the independent variables. GNP served as a proxy for the log-linear trend in the dependent variables that dominated the middle half of the period. Changes in the stock market index correlated rather well with the timing of the cyclical variability of the level of mergers, although with a very attenuated amplitude. The prime rate had appropriate amplitude, but its timing was often out of phase with the dependent variables. What these variables, separately and together, did not do is to pick up the sharp downturn between 1968 and 1970 shown between the dashed vertical lines. *But the dummy variable for those years did!* Because it was a one-time shift, the dummy variable overestimated the fall in 1969 and

TABLE 8-4

Selected Beckenstein Regression Coefficients

(t ratios shown in parentheses)

Dependent Variables and Period	Constant	Independent Variables						R^2	D-W
		GNP	ΔGNP	Standard and Poor's 500 Stocks	Prime Rate of Interest	Dummy for 1969 and after	Time		
A. Beckenstein I 1949–70									
1. Number of Acquisitions	−119	0.47	−0.29	2.49	9.14	−80.6	−7.4	.90	1.76
	(−4.40)	(3.10)	(−0.72)	(2.74)	(0.87)	(−2.67)	(−1.95)		
2. Dollar Value of Assets Acquired	−11143	47.8	−30.6	47.8	449	−4180	−992	.87	1.56
	(−5.2)	(4.03)	(−0.99)	(4.03)	(0.55)	(−1.78)	(−3.33)		
B. Beckenstein II 1949–71									
3. Number of Acquisitions	−107	0.31	−0.49	1.82	28.9	−117	−6.2	.86	1.50
	(−3.39)	(1.94)	(−1.07)	(1.75)	(3.21)	(−3.77)	(−1.39)		
4. Dollar Value of Assets Acquired	−9912	31.2	−50.4	124	2403	−7719	−863	.78	1.37
	(−3.66)	(2.24)	(−1.28)	(1.40)	(3.13)	(−2.90)	(−2.27)		

TABLE 8–5

Beckenstein Models: Estimated Values and Forecasts 1968–72

A. Number of Large Mergers in Manufacturing and Mining				B. Dollar Value of Assets Acquired (millions)			
Year	Actual* (1)	Beckenstein I (2)	Beckenstein II (3)	Year	Actual* (1)	Beckenstein I (2)	Beckenstein II (3)
1968	207	181	176	1968	$13,297	$10,963	$10,209
1969	155	125	120	1969	11,353	8,463	7,863
1970	98	110	109	1970	6,346	7,793	7,439
1971	66	179	91	1971	2,544	13,912	4,887
1972	64†	191	77	1972	1,820†	15,522	3,868

Note: Forecasts enclosed in dotted lines.

* Based on FTC, *Current Trends in Merger Activity, 1971*, Statistical Report No. 10 (Washington, D.C., May 1972).

† Because the 1972 data as reported exclude "companies for which data was not publicly available," it has been necessary to estimate statistically 1972 data comparable to those for 1968–71. The raw 1972 data reported 56 mergers with $1,749 million in assets. Since Beckenstein used the earlier series it is appropriate to offset the exclusion. The reported data have been inflated assuming nonreporting in 1972 was proportional to that in 1971.

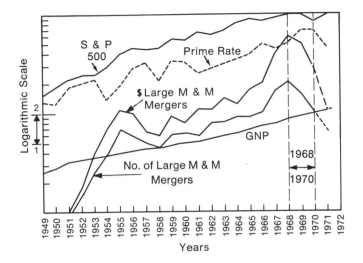

Fig. 8–1.   Selected time series 1949–71 (logarithmic scale).

underestimated it in 1970. But notwithstanding, all of this leads to a pretty good fit, for series that end in 1970.

However, when the stock market recovered sharply in 1971 and 1972 with GNP continuing to grow (in money terms) at its normal rate, even the depressing effect of the dummy variable could not prevent the predicted level of merger activity from rising sharply. The real world merger rate did not.

This exercise can be criticized in many ways. Importantly the proxy for 1969 and 1970 represented more than the Tax Reform Act. Nineteen sixty-nine was also the year of the beginning of the Nixon Administration, and of many other things which may be more (or less) relevant than the passage of a tax bill to explaining changes in merger activity. A period dummy variable picks up all the influences operating in the period, not just the hypothesized ones. Some of these influences clearly required not a one-time downward shift in the function, but a steadily increasing depressing effect.

Beckenstein II.   Faced with the 1971 data when they arrived, Beckenstein I needed help. One might have added a new proxy for 1971 and later years (calling it, e.g., a proxy for the unfavorable effect on conglomerate mergers resulting from the revelations about ITT); if one had, the variable would surely have shown a significant negative coefficient. But that would have been cheating. Instead Beckenstein chose simply to reestimate the model using the additional year of information. The regression results are shown in part B of table 8–4. Changes in the stock market index and the level GNP seem much less important than they did in the first run, the 1969 ("Tax") dummy seems even more important, and the previously not significant prime rate suddenly assumes major importance. What a difference a year makes! Does this tell us that credit conditions were after all a major factor all along or simply that the prime rate (alone among the included independent variables) fell sharply in 1970–71? Clearly it is the latter. Does this tell us that after 1971 the stock market was hardly significant any longer? I think not. Clearly the stock market, and thus speculative considerations, have played a role in the postwar merger movement. The loss of significance of the regression coefficient of the stock market index in Beckenstein II cannot refute this any more than can the significant coefficient in Beckenstein I prove it.[33] We know or believe that the stock market played a role on the basis of other evidence. But so have other things played roles. For much of the period the changes in the stock market index appear to have served as a proxy for a whole set of forces which were in a stable relationship to one another. When the merger wave erupted in 1966–68 and collapsed in 1969–70, the adequacy of any variable that showed a different cyclical pattern was threatened. This happened to the stock market index used. In combination with the so-called tax-reform dummy variable it didn't work too badly for 1969 and 1970 (unless you were focusing on the change from 1969 to 1970). But when the stock market revived in 1971 and the merger wave did not, there was lots of unexplained variance to account for. The prime rate, which had been positively (but not significantly) related to merger activity over the period 1949–70 suddenly came into its own, and the stock market variable lost significance.[34]

---

33. One possibility is that the wrong stock market variable was being used. After 1968 the price-earnings ratios of many of the major acquirers slumped relative to the general market, as we saw in chapter 5. Another possibility is that when small (and perhaps gullible) investors left the market after 1969, the speculative influences which the stock index reflected really did play a much smaller role. In a multiplicative model this decline in importance of a variable that had previously been important would itself decrease the merger rate.

34. The model estimated with 1971 data, with its greatly increased role for the prime rate proved disastrous as a predictor for 1973 as the

These difficulties are not matters of sophistication. One competent investigator[35] estimated a distributed lag adjustment model with a stock market index the sole regressor of deviations of the number of mergers from their trend value for the period 1946–66. He found the co-efficients of the index for the current year and each of the two prior years significant at the 1 percent level, with an R^2 of .66. Moreover adding, singly and in combination, seven other variables to his basic variables added very little to the model's explanatory power. As to prediction, the model was highly successful in predicting the spurt in merger activity after 1966 (although with a one-year lag) but failed to pick up the downturn and subsequent collapse. None of this is surprising when you look at the time series shown in figure 8–1.

My concern is with what, at best, such a study might have told us. Forget for a moment the post-1968 behavior. When the model was working it could be used to test the hypothesis that stock market variations were the principal-cause or correlate of merger activity against the hypothesis that *something else* was the principal-cause or correlate. But it could not really test it against a multiple-cause hypothesis. The importance of stock market prices is suggested by the fact that stock market prices proved for a long period to be the best single variable to use in explaining variance in merger activity, most of the time. But nothing in a multiple-cause hypothesis denies this. Moreover, the failure of the predictor in recent years is at least as compatible with a multiple-cause hypothesis as with the possibility that in 1968 some fundamental structural shift occurred after which stock market prices no longer exercised any significant influence.

This is not to render even relatively simple regression analyses useless. While regression analyses of this kind are not capable of telling us whether stock market fluctuations, or the rate of interest, or the Tax Reform Act are (or were) major causes of the level of merger activity, they can define data points that ultimately contribute to discovering how each of these things, and others, are linked, in some complex way, to the web of forces that condition the propensity to merge. It may seem a pity to have to crawl instead of to run, but it is a necessary stage in development.

---

sharp rise in the prime rate led to a predicted great upsurge in mergers that did not occur.

35. Since he chose not to publish his results because he does not think his regressions show enough to talk about, I shall leave him un-named. The results seem to me to have methodological importance.

CHAPTER NINE

Economic and Legal Theories of the Effect on Competition I: Reciprocity

IN the final section of chapter 3 (pp. 69–74), I identified three areas of potential adverse impact of a conglomerate merger: (1) the market of the acquired firm, (2) the market of the acquiring firm, and (3) other "markets" including the "macro-market" that is the economy (and body politic) as a whole. Performance in any or all of these areas might result from a particular form of induced behavior, or from a particular change in market structure. For example, suppose as a result of a particular merger, sales were made in large quantity by the acquired firm to the acquiring firm's suppliers as a result of "reciprocity." Such reciprocity might permit the acquiring firm better to exploit its monopsony position in *its* market (thus giving it an advantage vis-à-vis its rivals, who lacked such opportunities); instead (or in addition) reciprocity might be a predatory tactic in the market of the acquired firm, intended to take customers from existing competitors of the acquired firm, and/or to make entry into that market more difficult by foreclosing part of a potential entrant's market; in addition, by increasing the sales and/or profits of the combined firm, such reciprocity might increase its influence in other markets including capital markets, or in the political arena.

The example shows only that there is no neat correspondence among area of impact, form of behavior, and market structure. Indeed legal and economic theory often differ most sharply in how they define the "relevant linkages." For one example, legal theory has given a much more prominent role to the possibility of predatory behavior than most economists believe is justifiable either theoretically or empirically.

While any ordering of topics is to a degree arbitrary, and perhaps artificial, legislative or judicial policy is likely to take its point of departure from the contemporary legal stance. Thus it seems to me most appropriate to organize the subsequent discussion around legal concepts. My plan is as follows: Chapter 9 will deal with reciprocity, both in its own right and as prototypical of other forms of behavior in which market power is utilized indirectly. A discussion of predatory behavior will be included. Chapter 10 will deal with the whole congeries of structural effects that the merger may have in the market of the acquired firm, under the general rubric of "potential competition," the currently fashionable legal concept for dealing with such effects. Chapter 11 will deal, albeit briefly and perhaps inadequately, with the relevance of "macro-concentration" to the merger phenomenon and to policy.

The Nature of Reciprocity

Reciprocity is not new. Barter—reciprocity par excellence—is surely the earliest form of commerce. Adam Smith described reciprocity in 1776 as one of the "sneaking arts of underling tradesmen."[1] Within the last decade it has received an enormous increase in attention, first as a part of the "trade relations" fad that blossomed in the early sixties (when it was regarded as legal) and during which "trade relations" was often a mere euphemism for reciprocal trading,[2] second as an increasingly illegal form of trade behavior under Sherman §1 and Federal Trade Commission §5, and third, during 1968–70 as the primary handle by which Mr. McLaren felt Section 7 was to be extended to conglomerate mergers.

The literature on reciprocity and its effects is voluminous, and more impressive in quantity than in quality.[3] I shall here suggest what

---

1. Adam Smith, *The Wealth of Nations* (1776), Edwin Cannan edition (New York, 1937), p. 460.

2. It is from that period that the widely reproduced table derives, showing that more than half of 300 sampled purchasing agents found reciprocity a factor in their business. See e.g., FTC, *Economic Report on Corporate Mergers* (Washington, D.C., 1969), p. 740, citing *Purchasing Magazine,* November 20, 1961 (!).

3. A short list of papers that seem to me worth reading include: Stocking and Mueller, "Business Reciprocity and the Size of Firms," *Journal of Business of the University of Chicago* 30, no. 2 (1957): 73–95; Harsha, "The Conglomerate Merger and Reciprocity—Condemned by Conjecture?," *Antitrust Bulletin* 9, no. 2 (1964): 201–30; Ferguson, "Tying Arrangements and Reciprocity: An Economic Analysis," 30 LAW AND CONTEMPORARY PROBLEMS 552–80 (Summer 1965). Among the interesting court opinions are the Supreme Court opinions in *FTC v. Consolidated Foods Corp.,* 380 U.S. 592 (1965); the district court opinions of Judge Timbers in *United States v. ITT (Hartford and Grinnell),*

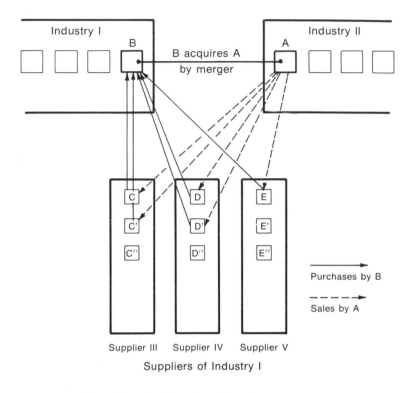

Fig. 9–1.   Reciprocity arising from merger.

seem to me to be the important aspects of the problem, without attempting systematically to cite earlier writers.

Reciprocity, to be understood, must be recognized to be not one but several different things. Figure 9–1 is a schematic representation of the whole congeries of things that are called "reciprocal dealing." Firm B in Industry I is assumed to have many suppliers who seek its custom, and over which it exercises some monopsony power. It acquires firm A in Industry II which produces a product that many of B's actual or potential suppliers can or must purchase from someone. One way or another, B lets it be known (or its suppliers come to believe) that the best way to sell supplies to firm B is to purchase the

---

306 F.Supp. 766 (D. Conn. 1969), appeal dismissed, 404 U.S. 801 (1971), and 324 F.Supp. 19 (D. Conn. 1970), appeal dismissed, 404 U.S. 801 (1971); and of Judge Austin in *United States v. ITT* (*Canteen*), 1971 *CCH Trade Cases* ¶73,619 (N.D. Ill. 1971).

products of its subsidiary A. Thus selling to B requires, reciprocally, buying from A. As a result of this, firm A's sales are greater than they otherwise would be.

In order to look at a variety of types of reciprocal dealing, and a variety of possible motives that might lead to it, it is useful to use four examples, each of which fits figure 9–1 but which differs from the others in important ways. Each is based on a real case. Since my intent is to create examples, not review the cases, the factual setting is far from complete but in no case do I think it is misleading.

EXAMPLE 1.   ARMOUR (B) AND WAUGH (A)[4]

Two employees of Armour & Company, responsible for arranging railway freight services for the giant meatpacker who was their employer, acquired stock in Waugh Equipment Company, a small manufacturer of draft gears, two of which are used in every railroad freight car. These freight agents gave Armour's freight business to railroads which in turn agreed to purchase their draft gears from Waugh. Within six years Waugh rose from a tiny role in the draft gear market (less than 1 percent) to the largest seller. Presumably its stockholders benefited greatly.

EXAMPLE 2.   CONSOLIDATED FOODS (B) AND GENTRY (A)[5]

Consolidated Foods, a large food wholesaler and retailer, acquired Gentry, one of two dominant manufacturers of dehydrated onion and garlic, products used by soup manufacturers (and others) in products they sold to Consolidated. After the acquisition, Consolidated undertook to assist Gentry in selling, by urging its purchasing agents to be aware of the Gentry connection. The court found that some suppliers responded and gave reciprocal orders. Some of these later reduced or abandoned them.

As to long-run effects, Gentry's share of the garlic business rose slightly at first but soon fell below the premerger level. Its share of the

4. Cf., *In re Waugh Mfg. Co.*, 15 FTC 232 (1931). See also, *In re Mechanical Mfg. Co.*, 16 FTC 67 (1932), where traffic managers at Swift did the same sort of thing, and a similar case involving a packer of food stuffs, *In re California Packing Corp.*, 25 FTC 379 (1937).
5. *FTC v. Consolidated Foods Corp.*, 380 U.S. 592 (1965).

dehydrated onion business rose gradually and seven years after the merger had increased from 27 percent to 35 percent.

EXAMPLE 3.   GENERAL DYNAMICS (B) AND LIQUID CARBONIC (A)[6]

General Dynamics, a firm whose principal customer is the United States Government, is an enormous and diversified purchaser. In 1957 it had roughly 80,000 industrial suppliers from whom it purchased in aggregate $500 million per year. Liquid Carbonic, a manufacturer of carbon dioxide and other industrial gases, was the largest firm in its market, with a share that was in 1957 roughly 35 percent of the total market (but slipping). The four-firm-concentration ratio was about 75 percent. In 1957 Liquid Carbonic was operating at about 65 percent of capacity and sought a merger with General Dynamics primarily because it believed its production could be increased via "the additional sales that will be generated with the assistance of General Dynamics." The merger took place, reciprocity was used, and Liquid Carbonic's sales increased enough to halt the decline and slightly increase its market share. The court was persuaded that General Dynamics intended to use and did use both persuasion and coercive tactics to assure that its leading suppliers purchased their requirements of carbon dioxide from Liquid Carbonic.

EXAMPLE 4.   INTERNATIONAL TELEPHONE AND TELEGRAPH (B) AND CANTEEN CORPORATION (A)[7]

International Telephone and Telegraph, the conglomerate giant, had sales in 1969 in excess of $5 billion, and purchased large amounts of supplies from numerous domestic suppliers. In 1967 ITT purchased more than $100,000 in goods or services from each of 725 companies including 61 of the top 100 corporations on the Fortune list. Canteen is a supplier of vended and manual food service of a kind used by virtually every commercial and industrial establishment—including all of ITT's suppliers. A large fraction of Canteen's sales were to industrial and commercial establishments.

---

6. *United States v. General Dynamics Corporation,* 258 F.Supp. 36 (S.D. N.Y. 1966).

7. *United States v. ITT (Canteen),* 1971 *CCH Trade Cases* ¶73,619 (N.D. Ill. 1971).

ITT acquired Canteen in 1969 as part of its conglomerate acquisition program. While there is no evidence that ITT intended to use, or did use, its purchasing power to urge or coerce its suppliers into purchasing Canteen's products, it is clear that the opportunity for reciprocity between ITT and its suppliers was increased by this addition to its product line of a product that all of its suppliers used.

Types of Reciprocity

The examples above are sufficient to show that "reciprocal dealing" may cover a variety of forms of selling to one's suppliers or purchasing from one's customers. Let me define seven for analytic purposes, although some of them may be difficult to distinguish in practice, and a smaller number may well serve for policy purposes.

Fraudulent reciprocity.   Purchasing agents or other employees of a firm (B) with monopsony power use some of that power to acquire a payoff to *themselves* in the form of purchases by B's suppliers of a product which is produced by a firm (A) in which these employees have a significant financial interest. This is clearly a form of bribe to the purchasing agent, and comes at the expense of B's stockholders, among others. Essentially this situation occurred in Waugh (example 1). Armour had unexerted monopsony power which was arrogated by its purchasing agents, for their own benefit. (I use the term "fraudulent" in a loose, nonlegal sense. The legal offense involved is properly preemption of corporate opportunity.)

Coercive reciprocity.   The firm with monopsony power uses covert or overt threats of shifting its purchases unless the supplier purchases some of the products which the monopsonist sells in return. This (the courts found) clearly occurred in both Waugh (example 1) and Liquid Carbonic (example 3) cases.

Consensual or contractual reciprocity.   It proves to the advantage of both firm B and its suppliers to contract or otherwise to agree to engage in reciprocity. Sometimes this sort of reciprocity follows recognition by both parties that there are real economies to be had in avoiding selling and purchasing expenses and in assuring stable supplies and sales, sometimes it is purely inertial. It is difficult to distinguish between mutually beneficial, and merely inertial forms, though it may be important in evaluating the effect. This kind of reciprocity may be contractual (for one example, by requirements contracts that are reciprocally negotiated) or simply tacit. In some, but not all cases, a condition is imposed that the supplier will meet the price and quality of any offered alternative source of supply.

Whether or not it is possible to distinguish coercive from non-coercive reciprocity is unclear. Mere discussions of possible shifts of business may be implied threats, etc. But the purpose of seeking to distinguish them is that truly voluntary reciprocity may be socially beneficial if it is motivated by a search for real economies,[8] whereas coercive reciprocity lacks any presumption of social value. Non-coercive reciprocity appears to figure prominently in the Consolidated Foods-Gentry case (example 2) and may have played a role (along with the coercive) in the Liquid Carbonic case (example 3).

Hortatory reciprocity.   Salesmen of firm A attempt to get their foot in the door of potential customers by calling their attention to the purchases B (A's parent) makes from them, but with no credible threat of retaliation if their plea is rejected. Salesmen use many forms of persuasion, and identification of trade relations is not exempt. Obviously this sort of behavior, if identifiable, is without significant adverse effect. The problem in practice is to distinguish it from other forms. This sort of salesmen's behavior is sometimes offered as evidence in support of coercive reciprocity, and *per contra,* coercive efforts are often defended as mere examples of salesmen's zeal. Defendants in Consolidated Foods (example 2) urged this as an explanation of the documents that the government claimed showed less benign activities. A few such episodes play a role in the Canteen case (example 4).

Reciprocity effect—requited.   Potential suppliers of a large purchaser (say Consolidated Foods) might, wholly unilaterally, seek to curry favor with that firm's purchasing agents by becoming customers of that firm's subsidiary, Gentry. This would create the opportunity for hortatory reciprocity by the suppliers. Consolidated in turn, while initiating no reciprocity, might shift its custom to those suppliers who

---

8. I intend this as the weak statement it is. The fact that it may be socially beneficial does not mean it is presumptively socially beneficial, because of the possibility of third-party effects.

purchased from it, thus establishing reciprocity. In the Consolidated case, the FTC found:

merely as a result of its connection with Consolidated, and without any action on the latter's part, Gentry would have an unfair advantage over competitors enabling it to make sales that otherwise might not have been made.

This "reciprocity effect," if requited, is identical in effect to consensual reciprocity, although the initiating party may be different.

Reciprocity effect—unrequited. This is distinguishable from re-quited reciprocity effect in that the large purchaser is unmoved by the fact that some suppliers or potential suppliers newly purchase from it. In ITT-Canteen (example 4), ITT claimed its purchasing procedures were reciprocity-proof, but the government claimed that potential suppliers of ITT might and did become customers of Canteen nonetheless, and quite unilaterally produced the same effect as if reciprocity had been an ITT objective. Unrequited reciprocity effect may be expected to prove transitional and to disappear as the supplying firms realize that they are limiting their choice but achieving no benefit to themselves. Unrequited reciprocity effect, like hortatory reciprocity, is clearly not harmful.

Coincidental reciprocity. This relationship occurs when two firms purchase each other's products simply as a result of market choices. Many of ITT's suppliers purchased food service from Canteen before the merger, and others would have purchased it in the years following the merger whether or not Canteen was acquired by ITT. This kind of reciprocal relationship would exist with or without other forms of reciprocity. The problem is that it creates legal confusion in statistics showing sets of reciprocal dealings. These problems are, indeed, amenable to statistical treatment,[9] but such showings often have tough going in the courts.

The Economic Theory of Reciprocity Motivation and Effects

A few of the types of reciprocity identified above can be dealt with quickly. Fraudulent reciprocity is surely undesirable per se; coinci-

---

9. One can estimate the fraction of A's sales to B's suppliers that would occur if there were random pairing of buyers and sellers, etc.

dental reciprocity should be regarded as a normal market phenomenon and presumed benign (indeed efficient) unless something other than reciprocity has distorted the market mechanism; hortatory reciprocity and unrequited reciprocity effect seem to be without lasting effects.

Beyond these easy answers lie the hard ones. Will a merger increase the likelihood of reciprocity, and if so will the effects be beneficial or adverse? Because reciprocity is not a single phenomenon, the answer is not unqualified. But if there are cases and cases, then it is the challenge to policy to effectively discriminate between the beneficial and the adverse. In this section I am concerned with motives and predicted effects; in the following section with the law as it has emerged and now stands, and in the final one with such guidelines for policy changes as emerge from the inadequacies of the existing legal stance.

MERGERS AND POSSIBILITIES FOR INCREASED RECIPROCITY

Reciprocity, of course, can exist without merger. Our concern is with merger-induced reciprocity and it is well to start with the obvious proposition that the opportunities for reciprocity may be greatly increased by merger.

Whenever a merger occurs in which an acquired company produces a widely used service or product, the suppliers of the acquiring company are likely to be potential or actual consumers of the products of the acquired company. If they are actual customers, the merger will initially create coincidental reciprocity. When they are potential customers, the opportunity for reciprocity is created. The bare opportunity for reciprocal trading must be present to some extent in virtually every merger, and must be greater the more diversified are a company's products and suppliers. Consider the ITT acquisition of Canteen. Since Canteen provides food service of a kind purchased by virtually every factory, plant, office, school, or hospital, its acquisition by any firm would create opportunity for reciprocal trading. When acquired by a large diversified company these possibilities are more numerous in the sense that the number of reciprocal buying opportunities is directly proportional to the number of potential suppliers of the acquiring firm.[10] But it is probabilities not mere possibili-

---

10. Formally, if a company produces n products using m potential suppliers it already has $m \cdot n$ opportunities for reciprocal buying since any one of its m suppliers might purchase any one of its n products. If the

ties that matter, both in leading to expected effects and in defining the need for policy action.

A mere increase in the number of reciprocal trading opportunities compels only a prediction of a greater number of cases of coincidental reciprocity.[11] For more there must be a decision to utilize the opportunities.

The FTC view,[12] which gained a brief ascendancy within the Department of Justice as well during the McLaren years, is that reciprocal trading opportunities offer a company a new and valuable weapon that is likely to be used. In particular reciprocity is thought to offer a firm a chance to utilize otherwise unutilizable monopsony[13] power to increase its profits.

This view has at least a superficial appeal, and has been embraced by some judges. It is concisely embodied by Judge Cannella in Liquid Carbonic:

> That the merger created the power to procure sales via the systematic application of purchasing power, is clear. The dollar volume of purchases by General Dynamics totalled approximately one-half billion dollars at the time of the merger. Yet it sold the great bulk of its products to the

---

company now acquires a company which produces a single product using r additional potential suppliers, its opportunities for reciprocal dealings increase to:

$$(m + r)(n + 1) = m \cdot n + r \cdot n + r + m.$$

The premerger reciprocity opportunities were $m \cdot n$ and r. The additional reciprocity opportunities are that each old potential supplier may buy the newly added product, which thus creates m potential reciprocal arrangements, and that each of the r new suppliers is a potential customer for each one of the original n products. For numerical illustration suppose $m = 2000$, $n = 10$, and $r = 10$. The premerger reciprocity possibilities are 20,010. The postmerger possibilities rise to 22,110, an increase of 10 percent.

11. If one assumes that there is as well a certain fraction of all trading that is reciprocal due to inertia or irrationality, that fraction too might be maintained as the opportunities increase. I shall neglect this, not as improbable, but as without significant consequence.

12. See generally FTC, *Economic Report on Corporate Mergers*, pp. 323–98.

13. Monopsony is the purchasing equivalent of monopoly power.

United States government. *This state of events deprived the defendant of gaining any competitive advantage from its large scale purchasing power.* The situation was remedied by the acquisition of Liquid Carbonic. This union *permitted the purchasing power to be asserted* against the vendors of the defendant who now used, for the first time in any significant degree, a product manufactured by General Dynamics. [Emphasis supplied.][14]

This theory can be illustrated by a look at facts developed in the case. Raytheon supplied roughly $10 million of product annually to General Dynamics, and purchased roughly $250,000 annually of carbon dioxide (CO_2), Liquid Carbonic's principal product. General Dynamics was presumed to be able to coerce or persuade Raytheon to purchase its CO_2 from Liquid Carbonic. This was, so the argument goes, a small concession for Raytheon to make to such a good customer. The ratio of purchases from Raytheon by General Dynamics (10 million dollars) to sales to Raytheon by CO_2 suppliers (one quarter million dollars) is 40. This number is defined as the "leverage ratio." In the leverage argument, the higher the ratio, the more persuasive the suggestion by GD that Raytheon buy its CO_2 from Liquid Carbonic. (See *United States v. General Dynamics,* p. 61, for examples of selected leverage ratios running from 17 to 693.) According to this theory, the higher the leverage ratio the greater the probability of reciprocity in one form or another. A closer look, however, modifies the conclusion.

Accept the General Dynamics-Raytheon facts as here stated, and suppose that as a result GD did have substantial monopsony power over Raytheon. It might have utilized its power *directly* by compelling Raytheon to sell to it more cheaply, to improve the quality of its product, etc. It might have done so *indirectly* by requiring Raytheon to provide GD with some additional product or service at less than market cost as a condition of its basic purchase. This would be a form of a *tying* arrangement. Alternatively it might have done so *indirectly* by compelling Raytheon to buy from GD a product that GD produces, even if Raytheon otherwise would have purchased it not at all, or elsewhere. This is noncoincidental reciprocity. That direct and indirect uses of this power are alternatives to one another may be quickly seen. If Raytheon's profits (direct or indirect) on its sales to General Dynamics amount to (say) 5 percent or $500,000, the maximum GD can extract from Raytheon by using its power is $500,000. If GD

---

14. *United States v. General Dynamics,* 258 F.Supp. 36 (S.D. N.Y. 1966) at 61.

does it by a direct price concession, it cannot also do it via reciprocity, or tying. If GD forgoes demanding direct price concessions, it can use its power indirectly, but it cannot disadvantage Raytheon by more than $500,000 per year, since the alternative of losing the GD business would only cost Raytheon $500,000 per year.

The interesting question is not *whether* a firm with monopsony power can use its market power indirectly, but *when* it will pay it to do so. Consider further the example. Assume that General Dynamics's profits on the sales of carbon dioxide are 25 percent of sales (to make the argument I am here assuming an unrealistically high rate). Then the acquisition of $250,000 of new Raytheon business for Liquid Carbonic would be worth $62,500. But this amounts to only ⅝ of 1 percent of the total dollar volume of its *purchases* from Raytheon. Even a 1 percent decrease in the price of the supplies it purchased from Raytheon would be more profitable to General Dynamics than a reciprocal requirement.[15] Given its monopsony power, such a negotiated price reduction was possible. It is this alternative of *direct* use of its purchasing power that Judge Cannella and the leverage theory neglect.

More formally let L (the leverage ratio) be the ratio (for a firm with monopsony power) of its purchases from a company to its potential sales to them.[16] Let π be its rate of profits on such sales. If firm can achieve a discount, d, on its purchases it will be better off using its purchasing power directly whenever $d > \pi/L$.[17] Notice that d is *inversely* related to L, and thus, contrary to the argument above, high leverage (which brings power) makes it relatively attractive to seek a direct discount. Where leverage is *low*, reciprocity may pay, but here monopsony power is likely also to be low.

---

15. I neglect here the possibility (which may in fact have been germane to this case) that profits on government sales would be *less* since such sales were on cost-plus contracts. I am concerned with direct versus indirect use of power not with the special problem of compelling efficient and competitive behavior of firms operating without any incentive to keep costs down.

16. Obviously there is more to monopsony power than the leverage ratio, as here defined. Thus even on its own terms the leverage theory of reciprocity would be subject to criticism. But the criticism in the text seems to me to be decisive.

17. If P and S are, respectively, dollar volume of purchases and potential sales, $L = P/S$. Direct discounts are preferred if $dP > \pi S$, from which, $d > \pi/L$.

This refutation of the leverage theory is sometimes extended to provide an alternative polar view: that direct use of market power is *always* simpler than indirect and thus that the use of indirect means (such as tying or reciprocity) is never used to exercise monopsony power, but instead is presumptive evidence of a real efficiency in such a use.[18]

POSITIVE MOTIVES FOR PRACTICING MERGER-INDUCED RECIPROCITY

While the Everest theory of reciprocity ("because it is there") and the leverage hypothesis seem unpersuasive, there *are* a variety of real situations in which profit seeking firms may be motivated to enter into reciprocal dealings—coercively or consensually—and they are not equally adverse or benign from the social point of view. I mean here to suggest several motives, rather than to treat them exhaustively.

Exercising otherwise unexercisable monopoly or monopsony power. It may not always be possible for holders of market power to exercise it directly, either because some prices are fixed by regulation, or because the price discrimination required for its full utilization would be difficult or illegal. For example, in the Waugh case, the Armour Company evidently held monopsony power against the railroads. Because railroads were not permitted by the ICC to grant rebates to large shippers, an offer to cut rates was not an available response to the threat of a shipper to shift his freight business elsewhere. But an indirect rebate—giving up one's freedom of choice and thus arguably paying too much for draft gears—was available. Thus neglecting the fraudulent aspects (Armour's unutilized monopsony power was used

---

18. This view is perhaps most widely associated with the Bowman-Bork view of vertical restraints. See generally Ward Bowman, "Tying Arrangements and the Leverage Problem," 67 YALE LAW JOURNAL 19 (1957); Robert H. Bork, "The Rule of Reason and the Per Se Concept: Price Fixing and Market Division II," 75 YALE LAW JOURNAL 373 (1966); Ferguson, "Tying Arrangements." This criticism is also implicit in the Stigler Task Force's (reprinted in BNA, *Antitrust and Trade Regulation Report,* no. 413 [June 10, 1969]) conclusion about reciprocity: "The economic threat to competition from reciprocity (reciprocal buying arrangements) is either small or nonexistent: monopoly power in one commodity is not effectively exploited by manipulating the price of an unrelated commodity." For a more extended statement see Stigler's "Working Paper" on reciprocity.

by agents on their own account rather than by the company) this seems a clear use of directly unutilizable market power. If the regulations against rebating had social merit, this use of reciprocity was antisocial. In this case, railroads were the victims of the meatpacker's market power. Notice that if the railroad had had monopoly power over the meatpacker it might have used reciprocity by forcing, e.g., Armour to acquire Waugh and then to sell it draft gears at below cost, as a condition for the railroad permitting Armour to ship its products at the established rates.[19]

Whether, generally, use of otherwise unutilizable market power is socially desirable depends upon allocative and redistributive values. Our general bias is that use of market power to raise prices is inefficient allocatively, and unless the redistribution is from advantaged to disadvantaged (e.g., farmers, workers) it is unlikely to be sufficient to offset an adverse presumption.

Achieving real economies in purchasing or selling in either market. Because buying and selling are necessary but not costless activities for many firms, it may be that the transactions costs involved in repeated search and contracting are high and that long-term contracts (implicit or explicit) reduce costs. Reciprocal trading may provide a convenient, search-free pairing device for buyers and sellers in which each party is kept honest by the other's reciprocal position. This sort of reciprocity would surely be regarded as reducing socially excessive transactions costs and thus providing a beneficial real economy. If the economy is passed on to consumers in part or in whole, it may benefit them as well.

It may be argued that any such benefit is alternatively attainable, by long-term requirement contracts or by vertical integration. That is true enough, but hardly decisive: such alternatives may be more costly, and indeed may be more restrictive because they are more rigid.

---

19. Thus reciprocity can represent use of indirect market power *in either direction.* A railroad's indirect uses of market power, via tying, play an important role in the legal side of our story. See *Northern Pacific Railway Co. v. United States,* 356 U.S. 1 (1958), a key tying case that is cited as a precedent for the Court's stand on reciprocity in *FTC v. Consolidated Foods Corp.,* 380 U.S. 592 (1965). Here Northern Pacific compelled buyers of its land to ship on its railroad. Why did they not merely raise the price of land? Because there was other land available. Their monopoly power lay not in land, but in railroading. Why did they not raise their rates? The ICC would not permit it.

The presence of this sort of a real economy seems most persuasive in an industry with high selling costs, and relatively little market power in particular firms. Colluding firms would agree, and a monopolistic firm would choose, to avoid such excessive expenditures. But an individual seller (buyer) cannot unilaterally retreat from such expenditures if his customers (suppliers) are influenced by things other than price, quality, and service. If, for example, other things being equal, a potential customer will buy from the seller who entertains him most lavishly, the firm must either entertain, lose sales, or cut price, etc. If price cutting is habitually met immediately, or if buyers prefer a world in which they are entertained, the industry may be characterized by excessive selling expenses. Here reciprocity may provide a preferred alternative.

Whether this sort of economy is even to be expected will be related to the market structure of the acquired firm's market, its selling costs, and the acquiring firm's purchasing costs.

Achieving entry into a new market, or efficient scale therein.   If Armour had wanted to enter the draft gear industry, the facts of the Waugh case suggest that it could have used reciprocity as a device to get a sizable toehold in such a market.[20] More generally any firm with monopsony power over suppliers could use that power to get a subsidiary established in an industry supplying its suppliers. Moreover, reciprocity might provide both the necessary minimum scale and the stability of demand requisite for efficient operation.

For evaluation, we need more information as to why the firm wished to enter, and why it utilized this device. If the market being entered were a tight oligopoly with significant entry barriers, such entry might be the most effective way to forge a vigorous new competitor; alternatively such entry might be designed to tighten a loose oligopoly, or even to monopolize. (The last possibility is considered more fully below.)

If reciprocity permits competitor-increasing entry, or if it rationalizes production in an overly fragmented industry, it may prove procompetitive and socially beneficial; if instead it provides a focal point for quasi-agreement, it might well be anticompetitive. If it sta-

---

20. Such an opportunity might exist as well if it entered *de novo* and then practiced reciprocity to gain market share. This alternative may or may not have been viable. See chapter 10.

bilizes one firm's market share and increases the volatility of all other firms' share it may well give that firm a dominant competitive advantage. Here one test seems relatively specific: what is the market structure in the acquired firm's industry and how does reciprocity affect it?

Reciprocity as a predatory device in the acquired firm's market. The use of reciprocity to gain market share, to foreclose competitors, and to raise barriers to future entrants is certainly a possibility. This device might be used along with or instead of predatory price cutting in an attempt to monopolize.

The predatory hypothesis, generally, has been given short shrift by most economists lately, reacting against a dominant legal tradition that regarded the propensity to cut prices below costs in order to drive competitors from the market as a real and present danger. Section 2 of the Sherman Act embraces the practice within the monopolization and attempts to monopolize concepts, and the legislative history and continuing legal interpretation of the Robinson-Patman Act, "reveal a continuing dread of the device."[21]

Given an impressive array of authorities relegating the predatory hypothesis to a back burner, one is tempted to apply the conclusion to possible predatory use of reciprocity, and indeed at one point I did just that. On reflection I think this may be inviting error by analogy. For that reason, before looking at *reciprocity* as a predatory device, it is worth looking at the problem in the more usual context: price cutting by a firm with a "deep pocket" that permits it to subsidize ("cross-subsidize") losses in a market while its less well-endowed rivals are forced to bankruptcy, merger, or (at least) a subservient position.[22]

---

21. John S. McGee, "Predatory Price Cutting: The Standard Oil (N.J.) Case," 1 JOURNAL OF LAW AND ECONOMICS, no. 1, 137–38 (October 1958).

22. There is a large literature both on the law of "attempts" cases, and the economic sense of it all. I do not attempt more than a capsule statement in the text. With respect to the economic literature, see in addition to McGee, ibid., and Turner (whose conclusion was cited on p. 71 above), "Conglomerate Mergers and Section 7 of the Clayton Act," 78 HARVARD LAW REVIEW 1339–48 (May 1965); M. A. Adelman, *A & P: A Study in Price-Cost Behavior and Public Policy* (Cambridge, Mass., 1959), pp. 372–79; Lester G. Telser, "Abusive Trade Practices: An Economic Analysis," 30 LAW AND CONTEMPORARY PROBLEMS 488 (Summer 1965); Telser, "Cutthroat Competition and the Long Purse," 9 JOURNAL OF LAW

I shall then argue that predatory reciprocity is a good deal less improbable (a priori) than predatory pricing.

The central question in the context of merger policy is not whether predatory behavior is possible (which it surely is), nor whether it is ever profitable (which it surely may be), nor yet whether it is always or usually sensible (which it surely is not); it is instead whether the conditions that might make it profitable are sufficiently likely that anticipation of predatory behavior ought to play a role in Section 7 cases where it can be reached "in its incipiency." Predatory behavior, if it is proven, is reachable under Section 2 and under the Robinson-Patman Act where some likely examples are to be found.[23]

The a priori case against merger-induced predatory behavior has three prongs: (1) a firm with market power in one market may use it there directly or in another market (or divide it), but not use it fully in both; in general it does not pay to use it indirectly; (2) the notion of subsidizing losses in one market by profits earned elsewhere does not generally commend itself unless a small investment in a "war of survival" promises handsome long-term re-

---

AND ECONOMICS, no. 2, 259–77 (October 1966); Richard Zerbe, "The American Sugar Refinery Company 1887–1914: The Story of a Monopoly," 12 JOURNAL OF LAW AND ECONOMICS, no. 2, 339–75 (October 1969); Kenneth G. Elzinga, "Predatory Pricing: The Case of the Gunpowder Trust," 13 JOURNAL OF LAW AND ECONOMICS, no. 1, 223–40 (April 1970); Basil S. Yamey, "Predatory Price Cutting: Notes and Comments," 15 JOURNAL OF LAW AND ECONOMICS, no. 1, 129–42 (April 1972). Yamey resists the general tide, with a case study showing use of predatory tactics to inhibit future entrants. The most steadfast economic voice in support of predatory behavior has been the Bureau of Economics, Federal Trade Commission.

With respect to the legal literature, an introduction to "attempts" may be found in Hibner, "Attempts to Monopolize: A Concept in Search of Analysis," 34 ABA ANTITRUST LAW JOURNAL 165–77 (1967); and Smith, "Attempt to Monopolize: Its Elements and Their Definition," 27 GEORGE WASHINGTON LAW REVIEW 227–44 (1958). A most impressive survey is Cooper, "Attempts and Monopolization: A Mildly Expansionary Answer to the Prophylactic Riddle of Section Two," 72 MICHIGAN LAW REVIEW 373–462 (January 1974).

23. The paucity of successful Section 2 cases might be argued either to support the notion that predatory behavior is highly infrequent, and therefore not worth too much concern, or that it is so difficult to detect that it ought to be caught in its incipiency before it is too late.

turns, conditions which rarely occur; and (3) where such conditions are found, there is almost always a cheaper alternative such as acquisition of one's rivals, collusion with them, or simply finding an accommodation. Consider each briefly.

1. While it is quite true that market power can be used directly or indirectly, this only serves to refute naïve arguments that suggest it can be used in market after market by a firm which thus extends its initial monopoly power to an ever-widening sphere.[24] Are there not times when a firm may profitably choose to *shift* its power from one market to another? Three possibilities come to mind. First it may find its power partially unutilizable in the original market, for any of a number of reasons (regulated prices, statutes limiting price discrimination, fear of antitrust prosecution) and thus be seeking a place to use it; second, the same degree of market power may be more effective in one market than another because the barrier to future entry is greater. In such a case the same degree of monopoly power provides a longer stream of monopoly benefits in the better blockaded industry.[25] Moreover, the predatory behavior may itself be a way of deterring entry.[26] Third, the same expenditure may yield quicker and richer results one place than another. For one example, the conditions of demand and cost may be such that one potential monopoly is more quickly achievable and much more profitable than another. These conditions are not necessarily so improbable as to be negligible.

2. The contention that investment in cross-subsidization is likely to be unwarranted, is not a logical conclusion. The possibility of this as a conglomerate phenomenon was noted as early as 1955 by Corwin Edwards,[27] and it is dealt with extensively in the FTC

---

24. A not routinely refuted possibility is that a firm might use its market power one year in Market A, and another year in Market B. If one year's predatory use of market power could permanently cripple rivals, it might thus widen its monopoly to both markets.

25. This is most easily seen in vertical situations, but it is generalizable. A manufacturing firm with 50 percent of its market may be unable to raise price toward monopoly levels without inducing a flood of entrants. By vertically integrating to acquire 50 percent of a limited basic input, it may effectively assure its 50 percent share, independent of the number of competitors for the rest.

26. See Yamey, "Predatory Price Cutting."

27. Corwin Edwards, "Conglomerate Bigness as a Source of Power," National Bureau of Economic Research, *Business Concentration and Public Policy* (New York, 1955), p. 350.

Economic Report.[28]   The following excerpt concisely states the hypothesis:

> Selling in many markets, a conglomerate firm has profit centers relatively insulated from each other. . . . Conglomerates consequently have options for strategies in individual markets that are unavailable to other firms. . . . Among the options open to conglomerates is "cross-subsidization."
>
> This is the ability to offset losses in one profit center by gains in another. Its practice depends on the extent of a firm's diversification compared to that of its competitors, as well as on the structure of the various markets in which it operates. . . . A large multimarket firm operating in competitive markets only is unable to subsidize expansion in one market by gains from another. But when a large conglomerate firm operates substantially in highly concentrated industries, it can earn profits above competitive levels. The greater these "excess" profits, the greater is the ability to employ cross-subsidization tactics to enter, condition, expand, or defend any of its markets.

This might make sense in overcoming an entry barrier into a profitable industry, a nonpredatory case dealt with above, or it might make sense in a predatory context in rather special conditions: where exit of rivals might be relatively quick, but entry or re-entry both slow and impeded. In such a case a small investment in below-cost pricing, with its attendant short-term losses, might drive one's rivals quickly to bankruptcy, destruction of their capacity, and be followed by a long period in which the predator would be able to charge high prices and enjoy the fruits of having created a monopoly.

3.   The "available alternative" doctrine may be concisely stated this way: since both predator and victim lose money during the predatory period, there is an available bargain that is superior for both and therefore a division that is superior for each. Victim, if he is rational, ought to accept a bribe to exit, merge, or behave rather than struggle in a manifestly losing cause. I am left largely unpersuaded by this sort of logical argument, because it seems to apply a fortiori to wars, strikes, and other observable phenomena; phenomena that can be understood as rational in terms of the absence of acceptable agreement mechanisms, varying perceptions, and the role of threat reinforcement to keep threats credible.

What *is* impressive to me about the attack on the predatory pricing hypothesis is not the a priori case sketched above, but the lack of

---

28. FTC, *Economic Report on Corporate Mergers*, pp. 398–457.

documented cases in which predatory pricing has been proven, and the substantial doubt raised about even those cases, such as Standard Oil and the Gunpowder Trust that were widely thought to be classics of their kind. For this reason it seems sensible to accept the view that there is time enough to deal with predatory pricing when it occurs, rather than as an incipient danger in conglomerate acquisitions.

But the possibility of predatory reciprocity via conglomerate acquisition seems to me much more likely, a priori, and thus to deserve close attention empirically to see if indeed it has occurred. Referring to the three kinds of arguments cited:

1. Unutilized or unutilizable purchasing power may well exist for large companies like General Dynamics or ITT. Their suppliers may be unable to give direct price concessions without having them spread to all of their customers, or without running the risk of Robinson-Patman Act violations. Moreover, the suppliers may, at relatively little cost to them but at relatively great benefit to the acquired firm, shift to purchasing from the acquired firm, particularly if it is understood that the latter will meet competitive terms. Thus, it may pay the monopsonist to use his power indirectly.

2. The required cross-subsidy may be relatively small (in direct purchasing power forgone) but provide a quick increase in market share for the subsidiary that is the beneficiary of the reciprocity. Moreover, increasing one's market share at fixed prices does create a barrier to future entrants, except to those able to utilize similar reciprocal relationships.[29]

3. Finally, the device may impose a difficult burden on competitors in the acquired firm's market, without great cost to the parent company. Competitors losing market share to the reciprocating giant may cut prices in return, but with the certainty of inviting matching cuts by the reciprocator. Smaller, poorer rivals are unlikely to be able to gain in the long run by starting a price war with a larger, richer competitor. Their most attractive option may be to seek their own merger partner, if a suitable one exists, or seek an accommodation with the reciprocating firm.

In short, while the conditions for predatory behavior being sensible are somewhat special, those special conditions seem much more realistic with respect to indirect use of purchasing power than with

---

29. The government, as one of its bases for opposing some mergers, has argued precisely this: that if permitted they will trigger further mergers which will in the end transform industry structure.

direct price warfare. As an empirical matter, I have found no evidence that predatory reciprocity occurs on a large scale or is a problem. This may be due more to the fact the problem has not been closely studied than to the fact that it is conclusively shown to be unimportant, and in any event the vigorously hostile stance of the McLaren years (and since) would surely have inhibited any attempt to use it. Whether if reciprocity were not anathematized it would occur, remains to be seen.[30]

Reciprocity as an alternative to price competition in the acquired firm's market. For any of a variety of reasons a firm may not wish (or be able) to cut prices as a means of increasing sales. In such circumstances its offer to its potential customers to buy from them reciprocally (on terms favorable to the customer as seller) may be an indirect means of increasing its sales.

Such a desire to avoid direct price cutting can arise in numerous ways: (1) The seller may be (undesirably) attempting to evade a public policy that has fixed a minimum price. A firm can evade minimum wage legislation by forcing its employees to live in company-supplied housing as a condition of employment, and charging over-market rentals. A broker may hold excessive balances in a bank with a large trust department because the broker is not allowed to give the bank a cut-rate brokerage commission; (2) sellers may tacitly agree (usually undesirably) to avoid price competition in an oligopolistic setting because in that way they can prevent breakaway competition. Reciprocity, like advertising and product differentiation, is a form of nonprice competition that can be used to prevent more vigorous direct competition; (3) an oligopolist can (desirably) evade a tacit agreement not to compete, by secret concessions in the form of reciprocal dealing. Like unsystematic price discrimination, this may be a pro-competitive force in a noncompetitive market; (4) the danger of ex-

---

30. With respect to conglomerate cross-subsidization more generally, it is all but impossible to evaluate on the basis of published data because most companies do not make public operating statements that permit distinguishing performance of separate divisions. Requiring such division-by-division reporting, if it could be accomplished on a uniform and economically sound basis, would certainly be useful for research in this area. Whether data collected by the Census of Manufacturers would serve these purposes, and if so whether it could be conveniently utilized might repay inquiry. A study, once and for all establishing or refuting cross-subsidization assertions, would be a welcome addition to the literature.

cessive competition in periods of general excess capacity and cyclically depressed economic conditions may make competitors (desirably or undesirably) look for more restricted—even more genteel—forms of competition—including reciprocity.

Once again, a key discriminating clue to the effects of such behavior if it occurs is likely to be found in the market structure and behavior in the market of the acquired firm. But here prediction is more complex, for (2) and (3) both are characterized by oligopolistic structure.

SUMMARY ON EFFECTS

Reciprocity is potentially many things, and with varied effects. Enough has been said to suggest that the "sneaking art" of reciprocity may in some circumstances be profitable to the practicer. In such cases the effect may be pro- or anticompetitive. Additionally, it may simply be an unproductive aspect of a market system that is imperfect, in which purchasing and sales agents pursue an easier life.[31]

For policy purposes it would be nice to be able to discriminate between the beneficial and the harmful. Ideally, this is what the legal standards achieve.

The Legal Status of Reciprocity

The CCH *Trade Regulation Reporter* currently characterizes reciprocity as a "recent and not thoroughly explored area of antitrust" (¶1665). As of the early sixties the practice was arguably legal, except where demonstrably coercive efforts had been used. The Waugh, Mechanical Mfg., and California Packing cases, cited on page 221, were the only ones and the most recent of them was 1937. All three were FTC Cease and Desist orders charging violations of FTC §5, all involved manifestly coercive behavior, and none was appealed to the courts. As the trade relations fad spread in the early 1960s, consensual reciprocity seemed legal—regrettably so to observers such as Hausman who urged new legislation,[32] less so to others such as

---

31. Patrick O'Malley, President of Canteen, in his testimony in the ITT case denigrated reciprocity for providing "an excuse to purchasing and a crutch to salesmen."

32. R. M. Hausman, "Reciprocal Dealing and the Antitrust Laws," 77 HARVARD LAW REVIEW 873 (1964).

Harsha[33] who saw a rising and perhaps unthinking adverse reaction. By the end of the decade all this had changed. Allegations of illegality had been made in a variety of cases, under various statutes, including Sections 1 and 2 of the Sherman Act and Section 7 of the Clayton Act, and the FTC announced (on Sept. 1, 1970) that reciprocal dealings involving not insubstantial amounts of commerce would be regarded by it as unmistakably violative of FTC §5.

SOME STATUTORY CONFUSION

If today reciprocity law suffers from some confusion, part of the cause is in the multiplicity of statutes. The first important court-decided reciprocity case was Consolidated Foods.[34] This was a §7 case, and the Supreme Court's 1965 opinion makes the very basic holding that reciprocity (including contractual and consensual) is "one of the congeries of anti-competitive practices at which the antitrust laws are aimed." The key cases cited in support of this proposition are, however, *tying* cases, although to my knowledge tying has never played a major role in decided §7 cases. Of the cited cases, the International Salt case[35] had found tying illegal under both Sherman §1 and Clayton §3 while the later Northern Pacific case was only a §1 case.[36] The first (and so far only) tried Section 1 *reciprocity* case was not to be decided until 1966. This was the General Dynamics (Liquid Carbonic) case, a district court opinion never appealed.

The linkage between Sherman §1, Clayton §7, and Clayton §3 made implicitly by Justice Douglas in Consolidated Foods, and explicitly by Judge Cannella in Liquid Carbonic, comes by analogy with tying contracts which by this stage were virtually per se illegal if an

---

33. Harsha, "The Conglomerate Merger."

34. The first of the modern cases is *United States v. Ingersol Rand Corp.,* 320 F.2d 509 (3d Cir. 1963), affirming an opinion of the District Court, 218 F.Supp. 530 (W.D. Pa. 1963), granting a preliminary injunction against a merger which might have been anticompetitive in a number of ways, one of which involved reciprocity. Both because reciprocity plays a small role, and because it is a preliminary injunction case, it is not later relied upon.

35. *International Salt Co. v. United States,* 332 U.S. 392 (1947).

36. *Northern Pacific Railway Co. v. United States,* 356 U.S. 1 (1958). Because this involved tying of a service (freight) it is not covered under the provisions of Clayton § 3, which do not apply to services.

agreement could be inferred covering a not insubstantial amount of commerce. I shall consider the analogy briefly below.

To complete this statutory run-down, Sherman §2 has been used once in a monopolization case, involving allegations that General Motors used reciprocity as part of its monopolization of the loco-motive industry, a case, however, that was subsequently dropped.[37] And §2 attempt charges are now included in all the Department of Justice reciprocity suits.

THE ANALOGY OF TYING AND RECIPROCITY

The formal symmetry between tying and reciprocity is complete. If I have monopoly power over you in terms of a primary product P which I sell and you want, I may well be able to exercise it in one of three ways, or in some combination thereof: (*a*) by the terms of sale of P; (*b*) by requiring you also to purchase some product S_1 at terms favor-able to me (tying); (*c*) by requiring you to acquire and sell me some product S_2 at terms favorable to me (reciprocity). Similarly if I have monopsony power over you in my purchases of your product P, I can exercise it (*a*) by the terms of purchase of P; (*b*) by requiring you to purchase some product S_3 at terms favorable to me (reciprocity); (*c*) by requiring you also to sell me some product S_4 at terms favorable to me (tying). With respect to either monopoly or monopsony power, cases (*b*) and (*c*)—tying and reciprocity—are alternatives to each other and to direct use of market power. To each of the earlier listed forms of reciprocity there is a precisely analogous form of tying contract.

But formal symmetry need not sensibly dictate legally symmetri-cal treatment, even in the absence of particular statutory language. Possibilities are not probabilities, and different expectations may well surround tying and reciprocity. Thus, Ferguson (see footnote 3) after considering their effects found reciprocity much less anticompetitive than tying, whereas Turner (see footnote 22, p. 1387) felt that "reciprocity, even more than the tying arrangements it so closely resembles, has little or nothing to be said in its favor."

---

37. *United States v. General Motors Corp.,* [1961–1970 Transfer Binder], *CCH Trade Regulation Reporter* ¶45,063 (Case 1733) (1963). The charge was brought in 1963 and dropped in 1967.

Despite the use of the tying analogy to bring consensual reciprocity into the antitrust ambit, it has led a separate legal life. To be sure the Sherman §1 (and FTC §5) per se ban on tying if agreement can be inferred has been extended to reciprocity.[38] But Clayton §3, which covers tying, uses language that seems to exclude reciprocity,[39] and all the recent decided reciprocity cases have involved mergers, an area where tying has been virtually ignored.[40]

CONSOLIDATED FOODS

I have already noted that Justice Douglas swept reciprocity into the picture by analogy to the Section 1 treatment of tying. The Consolidated Foods case involved the *merger* of a large food processor and distributor with a leading manufacturer of dehydrated onion and garlic, products utilizable by many of Consolidated's suppliers, and thus created the possibility of reciprocity. Because it was a Section 7 case it needed to be "concerned with probabilities not certainties," and as a

---

38. The General Dynamics (Liquid Carbonic) case, *United States v. General Dynamics,* 258 F.Supp. 36 (S.D. N.Y. 1966), is the only decided case. But a flood of reciprocity consent decrees in the years since underline this conclusion. The Canteen opinion, *United States v. ITT (Canteen),* 1971 *CCH Trade Cases* ¶73,619 (N.D. Ill. 1971) at footnotes 43 and 44, cites 10 consent Sherman Act decrees prohibiting reciprocity and reciprocity-related activities and 7 affidavits of voluntary compliance with the FTC containing similar prohibitions, all subsequent to 1968. At least 10 more Sherman Act consent decrees on the subject have been entered since. See generally *CCH Trade Cases* Special Index on U.S. Antitrust Consent Decrees, annually, for a complete listing. As prototypical of these see *United States v. United States Steel,* 1969 *CCH Trade Cases* ¶72,826 (W.D. Pa. 1969).

39. Section 3 says, in pertinent part: "That it shall be unlawful for any person engaged in commerce, in the course of such commerce, to lease or make a *sale or contract for sale* of goods, wares, merchandise, machinery, supplies, or other commodities, . . . on the condition, agreement, or understanding that the lessee or purchaser thereof shall not use or deal in the goods, wares, merchandise, machinery, supplies, or other commodities of a *competitor or competitors of the lessor or seller,* where the effect of such lease, sale, or contract for sale or such condition, agreement or understanding may be to substantially lessen competition or tend to create a monopoly in any line of commerce." [Emphasis supplied.]

40. It is treated *en passant* in the ITT Grinnell and Hartford cases where the sale of Grinnell sprinkler systems might be tied to the sale of fire insurance.

result an acquisition would violate Section 7 if as a result "the probability of a lessening of competition is shown."[41] Thus, the Court asserts
but never discusses whether practicing noncoercive reciprocity is illegal. It turns instead to the question of whether a merger creates the
probability of illegal reciprocity. Justice Douglas, for the Court, extended the legal prohibition well beyond the probability of practice of
coercive reciprocity that would be directly covered by the old FTC
cases. First he was prepared to infer a sufficient probability from (*a*)
the increased opportunities for reciprocity, (*b*) Consolidated's indicated intent to urge its suppliers to purchase from Gentry, and (*c*) a
limited number of episodes in which these urgings succeeded. This
opinion reversed the Court of Appeals's conclusion that overall the
attempt to practice reciprocity had proven ineffective. Second, and
more significantly, the Court was prepared to treat consensual reciprocity as all but indistinguishable from coercive:

> We do not go so far as to say that any acquisition, no matter how
> small, violates §7 if there is a probability of reciprocal buying. Some
> situations may amount only to *de minimis*. But where, as here, the acquisi-
> tion is of a company that commands a substantial share of a market, a
> finding of probability of reciprocal buying by the Commission, whose
> expertise the Congress trusts, should be honored, if there is substantial
> evidence to support it.
> The evidence is in our view plainly substantial. Reciprocity was tried
> over and again and it sometimes worked. The industry structure was
> peculiar, Basic being the leader with Gentry closing the gap. Moreover
> there is evidence, as the Commission found, "that *many buyers have de-
> termined that their source of supply may best be protected by a policy of
> buying from two suppliers.*" [Emphasis supplied.]

This seems to me to have broken new legal ground. Hortatory
evidence carried great weight, and consensual reciprocity and reciprocity effect were included without any attempt to demonstrate the
existence of an agreement. If the previous analogies with the status
of tying were valid, Consolidated Foods extended the provisions
against tying arrangements beyond agreements, whether coerced,
contracted, or simply inferred from a course of dealings, or it pushed
reciprocity beyond the tying rules.

---

41. Both quotes are from the second paragraph of Court's opinion,
and define the central issue of the case. The first is itself a quote from
Brown Shoe Co. v. United States, 370 U.S. 294 (1962).

Mr. Justice Stewart, in a concurring opinion,[42] attempted to avoid this extension of the illegality. He deplored reliance on "slipshod information confusingly presented and ambiguous in its implications." His central point is stated as follows:

Certainly the mere effort at reciprocity cannot be the basis for finding the probability of a significant alteration in the market structure. Section 7 does not punish intent. No matter how bent on reciprocity Consolidated might have been, if its activities would not have the requisite probable impact on competition, it cannot be held to have violated this law. And, I think, it is not enough to say that the merger is illegal merely because the reciprocity attempts "sometimes worked." If the opportunity for reciprocity itself is not a violation of the Act when the merger occurs, then some standard must be established for determining how effective reciprocity must be before the merger is subject to invalidation.

Notice that while Stewart resisted the first of the Douglas extensions—inferring sufficient probability from opportunity and intent—he apparently acquiesced in the second—the extension of illegality to consensual reciprocity as a matter of course if in fact it occurred, if one found substantial evidence to suppose it had occurred to a significant number of suppliers.

LATER CASES

While these two opinions in Consolidated Foods map the range of most of the subsequent debate about the Section 7 reciprocity cases a more extreme position was urged by the McLaren Antitrust Division, and has proven persuasive in two preliminary injunction cases. The extreme position went beyond the Douglas position (opportunity plus intent, plus some demonstrated effect) to urge a finding of probability on the grounds of opportunity alone. In the three ITT cases, the Department of Justice argued that merger-created opportunities for reci-

---

42. The case had come up from the FTC via the U.S. Court of Appeals for the Seventh Circuit. The FTC had ruled the opportunity for reciprocal buying was sufficient to violate Section 7. The Court of Appeals, looking to ten years of postacquisition evidence, found that although reciprocity had been tried, it had had no effect. Stewart (and Harlan) concurred (rather than dissenting) on the ground that FTC conclusions of fact should not be easily overturned.

procity plus leverage were a primary basis for a finding of probable adverse effect of the merger. Despite the fact that ITT had well-established policies against reciprocity, and a profit center organization that would have made systematic reciprocity difficult to achieve, and counter-productive for purchasing centers, the acquisitions increased the possibilities for reciprocity by a company with great purchasing power.[43] This the government urged should be enough.[44] Had they succeeded generally in this attempt, Mr. McLaren's view that Section 7 could readily embrace conglomerate acquisitions, would have been confirmed.

The first case after Consolidated (decided only two months later) was Penick & Ford,[45] wherein Judge Coolahan, in the District Court of New Jersey, took a Stewart-like view in denying possible reciprocity as a sufficient basis to stop a merger with R. J. Reynolds Tobacco Company. But in Allis-Chalmers, the Court of Appeals for the Third Circuit in a 2-1 decision moved toward the Douglas view and indeed relied principally on the possibilities of reciprocity effect in granting preliminary injunctive relief to stop a takeover of Allis-Chalmers by White Consolidated Industries.[46] The dissenting judge in Allis-Chalmers echoes and amplifies Stewart's dissent in Consolidated, "From the barest of facts, the majority have conjured vivid overtones of reciprocity in the rolling-mill industry."

---

43. ITT's practices were even more inhibiting to reciprocity than the kind the government was to later insist on as part of the consent decrees that have become so common.

44. They might have argued, but did not, that the present use of a profit center organization did not assure that at some point in the future the company would not reorganize and attempt to utilize its power to practice reciprocity.

45. *United States v. Penick & Ford and R. J. Reynolds Tobacco Co.*, 242 F.Supp. 518 (D. N.J. 1965). Reynolds, a leading cigarette manufacturer, had acquired Penick & Ford, the fourth largest producer of cornstarch. Cornstarch is used as an adhesive in the paper-box industry, which supplies cigarette manufacturers.

46. *Allis-Chalmers Mfg. Co. v. White Consolidated Industries,* 414 F.2d 506 (3d Cir. 1969), cert. denied 396 U.S. 1009 (1969). The district court had been entirely silent on the reciprocity issue. See 294 F.Supp. 1263 (D. Del. 1969). Because the case involved preliminary injunctive relief in a takeover rather than a final determination on the merits, the significance of the opinions in this case on the role of reciprocity is perhaps diminished.

246 Mergers: Motives, Effects, Policies

All but one of the more recent decisions have retreated toward the Stewart view.[47] Judge Will in Northwest Industries finds (in relevant part):

4. The potential for the practice of reciprocity would be greatly increased since the combined Northwest-Goodrich would have substantial additional purchasing power and more diversified products and services to sell to its suppliers.

5. While it is clear that the potential for reciprocity would be substantially increased, the extent to which actual reciprocity would be practiced and, therefore, the probable actual anti-competitive effect thereof is, on the basis of the present record, difficult if not impossible to forecast.

The court concluded that this was *not* sufficient basis to provide even a preliminary injunction to block Northwest's takeover attempt.[48] Judges Timbers (in Hartford and Grinnell) and Austin (in Canteen) give the reciprocity arguments equally short shrift. A more recent district court case, however, swings back the other way.[49] Judge Battisti, in the Northern District of Ohio, granted a preliminary injunction against White Consolidated Industries's attempt to merge with White Motor Corporation. He relies almost entirely on the mere opportunity for reciprocity effect, citing with approval the earlier Allis-Chalmers decision, although noting that the theory there announced has failed to gain acceptance outside of the Third Circuit.

Where this line of cases leaves us is perhaps in doubt. Table 9–1 summarizes three alternative legal stances. It is my guess that, in §7 cases we are somewhat closer to the Stewart standard than the other ones, but this is not going to be quickly tested, for none of the recent district decisions has any prospect of being appealed,[50] and the Justice

---

47. See the opinion of Judge Will in *United States v. Northwest Industries,* 301 F.Supp. 1066 (N.D. Ill. 1969), and the three ITT opinions cited in footnote 3 above.

48. Courts' reluctance to use the preliminary injunction in takeover attempts was discussed in chapter 7. Thus one might wish to take this case less seriously, particularly since the opinion recognizes that while the government had failed to show probable success of its theory—there was "a very real possibility" that it might win on that theory at trial.

49. *United States v. White Consolidated Industries Inc. and White Motor Corp.,* 323 F.Supp. 1397 (N.D. Ohio 1971).

50. The ITT cases have been settled. Northwest abandoned its takeover attempt and has already reduced its holdings of Goodrich stock from 16.4 to 9.5 percent, and is likely to dispose of the rest. The White Consolidated-White Motor Company merger has been abandoned.

TABLE 9-1

ALTERNATIVE LEGAL STANDARDS WITH RESPECT TO MERGER-INDUCED RECIPROCITY

Types	A. Stewart in Consolidated Foods (1) Opportunity (2) Substantial Evidence of Past or Present	B. Douglas in Consolidated Foods (1) Opportunity (2) Intent (3) Some Episodes	C. Third Circuit, Battisti (1) Opportunity
Fraudulent	Illegal	Illegal	Illegal with opportunity
Coercive	Illegal	Illegal	Illegal with opportunity
Contractual	Illegal	Illegal	Illegal with opportunity
Consensual–agreement including requited reciprocity effect	Illegal	Illegal	Illegal with opportunity
Consensual–agreement in doubt	Legal	Illegal if opportunity and intent	Illegal with opportunity
Nonagreement, hortatory	Legal	Evidence of intent. May be illegal with opportunity	Illegal with opportunity
Reciprocity effect–unrequited	Legal	Illegal if opportunity and intent	Illegal with opportunity
Coincidental	Legal	Legal	Illegal with opportunity

247

Department seems content (at least for the moment) to let stand the retreat from both the Douglas position in Consolidated Foods and the McLaren position in the conglomerate complaints that several of the cases represent. Given the changes on the Supreme Court since 1965, it is not clear what the Court would do on a new case, and no test seems yet on the horizon. It seems likely that further changes on the Court will occur before the issue arises again.

The other important case in the conglomerate merger context is the General Dynamics-Liquid Carbonic case discussed at length previously. Its primary importance was to forge the Section 1 link that had been previously missing. But it was a merger case, and it did result in divestiture of Liquid Carbonic. Its primary importance in the merger-induced reciprocity context is the articulation and development of the leverage hypothesis for inferring opportunity for reciprocity in conglomerate acquisitions. Because opportunity plays a role in all the legal stances, this hypothesis, fallacious though I believe it to be, may continue to play an important role.[51] If the B or C views of table 9–1 prevail, it indeed provides an all but decisive weapon against conglomerate acquisitions by large firms.

Law versus Economics: The Policy Problem

It seems clear that the emerging legal standard for reciprocity concerns "agreement," under both Section 1 and Section 7. The unresolved question concerns when to infer the probability of such agreements in a prospective merger. Whether the agreement is coercive, contractual, or merely consensual matters not. As the earlier discussion of effects suggested however, agreement may provide no guide at all to effect on competition—for an agreement to engage in reciprocity may achieve beneficial economies, or forge an effective entrant into a tightly oligopolistic industry, but it may also provide focus for all sorts of anticompetitive agreement. Even coercive reciprocity, as was present in the Liquid Carbonic case, might have been socially beneficial if it had led to a rationalization of the carbon dioxide industry into a smaller number of efficient producers. Table 9–2 at-

---

51. The rather detailed discussion of what is required to reach an inference of the probability of reciprocity occurring in most of the recent cases mitigates against the single test being decisive. But, as Judge Battisti demonstrated in White Consolidated, the court can if it chooses apply a very simple test.

TABLE 9–2

Potential Conflicts Between Legal Status and Economic Effects

Column groups — Socially Beneficial Effects (cols. 1–6); Socially Adverse Effects (cols. 7–13); No Effect (col. 14).

Legal Status	Industry I — Achieve real efficiency	Industry I — Break tacit cartel	Industry I — Avoid excess competition	Industry II — Achieve real efficiency	Industry II — Foster entry into oligopolistic industry	Supplying Industries — Achieve real efficiency	Industry I — Exercise otherwise unexercisable market power	Industry I — Evade desired price fixing	Industry I — Substitute for price competition	Industry II — Horizontal foreclosure and monopolization	Industry II — Raise entry barriers	Supplying Industries — Squeeze suppliers and jeopardize survival	Supplying Industries — Make entry more difficult to supplying industries	No Effect
Probably illegal														
Fraudulent	X	X					X	X		X	X	X	X	
Coercive	X	X	X	X	X		X	X	X	X	X	X	X	
Contractual, non-coercive	X	X	X	X	X	X		X		X	X		X	
Consensual, agreement inferable	X	X	X	X	X	X		X		X	X		X	
Requited reciprocity effect	X	X	X	X	X	X		X		X	X		X	
Legality in doubt														
Consensual, agreement in doubt	X	X	X	X	X	X		X		X	X		X	
Hortatory														
Unrequited reciprocity effect														X
Probably legal														
Coincidental	X			X		X								X

249

tempts, impressionistically, to highlight the possible conflicts of legal standards and economic effects.

The conflict arises because agreement presumably occurs when it serves the interests of the two parties involved. But it is "third party effects" or externalities that condition economic desirability. The market system is justified because, often, agreements produce socially useful allocations; public policy in the form of legal constraints is required because markets sometimes fail. But to treat all reciprocal agreements as per se market failures, as the law does, represents an assumption not supported by economic analysis.

These effects, for good or for ill, can occur in the industry of the acquiring firm (Industry I in the notation of figure 9–1, page 220), in the industry of the acquired firm (Industry II), and in the supplying industries (Industries III, IV, V). Because extended discussion of the probable competitive effects of reciprocity when it occurs is found elsewhere,[52] I shall not further review this ground. Clearly it is *possible* that (in given circumstances), in each of the industries involved, reciprocal arrangements can lead to a change in the patterns of purchasing and selling, that such changes can affect market shares and concentration ratios, that entry can be stimulated or retarded, and that the likelihood of healthy and vigorous price competition may be enhanced or diminished. These changes may benefit one or both of the reciprocal dealers, and the third-party effects may be beneficial or adverse. Useful analysis, no less than Section 7, deals with probabilities not possibilities, but table 9–2 deals only with possibilities.

To go beyond this it is necessary to introduce either theory or evidence. For example, knowing something about market structures surely makes some outcomes more, and some less, likely. If the supplying industries to Industry I are already tight oligopolies with little price competition, reciprocity is more likely to prove beneficial by providing for some competition, than as a device to eliminate the nonexistent price competition. In Industry I, if the firms have unexercised market power, reciprocity may provide a (socially undesirable) outlet for such power; if their power is fully utilized, this danger seems slight. In the acquired firm's industry (Industry II) whether postacquisition

---

52. See especially Ferguson, "Tying Arrangements"; Turner, "Conglomerate Mergers"; and more complexly Markovits, "Tie-Ins, Reciprocity, and the Leverage Theory," 76 YALE LAW JOURNAL 1397–1472 (June 1967).

reciprocity is a beneficial entry-producing step, or a potentially anti-competitive one, depends importantly upon the market structure, behavior, and the ease of entry in the industry before and after acquisition. Whether there are real efficiencies of scale, of selling and purchasing expenses, etc., depends upon the nature of the product and upon how it is produced and sold.

This suggests the possibility of structural guidelines for legal policy, rather than the single criterion of "agreement." The problem with this is that guidelines may be poorly designed. This seems to me to be the case with the reciprocity guidelines of the Department of Justice.[53]

In addition to rejecting "economies" defenses, unless there are special circumstances and indicating that without more it will challenge mergers where *intent* to practice reciprocity is present, or where *either* party has practiced reciprocity prior to the merger, the guideline provides:

. . . the Department will ordinarily challenge any merger which creates a significant danger of reciprocal buying. Unless it clearly appears that some special market factor makes remote the possibility that reciprocal buying behavior will actually occur, the Department considers that a significant danger of reciprocal buying is present whenever approximately 15% or more of the total purchases in a market in which one of the merging firms ("the selling firm") sells are accounted for by firms which also make substantial sales in markets where the other merging firm ("the buying firm") is both a substantial buyer and a more substantial buyer than all or most of the competitors of the selling firm.

This structural standard however goes wholly to *opportunity* and likelihood of reciprocity, not to effect.

Table 9–3 presents my subjective set of impressions, based on theory, of probable social results of reciprocity, if it is practiced. Its purpose is merely to suggest that looking at market structure in one industry alone is not sufficient for a general set of guidelines. Going beyond this kind of theorizing to empirical verification is a major unfinished task. Until it occurs announcing "guidelines" invites counter-productive results. Suppose table 9–3 is roughly correct; what would it imply about policy? In general, an all but irrebuttable presumption against a merger likely to produce reciprocity

---

53. United States Department of Justice, *Merger Guidelines* (May 30, 1968), ¶19.

TABLE 9–3

Predicted Effects of Reciprocity under Various Market Structures (selected possibilities)

Market Structure in Industry II (Acquired Firm, Selling Firm)	Market Structure in Industry I (Acquiring Firm, Buying Firm)*		
	Market without Unutilized Market Power. Tight Oligopoly or Competitive Market	Loose Oligopoly	Market with Unutilized Market Power
Competitive market Homogeneous product Low-selling costs Easy entry	Neutral or Adverse (probably no effect, but any effect bad)	Adverse (any change will be bad)	Adverse (any change will be bad)
Competitive market Heterogeneous product High-selling costs Easy entry	Beneficial (economy achieving)	Beneficial or Neutral (economy achieving)	Unclear (might achieve economies, but might raise entry barrier and use market power)
Loose oligopoly with impeded entry	Unclear (might tighten oligopoly, but by creating entry may bring efficiency, or more competition)	Unclear (any outcome possible)	Adverse (entry may rigidify)
Tight oligopoly with impeded entry	Beneficial or Neutral	Beneficial (most likely to add competitive element to noncompetitive market)	Unclear (entry may be beneficial but may also rigidify)

* All assume some monopsony power.

should be held only in cases where unambiguously adverse effects are expected. These situations are twofold, in the schema of table 9–3.

1. Acquisition by any firm (with appropriate opportunity to practice reciprocity) of a firm in a highly competitive industry with relatively homogeneous product and low selling costs. In such a case there is so little possibility of an improvement in performance, and some chance of a worsening, that a per se rule seems appropriate. The one exception I can think of is where the industry is overcompetitive and thus chronically depressed. That exception is readily identifiable.

2. Acquisition by a firm with unutilized market power in its original market, of a firm that is in a loosely oligopolistic market. Here foreclosure and an established market share may create a focal point to transform a loose oligopoly into a tight one, and thus provide a profitable but socially undesirable use of market power.

In stopping there I do not mean to suggest that other uses of merger-induced reciprocity are necessarily benign; but only that the probability of occurrence provides a poor basis for invalidating mergers. Obviously, if a merger occurs, the law can, at a later date, attack invidious behavior, including undesirable reciprocity. Indeed the merger itself can be attacked at a later date.

Clearly, Section 7 provides a more permissive standard ("probable effect" rather than "effect") for stopping certain activities. But it is the probable effect on *competition,* not on *behavior* that ought to be controlling, even under Section 7. And the "probable effect" of a "probable use" of reciprocity tends to make the presumed adverse effect on competition somewhat remote.

Summary

Merger-induced reciprocity is potentially many different forms of behavior, and there is no easy association between form and effect beyond the extreme forms of fraudulent and coincidental reciprocity. Even such conclusions as that hortatory reciprocity and unrequited reciprocity effect are unlikely to have any significant effect whatsoever are of limited use because to distinguish them in practice from other forms of reciprocity that have greater effect is difficult and, even where possible, may require more statistical sophistication than the judicial process is likely to accept. Both of these points suggest that, without more, the use of per se rules toward either legality or illegality of mergers, based on their potential for creating reciprocity, is not desirable.

Nor does the emerging legal standard focusing on the probability of *agreement* to engage in reciprocal transactions serve a constructive policy function, for it is *third-party* effects, with or without agreement, that should control policy. Because the first two parties agree creates no presumption of adverse effects on competition. I would not go so far as to urge the reverse, that it creates a presumption of beneficial economies.

So far as efficiencies are concerned, consensual reciprocity seems more beneficial than, say, contractual reciprocity, long-term requirements contracts, or vertical integration, if only because it is a more flexible, more readily reversible arrangement if the mutual advantage should diminish or disappear.

If one were to strive for guidelines one might proceed sequentially by identifying:

1. The opportunities for reciprocity
2. The likelihood of particular forms of reciprocity being practiced
3. The probable effects of such reciprocity in each of the markets involved
4. The consequences of such effects

At that stage creating a presumption against mergers with a high probability of producing adverse effects would be desirable.

The present legal debate has occurred in the neighborhood of point 2. While that seems a more promising neighborhood than point 1, which the Justice Department and FTC once urged, it does not promise a *generally* sensible outcome, from the policy point of view. We are thus a long way from the point of writing definitive guidelines. Here ignorance and uncertainty *do* have a clear policy implication for, most importantly, merger policy is not needed to control reciprocity—that can be dealt with on its merits with or without merger.[54] Nor is reciprocity needed to control mergers. Happily, I think, the trend toward reliance on it is on the wane.

---

54. I refrain from an extended comment on the wisdom of reciprocity law as beyond the scope of the discussion. But it seems to me still that "agreement" is a poor criterion. I can see why it may be sound policy to bar fraudulent or coercive reciprocity, even should it prove efficient, and I can see some case against allowing contracts that extend well into the future. But agreement per se is as much a part of free market transactions as it is of illegal conspiracy.

CHAPTER TEN

Economic and Legal Theories of the Effect on Competition II: Potential Competition

IF RECIPROCITY was the primary avenue by which Mr. McLaren expected to bring conglomerates within the ambit of Section 7, potential competition was a secondary one. As of 1974 it seems the more likely to prevail. As we shall see in some detail, the current legal trend is to make the conglomerate acquisition, which has legally survived the attacks on it via reciprocity, increasingly vulnerable to attack by virtue of a broadening of a potential competition doctrine.

Potential competition emerged as an important element in Section 7 merger cases in the years after 1950. As Markham noted in 1957,[1] most of the cases filed after 1950 invoked the notion of injury to potential competition, as one of the harms to be avoided by barring the merger. Just what the concept meant, or ought to have meant became a matter of lively speculation, none of it more cogent than that of Professor James Rahl in a 1958 article,[2] and of Donald Turner in his 1965 article.[3]

Rahl starts from the clear recognition of "potentiality" as an outgrowth of the incipiency doctrine that distinguished the Clayton Act from the Sherman Act by recognizing and inhibiting potential harm to competition. But, he asked, does the potential in question refer to potential competitors, to potential effect on present competition, or to potential effect on future competition? In particular, Rahl urged a distinction between: (1) a condition of freedom of future entry in the market concerned, (2) an existing positive competitive force supplied by the immediate threat of new entry by an identified firm.

---

1. Jesse Markham, "Merger Policy Under the New Section 7: A Six-Year Appraisal," 43 VIRGINIA LAW REVIEW 489 (1957).
2. James A. Rahl, "Applicability of the Clayton Act to Potential Competition," 12 ABA ANTITRUST LAW JOURNAL, §143 (1958).
3. Donald F. Turner, "Conglomerate Mergers and Section 7 of the Clayton Act," 78 HARVARD LAW REVIEW 1313–95 (May 1965).

The first involves inquiry into what the economist calls the condition of entry, and was, Rahl felt, a perfectly legitimate part of market analysis of the state of existing competition. The second he regarded as inviting a new legal theory of violation that substitutes potential competition for actual competition. This he regarded as illegitimate, absent a showing that the potential competition eliminated was quite as effective as actual competition.

Rahl's careful analysis seems to have been badly dated by intervening events. A merger demonstrably lessening potential competition in either of his two senses would surely be stopped by contemporary courts. The change in the frontier at which the debate is occurring is most easily seen by reproducing Rahl's dismissal of potential competition with respect to conglomerate acquisitions:

A pseudo-potential competition idea has begun to appear as enforcement authorities struggle for some kind of handle with which to grasp conglomerate acquisitions. The idea runs along the following lines. The acquiring firm has entered a new product or geographical market. It had a choice of two methods of achieving this entry—to acquire an existing firm, or to build its own new facilities, thus adding to the number of competitors in the new market. Its decision to enter by acquisition has resulted in a loss of an opportunity to increase competition in the industry. Therefore, it may be argued, the acquisition has lessened competition. The competition lessened is competition which did not exist, but which was "potential" in the sense that it is competition which the firm in question might have created itself. This ingenious use of the "potential competition" language illustrates the pitfalls which always lurk in so ambiguous a phrase.

Once again, we need to remind ourselves that the Clayton Act does not deal with all kinds of possibilities, nor does it protect mere "chance." Further, it does not prescribe a program for increasing competition. Its prohibition runs to conduct which actually or probably *lessens* competition. To treat an election not to augment competition as a lessening of competition is a neat trick, perhaps facilitated by the enveloping propensities of the phrase, "potential competition." It is, however, plainly not authorized by the language of the statute, nor by the philosophy of antitrust, which does not affirmatively seek to compel competition.[4]

Yet it is precisely this "pseudo-potential competition" that is at the heart of the emerging doctrine.

---

4. Rahl, "Applicability of the Clayton Act," pp. 142–43.

The Concept of Potential Competition

Potential competition is both an elastic and an elusive concept. While elasticity is desirable if it is used by the courts to stretch or contract the concept to provide a sensible middle ground between per se rules, elusiveness only invites confusion. Yet both elasticity and elusiveness seem to me to rest on the fact that "potentiality" involves several distinct concepts not one. One of these concerns a distinction between present effect on competition and future effect; another concerns a distinction between present competitors and other firms; another concerns a distinction based on the probability of effects occurring, with potential being distinguished from certain; and yet another concerns effects on potential competitors. The logical possibilities quickly become staggering as the following suggests.

$$\text{The} \begin{Bmatrix} \text{possible} \\ \text{probable} \\ \text{certain} \end{Bmatrix} \begin{Bmatrix} \text{present} \\ \text{future} \end{Bmatrix} \text{effect on} \begin{Bmatrix} \text{actual} \\ \text{potential} \end{Bmatrix}$$

$$\text{competitive} \begin{Bmatrix} \text{behavior} \\ \text{structure} \end{Bmatrix} \text{of} \begin{Bmatrix} \text{present} \\ \text{potential present} \\ \text{potential future} \end{Bmatrix} \text{competitors.}$$

Choosing all combinations involving one of the choices in each brace leads to 72 different questions, few of which are without some interest in assessing the effect of a merger and many of which seem to me to characterize allegations involved in particular cases.

This sort of game serves only to define the problem. My own shorter list of relevant possibilities involves each of the following alleged mechanisms for competitive harm:

1. Elimination of the acquiring firm as an additional competitive force because, absent acquisition, it would have been:

   a) a present *de novo* entrant
   b) a present entrant by a less restrictive acquisition
   c) a probable future *de novo* entrant
   d) a probable future less restrictive entrant.

2. Elimination of present competitive restraints on exercise of market power by existing competitors:

   a) by removing the presence of a perceived potential entrant

b) by the acquiring firm's restructuring the industry of the acquired firm by monopolizing it, or by creating a focus for
tacit collusion not previously present.

3.   Changing the market structure of the industry of the acquired firm in such a way as to raise the barriers to entry of firms
other than the acquiring firm who may have been potential future
competitors, or who may have exerted present restraining forces by
being perceived potential entrants.

The point about these different formulations is not that some are
inherently sensible and others not, for all can bear on the question of
whether the acquisition has the effect of substantially lessening competition, but rather that they look to very different kinds of evidence.

The first set of questions concerns crucially the identity, perceptions, and intentions of the acquiring firm, and the sense in which it is
particularly situated as a potential entrant. To see the importance of
this, notice that the effect of a policy barring the acquisition will be
procompetitive if the firm is a probable *de novo* entrant, but will remove any influence of it on the market if there is no possibility whatever of its entering unless it can do so by leading firm acquisition.

The second set of questions depends crucially on the market
structure and the state of competition in the acquired firm's market
before the acquisition. Contrary to the usual view, the more tightly
oligopolistic the industry before acquisition, the less the loss of competition is likely to be. Acquisition by a powerful new firm might
destabilize a tight, inefficient oligopoly and thus increase competition.
The greatest danger to competition is that entry of a powerful firm
into a loosely oligopolistic industry might provide the focus for price
leadership or for some other lessening of competitive behavior. Here
relevant evidence concerns both the status quo ante and the business
practices of the acquiring firm. One should be able to infer something about firm X's behavior in a new industry from its prior behavior in other industries.

The third set of questions is a degree more remote. It concerns
the perceptions and intentions of firms other than those now in the
industry, or parties to the acquisition. When one of a set of potential
present entrants actually enters a market it may change sharply the
likelihood of the others entering. Harm to competition has been argued
to result from a change, in either direction. If firm X's entry triggers a

series of acquisitions, it may foreshadow a merger trend that needs to be stopped in its incipiency. If, contrariwise, X's entry discourages entry by others it removes the restraint on present competitors that was part of competition before the acquisition. The potential entry that is discouraged may be contemporary or remote in time.

The courts' view of potential competition shifts from one to another of these conceptions of the problem, thus inviting as many definitions of potential competition as the blind men's descriptions of the elephant.

Potential Competition in Economic Theory

If the legal discussion of potential competition has been less than lucid, so too has the economic. I think this also results from the multiplicity of concepts. There seem to me to be three (not one) areas of economic theory relevant to evaluating the multiplicity of possible effects of "potential competition" on competition. They are (1) the so-called limit-price analysis concerning the effect of the presence of potential entrants; (2) the theory of oligopoly, with particular reference to what conduces to tight or loose oligopolistic behavior; and (3) the theory of what kinds of things increase barriers to entry. My immediate purpose is to show how these differ from one another, and how they bear on evaluation of leading firm conglomerate acquisitions.

LIMIT PRICING, AND THE GENERAL CONDITION OF ENTRY

The notion of the "limit price," due to Joe S. Bain, is that the threat of entry may lead the price in an oligopolistic industry to be set below the level existing sellers would set, absent the threat of entry, in order to forestall entry.[5] In such a situation, elimination of a potential entrant may change the condition of entry and lessen this restraint on the ability of the existing sellers to raise their prices.

The key concepts in this analysis are the "immediate condition of entry" (*ICE*), defined as the cost disadvantage of the most favored

---

5. Bain's work on entry and potential competition goes back at least to J. S. Bain, "A Note on Pricing in Monopoly and Oligopoly," *American Economic Review* 39, no. 2 (March 1949): 448. But the modern reader would do well to start with his *Barriers to New Competition: Their Character and Consequences in Manufacturing Industries* (Cambridge, Mass., 1956).

potential entrant over the firms already in the industry, and the "general condition of entry" (*GCE*), which is the schedule of *ICE*'s for successive entrants arranged in order of increasing disadvantage. Figure 10–1 shows several different hypothetical sets of entry conditions. The vertical axis represents costs (or prices) per unit. C^* is the level of average total cost for existing sellers, and thus approximates the level of competitive price. p^* reflects the monopoly price level which existing sellers would like to charge. The several curves labeled *GCE* each represent levels of average total cost, after entry, of successive potential entrants.

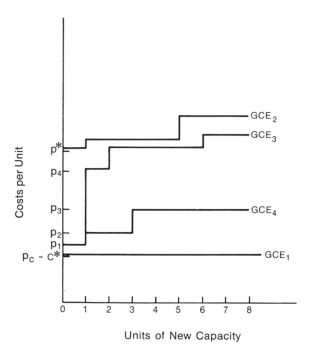

Fig. 10–1. Alternative patterns of the General Condition of Entry (GCE).

GCE_1 represents a situation of wholly unimpeded entry. Presumably entry would occur if price ever rose significantly above the competitive level, p_c. GCE_2 represents wholly blockaded entry: price can rise to p^* without any restraint from potential entrants and without inducing entry. GCE_3 and GCE_4 represent intermediate and more interesting situations. If GCE_3 pertains, a low limit price of p_1 would be required to forestall any entry, and thus the most probable potential entrant might be exercising a very great restraining effect on price. If this potential entrant disappeared, the limit price to forestall further entry would rise to p_4, the cost of the next most favored entrant.[6] For GCE_4 the loss of the most probable entrant would also have some effect, but a much smaller one since the second and third potential entrants themselves would restrain price to the level p_2, and there would be free entry above p_3.

This analysis suggests why looking at the nature and number of perceived potential entrants may be of fundamental significance. Perceived potential entrants whose entry-inducing price is well below p^* may constitute a real present competitive force. Whether the loss of *one* such potential entrant is serious depends upon whether it is the most—or one of a few most—favored potential entrants and whether the barriers to others are significantly higher. These are the considerations that led Turner to state as one of the minimum necessary conditions for prohibiting a merger:

> The merging firm at the edge of the market must be recognized by those in the market as the most likely entrant or one of a very few likely entrants, with barriers to entry by new companies or by other established firms being significantly higher.[7]

THE STATUS QUO ANTE IN THE ACQUIRED FIRM'S MARKET

The discussion above deals with the potential effect of the presence or absence of a potential competitor. Suppose conditions of GCE_3 apply, price in the industry is at the level p_1, and then the first potential entrant disappears from the scene. What will happen to price? If the structure of the industry is such that price cannot rise above p_1 because of internal competitive conditions, the loss of the potential entrant has had no adverse effect: the restraint it imposed was redundant. If, on the other hand, the industry was a tight oligopoly restrained only by the entry threat, the effect of the loss of the perceived potential

6. With GCE_3 the existing sellers might well choose to price at p_4, even though it invited entry of the most probable entrant, for the loss of market share might be less costly than the long-run loss of profits necessary to remove its motivation for entry.

7. Turner, "Conglomerate Mergers," at 1363.

entrant might be immediate and adverse, with price rising to p_4, as we have seen. This is the consideration that leads Turner to a second condition for prohibiting mergers:

The market concerned must be an oligopoly market; the number of actual sellers must be sufficiently small for them to be able collectively, though not necessarily collusively, to maintain prices above competitive levels.[8]

So far so good. But this case—elimination of the perceived potential entrant into a tight oligopoly whose propensities to raise price are restrained only by a perception of an entry threat—is but one among many.

Suppose instead that the relevant perceived *GCE* looks like that of GCE_5 in figure 10–2, and assume price is p_4, reflecting the fact that

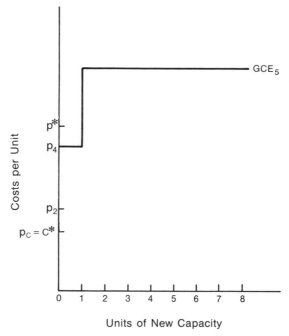

Fig. 10–2.   Hypothetical General Condition of Entry (GCE) where permitting acquisition may be beneficial to competition.

---

8. Turner, "Conglomerate Mergers," p. 433 nn. His third condition, "The barrier to entry by the firm in question must not be so high that the price it must expect to obtain before it would come in is above the price that would maximize the profits of the existing sellers," rules out cases such as shown by GCE_2 in figure 10–1.

the existing sellers are in fact a tight oligopoly. Now suppose that the most favored entrant acquires one of the existing sellers. The worst that could happen (from the competitive point of view) is that price after entry might rise from p_4 to p^*, but if p_4 is made arbitrarily close to p^* this will be of minimal adverse consequence. Alternatively, the new entrant might be the catalyst for upsetting the tight oligopoly, and leading to a price of, say, p_2. Clearly, such an entry by acquisition would be beneficial to competition. Finally, here, suppose the conditions of GCE_5, but suppose price is near the competitive level, say at p_2, due to the fact that the existing sellers are a loose oligopoly without any focal point for quasi agreement. It is internal competition not the entry threat that preserves competitive behavior. Now the entry by acquisition of the most probable potential entrant may be anticompetitive not because it removes any effective threat of entry, but because the new firm may be able to transform the market structure of the industry and cause price rise toward p^*.

Thus, Turner's rules seem to me to be insufficient. In general, the nearer the price before acquisition to the monopoly (or tight oligopoly) position, the *less* the present competitive harm of allowing an acquisition, whereas the nearer the price to the competitive level, the greater the potential competitive harm.

Obviously, looking only at current price is inadequate, for a low price today may foreshadow a higher one later, while the loss of a potential entrant now may be a loss forever. But what economic theory should lead us to look to is the expected direction of change in the market behavior of the acquired firm's industry as a result of the acquisition. The economic theory of oligopoly behavior does not generally lead to the conclusion that leading firm conglomerate acquisitions are presumptively anticompetitive.

This does not compel a rule of reason approach, but it does suggest attention to the opportunities for competitive benefit as well as for competitive harm.

THE EFFECT OF ACQUISITION ON THE GCE

In terms of formal analysis the acquisition of an existing seller by a perceived former potential entrant has two kinds of effects. First, it removes a potential entrant and thus shifts the vertical axis of charts like figures 10–1 and 10–2 to the right. Second, it may shift the GCE curve itself. This is illustrated in figure 10–3 where GCE_6 is the rele-

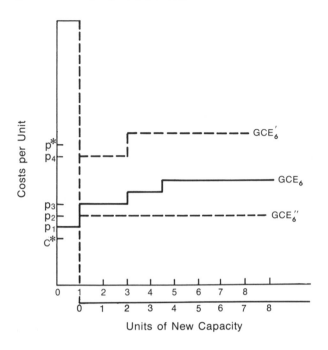

Fig. 10–3. Possible effects of an acquisition on the General Condition of Entry (GCE).

vant preacquisition curve. Now the most probable entrant enters by acquisition. If the curve does not shift, the axis merely shifts to the dashed vertical line, and the adverse effect of the acquisition will be at most to raise the limit price from p_1 to p_3. But if the entry increases barriers to further entry it may shift the *GCE* curve upward, say to GCE'_6, and have a further adverse potential effect. Even if the acquirer was not ever a perceived potential entrant (and thus was not represented by *GCE*), its entry could change the *GCE* by raising the barriers to entry. Assertions about upward shifts in the barriers to entry play an important role in a number of the cases discussed below, particularly Procter & Gamble, and General Foods. In both of these cases, assertions concern economies of marketing and advertising.

But the mere demonstration that an apparent outsider can successfully enter may increase the perceptions of existing sellers to other potential entrants and thus, since the limit price effect depends on the *recognition* by existing sellers of the entry threat, the threat of entry-by-acquisition on the behavior of managers may be a nonnegligible competitive force. Successful entry by acquisition may lead to a downward shift (say to GCE''_6) of *GCE,* and thus have no adverse effect, and might even have a beneficial one.

The Expanding Legal View of Potential Competition

The relatively recent—since 1963 or 1964—blossoming of the potential competition doctrine is most easily understood as mirroring the main line of development of antitrust doctrines. In area after area attention was first directed to clear and present dangers to competition, such as monopolization, collusion, and horizontal mergers of leading sellers in highly concentrated industries. But gradually attention was extended to less clear and less present dangers. The steadily widening role of the incipiency doctrine after 1914 for dealing with monopolization problems before they reached monopoly proportions and the injunction to act on the basis of probabilities, not certainties, foreshadow the more recent gradual broadening of the potential competition doctrine. A whole congeries of horizontal and vertical restraints were brought within the ambit of illegal behavior by finding a sufficient probability (well short of the certainty warranting a per se rule) that they would produce competitive harm. And both attempts to monopolize and mergers by firms without dominant positions have been included within the ambit of proscribed activities presumably because of the expectation of future harm to competition. Well before the great merger wave of the late 1960s the main-line tradition had incorporated the effect, incipient as well as actual, future as well as present, on competition in a market.

The acquisition of a firm in one market by an outsider—the essence of the conglomerate merger phenomenon—seems to me to be a difference in degree not in kind: the question is still what is the probable effect. The tricky part of the question—with respect to conglomerate acquisitions no less than with respect to single firm conduct—is how remote and how improbable the effect on competition can be and still be sufficient to proscribe the conduct in question. The trend has been to including less probable and more remote effects.

Potential competition started as the simplest of extensions of the prohibitions against horizontal acquisition of a competitor which had the effect of substantially lessening present competition. The first example of its use is the 1922 *ALCOA v. FTC* opinion,[9] in which the

---

9. *Aluminum Co. of America v. FTC,* 284 F. 401 (3d Cir. 1922), cert. denied 261 U.S. 616 (1922).

Third Circuit refused to allow an escape from the force of Clayton Section 7 by a device which turned an actual competitor into a potential competitor. Cleveland Company, a manufacturer of aluminum sheets, and a direct competitor of ALCOA, sold its plant to a newly formed corporation, Aluminum Rolling Mills Company, in which it would have a one-third interest. ALCOA subscribed for the other two-thirds of the new company's stock, and agreed to operate the plant. While an ALCOA stock acquisition of two-thirds of Cleveland would surely have been illegal, ALCOA argued that the effect of its acquisition of the new company could not be to lessen competition, since no competition existed between it and the new company, as the latter did not produce at the time of acquisition. The FTC and the court disagreed; the latter remarking "that in this defense the Aluminum Company stands on a ledge too narrow for safety" since the new corporation was being placed in commerce in a way which "forever prevented competition with [ALCOA]."[10]

Almost as easy as this case is the acquisition of a probable actual horizontal competitor. The El Paso case[11] which reached the Supreme Court in 1963 is almost classically simple. El Paso Natural Gas, the only out-of-state producer to supply natural gas to California, acquired Pacific Northwest Pipeline Company, which had once tried, but failed, to enter the California market. By acquiring Pacific Northwest, a potential competitor, El Paso had removed an ever-present threat to its market position in California. It seems clear that if Pacific Northwest had successfully entered the market, El Paso would not have been allowed to acquire it under Section 7. Thus acquisition of it, before its entry, was but a small further step. Nevertheless, it *was* an extension in two ways: first it presumed that Pacific Northwest (despite its earlier failure to enter) was a potential future entrant or was perceived so to be; second, it treated an undated future effect as of present concern. One view of the Supreme Court's position in El Paso is that it was effectively dealing with a horizontal acquisition—in Mr. Justice Douglas's view "unsuccessful bidders are no less competitors than successful ones."[12] It seems to me preferable to regard it as the first Supreme Court decision regarding market extension mergers, the

---

10. Id. at 407.

11. *United States v. El Paso Natural Gas Co. et al.,* 376 U.S. 651 (1964).

12. Id. at 660.

field in which the potential competition concept was to take seed and flourish.

In discussing the subsequent development of the potential competition doctrine and its application to conglomerate acquisitions, it is helpful to distinguish two concurrent lines of development. The first is a gradual broadening of the kinds of anticompetitive effect a merger might have via decreasing actual or potential competition. The second is a gradual erosion in the structural conditions that must be present to allow the inference that the adverse effects are sufficiently probable. These structural conditions concern both the nature of the acquired firm's market and the number and identity of the potential entrants thereto.

ANTICOMPETITIVE EFFECTS

Penn-Olin.   The Penn-Olin case[13] was a joint venture, not a merger, but its importance in understanding the use of potential competition doctrine is enormous, first, because the courts posed most explicitly many of the central issues, and second, because Turner used it, along with El Paso, to frame his insightful discussion of the problem.

Pennsalt, one of three United States producers of sodium chlorate, entered into a joint venture with Olin Mathieson, the chemical company, to build a sodium chlorate plant in what is known as the Southeastern United States market, where Pennsalt's two competitors (Hooker Chemical and American Potash) already had plants, but where Pennsalt did not. While this clearly added one actual competitor in the Southeastern United States sodium chlorate market, did it remove two potential entrants?

---

13. The most useful opinion is that of the district court in *United States v. Penn-Olin Chemical Company et al.,* 246 F.Supp. 917 (D. Del. 1965), where the case was on remand from a 1964 Supreme Court decision, 378 U.S. 158 (1964). The Supreme Court vacated and remanded the earlier decision of the district court 217 F.Supp. 110 (D. Del. 1963). The district court originally found no sufficient adverse competitive effect, but failed to answer what the Supreme Court found a vital question of fact: whether "one of the corporations would have entered the market by building a plant while the other would have remained a significant potential competitor," 378 U.S. at 175–76. The case came back to the Supreme Court in 1967, 386 U.S. 906 (1967), and the district court opinion was affirmed by a 4–4 vote, without opinion.

The district court posed three issues:

Issue 1: Whether if Penn-Olin had not been formed, there would have been a reasonable probability that (*a*) Olin would have constructed a sodium chlorate plant in the Southeast or (*b*) Pennsalt would have constructed a sodium chlorate plant in the Southeast?

Issue 2: Whether, if Penn-Olin had not been formed and either Olin or Pennsalt had constructed a sodium chlorate plant in the Southeast, the other, as a reasonable probability, would have maintained such continued interest in the Southeastern sodium chlorate market as to constitute it a significant potential competitor.

Issue 3: Whether the organization of Penn-Olin, as a reasonable probability, resulted in substantially less competition than would have existed if either Olin or Pennsalt had constructed a sodium chlorate plant in the Southeast while the other continued to have an interest in constructing such a plant.

Most importantly, the parties agreed, and the court held, that *both* Issues 1 and 2 required affirmative answers if the merger was to be violative of Section 7.[14] This view, which I shall describe as the theory of Penn-Olin, says that so far as competitive effect is concerned, one actual entrant is to be preferred to either one or two potential (but improbable) entrants, but not to one actual or probable entrant with another on the edge of the market. The theory implies (*a*) that an actual entrant is a more effective competitive force than a potential entrant, (*b*) that a potential entrant may have positive procompetitive influences even if it does not enter, and (*c*) that more competitors are better than less. This straightforward theory does not deal directly with whether some number of potential entrants (greater than two) might be preferred to one actual entrant, and it appears to reject the possibility that a potential competitor might be a more competitive influence than an actual one in some circumstances. Later cases were to explore those possibilities.

Applications of Penn-Olin theory.   A series of later cases in the spirit of the Penn-Olin theory has denied mergers on the ground either that

---

14. The district court did not reach Issue 3, because it was to find negatively on Issue 1. The defendants urged and the government opposed the necessity for an affirmative answer to Issue 3 as well. Whether the Supreme Court had implicitly rejected the necessity for an affirmative answer to Issue 3 by vacating and remanding the original order based on a negative finding to Issue 3 is not entirely clear. The alternative is to think the court was not satisfied that a proper factual examination had been made.

the acquiring firm was itself a probable *de novo* entrant, thus relying on implication (*a*), or that absent the acquisition it would have remained a potential entrant while the acquired firm remained an actual competitor—implications (*b*) and (*c*). In Wilson,[15] a leading sporting goods manufacturer was enjoined from acquiring a gymnastic equipment manufacturer, because the gymnastic equipment market was "ripe for entry" and Wilson was a leading potential entrant. In Procter & Gamble,[16] the Supreme Court ordered the divestiture by P & G of the acquired Clorox Company because "liquid bleach was a natural avenue of diversification" for P & G and because Procter "had considered the possibility of independently entering but decided against it because the acquisition of Clorox would enable Procter to capture a more commanding share of the market." And most recently in Kennecott[17] the Tenth Circuit found against the large copper mining company's acquisition of a giant coal producer (Peabody) on the ground, in part, that "the removal of Kennecott from the edge of the market and the substitution of it within the market for Peabody, the leading producer and distributor, eliminated a substantial potential competitive force." Both Procter & Gamble and Kennecott were, moreover, considered the most probable *de novo* entrants. Each of these cases broke new ground in other directions, as is discussed below, but as to the kind of effect, they are direct applications of the Penn-Olin theory, although of course opposite to Penn-Olin in the finding.[18]

Falstaff: elimination of a present or future competitive effect. The necessity for the acquiring firm to be a probable *de novo* entrant was

---

15. *United States v. Wilson Sporting Goods and Nissen Corp.*, 288 F.Supp. 543 (N.D. Ill. 1968).

16. *FTC v. Procter & Gamble Co.*, 386 U.S. 568 (1967).

17. *Kennecott Copper Corp. v. FTC*, 467 F.2d 67 (10th Cir. 1972). Petition for cert. filed.

18. *Allis-Chalmer Mfg. Co. v. White Consolidated Industries*, 414 F.2d 506 (3d Cir. 1969), reversing 294 F.Supp. 1263 (D. Del. 1969), cert. denied 396 U.S. 1009 (1969), is of interest in this connection only because the potential competition argument was used by a *target* firm in a contested takeover. Allis (the target) claimed it was a potential entrant into (among other markets served by White) the steel rolling mill industry where a White subsidiary (Blaw Knox) operated. The district court found no evidence to support this self-serving assertion. The Circuit Court remanded it to the district court for more inquiry, over a vigorous dissent. This case is like ALCOA and El Paso in raising as the issue potential entry by the *acquired* firm.

assumed by the district court in *United States v. Falstaff Brewing Corp.,*[19] but promptly rejected by the Supreme Court. In that case the government challenged the acquisition by Falstaff, the fourth largest beer producer in the nation, of Narragansett Brewing Corporation, the largest seller of beer in the New England market. The district court dismissed the government's action, finding that the only way that Falstaff intended to penetrate the New England market was by acquisition and that consequently its purchase of Narragansett would not substantially lessen competition in violation of Section 7 of the Clayton Act.

The Supreme Court, per Mr. Justice White, held that the lower court erred in assuming that because Falstaff would not have entered the market *de novo,* it could not be considered a potential competitor; rather, according to White, the district court should have considered whether Falstaff was a potential competitor in the sense that its position on the edge of the market exerted a beneficial influence on competitive conditions within it. It remanded the case for a finding on this matter.

This case is sufficiently recent, and its four opinions sufficiently diverse that its precise significance is not clear to me. But it has several interesting strands that may extend the notion of wherein lies the competitive harm. A first strand is that even if Falstaff was not a potential actual entrant, it might nevertheless be perceived by existing sellers to be one, and thus might exercise a present competitive effect.[20]

---

19. *United States v. Falstaff Brewing Corp.,* 332 F.Supp. 970 (D. R.I. 1971), reversed and remanded 410 U.S. 526 (1973). The import is clouded by the presence of four opinions for the seven participating Justices. The Court's opinion is in many ways less interesting than the longer concurring opinion of Justice Marshall. Justice Douglas also concurs, while Justices Rehnquist and Stewart dissent, and Justices Brennan and Powell did not participate. For an excellent discussion of the case see "United States v. Falstaff Brewing Corporation: Potential Competition Re-examined,"72 MICHIGAN LAW REVIEW 837–67 (March 1974).

20. "Surely, it could not be said on this record that Falstaff's general interest in the New England market was unknown; and if it would appear to rational beer merchants in New England that Falstaff might well build a new brewery to supply the northeastern market then its entry by merger becomes suspect under §7. The District Court should therefore have appraised the economic facts about Falstaff and the New England market in order to determine whether in any realistic sense Falstaff could be said to be a potential competitor on the fringe of the market

A second strand is that Falstaff might be a potential future entrant even if it is not a present potential entrant. This view is expressed by Justice Douglas:

> ... Thus, although Falstaff might not have made a *de novo* entry if it had not been allowed to acquire Narragansett, we cannot say that it would be unwilling to make such an entry *in the future* when the New England market might be ripe for an infusion of new competition. At this point in time, it is the most likely new competitor.[21]

and by Justice Marshall:

> ... Even if it is true that management has no present intent of entering the market *de novo,* the possibility remains that it may change its mind as the objective factors favoring such entry are more clearly perceived. Of course, it is possible that management will adamantly continue to close its eyes to the company's own self-interest. But in that event, the chance remains that the stockholders will install new, more competent officers who will better serve their interests.[22]

A final strand concerns the irrelevance of a showing that the industry of the firm being acquired was presently competitive. As Justice Marshall put it:

> Still, even if the market is presently competitive, it is possible that it might grow less competitive in the future. For example, a market might be so concentrated that even though it is presently competitive, there is a serious risk that parallel pricing policies might emerge sometime in the near future. In such a situation, an effective competitor lingering on the fringe of the market—what might be called a *potential* perceived potential entrant—could exert a deterrent force when anticompetitive conduct is about to emerge.[23]

Without more, it is difficult to tell how far this decision goes. At one extreme it can be regarded as fairly limited because it involves an

---

with likely influence on existing competition." (*United States v. Falstaff Brewing Corp.,* 410 U.S. 526 [1973] at 533–34.) While this seems reasonable enough, the notion of remanding the case to determine if other New England beer manufacturers continued to incorrectly perceive Falstaff's intentions seems to present problems. Whatever they may have perceived originally, the evidence in the case surely was not overlooked by them.

21. Id. at 544.
22. Id. at 569.
23. Id. at 560 n. 15. See also Douglas at 538–39.

almost horizontal market extension merger by one of the few large brewers who did not have complete national coverage, in an industry with a trend toward increasing market share of national producers. In this view the whole United States, not New England, is the relevant market, and the merger increased concentration in that market. At the other extreme it can be argued that *simply by virtue of its acquisition,* Falstaff was revealed to be a potential present or future force in the market which might someday need such a force. But in that sense every acquisition thus eliminates a revealed potential competitor. For the time being it seems best to read it relatively narrowly.

Ford-Autolite: potential preferred to actual.   A different theory of competitive harm is raised in Ford-Autolite, where the Supreme Court affirmed the interesting opinion of the Court in the Eastern District of Michigan in 1968.[24] In 1961 Ford had acquired Autolite, the smaller of two significant independent spark plug manufacturers (the other was Champion, from whom Ford had purchased prior to its acquisition of Autolite), in an industry in which General Motors had long been dominant through its AC Division. Ford had concluded it could have entered *de novo,* but such entry would take five to eight years, and acquiring Autolite (with 15 percent of the market) seemed both quicker and cheaper.

The district court conceded that had Ford entered *de novo,* Autolite would have been likely to fail. Nevertheless it argued:

> An interested firm on the outside has a twofold significance. It may someday go in and set the stage for noticeable deconcentration. While it merely stays near the edge, it is a deterrent to current competitors. . . . This was Ford uniquely, as both a prime candidate to manufacture and the major customer of the dominant member of the oligopoly. Given the chance that Autolite would have been doomed to oblivion by defendant's grassroots entry, which also would have destroyed Ford's soothing influence over replacement prices, Ford may well have been more useful as a potential than it would have been as a real producer, regardless how it began fabrication. Had Ford taken the internal-expansion route, there would have been no illegality; not, however, because the result necessarily would have been commendable, but simply because that course has not been proscribed.[25]

---

24. *United States v. Ford Motor Company and The Electric Autolite Co.,* 286 F.Supp. 407 (E.D. Mich. 1968), 315 F.Supp. 372 (E.D. Mich. 1970), affirmed by the Supreme Court in *Ford Motor Co. v. United States,* 405 U.S. 562 (1972).

25. 286 F.Supp. at 441.

The argument here, countering the implication of the Penn-Olin theory, that one in the bush is better than one in the market, is intriguing, although arguably a fairly special case. But it has a more general counterpart in the purely conglomerate merger area. Suppose a large conglomerate is known to be considering entry by acquisition into only one of n industries, with sufficient probability that it exerts a beneficial competitive influence in all n. Once its plans are announced it has major impact in only one industry, and the other $n - 1$ industries can relax. If this is accepted, the policy challenge is clear but difficult: one should discourage actual acquisitions without destroying the credible threat of actual entry. Conceivably the frequent remedy imposed (or consented to) in the aftermath of Section 7 cases, of prohibiting or greatly limiting future acquisitions of acquiring companies achieves that result, by encouraging *de novo* entry instead of acquisition. However, it surely serves to *diminish* the competitive threat of takeover and whatever precompetitive influence that threat has. Whether such prohibitions increase the probability of *de novo* entry to the point where such entry is regarded as credible, and thus have on balance a procompetitive potential competition effect, is not clear. For conglomerates (as distinct from more nearly horizontal or vertical acquisitions such as Falstaff or Autolite) the potential for entry is probably credible only if the conglomerate can enter via acquisition. This is the province of the toehold theory of entry.

Bendix-Fram: toeholds. The recognition that entry by acquisition might increase competition rather than diminish it had been explicitly discussed by Commissioner Philip Elman of the FTC many years before the Bendix-Fram case. In Beatrice Food Co., he discussed this as part of a long essay on potential competition:

. . . On the other hand, a merger between a very small factor—not one of the few dominant firms—in the market and a small concern from outside the market may increase, rather than lessen, competition by making the merged firm a more viable competitor.

The competitive effects are more difficult to predict when a very small factor in the market is acquired by a substantial potential competitor. The merger may increase competition in the market by injecting a substantial firm, one capable of challenging the dominant firms in the market, in place of a firm too small to be a significant competitive factor. But much would depend on the industry setting of the merger.[26]

---

26. *In re Beatrice Foods Co.,* [1965–1967 Transfer Binder] *CCH Trade Regulation Reporter* ¶17, 244, at 22,332 (FTC 1965).

Bendix's acquisition of Fram raises the toehold question clearly.[27] Bendix, one of the seventy largest industrial companies, and a diversified manufacturer of components and assemblies for aerospace, automotive, automation, and scientific machinery, acquired Fram, the third largest United States manufacturer of filters, particularly automotive filters with 12.4 percent of the market. In its opinion, the FTC, per Elman, articulated the notion that Bendix ought to have entered by acquisition of a small competitor rather than a leading one, and used this toehold to expand into the industry. Because this is new and I think sensible legal ground it is worth quoting at some length from the opinion:

> No real dispute exists as to the imminence, likelihood, or ability of Bendix to have become a real and substantial competitor of Fram in the passenger car filter aftermarket. The only question was the form that new entry would take. Bendix had three choices: (1) to expand internally; (2) to make a toehold acquisition looking toward expansion on that base; and (3) to merge with a leading firm. If Bendix had taken either of the first two routes of entry, it would have become an actual competitor of Fram, and would have provided a beneficial new element in the market. Either of those two routes would have promoted competition; neither violated Section 7; indeed, either was the sort of entry into a new market which Congress intended to encourage. . . .
>
> If any barrier to [internal expansion] existed for Bendix, it was, as respondents contend, due to the mass marketing and promotional tech-

---

27. The important FTC decision, by Commissioner Elman, is at 3 *CCH Trade Regulation Reporter* ¶19,288 (FTC 1970). The 6th Circuit decision is *Bendix Corp. v. FTC,* 450 F.2d 534 (6th Cir. 1971). The Circuit Court, vacating and remanding, does so on procedural grounds, under the Administrative Procedure Act. It held that the FTC decided the matter on a theory which was never charged, raised, or tried during the administrative hearing, thus violating Section 5 of the Act. The Commission had explicitly acknowledged that it was breaking new ground: "Although previous cases have only involved potential entry in one form, i.e., by internal expansion, it is clear that the *form* of entry was not controlling in these decisions. What was determinative in each of these cases was (1) the actual elimination of the additional decision-making, the added capacity, and the other market stimuli which would have resulted had entry taken a pro-competitive form, such as internal expansion; and (2) the anti-competitive consequences of the removal of the disciplining effect of a potential competitor from the market's edge. We believe that these adverse effects on competition may result from the elimination of a potential entrant who might have entered by internal expansion or who might have entered by a toehold acquisition."

niques necessary to sell filters in the aftermarket. But this was precisely the barrier that Bendix could have surmounted by a toehold acquisition of a firm with substantial promotional facilities.

From the standpoint of Section 7, and the statutory policy of favoring mergers which may increase competition and prohibiting mergers which may lessen competition, it made a crucial difference whether Bendix merged with Fram or another leading firm, or with one of the various smaller and less established firms with which it unsuccessfully negotiated.

Instead, Bendix chose the third route—acquisition of Fram, a leading firm—and thus the likelihood of substantial competition between these two firms was forever eliminated. By the same token, the competitive input that Bendix could have brought to the entire market, had it entered by a toehold acquisition, was also lost.

This is the "pseudo-potential competition" doctrine Rahl dismissed a dozen years earlier. One may justify this theory in two ways. One is that the adverse effect on competition of a leading firm acquisition is the elimination of a large rather than a small rival. If one assumes that entry would have occurred in some form, it is always the acquired firm that is eliminated from competition (relative to the competition that would have existed after *de novo* entry). The other viewpoint focuses on differences in the postacquisition behavior of the same acquirer. If a large company such as Bendix entered via a toehold it might be motivated vigorously to enlarge its market share and thus to be a highly procompetitive force. That same company entering as a leading firm might be content to merely maintain its market share and thus to be an anticompetitive force.

Commissioner Elman's once lonely advocacy of the potentially procompetitive possibilities of toehold acquisitions is gaining legal support as a basis for attacking leading firm acquisitions. Clearly, the plaintiff can more easily prove that a less restrictive acquisition was available than that the acquirer was a potential *de novo* entrant. Whether a potential entrant ought to have the burden of proof that it had sought the least restrictive possible toehold, or whether instead guidelines should define permissible acquisitions is an important practical matter.

What is clear is that the Commission in Bendix-Fram is looking past the Penn-Olin theory in the direction of the quality of competition, not the number of competitors. Moreover it concerns the probable behavior of the firms after entry relative to competitive behavior before entry. Both of these seem, to an economist, major legal steps forward.

The particular relevance to conglomerate acquisitions is clear. If it ever makes sense to encourage conglomerate entry (and I believe it does), such entry may require permitting acquisitions. Obviously, counting numbers is not enough, for there may be a different competitive impact of different possible acquisitions.

Effect on subsequent entry: Procter & Gamble et al. A different broadening of the concept of competitive harm concerns the effect of the acquisition on what we have called the condition of future entry. This consideration plays a significant role in Procter & Gamble, discussed above, and in General Foods's acquisition of SOS scouring pads,[28] and is also invoked in the rambling Wilson opinion, cited above.

One element in each of these three cases was that entry of a large, diversified outsider into the industry of the acquired firm would raise the subsequent barriers to entry of other potential entrants.

This possibility had (I am tempted to say "of course") been anticipated by Turner:

When we turn to the effect of large firm acquisitions on future entry by new competitors, there is more cause for concern. Present competitors have made their commitments; their capital is already involved. Potential competitors have not made commitments; their capital can readily be diverted to other employment if there is any adverse shift in the risks of entering a particular market. Consequently, though present competitors might even heighten their competitive efforts on the arrival of a large firm in order to protect what is irrevocably invested, it is likely that potential new entrants will view this development as a substantial deterrent.[29]

He continues with the warning that "it is virtually impossible to estimate the probabilities of significant adverse effects on entry."

The barrier to further entry theory in both the Clorox and SOS acquisitions was asserted to occur through advantages of marketing and advertising but it can be readily extended to other entry barriers. It is concisely stated by Justice Douglas in the P & G opinion:

The acquisition may also have the tendency of raising the barriers to new entry. The major competitive weapon in the successful marketing of bleach is advertising. Clorox was limited in this area by its relatively small

---

28. *General Foods Corp. v. FTC,* 386 F.2d 936 (3d Cir. 1967), cert. denied 391 U.S. 919 (1968).

29. Turner, "Conglomerate Mergers," p. 1356.

budget and its inability to obtain substantial discounts. By contrast, Procter's budget was much larger; and, although it would not devote its entire budget to advertising Clorox, it could divert a large portion to meet the short-term threat of a new entrant. Procter would be able to use its volume discounts to advantage in advertising Clorox. Thus, a new entrant would be much more reluctant to face the giant Procter than it would have been to face the smaller Clorox.[30]

In sum. It now seems that the courts are willing to invoke Section 7 against an acquisition if competition is adversely affected by any one of: elimination of a probable *de novo* entrant, elimination of a threat on the edge of the market, replacement of a powerful threat on the edge of the market by a beefed-up competitor in the industry (the doctrine of Ford-Autolite), entry via acquisition of a leading producer rather than by an available smaller one, and an entry that increases the subsequent barriers to entry for other potential entrants. At least in terms of competitive effects this seems a sufficient arsenal with which to shoot down any merger that poses any threat to competition.

STRUCTURAL CONDITIONS FOR ADVERSE EFFECTS

Economists and lawyers agree that acquisition is more likely to lead to adverse competitive effect in some market structures than in others. The judicial list of structural conditions required to support an inference of probable adverse effect has been shrinking, concurrently with the broadening of the set of possible adverse effects.

As a starting point, consider again the three important minimum conditions that seemed to Turner obviously must obtain before there would be the likelihood of adverse effect arising from a firm at the edge of the market acquiring a firm in the market: (1) The market must be an oligopoly market; (2) the acquiring firm must be recognized as the most likely entrant or one of a very few likely entrants; (3) the acquiring firm must have low enough projected costs so that it was a real possible *de novo* entrant.[31] The significance of these conditions for treatment of pure conglomerate mergers is that neither the second nor the third minimum condition is likely to apply to the pure

---

30. *FTC v. Procter & Gamble,* 386 U.S. 568 (1967), at 579. But see Peterman, cited above on p. 66, on the merits of this fear.
31. Turner, "Conglomerate Mergers," p. 1363.

conglomerate acquisition. It is thus not surprising that Turner regarded the pure conglomerate as largely outside the reach of Section 7.

These conditions can be reasonably argued to have been present in El Paso, Penn-Olin, Procter & Gamble, Ford-Autolite, Falstaff, and Bendix-Fram, among the major cases treated above. But one or more were notably absent in General Foods, Wilson, and Kennecott.

General Foods.   General Foods's acquisition of SOS differed critically from the earlier cases (especially Procter & Gamble's acquisition of Clorox, to which it was compared) in two respects.

The first difference was that General Foods was not a perceived probable entrant. Unlike Clorox, where liquid bleach was a natural line of diversification for P & G, and everyone knew it, General Foods Corporation produces and distributes packaged foods. While it was thus a potential entrant into any low-priced, high turnover household consumer commodity sold to customers through grocery and supermarket outlets, its choice of scouring pads instead of razor blades, light bulbs, or dishcloths could hardly have been predicted, and it was not a perceived most probable entrant by the existing sellers.

The court was unimpressed:

It is true that G. F. was not a potential competitor lurking on the fringe of the soap pad market and exerting an effect on the actions of the actual competitors. However, we do not read *Clorox* as holding that "product extension" mergers must involve the elimination of this type of potential competition to run afoul of the Clayton Act.[32]

Thus in General Foods, the entry into an oligopolistic industry with some entry barriers, might be illegal even if the firm had not been perceived to be a highly likely potential entrant. (Arguably, the language quoted above limits this holding to product extension mergers, but I doubt it.) Illegality could occur, if the entry itself proved ex post to have anticompetitive effect, say, by raising further entry barriers.

The importance of this change for conglomerate acquisitions is immense. Few real conglomerates are perceived potential entrants into any industry in the terms of Turner's second condition, but all are potential entrants by acquisition into any oligopolistic industry where entry barriers exist and take the form of high capital requirements and

---

32. 386 F.2d at 946.

well-entrenched managements. If General Foods applies, the virtual exclusion of pure conglomerate acquisitions from Section 7 prosecution vanishes.

A second important difference from Clorox was that General Foods was not the most probable, but only one of many possible entrants into the scouring pad industry. Indeed Procter & Gamble was as likely a potential entrant, and any manufacturer of goods distributed to customers via grocery stores was a potential entrant.

The lurking trap to the government in a permissive definition of a potential entrant is manifest: the more loosely potential entry is defined, the greater the number of such entrants there are and thus the less serious is the loss of any one. The court in General Foods avoided the problem by acting as if it was unnecessary to inquire as to the number of alternative potential entrants. The reason was that the court apparently believed that once General Foods had entered, it so raised the barriers to future entry that *all* the preentry potential entrants were thus eliminated. Entry barriers previously significant but not decisive against unnamed other potential entrants, were supposed to have become insurmountable *because of* the dominant position a General Foods owned SOS commanded. If those were the facts, the court seems justified in concluding that the acquisition removed any beneficial effect of potential competitors in the market. In such circumstances, Turner's second minimum condition, a preentry condition, thus may need a postentry addendum, "or its entry must have the effect of raising the barriers to formerly potential entrants to the point where they are significantly less effective competitive forces in the market."

Turner himself rejects this approach on the ground that it would be all but impossible to demonstrate in a particular case. But that does not seem to me to be decisive. What is needed is some research on the question of how, in general, merger activity affects the propensities to subsequent entry. Conceivably this sort of effect is the rule rather than the exception.

Wilson. In Wilson, although Judge Marovitz quotes Turner at length and with approval, he further erodes the minimum conditions. In Wilson the court finds specifically that entry was easy, and that there were many logical potential entrants—McGregor, Rawlings, Spalding, and Medalist are named.

As we have previously stated, the gymnastic apparatus market is ripe for entry, due to its rapidly expanding demand and high profit margins. The technological and capital requirements for entry are not substantial, and a number of companies have become relatively serious competitors after entering with a nominal capital investment.[33]

Apparently in Wilson, entry into any oligopolistic industry is illegal if any of the effects discussed in the previous section are present. The decision itself appears to rest partly on the likely entrenchment of Wilson in the gymnastics equipment market, and partly on the assertion that potential horizontal competition between Wilson if it had entered *de novo* and Nissen, was eliminated.[34] It remains to be seen whether the Wilson decision is an aberration or whether it invites virtually total disregard of the need for a restricted condition of entry. General Foods had overlooked relatively easy entry before the General Foods's acquisition on the ground that entry subsequently became blockaded. Wilson eliminates the condition of entry entirely.

Kennecott. If General Foods and Wilson arguably loosened the structural conditions with respect to the condition of entry, Kennecott loosened them with respect to the market structure in the acquired industry.

The significance of Kennecott is that even the requirement for oligopoly may not be necessary! The Tenth Circuit in its finding that Kennecott's acquisition of Peabody was a violation, *via the potential competition route,* said:

Ordinarily the potential competition concept comes into play where the industry is regarded as an oligopoly. Admittedly, the industry as it existed at the time of trial was not a tight oligopoly. Based, however, on the findings of the Commission that the industry is on its way to becoming highly concentrated, the Commission determined that it was justified in acting so as to prevent the development of a tightly concentrated industry.[35]

33. *United States v. Wilson Sporting Goods and Nissen Corp.,* 288 F. Supp. 543 (N.D. Ohio 1971) at 560.

34. The Wilson case ended in a consent decree, 1968 *CCH Trade Cases,* ¶72,585 (N.D. Ill. 1968) that not only prohibited the Nissen merger, but barred Wilson from acquiring any other gymnastics manufacturers for at least five years.

35. *Kennecott Copper Corp. v. FTC,* 467 F.2d 67 (10th Cir. 1972) at 75–76.

Whether substituting "incipient oligopoly" for oligopoly as a structural condition here is a major extension of the potential competition doctrine depends upon one's view of the facts. The notion that the court should determine the effect on competition after entry, rather than merely looking at the structure beforehand, seems in line with the economic analysis offered above. But neither the court nor the Commission had evidence before it to suggest that Kennecott would create a tight oligopoly in a previously competitive market or that tight oligopoly was incipient. The hearing examiner had found the industry competitive, and the Commission's reversal of the examiner's finding rested primarily on a trend toward concentration and an asserted "deep pocket" effect of Kennecott's entry into the industry. By any reasonable reading of the facts about the bituminous coal industry in 1972 it was not likely to become in the foreseeable future the kind of tight oligopoly that is able to raise price above competitive levels, and that is contemplated in Turner's first condition. The rising concentration in coal is a product of the shift of the coal industry almost entirely into supplying fuel for electrical generation on long-term contracts.[36]

The decision thus seems to me to go too far on the facts of the case and the reasons adduced. Although Kennecott's acquisition of the nation's largest coal producer may be objectionable in the sense of creating a larger enterprise that was necessary for any efficiency, one might be more comfortable if the merger had been struck down in some other way—e.g., via the toehold theory.[37]

THE CURRENT LEGAL STATUS OF POTENTIAL COMPETITION

Table 10–1 schematically shows the cases discussed above. The courts have come a long way toward using potential competition to forge a general weapon for attacking conglomerate acquisitions whenever the acquirer is a large firm and the acquired firm is a leading producer.

While some of the decisions seem unsound to me on the factual situations involved, the notion involved in General Foods of looking

---

36. See generally *United States v. General Dynamics (United Electric Coal Companies and Freeman Coal Mining Corp.)*, 341 F.Supp. 534 (N.D. Ill. 1972), for a detailed discussion of the market structure of the coal industry.

37. Cf., *Kennecott Copper Corp. v. FTC*, 467 F.2d 67 (10th Cir. 1972), at 77 n8.

TABLE 10–1

Emerging Legal Bases for Use of "Potential Competition" in Section 7 Cases

Type of Effect	Structural Situation in Acquired Firm's Industry			
	1. Oligopoly 2. One of Few Most Probable Entrants 3. Entry Difficult	1. Oligopoly 2. ——— 3. Entry Difficult	1. Oligopoly 2. ——— 3. ———	1. Trend toward Concentration 2. ——— 3. Entry Difficult
A. Eliminate acquired firm as potential threat to acquirer	ALCOA (1922) El Paso (1964)			
B. Eliminate acquirer as a *de novo* entrant or a threat on edge of the market, in addition to acquired firm	Penn-Olin Theory (1965) Procter & Gamble (1967)			
C. Eliminate a threat on edge of the market which was not a probable *de novo* entrant but may have been perceived as one	Falstaff (1973)			
D. Eliminate a threat on the edge of the market, with no change in number of actual and potential entrants	Ford-Autolite (1968)			
E. Raise subsequent barriers to entry by entrenchment of a large acquirer	Procter & Gamble (1967)	General Foods-SOS (1967)	Wilson-Nissen (1968)	
F. Eliminate larger seller than necessary to enter	Bendix-Fram (1971)			Kennecott (1972)

at the *post-entry* condition of entry, and in Kennecott of inquiring as to the likelihood of creating a *post-entry* tight oligopoly even if the market were initially competitive, seems sensible.

Moreover, although the courts have opened up the possibilities, they have not gone all the way. The Supreme Court's affirmation of the district court's finding against the government in what is known as the Greeley Bank case[38] is perhaps a case in point. The district court had held that the acquisition of a bank in Greeley, Colorado, by a Denver bank holding company was not a violation of Section 7 because the acquiring bank was neither a potential *de novo* entrant, nor a force on the edge of the market, and that the acquisition did not promise to transform competition by virtue of the acquisition.[39] Similarly there are limits beyond which the FTC will not go, as evidenced in the recent Beatrice-Sexton decision.[40] Beatrice, a large diversified company, originally a dairy producer, now a conglomerate, ranking roughly two hundredth in assets and one hundredth in sales among industrial corporations, had acquired Sexton, a distributor of dry-processed foods to the food service industry with sales of roughly $100 million per year. The hearing examiner had found a violation of Section 7 because Beatrice was a likely or potential entrant into institutional dry wholesaling in which Sexton was a leading firm. The Commission reversed. The hearing examiner had found Sexton's industry was, and remained, unconcentrated, easy to enter, with a large number of potential entrants. The Commission held that even though Beatrice had been an obvious potential entrant, no probability of competitive harm could be inferred.

Thus the present legal stance appears open enough to embrace a variety of legal positions. If the Court's position on potential competition is inchoate, it seems possible that it may be shaped into a sufficiently embracing concept to deal with those conglomerate mergers that promise present or future harm to competition.

---

38. *United States v. First National Bancorporation,* 410 U.S. 577 (1973), affirming by an equally divided court 329 F.Supp. 1003 (D.C. Colo. 1971).

39. The government has tended to fare badly at the district court level in bank merger cases in recent years. See, Trier and Snider, "United States v. Falstaff Brewing Corporation: Potential Competition Re-Re-examined," 72 MICHIGAN LAW REVIEW 837–68 (March 1974).

40. *In re Beatrice Foods Co.,* [1970–1973 Transfer Binder] *CCH Trade Regulation Reporter,* ¶20,121 (FTC 1972).

Is Potential Competition a Satisfactory Policy Guide?

Potential competition appears to be an available legal handle for conglomerate merger policy. Can it be fashioned into an economically sensible one? I think the answer may well be yes. Such a policy must define rules that satisfy public goals by changing private behavior in desired directions. To see the dimensions of the problem, consider three policy stances that might be applied to firm X's desire to enter a particular industry. In Policy A no acquisition is permitted; in Policy B toehold acquisitions only are permitted, and in Policy C, any acquisition is permitted.

Next specify five actions by the potential acquirer/entrant:

1. *De novo* entry
2. Entry via toehold acquisition
3. Entry via large or leading-firm acquisition
4. No entry now, but subsequent potential entry if prices and profits rise significantly
5. No entry or acquisition reasonably foreseeable

Suppose that public preferences are such that lower numbered actions are always preferred to higher numbered ones, except that action 3 may in some circumstances be worse than 4 or 5.

Further assume that entrant/acquirers (absent legal barriers) prefer entry into an industry by large or leading-firm acquisition rather than toehold entry, and further prefer toehold acquisition to *de novo* entry.[41]

These assumptions are sufficient to define a sensible policy only if one can predict firms' responses if their preferred actions are prohibited. If one bars large-firm acquisitions, will the potential acquirer become a toehold acquirer, or will he withdraw to the sidelines? If one bars toehold entry will one induce *de novo* entry or loss of interest in entering in any form?

---

41. This need not be factually correct in all cases, but it is the theoretically interesting case. If a policy has any effect it is in such cases. For example, a policy that forbids large or leading-firm mergers but permits toehold acquisitions does not affect the probability of a *de novo* entry that would have occurred in any event, nor a toehold acquisition that was in the works. But it does force those who had planned a larger or leading-firm acquisition to choose between no entry and toehold acquisition.

One can go some distance toward a successful policy if one is prepared to regard leading-firm acquisitions as without redeeming value or as an outcome with less merit than nonentry: one need only define leading-firm acquisitions and prohibit them. While there are some economists who would go that far, I have two major reservations. The first is that the threat to large firms of being taken over may be a powerful control on their market behavior and their efficiency. The second is that the competitive role of the target firm before and after entry deserves to be considered. If competition is vigorous (whether or not it is structurally oligopolistic) and the industry is efficient there is little to be gained and much potentially lost by allowing a leading-firm acquisition. If, contrariwise, the industry is inefficiently run (whether or not it shows signs of being monopolistically controlled) an aggressive new firm might be beneficial. Entry by acquisition may be better than no entry. Moreover, if a tight oligopoly is already entrenched, there may be less hazard in a potential farther entrenchment than in the possibility that the new firm may upset established patterns. Just as acquisition of a failing company may be benign or positively beneficial so may acquisition of a competitively moribund one in a sluggish industry.

Policy may also be easy if one assumes that forbidding leading-firm acquisitions will virtually surely rechannel acquisitive instincts into toehold entry. This is a more common view, and seems to have gained great support at the FTC lately.[42]

In general if entry of a new firm is expected to invigorate competition, the choice among forms of entry will be on the basis of which form looks most promising in terms of a prompt and significant increase in the number of *vigorous* competitors.

But how can the policy maker who wishes to encourage entry determine the least restrictive form of entry? Here I expect looking closely at the identity of the potential entrants can be of great help. As a first approximation I would suggest that nearby market extension mergers may have a genuine *de novo* alternative; more distant market extension mergers and most product extension mergers would have a

---

42. A cynical prediction: If this view prevails and leads to the acquisition of many small businesses, I predict it will add fuel to the fears, discussed in chapter 11, that conglomerates do their real harm to the quality of society not to the quality of competition. When it does, the FTC is likely to find a way to oppose every toehold acquisition if the owners are small, or the acquirer is not locally controlled.

toehold acquisition alternative. At least, rebuttable presumptions in those directions might be warranted.

A different problem arises if the probabilities of both *de novo* and toehold entry are negligibly small. While toehold acquisitions may be attractive to acquirers in many market or product extension mergers, this is not the case in many pure conglomerate acquisitions. Suppose that because of high entry barriers and unaggressive management a particular industry has become notably inefficient. This was arguably the case in steel. Suppose now that a large conglomerate firm is willing to enter by a leading-firm acquisition but neither it nor anyone else will enter on a *de novo* or toehold basis. Prohibiting such acquisitions eliminates the takeover itself, for good or for ill, depending upon the market structure and the expected pro- and postacquisition market behavior. But it also removes whatever effect the threat of such acquisition might have on the leading firms in the industry. This last, the insulation of entrenched managements with large and/or leading-firm positions in oligopoly markets from effective challenge, may well be the most serious competitive consequence of a virtual per se rule against leading-firm acquisitions.

This argument against presumptive illegality of leading-firm acquisitions is all the stronger when the probability of such entry is small but not wholly negligible. A general policy against leading-firm acquisitions, or a series of consent decrees in which the principal conglomerate acquirers agree to abstain from major acquisitions, probably lifts the shadow of fear from a dozen corporate boardrooms for every merger it actually prevents.[43] If, as suggested earlier, one wishes to retain a credible threat of entry but not encourage much actual entry, *permitting* unexpected acquisitions may be highly desirable.[44] Fear of takeover may be a socially useful element in the

---

43. Some commentators, who have puzzled over why it was a conservative Republican Administration that took on the conglomerates, suggest the answer may lie in the protection such an attack provides to the conventional business establishment.

44. The threat can go beyond socially desirable ends. A large company (which must remain unnamed) was generating a high cash flow from current operations, and its best analysis suggested the funds ought to be held in relatively liquid form in anticipation of major needs three to five years ahead. The directors, in 1967, decided they could not afford to follow the optimal path because their improving liquidity made them a sitting duck for certain conglomerate acquirers. As a result they engaged in a series of acquisitions, whose main merit was to reduce the attractiveness of their own company as a target by decreasing its liquidity.

life of the manager of a large, established, profitable company. If the easy life is one of the rewards of the monopolist and a threat to competition, anything that makes him reluctant to enjoy those rewards may be competitively beneficial.

All of the above can be interpreted to say "it depends," and so, indeed, it does. Is there enough predictability to make general rules sensible? I believe there may be, as I will suggest in chapter 12.

CHAPTER ELEVEN

Economic and Legal Theories of the Effect on Competition III: Macro-concentration

MACRO-CONCENTRATION, unlike market concentration, is concerned with social rather than market structure, with the health of the enterprise system, rather than with the degree of monopoly power. So to classify the concerns does not diminish them, but it does warn of the dangers of substituting verbal characterization for analysis. Macro-concentration focuses attention upon a host of fears related to the growth and influence of the giant corporation; fears that promise to continue to play an important role in the public attitude toward conglomerate merger policy.

Consider the following, part of a speech delivered on June 6, 1969, in Savannah, Georgia:

> I believe that the future vitality of our free economy may be in danger because of the increasing threat of economic concentration by corporate mergers.
> In 1948, the nation's 200 largest industrial corporations controlled 48 percent of the manufacturing assets. Today, these firms control 58 percent, while the top 500 firms control 75 percent of these assets.
> The danger that this super-concentration poses to our economic, political and social structure cannot be overestimated.[1]

These words were delivered by the then Attorney General of the United States, John N. Mitchell, as he announced the new antitrust stance the Nixon Administration proposed to take.

The Attorney General of a conservative Republican Administration was thus picking up a theme more usually associated with the FTC, Ralph Nader, and others of the liberal establishment. It was less surprising that the opening sentence of the FTC *Economic Report on Corporate Mergers* (1969) read: "In unprecedented fashion the current merger movement is centralizing and consolidating corporate control and decision-making among a relatively few vast companies."

---

1. Speech reproduced in BNA *Antitrust and Trade Regulation Report,* no. 413 (June 10, 1969): X–9.

This view, by whomever expressed, echoes concerns that can be traced back at least to the nineteenth century.[2]

These concerns involve both economic and noneconomic values, and they relate both to giant corporations (where *size* is the essence of the concern) and to multiproduct, multimarket, multiindustry, and perhaps also multinational enterprises (where *diversity* heightens the concern with size).

Macro-concentration and Mergers: Some Statistics and Their Interpretation

SIZE OF LARGE MANUFACTURING AND MINING COMPANIES

Table 11–1 shows both the growing size of large corporations and the size of large acquisitions.[3] As can be seen the average asset size of the large manufacturing and mining (hereafter M & M) corporation increased dramatically between 1961 and 1971—by an amount roughly twice the increase in price levels of investment goods over the period. For our present concerns it is important to ask how significant a role mergers played in this growth.

Figure 11–1 gives a first perspective on this question for the period 1964–71, by comparing the level of and growth in total assets both to large assets acquired and to the new M & M investment in plant and equipment.[4] It is clear that even at its peak the great merger wave did not explain much of the growth in assets. This is perhaps most clearly seen by the comparison of the top-most (total assets) and bottom-most (merger acquired assets) lines in figure 11–1. Whatever the source of the growth in total assets, merger activity had little to do with it. The reason is suggested in table 11–2: many new large companies were "born," by internal growth of companies previously under $10 million in size, by mergers of smaller companies, and by

---

2. See footnote 18 below.

3. Certain computations on these data were looked at in chapter 1. See table 1–2.

4. These measures are not directly comparable in the sense of being components of one another. For one reason, the growth in total large firm M & M assets do not include M & M assets acquired by already large M & M companies. For another, the "new investment" series available covers *all* M & M companies (small as well as large) but covers only a portion of new investment.

TABLE 11–1

LARGE MANUFACTURING AND MINING ACQUISITIONS COMPARED TO
ALL LARGE MANUFACTURING AND MINING CORPORATIONS 1961–71
(ASSETS IN MILLIONS OF DOLLARS)

	CORPORATIONS OVER $10 MILLION IN ASSET SIZE			LARGE ACQUISITIONS*		
Year	*Total Assets*	*No. of Cor-pora-tions*	*Average Asset Size*	*Total Assets*	*No. of Com-panies*	*Average Asset Size*
1961	$222,938	2,100	$106.2	$2,356.4	60	$39.3
1962	238,002	2,178	109.3	2,447.9	80	30.6
1963	249,018	2,244	111.0	3,148.5	82	38.4
1964	264,448	2,307	114.6	2,727.6	91	30.0
1965	285,197	2,403	118.7	3,845.2	91	42.3
1966	319,845	2,518	127.0	4,170.6	101	41.3
1967	357,368	2,659	134.4	9,090.8	168	54.1
1968	398,847	2,646	150.7	13,297.3	207	64.2
1969	451,610	2,802	161.2	11,352.8	155	73.2
1970	504,543	2,930	172.2	6,346.4	98	64.8
1971†	538,216	2,962	181.7	2,544.3	66	38.6

SOURCE: FTC, *Current Trends in Merger Activity, 1971,* Statistical Report
No. 10 (Washington, D.C., May 1972), table 7. The FTC, Bureau of Economics, *Report on Mergers and Acquisitions* (Washington, D.C., October 1973),
table 18, issued as this manuscript went to press revises these series and the
absolute changes are significant. However, all trends are unaffected.

* Acquired firms with assets of $10 million or more.
† Figures for 1971 are preliminary.

new entry. For example, during the peak of the merger wave in 1967,
1968, and 1969 there were 530 large acquisitions. Yet by the end of
1969 there were 284 more large companies than in 1966, a *net* increase of more than 10 percent. If all 530 acquired companies were
subtracted from the list by virtue of acquisition, this means 714 new
companies were created. Because new companies might be smaller
than acquired companies, mere numbers while providing a simple
first test are not decisive.

In order to deal with "real" size I have deflated asset data introduced above by an appropriate price index.[5] Table 11–3 presents these

5. For total assets and assets acquired by merger, I have used the
implicit GNP deflator for all nonresidential fixed gross private domestic
investment. For plant and equipment I have used the producer's durable
equipment deflator.

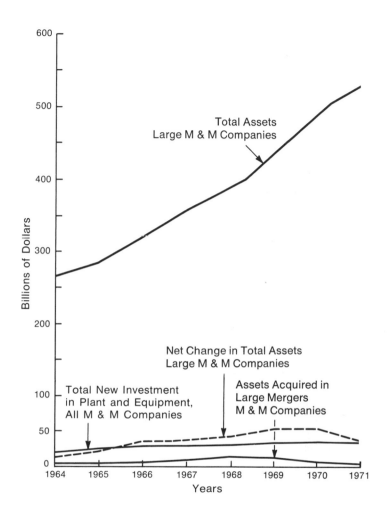

Fig. 11–1.   Assets acquired, 1964–71, in perspective.

data. Perhaps most revealing are the averages computed in the final two columns and plotted in figure 11–2. The first of these is the actual asset size, the second a measure from which any merger-caused growth has been eliminated. The average size of large corporations would not have been very different if none of the large mergers had occurred and the acquired companies had remained independent. If there is a "mere size" problem, it is not primarily a *merger* problem. The dramatic statement (cited earlier, and characteristic of a whole genre), "In unprecedented fashion the current merger movement is centralizing and consolidating corporate control and decision-making among a rela-

TABLE 11–2

NUMBERS OF LARGE MANUFACTURING AND MINING CORPORATIONS

			EXTREME ASSUMPTION: ALL LARGE ACQUISITIONS BY OTHER LARGE M & M COMPANIES	
Year	*Actual Number of Large Corporations* (1)	*Large Acquisitions* (2)	*Maximum Number of Companies If Large Mergers Prohibited** (3)	*Minimum Gross New Large Company Forma- tion†* (4)
1961	2,100	60	2,160	n.a.‡
1962	2,178	80	2,258	158
1963	2,244	82	2,326	148
1964	2,307	91	2,398	154
1965	2,403	91	2,494	187
1966	2,518	101	2,619	216
1967	2,659	168	2,827	209
1968	2,646	207	2,853	194
1969	2,802	155	2,957	311
1970	2,930	98	3,028	126
1971	2,962	66	3,023	98

SOURCE: Table 11–1.

* Column (1) + column (2).
† Column (1) + column (2).
‡ Not available.

tively few vast companies" must be understood to be hyperbole. Whether this fosters sound policy formulation is debatable.

THE 200 LARGEST M & M COMPANIES

Concentration, generally, focuses on the share of something controlled by the largest companies. Usual measures of *market concentration* use the share of production, or shipments, or sales of the 4 or 8 largest sellers. Macro-concentration which relates to no well-defined market usually concerns share of total assets, total sales, or total employment in the economy or in a sector of the economy, of the largest 100 to 500 firms.

I shall without loss of generality focus on the "200 largest" firms and asset measures in discussing macro-concentration. Table

TABLE 11-3

SELECTED ASSET MEASURES IN CONSTANT DOLLARS 1961–71

Year	Total Assets, All Large M & M Corporations (billions of 1958 dollars)	Yearly Change in Total Assets (billions of 1958 dollars)	Assets Acquired in Large M & M Acquisitions (billions of 1958 dollars)	Total New Investment for Plant and Equipment, All M & M Firms (billions of 1958 dollars)	Average Size of Large M & M Corporations (millions of 1958 dollars) Actual	Modified*
1961	$213.8	—	$ 2.257	$15.28	$101.7	$ 98.8
1962	225.2	$11.4	2.315	16.12	103.4	99.7
1963	231.6	6.4	2.928	17.10	103.2	99.6
1964	241.4	9.8	2.490	20.10	104.6	100.7
1965	256.6	15.2	3.460	23.97	106.8	103.0
1966	282.0	25.4	3.678	28.11	112.0	107.6
1967	302.7	20.7	7.702	27.63	113.9	107.1
1968	323.3	20.6	10.778	26.78	102.2	113.3
1969	347.7	24.4	8.740	29.08	124.1	117.6
1970	375.4	27.7	4.720	28.14	128.1	123.9
1971	378.1	2.7	1.787	25.90	127.7	125.0

* Modified mean uses column (3) of table 11–2 instead of column (1) for number of firms. It thus provides a minimum estimate of the asset size of large M & M corporations if all large M & M acquisitions had been prevented.

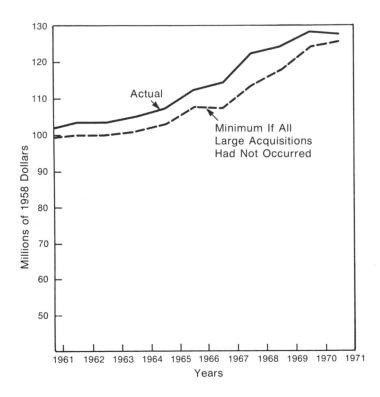

Fig. 11–2.   Average asset size of large manufacturing and mining companies (1958 dollars) 1961–71.

11–4 is a representative tabulation of the genre,[6] and I cite it without endorsing it. Everyone knows, and data of this sort confirm, that giant corporations exist and play major roles in the manufacturing industries. For half a century (at least) the largest 200 companies have collectively accounted for roughly half of all manufacturing assets. Recently that percentage has risen to about 60 percent.

There are many ambiguities involved in measures of this kind, and in interpreting what they show.[7] These are discussed in insightful

---

6. It is taken from the FTC, Bureau of Economics, *Economic Report on Corporate Mergers* (Washington, D.C., 1969), table 3–3. The report provides a wide variety of measures of macro-concentration in chapters 3 and 4.

7. There is a long literature on this topic dating at least from M. A. Adelman, "The Measurement of Industrial Concentration," *Review of Economics and Statistics* 33, no. 4 (November 1951): 269–96. It does

TABLE 11–4

SHARE OF MANUFACTURING ASSETS HELD BY THE 200
LARGEST CORPORATIONS,* 1929–41 AND 1947–68

| Year | PERCENTAGES | |
	Total Assets	*Corporate Assets*
1929	45.8	47.7
1931	49.0	50.9
1933	49.5	51.4
1935	47.7	49.6
1937	49.1	50.9
1939	48.7	50.5
1941†	45.1	46.7
1947	45.0	47.2
1948	46.3	48.3
1949	47.1	49.0
1950	46.1	47.7
1951	46.1	47.7
1952	47.7	49.2
1953	48.7	50.3
1954	50.4	52.1
1955	51.6	53.1
1956	52.8	54.1
1957	54.3	55.6
1958	55.2	56.6
1959	54.8	56.0
1960	55.2	56.3
1961	55.4	56.3
1962	55.1	56.0
1963	55.5	56.3
1964	55.8	56.6
1965	55.9	56.7
1966	56.1	56.7
1967	58.7	59.3
1968	60.4	60.9

SOURCE: Federal Trade Commission, Bureau of Economics, *Economic Report on Corporate Mergers* (Washington, D.C., 1969), p. 173.

* Ranked according to asset size in each year.
† Data are not available for the years between 1941 and 1947 because some large corporations did not publish balance sheets for reasons of wartime security.

not seem necessary here to review or cite it. In particular, I shall neglect important, though minor, sources of confusion—such as the inclusion of foreign assets of these large corporations and inclusion of nonmanufacturing assets of manufacturing firms—in favor of major ones. This is justi-

detail by Betty Bock.[8] Of particular importance is the fact that the identity of the largest 200 industrial firms changes year by year, for a variety of reasons. Firms may disappear due to merger, or failure, or because they become nonindustrial; they may survive but be displaced by other originally smaller firms, by entering ones, or by firms newly classified as industrial, etc. Data which compare the assets of whatever group is the largest 200 in one year with another group that is the largest in a second year (what Bock calls "an each year game"), tell more about the role of large firms in the economy (or in the manufacturing sector) than about the behavior of individual firms. Obviously it makes a difference if the same 200 firms are largest or if their composition changes sharply.

Table 11–5, from the more recent Bock study, illustrates some of the complexities involved in comparing two years some distance apart. Two hundred and fifty-nine different individual corporations were in the 200 largest in either 1954 or 1968. The first line shows that the total assets of the 200 industrial corporations which were largest increased by 232 percent. Since all manufacturing corporations (line 15) increased their assets by only 171 percent, the largest 200 increased their relative share of total assets. *Macro-concentration* thus increased.

In order to provide a path through the maze created by a changing set of firms, look at table 11–6, derived from the Bock data, and some analysis thereon by Lee Preston, cited just below. Bear in mind, as a benchmark, the 171 percent increase of assets of all manufacturing firms between 1954 and 1968 (shown on line 15 of table 11–5). A "continuing giant" is a company that was on the list of the largest 200 in both years. Line 8 of table 11–6 shows their assets increased by 182 percent, slightly above the benchmark rate of increase, but at least roughly proportional to overall growth. In sharp contrast great increases in assets were achieved by the *additions* to the giants' list, as shown on lines 9 to 12 of table 11–6.

---

fied, in my view, in this context because I will conclude that whatever macro-concentration shows in general, it is not very significantly a *merger* or merger-related phenomenon.

8. Betty Bock, *Statistical Games and the "200 Largest Industrials," 1954 and 1968,* Studies in Business Economics No. 115 (New York, 1970); and Bock, *Antitrust Issues in Conglomerate Acquisitions: Tracking a Moving Target,* Studies in Business Economics No. 110 (New York, 1969).

TABLE 11-5

259 INDUSTRIAL CORPORATIONS THAT WERE THE "200 LARGEST" IN TOTAL REPORTED ASSETS IN 1954 OR 1968, SUMMARY DATA

Corporate Sets	ASSET DATA			ACQUISITION DATA ASSETS ACQUIRED THROUGH "LARGE" ACQUISITIONS, 1955-68	
	TOTAL ASSETS ($ millions)		Percentage Change in Total Assets, 1954-68	Total ($ millions)	As a Percentage of Change in Assets, 1954-68
	1954 (1)	1968 (2)	(3)	(4)	(5)
(1) The "200 Largest" in 1954 and in 1968: an each-year game	$91,126	$302,772	232	$14,892	9
(2) The "200 Largest" in 1954: an initial-year game	91,126	249,173	173	14,694	9
(3) 141 corporations among the "200 Largest," 1954 and 1968	80,489	241,763	200	14,694	9
(4) 59 corporations not among the "200 Largest" in 1968	10,637	7,410	−30	—	—
(5) 27 corporations below the "200 Largest" in 1968	3,959	7,410	87	198	6
(6) 32 corporations acquired by other corporations, 1955-68	6,678	—	—	—	—
(7) The "200 Largest" in 1968: an end-year game	86,989	302,772	248	28,100	13
(8) 141 corporations among the "200 Largest," 1954 and 1968	80,489	241,763	200	14,694	9
(9) 59 corporations not among the "200 Largest" in 1954	6,500	61,009	839	13,406	25
(10) 43 corporations for which 1954 asset data were available	2,638	28,712	988	8,857	34
(11) 3 corporations for which 1954 asset data first appeared after 1954 and were below the 1954 cut-off		5,464		2,212	41
(12) 5 corporations incorporated after 1954		3,564		754	21
(13) 5 corporations not classified as industrials in 1954	1,493	12,002	703	1,271	12
(14) 3 other corporations	2,369	11,267	376	312	4
(15) All manufacturing corporations (cols. 1, 2, and 3)	178,986	485,901	171		
(16) All "large" manufacturing and mining acquisitions (cols. 4 and 5)				38,439	13

SOURCE: Betty Bock, *Statistical Games and the "200 Largest Industrials," 1954 and 1968*, Studies in Business Economics No. 115 (New York, 1970), pp. 10–13.

NOTE: Original sources and footnotes omitted here.

297

TABLE 11–6

GIANT FIRMS (TOP 200) 1954 AND 1968

	Number	ASSETS ($ BILLIONS)		Percentage Increase in Assets
		1954	1968	
1954 Giants				
1. Continuing giants	141	80.5	241.8*	200
2. 1954 giants acquired by 1954 giants	17	5.2	incl. above	n.a.
3. Surviving assets of surviving 1954 giants	158	85.7	241.8	182
4. Renamed giants†	11	0.9	2.7‡	
5. Continuing giants (adjusted)	169	86.6	244.5	182
6. Removed giants§	31	4.5	4.7	4.4
7. All 1954 giants	200	91.1	249.2	173
1968 Giants				
8. Continuing giants (adjusted)	169	86.6	244.5	182
9. Newly grown giants‖	32	1.7	26.0	1398
10. New giants#	8	—	9.0	—
11. Newly listed giants**	8	3.9	23.3	503
12. Subtotal: new giants	48	5.6	58.3	941
13. All 1968 giants	217††	92.2‡‡	302.8	228

SOURCE: Table 11–5, modified to divide differently certain categories, as described in the footnotes.

* Includes assets of firms in line (2).

† 1954 giants acquired by firms not previously on the list, that were 1968 giants under new corporate name.

‡ Estimated by me. I have attempted to include only the acquired companies' portion of the acquiring companies' assets.

§ 1954 giants not included in 1968 list. Of these four were acquired by other firms that did not subsequently make the 1968 list, and 27 retained their identity but fell below the size required to make 1968 list.

‖ Companies which in 1954 were too small for list, but whose growth warranted inclusion in 1968. Line (10) of table 11–5 less the eleven renamed giants.

Lines (11) and (12), table 11–5.

** Lines (13) and (14), table 11–5.

†† These "217" nominal companies represent 200 1968 decision makers. See line (2) above.

‡‡ Differs from table 11–5 line (7) because it includes assets of 17 companies shown on line (2) above. These assets are in both 1954 and 1968 lists and thus do not represent an increase in assets controlled between the two years.

This is significant, but hardly surprising; rapidly growing firms have a better chance of being on a "biggest" list than do firms that grow less rapidly or decline. The measure of growth shown in line 13 is made larger by the fact that the assets concerned included the assets of what were in 1954 more than 200 firms.

Returning to table 11–5, it is clear from a comparison of columns (4) and (5) that large acquisitions accounted for under 10 percent of the growth of assets of the largest 200 firms, except for the "emerging" giants—those not on the list at the beginning of the period. Evidently mergers provided an important source of upward mobility to firms below the top-size group.

These data have been extensively analyzed. Let me briefly cite two somewhat different conclusions, by two highly competent analysts.

The [data] suggest that internal growth and small acquisitions have played a more significant role in the growth of the "200 largest" industrial corporations as a group than have "large" acquisitions, and this is so regardless of whether one takes the "200 largest" in 1954, the "200 largest" in 1968, or the "200 largest" in both years.

The [data] also suggest that "large" acquisitions played a more substantial role in permitting companies below the "200 largest" to challenge the positions of those originally among the "200 largest" than in supporting the growth of corporations already in the set.[9]

Professor Preston analyzed these same data more fully by distinguishing among several groups. One hundred and two of the 141 continuing giants were engaged in at least one large manufacturing and mining acquisition. These "acquiring giants" were contrasted to 39 "non-acquiring giants" and to two sets of 59 "turn-over giants." Table 11–7 reproduces his tabulation. He interprets the findings as follows:[10]

Mergers did not account for the major portion of the growth of these firms over the period, but merger-acquired assets accounted for more than half of the *relative* growth of the Acquiring Giants as compared to all manufacturing corporations. It would not, of course, be correct to conclude that the Acquiring Giants would have increased their share of corporate assets less than half as much as they did during this period—still less that their shares, like those of the 39 non-merging giants would have

9. Bock, *Statistical Games,* pp. 22, 24.

10. Lee E. Preston, "Giant Firms, Large Mergers and Concentration: Patterns and Policy Alternatives, 1954–1968," *Industrial Organization Review* 1, no. 1 (1973): 39.

declined—if they had not engaged in large mergers. Other growth alternatives might have been pursued with equal or even greater success. On the other hand, the impact of mergers on corporate growth may be understated by simple asset comparisons, since these take no account of the postmerger growth of the acquired activities. It is indisputable, however, that the Surviving Giant firms over this period were heavily involved in merger activity. Thus, although it is probably not true that *all* of the increase in aggregate concentration, either among the 102 Acquiring Giants or among all giant firms, was due to merger activity, the strong association between giant firm survival and growth, on one hand, and large mergers, on the other, is undeniable.

TABLE 11–7

AVERAGE RANKS AND ASSET SIZES OF 200 LARGEST FIRMS, 1954 AND 1968

	Number of Firms	1954	1968
		Average Rank (assets)	
Acquiring giants	102	81	81
Nonacquiring giants	39	88	107
Turnover giants			
1954	59	142	—
1968	59	—	130
		Average Asset Size (millions)	
Acquiring giants	102	$570	$1,809
Nonacquiring giants	39	574	1,467
Turnover giants			
1954	59	180	—
1968	59	—	1,034
200 giant firms	200	456	1,514

SOURCE: Lee E. Preston, "Giant Firms, Large Mergers and Concentration: Patterns and Policy Alternatives, 1954–1968," *Industrial Organization Review* 1, no. 1 (1973): pp. 35–46, table 2.

Although Bock and Preston put somewhat different glosses on their interpretations, it seems to me that they are both correct, and that each puts the factual picture in better perspective than the FTC report or the alarmist rhetoric. Clearly large firms do play a major role in American industry; clearly large firms grow both internally and by merger; clearly not all firms grow at the same rate and thus new and rapidly growing firms intrude into the list of largest companies displacing others that have grown less rapidly and replacing large firms that have disappeared. While mergers play a role in the activities of many large companies, they play on average a lesser role than other forms of growth.

The phenomenon of the large firm and of macro-concentration is thus not exclusively or primarily a product of the large merger. Preston in an interesting further analysis[11] shows that if the Neal Task Force proposal barring all acquisitions between "very large firms" and "leading firms"[12] had been in effect, roughly 27 mergers involving $3 billion of assets (less than 8 percent of all assets acquired in large acquisitions over the period) would not have occurred. This would not have changed significantly the structure of American manufacturing, nor even the role of mergers in affecting it. Yet the Neal proposals seem to me to represent the outer limits of public policies toward mergers that we might expect. If large size firms and their share of total assets really pose a danger that "cannot be overestimated," the problem is not in dominant part a failure of merger policy.

The Effects of Macro-concentration

THE RELATIONSHIP OF MACRO- AND MARKET CONCENTRATION

Despite a recent challenge to the view, there is a very widespread belief in an inverse relationship (at least in some ranges) between concentration, represented by the market shares of the n (usually 4 or 8) largest firms, and the intensity of competition in the *market*.[13]

---

11. Preston, "Giant Firms."

12. The Task Force defined a "very large firm" to be one with sales in excess of $500 million or assets in excess of $250 million. A "leading firm" was defined as having both (*a*) a market share of more than 10 percent *and* (*b*) position as one of the top four firms in a market with four-firm concentration above 50 percent. The statute would apply only to markets in which aggregate sales amounted to more than $100 million.

13. The theoretical notion that concentration ratios provide a proxy measure for the inherently unmeasurable "intensity of competition" hardly needs documentation. The central empirical linkage that high concentration ratios are associated with high and persistent profits, and thus with monopoly power was first presented by Joe S. Bain, "Relation of Profit Rate to Industry Concentration: American Manufacturing 1936–40," *Quarterly Journal of Economics* 65, no. 3 (August 1951): 293–324. Yale Brozen challenges the findings and the hypothesis of Bain and the subsequent literature, in Yale Brozen, "The Antitrust Task Force Deconcentration Recommendation," 13 JOURNAL OF LAW AND ECONOMICS, no. 2,

In contrast, the share of assets, sales, or profits controlled by the *n* (usually 100 to 500) largest firms, on increases therein, does not necessarily say anything about the level of concentration in any individual market. The uncertain linkage of macro-concentration to market concentration is nicely illustrated by an example of Neil Jacoby.[14] Suppose there are 500 industries (analogous to the SIC four-digit ones) which are aggregated into 20 broad industry groups (analogous to the SIC two-digit industries). Suppose there are only 500 firms in the economy, all giants. Visualize three alternative organizations of them—each of which exhibits the same macro-concentration:

a)   *A single industry structure* in which there is one large firm in each industry. Each such firm would have a high degree of monopoly power in its market.

b)   *A concentric industry structure* in which each firm operates to some extent in all of the industries of *one* of the major industry groups into which the industries are aggregated. Each industry would have an average of 25 firms and its market structure might be highly competitive or highly oligopolistic. The particular form of market structure would depend upon the number and relative sizes of firms, their product specializations, etc. Some of these industries might be highly concentrated, others not.[15]

c)   *A totally conglomerate structure* in which each firm operated approximately proportionally in each of the 500 industries. Whatever might be true of the efficiency of such an arrangement, market concentration would surely be negligible.

270–92 (October 1970). This paper has begun a new controversy, of which the following two articles are but the opening shots. See Paul Mac-Avoy, James W. McKie, and Lee E. Preston, "High and Stable Concentration Levels, Profitability, and Public Policy: A Response," 14 JOURNAL OF LAW AND ECONOMICS, no. 2, 493–99 (October 1971); and Yale Brozen, "The Persistence of 'High Rates of Return' in High-Stable Concentration Industries," 14 JOURNAL OF LAW AND ECONOMICS, no. 2, 501–12 (October 1971). For present purposes this debate need not concern us, though if Brozen is correct that concentration measures nothing, much antitrust law and industrial organization theory needs recasting.

14. See Neil H. Jacoby, "The Conglomerate Corporation," *Center Magazine* 2, no. 4 (July 1969): 51.

15. Four-firm concentration in a 25-firm industry could be as low as 16 percent but could also approach 100 percent. The more diversified these firms were, the lower the concentration ratio.

While there is thus no necessary theoretical link between macro-concentration and market concentration, there may be an empirical one. Many of the real-world giant corporations are specialized in relatively few industries, and the power their size confers is in good part market power. General Motors, General Electric, U.S. Steel, Goodyear, Boeing, R. J. Reynolds, DuPont—to name a few—are familiar manufacturing giants and while each is diversified, its major product lines can be correctly specified without much research. While not all large firms have large market shares, and not all large market shares are held by large firms, it is empirically correct that overall there is a strong positive relationship between size of firm and market share. This positive, albeit imperfect, relationship implies a positive relationship between size of firm, the *level* of macro-concentration and the *level* of market concentration in at least some markets. But it need say nothing about the relation of *changes* in macro-concentration to *changes* in levels of market concentration; yet this latter is what a conglomerate merger may affect.

To what extent do increases in macro-concentration lead to increases in market concentration? Preston looked at the shares held by the 200 largest firms of the total assets of all firms in each of 19 two-digit manufacturing industries in both 1954 and 1968, a period over which macro-concentration increased.[16] Table 11–8 crossclassifies these 19 industry groups according to the level and direction of change of the giant firms' share of their industry groups' assets.

While two-digit industries are not ideal proxies for economic markets, if there were a market pattern of increasing market concentration in concentrated industries it would be expected to show up in such a tabulation. No such showing occurs.[17] In only five industry groups did the giant firms' share increase appreciably and in only two

---

16. Preston, "Giant Firms."

17. This is not, of course, to say that during this period mergers (or other changes) did not increase market concentration in particular industries. Much of the antimerger litigation of the period was concerned with such cases and with trends toward increased concentration brought about by mergers in such areas as retailing, food service, and coal production. At the same time, a 1965 study by Leonard Weiss suggested that in six major industries mergers occurred but had little effect on concentration. Cf. Leonard W. Weiss, "An Evaluation of Mergers in Six Industries," *Review of Economics and Statistics* 47, no. 2 (May 1965): 172–81. His six industries were steel, automobiles, petroleum refining, cement, flour, and brewing.

TABLE 11–8

ASSET SHARE OF GIANT CORPORATIONS IN MAJOR INDUSTRY GROUPS
(BY LEVEL AND CHANGE BETWEEN 1954 AND 1968)

Giant's Share of Assets of Group, in Year in Which Share Was Higher	CHANGE IN SHARE BETWEEN 1954 AND 1968			
	Decreased by 5 Percentage Points or More	Stayed within ±5 Percentage Points	Increased by 5 Percentage Points or More	All
Less than 10%	—	3	—	3
10–29.9%	1	1	1	3
30–49.9%	—	3	2	5
50–69.9%	1	1	2	4
70% or more	3	1	—	4
All	5	9	5	19

SOURCE: Preston, "Giant Firms, Large Mergers and Concentration: Patterns and Policy Alternatives, 1954–1968," *Industrial Organization Review* 1, no. 1 (1973).

did it both increase and reach 50 percent, precisely the expected number of cases if levels and directions of change were uncorrelated.

As an empirical matter, then, there is no weight of evidence to suggest that whatever increases in macro-concentration have occurred in the past two decades have led to a general pattern of increase in market concentration.

SIZE PER SE

The distinction between size and diversity is particularly important when looking at the significance of conglomerate mergers and conglomerate firms. For while some conglomerates are giants, most large companies are not in any sense conglomerates. In 1968, at the height of the conglomerate wave there were 5 large conglomerates in the top 60 firms (ranked according to sales). They ranked 14 (ITT); 30 (LTV); 45 (Tenneco); 48 (Litton); 59 (Textron). If size is the major concern, the conglomerate firms are only part of the problem. In the 1969 list of the 200 largest industrials, only 8 were conglomerates.

Concerns with size per se are neither new nor surprising in a society that theoretically reveres the invisible hand, but often witnesses the all-too-visible paw.[18] These concerns have been part of our political and economic heritage at least since Berle and Means's seminal contribution of four decades ago.[19]

Behind the concern is, partly, a notion of competitive fairness. Corwin Edwards, just after completing a seven-year stint as chief economist for the FTC, suggested a smorgasbord of advantages of large size firms each of which disturbed him:

. . . the large enterprise has advantages over the small in its capacity to spend money or take losses at any selected point at which it encounters a small rival, in its enjoyment of discriminations and preferences, in its ability to control distributors, customers and sources of supply by tie-in sales and exclusive dealing arrangements, and in its opportunities to strengthen its position through exchanges of favors with other large enterprises. . . .

The large company's advantage in litigation is derived from the fact that it can afford to maintain its own law office and to disregard the costs of litigation in determining its legal tactics. . . . The campaign contributions of large companies and the occasional case of direct or indirect bribery are probably the least significant sources of the large company's political power. . . . Within wide limits, it can buy its own reputation. Good repute, in turn, may be used for market advantage, political advantage or advantage in controversies with other economic groups.

The large concern also has an advantage in finance. It is a large user of the services of commercial banks and investment banks, keeps large sums on deposit and therefore receives the consideration given a valued customer.[20]

Edwards's list ranges from the anticompetitive and the unfair through the achievement of real efficiencies to the use of political power and influence. Suppose that many of these effects do occur, and

---

18. As an indication of how long these concerns have been articulated, let me note the dictum of Judge Hand in *United States v. Aluminum Co. of America*, 148 F.2d 416, 428 (2d Cir. 1945), "industrial consolidations are inherently undesirable, regardless of their economic results." Hand cited Senator Sherman (1890), and Mr. Justice Peckham in *Trans-Missouri Freight* (1897) in support. I dare say neither Sherman nor Peckham were regarded as breaking new doctrinal ground, at the time of their remarks.

19. A. A. Berle and G. C. Means, *The Modern Corporation and Private Property* (New York, 1932).

20. Corwin D. Edwards, "Conglomerate Bigness as a Source of Power," National Bureau of Economic Research, *Business Concentration and Price Policy* (New York, 1955): 344–48.

are in fact judged undesirable. Why then do we tolerate large firms rather than prohibiting firms beyond a certain size? Presumably this is because we cannot extirpate such firms without risk to the benefits that large size firms confer, or because the costs of attacking them are themselves regarded as too high. In either case it suggests that, on average, the social benefits of much of the large size that we have in the economy are judged to exceed the costs. To say that fears of size are not decisive is (of course) not to say that they are groundless, as some have urged, nor that they are in a fundamental sense less worthy than fears about market power narrowly conceived. But a mere listing of legitimate concerns about size does not itself provide a viable or sensible policy.

In any event, it seems clear that concerns about size are not exclusively, nor indeed primarily, a concern with mergers. As we have seen (table 11–7), acquiring giants were not materially different in size or rank within the top 200, from nonacquiring ones, and many of the largest firms in the economy have not engaged in major mergers for at least half a century. Moreover even merging firms have grown much more by internal growth than by acquisitions.[21]

A widely held belief however is that size achieved by merger is less likely to achieve economies than is size achieved by internal growth,[22] and thus the concerns about disadvantages of large firms become more compelling. From this it is but a small step to the argument that growth by *conglomerate* merger is least likely to produce desirable synergies, and thus that such mergers provide the first line of attack on size per se, and the macro-concentration that reflects it.

I cannot assess the implicit factual assertion that underlies this line of argument, but perhaps I can usefully restate it. It is that, other things equal, large firms that achieved their size by internal growth will prove to be more efficient than those that achieved their success by merger, and further that among the latter group, the least efficient subgroup will be those whose growth has been conglomerate. This is a testable hypothesis, but it has not yet been shown to be valid. It is important to distinguish this hypothesis from the demonstrably correct but much less interesting statements that not all increases in

---

21. There may nevertheless be practical reasons why, if size is a concern, merger induced growth is a particularly attractive point of attack. See below, page 316.

22. Weiss, "An Evaluation of Mergers," argues that this belief is not confirmed by his studies of six major industries.

size are motivated by efficiency considerations, and that not all giant firms have proven efficient.

CONGLOMERATENESS PER SE

As of 1973, not a little influenced by the revelations concerning ITT, the conglomerate corporation suffered from a bad press. A year earlier both the Republican and Democratic 1972 platforms gave the conglomerates a major portion of the attention they devoted to business organization.

The Republican plank said:

We will press on for greater competition in our economy. The energetic antitrust program of the past four years demonstrates our commitment to free competition as our basic policy. The Antitrust Division has moved decisively to invalidate those "conglomerate" mergers which stifle competition and discourage economic concentration.

The Democratic plank said, in relevant parts:

The Democratic Party deplores the increasing concentration of economic power in fewer and fewer hands. Five percent of the American people control 90 percent of our productive national wealth. Less than one percent of all manufacturers have 88 percent of the profits. . . . The rest of the population—including all working men and women—pay too much for essential products and services because of national policy and market distortions. . . .

To this end, the Federal government should:

Step up anti-trust action to help competition, *with particular regard to laws and enforcement curbing conglomerate mergers* which swallow up efficient small business and feed the power of corporate giants;

Strengthen the anti-trust laws so that the divestiture remedy will be used vigorously to *break up large conglomerates* found to violate the anti-trust laws. [Emphasis supplied.]

Before looking briefly at the sources of this bipartisan aversion, it is interesting to note that a handful of years previously, the conglomerates were cherished rather than excoriated by the press, and by much of the public.[23] The transformation (in my view) occurred

---

23. I can demonstrate this most easily by quoting from an article of mine in 1969. Cf. "Conglomerates and the Public Interest," 14 LAW QUADRANGLE NOTES 16–17 (Spring 1970): "The personality cult of the conglomerators—the Ling's, the Geneen's, the Ash's, the Bluhdorn's that

primarily not in response to some newly published basic research nor even because of particular scandalous behavior but, more mundanely, because of the reversal of the fortunes of those who gambled on the stocks of the conglomerates.

Are there substantive reasons for concern with the *conglomerate* aspect of macro-concentration? The possibility of unilateral anti-competitive activities by the conglomerate firm was discussed in chapter 9 with reference to predatory pricing, reciprocity, and cross-subsidization. Beyond these, the fears I have identified are of three principal kinds.

"Community of interest."   The nature of what is feared was succinctly restated in the FTC, *Economic Report:*

When firms meet each other as rivals in many markets, in some of which they are dominant firms and in others in which they may hold more vulnerable positions, their conduct options are no longer constrained solely by what happens in particular markets. Other firms in the markets may adjust their strategies in various ways to accommodate to the presence of multi-market competitors. Thus, the presence of multi-market firms introduces a new element of market structure.[24]

Fortune, Time, and even the *Wall Street Journal* and the *New York Times* profile with such attention and loving care—is characterized (in restrained moments) by phrases such as 'exuberant,' 'dynamic,' and 'high riding.' Compare: 'quietly competent,' 'shrewd,' and 'imaginative,' adjectives recently used to describe the new Ford troika. Whether there is a real difference underlying such semantics is incidental to me and I leave the matter to the psychologists. But the attitude of the press and the public *is* revealing. For if it is true, as I believe, that these men and their companies excite more admiration than apprehension on the part of the public at large, it argues against the existence of a latent demand for public action to close the outlets for the dynamism. I am not enough of a social historian to know when Vanderbilt, Carnegie, Ford and Rockefeller, and others of those now called robber barons, were transformed from folk heroes into sinister oligarchs, but it is clear that such a shift did occur sometime after the era of Horatio Alger, and before the time of FDR—helped no little by Ida Tarbell, Upton Sinclair and by the crash of 1929." (The fact that as this book is published a Ford and a Rockefeller are President and Vice-President is the sort of coincidence that makes strong men tremble.)

24. FTC, *Economic Report,* p. 220. A number of episodes allegedly illustrative of such behavior are presented on pages 458–71. Corwin Edwards made this charge twenty years ago. See Corwin Edwards, "Conglomerate Bigness as a Source of Power," National Bureau of Economics, *Business Concentration and Public Policy* (New York, 1955).

These concerns are an extension of an old and traditional fear that competition can be frustrated at the highest levels of corporate control, by explicit or tacit willingness to refrain from vigorous competition with other large companies, and/or to compete unfairly with smaller ones. Section 8 of the Clayton Act (1914) limited interlocking directorates between competitors.[25] The concern was that two companies that were in vertical or horizontal relationships would, via interlocking directorships, find opportunities for anticompetitive actions not otherwise available. The present charge is broader and involves a less explicit link; it is that the multiproduct conglomerates are inherently in competition with one another in many markets and thus need no common directors, etc., to make them aware of their competitive interlocks. The FTC *Economic Report's* most telling example relates to duPont's relations with the British Imperial Chemical Industries in the 1920s. It cites duPont documents as follows:

It is not good business sense to attempt an expansion in certain directions if such an act is bound to result as a boomerang of retaliation. It has been the DuPont's policy to follow such lines of common sense procedure. . . . This was done on the broad theory that cooperation is wiser than antagonism, and that in the matter of detail the chances in the long run were that the boot was just as likely to be on one leg as on the other.[26]

Whether this example shows *conglomerate* tacit agreement or simply ordinary oligopolistic recognition of interdependence is almost beside the point. This example and a handful of others certainly confirm the possibility of systematic self-restraint, implicit conspiracy, or even covert agreement, but they hardly prove these are the normal

---

25. This problem did not catch much popular fancy until the TNEC investigations of the late thirties. It was the subject of an FTC monograph published in 1951. See FTC, *Report of the FTC on Interlocking Directorates* (1951). See also Federal Trade Commission, Bureau of Economics, *Annual Report* (Washington, D.C., 1950), p. 19. Section 8 while seldom used is not entirely a dead letter, as the November 1972 Complaint by the FTC against ALCOA shows. Two complaints were issued under Section 8, one concerning ALCOA and Kennecott Copper, the other, ALCOA and ARMCO Steel. See *In re Georgia-Pacific Corp.*, 3 *CCH Trade Regulation Reporter*, ¶20,147 (FTC order 1972).

26. FTC, *Economic Report*, p. 462, citing originally: *United States v. Imperial Chemical Industries*, 100 F.Supp. 504 (S.D. N.Y. 1951), Government Exhibit 37, pp. 198, 200.

or expected forms of behavior.[27] Nor do they suggest why tacit collusion among ITT, LTV, and Tenneco is more likely because they are all giants than between General Electric and Westinghouse. Once again, while almost anything is possible in behavior, I am aware of no evidence supporting the sort of deferential treatment of *one conglomerate by another* that appears to be alleged as a special danger of conglomeration.

Political influence.   The involvement of ITT with the Nixon administration in financial contributions to the proposed 1972 San Diego convention, in negotiating a settlement of its three outstanding antitrust suits, and in its offer to provide funds to the CIA for anti-Allende operations within Chile (and quite possibly in yet to be disclosed other ways), are truly disturbing elements on the national scene. But do they indict conglomerates? My own view is that they tell us more about the unusual morality of the Nixon Administration (on which we have some corroborative evidence) and of Harold Geneen than about conglomerate corporations generally.

That giant corporations can and do exert influence and political power is hardly to be denied in a year such as 1972 in which Boeing, Lockheed, and the Penn Central Railroad, as well as ITT, were repeatedly on the front pages of the newspapers by virtue of government involvement in their affairs, and vice versa. Political power conferred by size arises in part simply because the welfare of the large company looms decisive in the consciousness of legislators whose constituencies lie in the shadow of its plants. The firm with plants in fifty congressional districts has many spokesmen. Whenever a major company is in trouble, whether by virtue of financial mismanagement, foreign competition, loss of a government contract, or government regulation, its stockholders and managers, and also its employees, its suppliers (and their employees and suppliers), see themselves as bearing the brunt of the costs, and turn to their political representatives for help. Obviously too, the political power of large contributions, small favors, and indefatigable lobbyists cannot be ignored. Presumably companies

---

27. Interestingly each of the examples used by the FTC at the place cited, except the one quoted, involved conduct that if proved would have been manifestly illegal. They thus tend to suggest the not-very-surprising conclusion that some giant firms violate the antitrust laws some of the time.

do those things because they pay, and there may well be economies of scale in lobbying.

But granting all of these possibilities, there seems little evidence that political amorality or immorality is primarily a conglomerate problem, or a merger-induced problem, or even a corporate problem. Obviously, size and diversity that are otherwise without redeeming value may be harmful—but if this is the case we are back to the sort of polar position discussed in chapter 3 and sound policy is obvious and easy. This view does not command instant adherence because its postulates are not met.

Political concerns seem to me to deserve inclusion in the balance, but they hardly dominate it. Certainly they do not seem the sole province of the conglomerate merger, nor is merger policy the most likely basis of attack on corruption in political decision making.

Conglomerate centralization. The replacement of independent, decentralized decision making by a smaller number of centralized decision makers may be accelerated under a conglomerate structure.[28] The financial orientation of the conglomerate corporation may tend to concentrate the headquarters locations of scattered activities into major financial centers. This has concerned such diverse commentators as Mr. Justice Douglas and Richard McLaren.

Mr. McLaren, shortly after taking over the Antitrust Division, put it this way:

I am concerned also about the increasing size of these mergers. Aside from the competitive impact of increased economic concentration, I am concerned over the human dislocations which result from these mergers. When the headquarters of one or two large companies are removed from the nation's smaller cities to New York or Chicago or Los Angeles, I think we all recognize that there is a serious impact upon the community.

The loss is felt by its banks, its merchants, its professional and service people—accountants, lawyers, advertising agencies. The community loses some of its best educated, most energetic and public spirited citizens.

I am concerned that even some of our cities may become "branch

---

28. John Narver, *Conglomerate Mergers and Market Competition* (Berkeley, Calif., 1967), *defines* conglomerates as the application of financial resources to multimarket activities. This interesting insight causes him to overlook almost all other aspects of the conglomerate phenomenon.

house cities," whose major business affairs are directed by absentee managers.[29]

Those words echo those of Justice Douglas two decades earlier in the Standard Stations case:

But beyond all that there is the effect on the community when independents are swallowed up by the trusts and entrepreneurs become employees of absentee owners. Then there is a serious loss in citizenship. Local leadership is diluted. He who was a leader in the village becomes dependent on outsiders for his action and policy. Clerks responsible to a superior in a distant place take the place of resident proprietors beholden to no one. These are the prices which the nation pays for the almost ceaseless growth in bigness on the part of industry.[30]

A quarter century later, in Falstaff, Justice Douglas was even more eloquent:

A case in point is Goldendale in my State of Washington. It was a thriving community—an ideal place to raise a family—until the company that owned the sawmill was bought by an out-of-state giant. In a year or so, auditors in faraway New York City, who never knew the glories of Goldendale, decided to close the local mill and truck all the logs to Yakima. Goldendale became greatly crippled. It is Exhibit A to the Brandeis concern, which became part of the Clayton Act concern, with the effects that the impact of monopoly often has on a community, as contrasted with the beneficent effect of competition.
A nation of clerks is anathema to the American antitrust dream. . . .[31]

How seriously one views these considerations is a matter of taste, and, in the end, of a collective political judgment. My reaction to this speculation is one of letdown. Surely the plights of displaced managers, disappointed city fathers and their constituent bankers, advertising men, and *a fortiori* their used car dealers are not the foundation of an overriding social concern. The transformation of the American scene, if it involves that, is another matter.

---

29. Richard J. McLaren, Statement to the House Ways and Means Committee. See the *New York Times,* March 13, 1969, p. 72.
30. *Standard Oil Company of California v. United States,* 337 U.S. 293 (1948) at 318–19.
31. *United States v. Falstaff Brewing Corp.,* 410 U.S. 526 (1973) at 543.

Macro-concentration in the Law

Of the three approaches to controlling conglomerate acquisitions attempted by the Nixon Administration—reciprocity, macro-concentration, potential competition—macro-concentration would surely have presented the most direct approach. The attempt, in the three ITT cases (cited in fnn. 22–24, p. 162) and in Northwest Industries, to generate judicial support for this view has been wholly without success at the district court level and since none of the tried cases is to be appealed, the issue is not likely to be reopened in the near future. Because it is direct and thus simple, it deserves a passing look.

In Northwest, the government argued that the merger of two of the 100 largest nonfinancial corporations constituted a violation, without more, of Section 7. Judge Will disagreed:

> We do not so read Section 7. . . . [T]he Government contends that [anticompetitive results] are inherent in such mergers because of the great economic power resulting therefrom even though there is no competitive relationship between them. . . .
> . . . There may be very good reasons indeed to limit the growth of this country's largest corporations, particularly through mergers and acquisitions. . . .
> . . . The law as it now stands, however, makes the adverse effect on competition the test of validity and until Congress broadens the criteria, the Court must judge proposed transactions on that standard.[32]

Judge Timbers echoed this in denying preliminary injunctions in the Hartford and Grinnell cases:

> . . . The alleged adverse effects of economic concentration brought about by merger activity, especially merger activity of large diversified corporations such as ITT, arguably may be such that, as a matter of social and economic policy, the standard by which the legality of a merger should be measured under the antitrust laws is the degree to which it may increase economic concentration—not merely the degree to which it may lessen competition. If the standard is to be changed, however, in the opinion of this Court it is fundamental under our system of government that that determination be made by the Congress and not by the courts.[33]

---

32. *United States v. Northwest Industries,* 301 F.Supp. 1066 (N.D. Ill. 1969) at 1096.

33. *United States v. ITT (Grinnell),* 306 F.Supp. 766 (D. Conn. 1969) at 796–97.

After trial on the merits of the Grinnell case, the court re-emphasized this stand and refused to follow the government when it "raised the same issue, but with a different and somewhat ingenious twist"—namely that the anticompetitive effects would appear in "numerous though undesignated individual 'lines of commerce.'" The court regarded this as an invitation to engage in judicial legislation, which it "most emphatically refused to do."[34]

Judge Austin in Canteen refused to admit macro-concentration data, despite an even more ingenious attempt by the government. It argued the relevance of such data on the ground that the greater the level of macro-concentration, the greater the opportunity for reciprocity, and thus the greater the potential competitive harm. Judge Austin would have none of it.

If the macro-concentration doctrine is thus moribund, it is not yet dead. Professor Harlan Blake has recently attempted to provide a legal rationale for interpretation of Section 7 that would result in the presumption that any substantial acquisition by a large firm would probably result in an injury to competition.[35]

The essence of his view is that the "strict constructionist" view of Section 7 based on the line of commerce language is both unfortunate and not compelled. In an ingenious re-reading of legislative history, he argues for an interpretation of antitrust objectives as preservation of a competitive *system*—"in which all economic units in the unregulated sector are subject to the continuing discipline of competitive market forces."[36] Equally ingeniously (some may feel bizarrely) Blake finds in three postwar Sherman Act cases—Fortner, Griffith, and Grinnell[37]—evidence of the Supreme Court's desire to

---

34. *United States v. ITT (Grinnell)*, 324 F.Supp. 19 (D. Conn. 1970) at 52.

35. Harlan Blake, "Conglomerate Mergers and the Antitrust Laws," 73 COLUMBIA LAW REVIEW 555 (1973).

36. Blake, "Conglomerate Mergers," p. 594. His most intriguing argument is that the original Section 7 covered *stock* acquisitions precisely because it was loose-knit agglomerations of power that were feared more than tighter-knit ones. An earlier attempt to show this broader legislative intent is in J. C. Thomas, "Conglomerate Merger Syndrome—A Comparison: Congressional Policy With Enforcement Policy," 36 FORDHAM LAW REVIEW 461 (1968).

37. *Fortner Enterprises, Inc. v. United States Steel Corp.*, 394 U.S. 495 (1969); *United States v. Griffith*, 334 U.S. 100 (1948); *United States v. Grinnell Corp.*, 384 U.S. 563 (1966).

bring remoter uses of economic power within the antitrust ambit, and thus to foreshadow a Section 7 move toward size per se as a basis for stopping mergers between very large companies.

Given the recent changes in the Court, Blake's view seems unlikely to be adopted soon. If a more sweeping size-based prohibition on mergers comes, it seems likely to require legislative action. Legally this seems unnecessary for dealing with many conglomerate mergers because of the imaginative development of the potential competition handle, discussed in chapter 10.

For the moment at least macro-concentration as a legal basis of antitrust action seems to be a *curiosum*. But when next the tides of populism rise it may well be brought forward again.

The Propriety of Merger Policy in Dealing with Concerns about Macro-concentration

Obviously, prescription depends upon diagnosis, and competent observers disagree as to the threat to our competitive and political system posed by large firms, and by merger-induced growth in firm size. I am among the more sanguine group, Harlan Blake among the more alarmed (though we are by no means at the extremes). But it is not merely a matter of ultimate values. There are several positive questions that merit continued research. Let me pose four.

1. Are political influence and immorality most sensibly attacked by controlling corporate size?

It is clear that lobbying, influence peddling, corruption, and worse occur, and require wealth, influence, and other things that large corporations have. It is also clear that the Jeffersonian ideal of a society of small businessmen, tradesmen, and farmers conflicts with the requirements of modern technology and the search for the high standards of material well-being to which we are accustomed. What is perhaps less clear is the empirical evidence with respect to whether abuses of public morality are in fact even roughly proportional in frequency or in magnitude to the size of companies, or whether instead they occur in some fraction of cases of all companies above *relatively* low (but absolutely substantial) size.

Suppose for the sake of argument that size per se is a correlate of abuse, but that the frequency of such abuse is relatively low even among large corporations. Before attacking size per se one must ask whether the average benefits that size confers are such that size per se should not be the basis for attack. This in turn depends upon the effectiveness of alternative policies—e.g., those concerning financing of campaigns, lobbying, and simple criminality—to deal with improper behavior in the political arena.

These are issues on which there is more assertion than evidence. They are only irrelevant if size is achieved that is without redeeming value.

2. Is merger policy an appropriate vehicle for seeking to limit size of firms, or to prevent further growth in average size?

Suppose that it is agreed that in some average sense size of firms is greater than the optimal balance between benefits and costs would dictate. Much size is achieved by internal growth not merger, and alternatives to merger prohibitions include prohibitions on size beyond some limits, and deconcentration statutes such as are periodically proposed in Congress.[38] The conventional argument against absolute size limitations is that "appropriate" size is very much a relative matter. An automobile company with sales or assets of \$1 billion per year is demonstrably a small company which must struggle to survive in its markets but would dominate most manufacturing industries. Thus efficiency, market power, and political influence respond to different concepts and measures of size and any rule would either penalize efficiency where scale is important, or encourage unnecessary size where scale is unimportant. Are industry-specific size guidelines derivable? If so, what is the measure of size that is appropriate?

If the problem is size beyond some "required" level is there a sensible basis for focusing on mergers, as distinct from internal growth? There may be. One argument for this view is that internal expansion creates new capacity (and thus the potential for more output and more competition) while merger-acquired capacity does not. (This is the potential competition argument that concerned us in chapter 10.) A second argument for distinguishing growth by merger from other growth, is that the former is more readily spotted, and easily prevented, for it occurs in discrete and publicly noticed chunks and it is announced in advance. Thus even if all large-size corporations were (marginally) equally sinister, a policy aimed at decreasing their number could most easily be implemented by preventing mergers that create such companies. A third argument (which we encountered above) is the unproved notion that size achieved by merger is less

---

38. See, for current example, the Hart Bill, now before the Senate.

likely to prove efficient. Accepting any or all of these arguments—
and the second seems to me the most compelling—argues for a discriminating use of merger policy along what I take to be present Section 7 lines, or the development of guidelines that attempt to anticipate
which mergers are likely to be on net balance undesirable. Several
sets of such guidelines will be examined in the next chapter.

3.   Do conglomerate mergers require special attention in connection with size?

At first glance it would appear that if size is the problem, conglomerate firms do not merit special attention. The per se argument
(see p. 55) that benefits are presumably negligible seems without
logical compulsion or empirical support. Nor do the harms allegedly
caused by diversity seem to provide a sufficient basis for a distinction.
But, to the extent that size is a problem, there is a basis for special
concern because of the lesser constraint imposed by existing antitrust
interpretation. Thus, large horizontal acquisitions or large vertical
acquisitions are likely to be restrained in a way that large conglomerate
ones are not. An interesting, but difficult empirical question concerns
the real differential in effect on size of company for firms of different
types. An effective size constraint might ideally be equal in its impact
on all firms.

While size is arguably one dimension of public concern with
corporate performance, it is surely not the only dimension. Even for
conglomerate firms and conglomerate acquisitions, a general policy
ought to be multidimensional and recognize significant differences
among firms classified as conglomerate.

Harlan Blake, Willard F. Mueller, and some others come close
to arguing that macro-concentration and firm size provide a suitable
single standard for a per se rule. This seems to me an appropriate
solution if, but only if, one views the threats of large size and corporate diversity as overriding social concerns. I am not yet at that
point.

CHAPTER TWELVE

Some Suggestions and Premises for Policy

THE dominant conclusion of this book is that what has come to be called the conglomerate merger wave of the 1960s reflected not a single phenomenon subject to a single dominant causal force but was instead a complex of many mergers with varied motivations and varied effects. In chapter 8 (pp. 205–8) I attempted to summarize our knowledge about motivation and causes and to suggest the frontiers of our ignorance.

What is an appropriate policy response in the face of partial ignorance? It is obviously appropriate to urge additional research, by enforcement agencies as well as by detached scholars, and the recent building up of the research capabilities of both the FTC and the Department of Justice are most encouraging signs. But while research remains to be done, knowledge accumulates slowly and it is necessary to have policies for this year and this decade as well as next. At this point there seems to me to be a relatively stable legal situation after a decade in which we have witnessed the shakedown of a series of innovative legal encounters with the problem of conglomerate mergers. It is an oversimplification, but perhaps a relatively insightful one, to characterize the legal status (in August 1974) of the conglomerate merger as being much less a thing apart from other mergers than it was even a few years ago. It was common before 1965 to regard conglomerate mergers as largely outside the reach of Section 7. Three legal avenues of attack on that position were discussed in chapters 9 through 11. The inability of the reciprocity and macro-concentration approaches to command significant judicial support is likely to prove much less important than the effective fashioning of the potential competition concept as a device to reintegrate market extension, product extension, and even unrelated acquisitions into the main line of antitrust enforcement: the probable effect on competition.

My purpose in this chapter is not to explore further the positive question of what our policy is, but to tilt, albeit cautiously, with what it ought to be, given the state of our knowledge. There has been no shortage of sets of policy prescriptions and proposed guidelines put forward. It is not my intention to summarize them, nor to labor their possible flaws, nor yet to replace them with guidelines of my own, though I will do a bit of each of those things.

I speak of guidelines reluctantly for fear of guilt by association with the merger guidelines issued in May 1968; but it is useful to use the phrase in its generic sense. Guidelines, properly formulated and flexibly interpreted, seem to me more conducive to groping toward an intelligent set of policies than new legislation, largely because of our ignorance. If we know enough to warrant a deconcentration statute, or a new merger bill, or a prohibition of acquisitions based on a measure of mere size, that consensus has escaped me.[1]

A chief advantage of guidelines that are explicitly limited by the state of our knowledge, is that they invite the systematic accumulation of insight and experience, and the use of these things to revise the guidelines.

While I have no blueprint to present, I do have certain views as to what the initial guidelines should look like. They have the following four features:

1. Guidelines ought to strive not to determine appropriate policy response in all, or even most, cases but instead to define two (possibly quite limited) subsets of cases. The first consists of those where the probability of significant adverse effect is *known* to be high enough to warrant a strong (but rebuttable) presumption against the acquisition. The second consists of those where the probability of significant adverse effect is *known* to be small enough to warrant a strong (but rebuttable) presumption against interfering with the market decision to merge. Whether these two sets are equally large, and whether they occupy 5 percent or 50 percent of the spectrum is not important at the outset. For other cases, where present knowledge is insufficient, the guidelines ought to remain silent. The existing legal channels for challenging such acquisitions would remain open. The purpose of guidelines is *not* to replace uncertainty by certainty, but to apply efficiently such wisdom as we possess. As knowledge increases, either or both covered subsets may be expected to expand and the "in doubt" middle ground to shrink. But I have no expectation that it will soon (or ever) be negligible.

---

1. In a similar vein, the 1968 merger guidelines, while perhaps unfairly characterized as "a lotus land of percentage tests," do appear to embody a great deal more hard knowledge about the effects of mergers than we have.

2.   While the bases for rebuttability of presumptive legality or illegality ought to be made as explicit as possible and be based upon accumulated knowledge of the kind of exception that is likely to be perversely treated by otherwise sensible guidelines, they ought never be regarded as closed. It may well be that the burden ought to be less on those who seek to demonstrate a well-established basis for rebuttal (e.g., a failing company defense) than on those who would advance a novel one, but the administrative convenience of outlawing certain sorts of showings (e.g., a demonstrated efficiencies defense) seems to me outweighed by the reductions in our ignorance that such attempts may provide. Bases for rebuttability that *are* stated ought moreover to be grounded in effects on competition and performance rather than on surrogates therefor. If, again for example, saving a failing company has merit, it is because of the positive effect on competition in that case; saving inefficient or ineffective competitors may be perverse.

3.   Guidelines need to be developed on an industry-by-industry basis rather than globally. This is not because a different competitive policy is appropriate for beer than for clothing, but instead because market and industry structure, market behavior, and the effect on competition are multidimensional things and, at this stage, our knowledge is far too limited to operate with a single set of rules. Formulation of this kind of guideline requires both academic input and industry knowledge. In proposing industry-by-industry guidelines, it is not necessary to have them for all industries at once, for their development may indeed be sequential. The enlarging domain should be paced by the ability to formulate with some confidence rather than merely by a desire to resolve ambiguity.

4.   Industry-by-industry guidelines need to pay attention not only to the acquired firm but also to the acquiring one with attention not only to size, but also to the probable alternative (for each merger partner) if the merger is prohibited.

Underlying these suggestions, and in further elaboration of them, are certain premises which must be made explicit.

Premise 1:   The Crisis Is Past

That the merger explosion of 1966–68 caused an atmosphere of crisis is hardly surprising when one looks at the statistics available in 1968 (see figure 1–1 on p. 4). But whether or not the worst anticipations were ever justified, they are no longer. This is shown not only by the merger statistics of the period 1968–72, but by virtually every recent study. Not only has the merger rate returned to prewave levels, the effects of the completed mergers on concentration and on competition proved to have been much less than was feared and less than might reasonably have been expected. This is a central conclusion of Jesse Markham's new book and of the second FTC study. Markham says in relevant part:

> Moreover, the rise of conglomerate enterprise (largely through acquisition) in the decade of the 1960's has surprisingly had little if any measurable effect on the overall structure of the manufacturing economy, or on the particular markets diversifying companies have entered through acquisition. Aggregate concentration, of dubious antitrust significance in any case, has remained virtually unchanged; and changes in concentration in the invaded markets have been marked more frequently by decreases than by increases, a pattern indicative of slightly less monopoly growth but statistically not distinguishable from that of markets generally.
>
> We are led then to the conclusion that highly diversified firms (or, if one prefers, conglomerates) present no special antitrust problems, and require no special antitrust policy. The decade of the 1960's witnessed the spectacular rise of about 25 new conglomerates, and a significant increase in overall company diversification. But in the marketplace they appear to behave no differently from other firms.[2]

The second FTC report, in marked contrast to the tone of the first report, says in part:

> The data show two interesting features of the merger activity of our sample companies. First, they apparently did not acquire substantial market positions in new areas. . . . [I]n 82.0 percent of the acquired product classes, the sample conglomerates had market shares of less than 5 percent.
>
> A second characteristic . . . is the level of concentration prevailing in the industries they entered. Our data show that most of the sample firms are engaged in industries which, on the average, do not appear to be highly concentrated. Moreover, it would appear that the average level of concentration of industries in which our sample firms participated declined between 1963 and 1969. . . .
>
> Looking specifically at product classes the conglomerates added through acquisition between 1963 and 1969, it does not appear that conglomerates followed a "toehold" strategy of making small acquisitions in concentrated industries. . . . More generally, [these data] show no

---

2. Jesse W. Markham, *Conglomerate Enterprise and Public Policy* (Cambridge, Mass., 1973), pp. 176–77.

evidence that conglomerates aggressively expand market shares after acquisition, either in a "good" toehold sense or a "bad" deep-pockets-predatory sense.

It seems difficult to imagine, therefore, on the basis of these data, that the picture held by many of conglomerates' expanding acquired market shares as an element of a purposeful and widespread developmental program can be true. Support for this position simply does not exist in our data. . . .

There is no evidence [either] that the conglomerates have made many improvements in the operations of acquired firms. On the other hand, it is not clear that these firms have necessarily declined in any consistent manner. We can say, however, that the alleged qualities of corporate synergism, if they exist, are not detectable from our data.[3]

Neither these studies nor others demonstrate that nothing changed, or that there is no possible long term adverse (or beneficial) effect—our knowledge is far too fragmentary for reaching or rejecting definitively such conclusions. But whether such things as the loss in information about particular markets, which the FTC study regards as a major cost of the increasing interindustry diversification, or the turnover in the makeup of the largest 200 corporations, are of major or minor consequence (or indeed are for good or for ill), there is nothing to suggest the need for hasty or drastic action. If there are benefits to a slow and sober approach to policy revision there is no longer a prospect of a runaway merger trend to force greater speed.

May not a new merger wave erupt at any time? I think not soon. The changes in tax laws, approved accounting practices, security laws, as well as increasing antitrust scrutiny and a major stock market slump have surely combined to dismotivate many of the kinds of mergers that figured in the great upsurge of the wave of the late 1960s. Whatever the half-life of investors' memories there is no possibility of it being shorter than the next five or ten years. Thus there is time to discuss policy with care before enacting it. The challenge to our attention is to evaluate (and if necessary repair) the structure when it is *not* under stress.

Premise 2: *Easy Solutions Are Inadequate*

Alternative extreme per se positions were sketched in chapter 3, pages 53–58. Neither the premises underlying per se legality (no anticom-

---

3. Federal Trade Commission, Bureau of Economics, *Economic Report on Conglomerate Merger Performance, an Empirical Analysis of Nine Corporations* (Washington, D.C., November 1972), chap. 6.

petitive effect, probable synergies) nor underlying per se illegality (probable anticompetitive effect, no synergies) have received sufficient support in the studies reviewed to prove decisive. Some, but by no means most, of the mergers completed have changed competitive conditions. Some, but by no means most, of the mergers completed have visibly led to more efficient operation of the companies or industries involved.

The absence of striking results in aggregate behavior or performance, which pervades the studies reviewed in chapter 8, and is as well the hallmark of the two most recent studies (cited just above), suggests that *on average* the conglomerate acquisition has not proven very important for good or for ill. *But it is not the purpose of merger policy to regulate the average merger*. It is, instead, to recognize the variance, if variance exists, and to inhibit the malign while not stifling the benign. The evidence suggests that there is such variance and that, therefore, there is scope for insightful policy guidelines.

A less extreme pair of views than the per se positions just mentioned that also lead to easy solutions are to regard either the beneficial effect of a merger as always alternatively available or the adverse effects as always alternatively reachable. In the first view, prohibiting beneficial mergers is of little consequence because of a nearly as good second-best solution (*de novo* entry); thus a tough merger policy is clearly sound. In the second view, permitting conglomerate mergers is virtually costless for the occasional adverse effect may be struck down after the fact as easily as before it.

The problem with these views is that they represent assertions not supported by the weight of evidence. No one has, to my knowledge, effectively disproved that it is easier to prevent a merger than to undo one. The incipiency notion, although often abused, is a sound basis for dealing with clear and future dangers. But also sound is the notion that acquisition may be a most efficient way of reorganizing resources or responding to change in the environment. A relatively sophisticated view of the firm is as a bundle of capabilities which it is expensive to accumulate or to disperse.[4] When the problems a firm faces change, it may find its bundles of capabilities partially inadequate and find an efficient solution in merging with a firm with a comple-

---

4. Transactions costs, often assumed away, strike me to be of the very essence of the matter. Assembling a going concern involves such enormous costs that it must generally promise larger benefits. Saving those benefits may thus be very valuable.

324   *Mergers: Motives, Effects, Policies*

mentary imbalance of capabilities and problems. The literature contains enough examples to compel respect for this position, without going to the unjustified extreme of supposing it is the characteristic merger situation.

Finally, one might argue that no policy action is required either because the merger wave has subsided never to arise again, or because present laws and present policy are themselves optimal. The first view seems to me a triumph of hope over evidence. Many mergers continue to be sought and consummated. In 1972 more than 2,000 mergers were completed and another 953 pending.[5] While the size and number of large mergers made in 1972 were a substantial retreat from the peaks of the 1960s, this statistic suggests that motives to merge remain and given the appropriate set of conditions, merger propensities could again increase. The view that existing laws and interpretations are fully adequate may (as Markham believes) in fact be correct, but the policy existing seems to me sufficiently inchoate that it is hard to say. The Burger Court is still all but untested in major questions of antitrust, and where tested it speaks with many voices (as in Falstaff) or by a sharply divided court. Moreover, the Nixon Department of Justice (itself unpredictable) is in the process of being replaced. While the 1968 merger guidelines (which I believe to be unsatisfactory) remain on the books no one knows the force they carry even within the Antitrust Division.

Premise 3: Uncertainty about Cause and Effect Dictates Limited Not Comprehensive Guidelines

Professor Turner long ago posed the relevant challenge: to formulate appropriate rules for determining the lawfulness of *particular* mergers. Given that mergers are a mixed bag of motives and probable effects, sensible specification of rules that separate the good from the bad depends crucially on our ability to relate identifiable characteristics of structure and/or behavior to probable effects.

Even with full knowledge of the underlying structure of cause and effect, rules would prove tricky to construct in a multivariate world. Such rules would need to define the measures used to distinguish one case from another, and in so doing not only invite some

---

5. Federal Trade Commission, Bureau of Economics, *Report on Mergers and Acquisitions* (Washington, D.C., October 1973), pp. 7, 8.

mergers that would otherwise not occur, but also invite avoidance of the ban by affecting the measures themselves. The ingenuity of men (and especially lawyers) in avoiding the intent of a set of fixed rules hardly needs explication.

But where knowledge is seriously limited a yet more compelling case for limited rule making exists. It is one thing to risk rigid rules when one is confident that the result is virtually always clearly beneficial (for then the occasional aberrant result may be regarded as a small price to pay for the characteristically beneficial results); it is quite another to provide rules if there is no consensus that they are beneficial, even if the rule is beneficial more often than it is adverse. The reason is that the existence of the rule prevents the search (judicial or otherwise) for a more discriminating criterion for judgment.

In my view then policy guidelines should embody real knowledge but be constrained by real ignorance. In the conglomerate area particularly, the limits of our knowledge are very large. Symmetry sometimes takes on a life of its own. But it is neither essential nor appropriate that conglomerate merger guidelines be as comprehensive as (say) horizontal merger guidelines. It is not appropriate because we know much less and perverse guidelines are worse than no guidelines. It is not necessary because, absent a guideline, there may be a healthy uncertainty that invites both caution in merging and search for knowledge. Since we must crawl before we walk and run, let us be content to crawl in the right direction while we determine where next to walk.

Premise 4: Appropriate Guidelines Require Both Regions of Doubt and Rebuttable Presumptions

Suppose for the moment that the market structure surrounding a proposed merger is somehow one dimensional (e.g., concentration) and monotonically related to the effect of the merger (i.e., the higher concentration the more anticompetitive the merger). One can then visualize a spectrum of effects from the unambiguously benign to the unambiguously malign associated with the measure of structure.

The simplest sort of guideline is one in which at some level of the measured characteristic one simply draws the line between legal and illegal. Conceivably in a world of perfect knowledge this would be an appropriate stance, although even here, unless the effects were discontinuous (clearly beneficial on one side of the point of illegality, clearly adverse on the other side of it), one might prefer a trichotomous guideline with an area of doubt in the neighborhood of the borderline to make more difficult evasion of the intent of the policy. While guidelines of legal/illegal form would give businessmen and lawyers the certainty they profess to want,[6] the conditions required certainly do not exist. Actually, virtually no one suggests guidelines of this kind. Harlan Blake[7] proposes a simple rule based on the prohibition of "substantial acquisitions by large firms," and it is possible that Blake intends this as the only guideline. Given his views more generally, I would infer that while he does not discuss other bases for attack on conglomerate mergers he intends this as an *additional* prohibition, to substitute for market-effect tests when the firm is large, rather than as license for conglomerate acquisitions when the firm is not large, independent of market effect.

More generally, what may appear to be a simple legal/illegal dichotomy in one or more dimensions need not result in a simple dichotomy. Given multiple bases for evaluation, even a legal/illegal guideline on several of them leaves the issue in doubt with respect to other reserved bases for attack. A case in point is the merger guidelines proposed by the Neal Task Force[8] which appear to be of this form, but they are not. The detail need not concern us but the Task Force proposed new legislation whose key feature was a prohibition on mergers between leading firms (market share of 10 percent or more in an industry with four-firm concentration ratio in excess of 50 percent) and large firms (sales in excess of $500 million or assets in excess of $250 million). While the proposals are genuinely unambiguous, mergers not falling under this prohibition, however, would still be subject to attack under existing provisions of Section 7.

A more common sort of dichotomous guideline is to regard some forms as plainly illegal and others as in doubt. This form (illegal/in

---

6. Whether businessmen really want certainty is arguable, though I suspect that given certainty of enforcement they would be worse off than with the possibility of undetected violations. That lawyers would suffer if there were no uncertainty seems so obvious as to require no defense. What lawyers perhaps want is certainty as to outcome with criteria revealed to them but not their clients.

7. Harlan Blake, "Conglomerate Mergers and the Antitrust Laws," 73 COLUMBIA LAW REVIEW 554 (1973).

8. "White House Task Force Report on Antitrust Policy" (Neal Report), submitted July 5, 1968, reprinted in BNA, *Antitrust and Trade Regulation Report,* no. 411 (May 27, 1969): pt. II.

doubt) is the hallmark of the 1968 conglomerate merger guidelines of the Department of Justice:

> At the present time, the Department regards two categories of conglomerate mergers as having sufficiently identifiable anticompetitive effects as to be the subject of relatively specific structural guidelines: mergers involving potential entrants (Paragraph 18) and mergers creating a danger of reciprocal buying (Paragraph 19).
>
> Another important category of conglomerate mergers that will frequently be the subject of enforcement action—mergers which for one or more of several reasons threaten to entrench or enhance the market power of the acquired firm—is described generally in Paragraph 20.
>
> As Paragraph 20 makes clear, enforcement action will also be taken against still other types of conglomerate mergers that on specific analysis appear anticompetitive. The fact that, as yet, the Department does not believe it useful to describe such other types of mergers in terms of a few major elements of market structure should in no sense be regarded as indicating that enforcement action will not be taken. Nor is it to be assumed that mergers of the type described in Paragraphs 18 and 19, but not covered by specific rules thereof, may not be the subject of enforcement action if specific analysis indicates that they appear anticompetitive.

Were the guidelines in paragraphs 18 and 19 exceedingly narrow the reservation of powers involved in the third paragraph quoted above might be only prudent. But consider the following excerpts from potential competition guidelines:[9]

18. *Mergers Involving Potential Entrants.*
   (*a*) . . . The Department will ordinarily challenge any merger between one of the most likely entrants into the market and:
      (*i*) any firm with approximately 25% or more of the market;
      (*ii*) one of the two largest firms in a market in which the shares of the two largest firms amount to approximately 50% or more;
      (*iii*) one of the four largest firms in a market in which shares of the eight largest firms amount to approximately 75% or more, provided the merging firm's share of the market amounts to approximately 10% or more; or
      (*iv*) one of the eight largest firms in a market in which the shares of these firms amount to approximately 75% or more, provided either (A) the merging firm's share of the market is not insubstantial and there are no more than one or two likely entrants into the market, or (B) the merging firm is a rapidly growing firm.

---

9. The reciprocity guidelines were quoted in some detail on page 251.

In determining whether a firm is one of the most likely potential entrants into a market, the Department accords primary significance to the firm's capability of entering on a competitively significant scale relative to the capability of other firms (i.e., the technological and financial resources available to it) and to the firm's economic incentive to enter (evidenced by, for example, the general attractiveness of the market in terms of risk and profit; or any special relationship of the firm to the market; or the firm's manifested interest in entry; or the natural expansion pattern of the firm, or the like).

(*b*) The Department will also ordinarily challenge a merger between an existing competitor in a market and a likely entrant, undertaken for the purpose of preventing the competitive "disturbance" or "disruption" that such entry might create.

While superficially specific, these guidelines are almost hopelessly vague. Given the very flexible market definitions which the Supreme Court had enunciated in previous cases (and the guidelines accepted and make yet more elastic) [10] it was difficult to find many mergers between large firms that were not covered. But this was not the only basis for attacking mergers. Any that were missed were likely to be picked up by the guidelines with respect to the potential for reciprocity. The more remote the product lines (and thus the less likely was potential entry), the greater the diversity and thus the more likely an opportunity for reciprocity.

One might characterize this kind of stance as close to a per se illegality criterion with the Justice Department in a position to grant exceptions simply by not prosecuting. It might be an appropriate stance if the presumptions underlying per se illegality were justified.

---

10. ¶3 of the guidelines says in part: ". . . A market is any grouping of sales (or other commercial transactions) in which each of the firms whose sales are included enjoys some advantage in competing with those firms whose sales are not included. The advantage need not be great, for so long as it is significant it defines an area of effective competition among the included sellers in which the competition of the excluded sellers is *ex hypothesis,* less effective."

This very permissive definition would not exempt the merger of producers of two differentiated products from scrutiny, but it might exclude the competitive impact of a third producer who was no more disadvantaged from the acquirer than the acquiree. For my view of a more satisfactory basis of market definition see P. O. Steiner, "Markets and Industries," *International Encyclopedia of the Social Sciences* 9 (1968): 575.

It does not seem appropriate in the face of existing evidence about the effects of conglomerate mergers.

These guidelines perhaps would be justified if the need was to have a high and uncertain inhibition against conglomerate acquisitions. I do not dismiss that as a sensible policy for 1968—when the guidelines were announced. They do not seem sensible in the general climate of the 1970s, yet they remain unwithdrawn.[11]

My strong preference ideologically, a preference I think amply justified by the weight of our knowledge, is for a trichotomous— legal/in doubt/illegal—guideline. If it is possible to define classes of acquisitions which are as presumptively benign as others are adverse, then the trichotomous view has much to recommend it, with the area of doubt being determined by the state of our ignorance. There seems no reason not to iterate to a sensible policy.

A possible and important potential objection to the three zone guideline is that while the potentially beneficial acquisitions in the "illegal" zone can be permitted by prosecutorial discretion, the potentially harmful ones in the "legal" zone cannot be so easily stopped. It compels the notion of these as rebuttable presumptions rather than per se rules.

The basic case *against* rebuttability of presumptions is that the resources devoted to attempts at rebuttal will exceed the benefits achieved. (See pp. 52–53.) But in as tenuous an area as conglomerate mergers, where the evidence is far from clear, this possibility seems less strong than another. Rebuttability may be required to deal with a class of situations where average tendencies are understood but individual variations are sufficiently important to warrant attention yet insufficiently understood to be structural exceptions. Rebuttability seems to me a most attractive way of dealing with our limited information.

---

11. A reverse sort of dichotomy, legal/in doubt, is sometimes suggested. E.g., with respect to horizontal mergers the Stigler Task Force said (reprinted in BNA, *Antitrust and Trade Regulation Report*, no. 413, [June 10, 1969]: 214) : "We agree with the basic premise of the horizontal-merger provisions of the Guidelines that market-share percentages are the appropriate touchstone of illegality for such mergers. We would favor levels of concentration modestly *lower* than those now used (but differently structured), with the purposes of (1) allowing all mergers below the Guidelines levels, and (2) not prohibiting, but reviewing, those above the critical level, with an implied probability that the more a proposed merger lies above the level of automatic approval, the less the probability of its acceptance."

How far to go in permitting rebuttal of a presumption of illegality is itself a major topic for debate. The case for allowing efficiency defenses has been discussed by Oliver Williamson;[12] the case against, as stated in the guidelines, is that an acceptable alternative means of achieving them is always available. Even if one rejects using positive justifications based upon efficiencies, there does seem to be a reasonable basis for allowing a showing of *pro*competitive effect, to rebut the presumption of *anti*competitive effect. There is a limited basis of this in the present guidelines with respect to failing companies. The exception is carefully circumscribed:

> The Department regards as failing only those firms with no reasonable prospect of remaining viable; it does not regard a firm as failing merely because the firm has been unprofitable for a period of time, has lost market position or failed to maintain its competitive position in some other respect, has poor management, or has not fully explored the possibility of overcoming its difficulties through self-help.
>
> In determining the applicability of the above standard to the acquisition of a failing division of a multi-market company, such factors as the difficulty in assessing the viability of a portion of a company, the possibility of arbitrary accounting practices, and the likelihood that an otherwise healthy company can rehabilitate one of its parts, will lead the Department to apply this standard only in the clearest of circumstances.

Shepherd and Campbell propose as grounds for rebutting their presumption against conglomerate acquisitions of leading firms, a somewhat broader class of cases—which they characterize as including moribund firms.[13] Unfortunately the extenuations they would admit—acquisition of firms with sharply declining market shares, or situations where demonstrable economies can be shown only to be achievable in this manner, or of firms in rapidly growing markets— seem to me to miss the most important case—the too comfortable firm in the too comfortable industry.

It is not the occasional and well-understood exception to the feared anticompetitive effect that is of major concern, but the larger subclass of cases that are not sufficiently understood to warrant a

12. Oliver E. Williamson, "Economies as an Antitrust Defense: The Welfare Tradeoffs," *American Economic Review* 58, no. 1 (March 1968): 18–36.

13. J. S. Campbell and W. G. Shepherd, "Leading-Firm Conglomerate Mergers," *Antitrust Bulletin* 13 (1968): 1361–79.

well-defined exception. My view is that at this stage a good deal less rigidity is warranted than the existing guidelines allow. Just as courts characteristically admit a good deal of disputed evidence "for what it is worth," so a parallel permissive (but skeptical) stand on exceptions might be appropriate.

Rebuttability, in a symmetric model, applies at the other end as well. The conglomerate guidelines paragraph cited above reserves the right to prosecute mergers not otherwise mentioned, "if specific analysis indicates they appear anticompetitive." This seems to me to be precisely the kind of consideration a prosecutor might adduce in rebutting a presumptively legal acquisition. But the government's burden of proof there ought to be higher the greater is the apparent departure from the usual guideline.

Premise 5: Probable Effect on Competition Requires Greater and Less Mechanistic Attention than It Has Received

While it is the essence of science to seek shortcuts to prediction of effects, it is the counsel of folly to use shortcuts that mispredict. Whatever the virtues of micro-concentration ratios, market shares, and similar structural characteristics as proxies for the intensity of competition in general or with respect to horizontal mergers,[14] there is a much less secure linkage in the case of conglomerate acquisitions where acquirer and acquiree are characteristically in very different markets. Any one of macro-concentration, reciprocity, or potential competition might provide a reasonable basis for some inferences about the probable effect of a merger on competition, but none of them is a substitute for explicit attention to the effect on competition. This is an empirical judgment not a theoretical one.

My reasons for largely rejecting the macro-concentration approach were summarized on pages 315–17. That discussion, however, may have failed to do justice to the "entrenchment effect" of an acquisition of a leading seller by a large seller. Concisely stated, whatever market power a firm may have may be entrenched by being

---

14. As noted above on page 301, even the very basic proposition of a linkage between concentration and competition in a well-defined market has its critics. See, e.g., Yale Brozen, "The Antitrust Task Force Deconcentration Recommendation," 13 JOURNAL OF LAW AND ECONOMICS, no. 2, 270–92 (October 1970).

acquired by a larger, richer company, both because such an acquirer has greater resources with which to fight (or discipline) competitors, and because its presence may inhibit smaller concerns from daring to compete. These concerns may certainly be justified in particular cases, but there is no evidence that most acquisitions by large firms of leading firms have this effect. Whether enough do that the appropriate policy stance is a rebuttable presumption against large-firm acquisitions on this basis alone or is instead a rebuttable presumption the other way is today an unresolved empirical question. The entrenchment argument seems to me to have been more asserted than documented to date.

That the mere possibility of reciprocity does not provide a satisfactory general basis for concern with conglomerate mergers was argued at length in chapter 9 and was summarized on pages 253–54. Except for a pair of well-defined exceptions (listed on p. 253), reciprocity seems to me to provide a poor guide to conglomerate policy.[15] The first of these exceptions is readily determined in terms of the market structure of the acquired firm's industry and thus should be easily defined in industry-by-industry guidelines. The second requires information about the potential acquirer as well, but it too seems manageable in terms of an industry-by-industry approach.

Potential competition provides the primary basis for dealing with conglomerate acquisitions. This approach invites focusing attention on the effect of the acquisitions in the market of the acquired firm. Most of the professional literature has focused here on very general guidelines concerning the number of potential entrants, the degree of concentration in the acquired firm's market and the relative size of the acquired firm. Turner's original minimum proposed rules (see pp. 261–62) are a case in point, but as there shown, they fail to deal sufficiently with the fact that entry into a tight oligopolistic market may be beneficial to competition if it upsets the tight oligopoly rather than entrenching it, and entry into an apparently competitive market by a large acquirer could provide a focal point of decreasing competition.

The fact is that "the condition of entry" is itself a highly complex set of structural conditions, and the effects on competition depend on

---

15. This is not to say, of course, that predatory reciprocal behavior cannot conceivably occur. It can, but if it does (and the result seems likely to be infrequent) it is readily reachable directly.

many things. Were there a simple measure and a dominant expected set of results, a general guideline with a right of rebuttal would be a satisfactory policy stance. But (as the tried cases suggest) potential competition is so many different things that an industry-by-industry approach seems necessary to avoid a procrustean policy. One does not have a great deal of difficulty thinking, one by one, about the effects of entry (and the set of potential entrants) into beer, food service, bleach, sporting goods, or automobile replacement parts. It is much more difficult to define a single yardstick for discriminating between real cases of adverse or beneficial effects on competition that apply to all of those industries.

My major reservation in urging an industry-by-industry approach is that such guidelines have been developed for selected industries by the FTC, and these do not necessarily inspire confidence in the process. While bad guidelines, or unnecessarily myopic ones, are worse than none, an alternative procedure, with guidelines arrived at after public hearings seems to me to merit serious debate. The recent reorganization of economic analysis within the Antitrust Division, and the appointment of F. M. Scherer as Director of the Bureau of Economics of the FTC provide a remarkable opportunity to harness research talent and ample data to a major policy challenge.

Two further comments may clarify this suggestion, and rebut possible opposition to it as an undesirable return toward a paralyzing "rule of reason." First, I here suggest an *industry* not a market standard. For the characteristics of beer, banks, cement, clothing, tires, etc., seem to be controlling whether there is one market or hundreds and whether the acquisition of the bank (or the brewery) is in Colorado or Wisconsin. The courts appear to be fashioning somewhat different criteria for banks than for other industries and the distinctions drawn by various courts are almost industry specific. The major enforcement agencies tend to develop specialized staffs for major industries. Obviously the various industry guidelines would themselves have to be reviewed for overall consistency with basic policies—the latter based on whatever general knowledge of links between structure and effects we have. Second, to the extent that interindustry regularities seem to emerge, industry-by-industry guidelines can be brought under general and overriding standards. Conceivably, after some time, a comprehensive (and effective) general set of guidelines with well-defined bases for rebuttal could replace the multiplicity of individual industry standards.

*Premise 6:   Attention Is Required to the
Probable Alternative to a Merger*

The effect of a proposed merger, or its prohibition, is different if the alternative to a proposed merger is, on the one hand, loss of an entrant
in any form or, on the other hand, a less restrictive form of entry.
This policy concern was discussed on pages 284–87.

Here one policy response might be to fashion specific general
prohibitory rules (say along lines such as those proposed by the Neal
Task Force), but to permit rebuttal of the adverse presumption by
showing that no less restrictive form of entry was feasible. This
seems to me to be rather more one-sided than is merited by the weight
of our knowledge, as well as encouraging all sorts of self-serving (but
difficult to disprove) assertions.

It seems to me that on this score we have *underutilized* our existing knowledge, and particularly the distinction among market extension, product extension, and pure conglomerate acquisitions. As
a first approximation let me suggest that within whatever overall
guidelines seem appropriate, the rebuttable presumptions be as follows: an available alternative to a nearby market extension merger
is *de novo* expansion; an available alternative to a distant market
extension merger or a product extension merger is a toehold acquisition; but the alternative to a pure conglomerate acquisition is entry-
by-acquisition into a different market or industry. These presumptions
would be rebuttable from either side, the burden resting on him who
chose to rebut.

Postscript

How will the conglomerate merger wave of the 1960s look from the
perspective of the year 2000? My guess is that to the historians it will
be regarded from that vantage point as an interesting episode, somewhat more important (in its long-run effects) than the Florida land
boom, and somewhat less consequential than the 1937 depression.
Perhaps, like the NRA, it will be regarded as an episode that threatened to achieve a lasting transformation of the industrial landscape,
but failed to do so.

It is my hope that to students of industrial organization and to
students of public policy, it will be seen to have provided the catalyst
and the key bits of experience out of which came a greater under-

standing of the American economy and a more nearly sensible set of policies for coping with mergers. To convert that hope to a realization will require more analysis, by more people, in and out of government than has yet occurred.

Bibliography

Books and Documents

Adelman, M. A. *A & P: A Study in Price-Cost Behavior and Public Policy.* Cambridge, Mass.: Harvard University Press, 1959.

Alberts, William W., and Segall, Joel E., eds. *The Corporate Merger.* Chicago: University of Chicago Press, 1966.

Ansoff, H. Igor, Brandenburg, Richard G., Portner, Fred E., and Radosevich, Raymond. *Acquisition Behavior of U.S. Manufacturing Firms, 1946–1965.* Nashville, Tenn.: Vanderbilt University Press, 1971.

Bain, Joe S. *Barriers to New Competition: Their Character and Consequences in Manufacturing Industries.* Cambridge, Mass.: Harvard University Press, 1956.

Berle, Adolf A., and Means, Gardiner C. *The Modern Corporation and Private Property.* New York: Macmillan Co., 1932.

Bock, Betty. *Mergers and Markets.* Studies in Business Economics No. 100. New York: National Industrial Conference Board, 1968.

———. *Antitrust Issues in Conglomerate Acquisitions: Tracking a Moving Target.* Studies in Business Economics No. 110. New York: National Industrial Conference Board, 1969.

———. *Statistical Games and the "200 Largest Industrials," 1954 and 1968.* Studies in Business Economics No. 115. New York: National Industrial Conference Board, 1970.

Federal Reserve Board. *A Study of Financing Small Business,* Part II. Washington, D.C.: United States Government Printing Office, 1958.

Federal Trade Commission, Bureau of Economics. *Annual Report.* Washington, D.C.: United States Government Printing Office, 1950.

———. *Current Trends in Merger Activity, 1970.* Statistical Report No. 8. Washington, D.C.: United States Government Printing Office, March 1971.

———. *Current Trends in Merger Activity, 1971.* Statistical Report No. 10. Washington, D.C.: United States Government Printing Office, May 1972.

———. *Economic Report on Corporate Mergers.* Washington, D.C.: United States Government Printing Office, 1969.

———. *Economic Report on Conglomerate Merger Performance, An Empirical Analysis of Nine Corporations.* Washington, D.C.: United States Government Printing Office, November 1972.

———. *Large Mergers in Manufacturing and Mining 1948–1971.* Statistical Report No. 9. Washington, D.C.: United States Government Printing Office, May 1972.

———. *Report of the FTC on Interlocking Directorates.* Washington, D.C.: United States Government Printing Office, 1951.

337

————. *Report of the FTC on the Merger Movement: A Summary Report*. Washington, D.C.: United States Government Printing Office, 1948.

————. *Report on Mergers and Acquisitions*. Washington, D.C.: United States Government Printing Office, October 1973.

Florence, P. Sargeant. *The Logic of Industrial Organization*. London: Kegan Paul, Trench Trubner & Co. Ltd., 1933.

Garoian, Leon, ed. *Economics of Conglomerate Growth*. Corvallis, Oreg.: Oregon State University, 1969.

Gort, Michael. *Diversification and Integration in American Industry*. Princeton, N.J.: Princeton University Press, 1962.

Kelly, Eamon M. *The Profitability of Growth Through Merger*. University Park, Pa.: Pennsylvania State University Press, 1967.

Larner, Robert J. *Management Control and the Large Corporation*. Cambridge, Mass.: Dunellen Publishing Co., 1970.

Markham, Jesse W. *Conglomerate Enterprise and Public Policy*. Boston, Mass.: Division of Research, Harvard Business School, 1973.

Marris, Robin. *The Economic Theory of Managerial Capitalism*. Glencoe, Ill.: Free Press, 1964.

Moody's Handbook of Common Stock. Quarterly Survey of Current Business, Issues 1963–71. New York: Moody's Investor Service, Inc., 1963–71.

Narver, John. *Conglomerate Mergers and Market Competition*. Berkeley, Calif.: University of California Press, 1967.

Nelson, Ralph. *Merger Movements in American Industry 1895–1956*. National Bureau of Economic Research, General Studies No. 66. Princeton, N.J.: Princeton University Press, 1959.

Reid, Samuel R. *Mergers, Managers and the Economy*. New York: McGraw-Hill, 1968.

Robinson, Edward A. G. *The Structure of Competitive Industry*. Rev. ed. Chicago: University of Chicago Press, 1959.

ST. JOHN'S LAW REVIEW. *Conglomerate Mergers and Acquisitions: Opinion and Analysis: Special Edition* 44 (Spring 1970).

Scherer, Frederic M. *Industrial Market Structure and Economic Performance*. Chicago: Rand McNally, 1971.

Singh, Ajit. *Takeovers: Their Relevance to the Stock Market and the Theory of the Firm*. Cambridge: Cambridge University Press, 1971.

Smith, Adam. *The Wealth of Nations* (1776). Edwin Cannan Edition; New York: Putnam, 1937.

United States Congress, House of Representatives. *Hearings before the Committee on Ways and Means,* 91st Congress, 1st Session on Tax Reform, Part 7. 1969.

United States Department of Justice. *Merger Guidelines*. May 30, 1968.

Weston, J. Fred, and Peltzman, Sam, eds. *Public Policy Toward Mergers*. Pacific Palisades, Calif.: Goodyear Publishing Co., 1969.

Williamson, Oliver. *Corporate Control and Business Behavior: An Inquiry into the Effects of Organization Form on Enterprise Behavior*. New York: Prentice-Hall, 1970.

Unpublished Manuscripts

Binder, Denis. "An Empirical Study of Contested Tender Offers: 1960–1969." S.J.D. thesis, Law School, University of Michigan, 1973.

Eis, Carl. "The 1919–1930 Merger Movement in American Industry." Ph.D. dissertation, City University of New York, 1968.

Gilbert, David. "Mergers, Diversification and the Theories of the Firm." Ph.D. dissertation, Harvard University, 1971.

Stone, James M. "Conglomerate Mergers: Their Implications for the Efficiency of Capital and the Theory of the Firm." Honors thesis, Harvard College, 1969.

Articles

Accounting Principles Board of the American Institute of Certified Public Accountants. Opinion No. 16. "Business Conditions." New York: American Institute of C.P.A.'s (AICPA). August 1970.

————. Opinion No. 17. "Intangible Assets." New York: American Institute of C.P.A.'s (AICPA). August 1970.

Adelman, M. A. "The Measurement of Industrial Concentration." *Review of Economics and Statistics* 33, no. 4 (November 1951):269–96.

Alberts, William W. "The Profitability of Growth by Merger." In *The Corporate Merger,* edited by William Alberts and Joel Segall. Chicago: University of Chicago Press, 1966.

Allan, Robert M., Jr. "Expansion by Merger." In *The Corporate Merger,* edited by William Alberts and Joel Segall. Chicago: University of Chicago Press, 1966.

Ammer, Dean S. "Realistic Reciprocity." *Harvard Business Review,* January-February 1962, pp. 116–24.

Archer, Stephen H., and Faerber, LeRoy G. "Firm Size and the Cost of Externally Secured Equity Capital." *Journal of Finance* 21 (March 1966):69–83.

Arnould, Richard. "Conglomerate Growth and Profitability." In *Economics of Conglomerate Growth,* edited by Leon Garoian. Corvallis, Oreg.: Oregon State University, 1969.

Asper, Lewis D. "Reciprocity, Purchasing Power, and Competition." 48 MINNESOTA LAW REVIEW 522–55 (1964).

Austin, Arthur Donald. "A Survey of the Problems Encountered in Combating Reciprocal Trading Under Existing Trade Regulation Laws." 41 INDIANA LAW JOURNAL 165–96 (1966).

Backman, Jules. "Conglomerate Mergers and Competition." 44 ST. JOHN'S LAW REVIEW, Special Edition, 90–132 (Spring 1970).

Bain, Joe S. "Advantages of the Large Firm: Production, Distribution and Sales Promotion." *Journal of Marketing* 20 (April 1956):336–46.

————. "A Note on Pricing in Monopoly and Oligopoly." *American Economic Review* 39, no. 2 (March 1949):448–64.

340 *Bibliography*

————. "Monopoly and Oligopoly by Merger, Discussion." *American Economic Review,* Papers and Proceedings 40, no. 2 (May 1950): 64–66.

————. "Relation of Profit Rate to Industry Concentration: American Manufacturing 1936–1940." *Quarterly Journal of Economics* 65, no. 3 (1951):293–324.

Berry, Charles. "Economic Policy and the Conglomerate Merger." 44 St. John's Law Review, Special Edition, 266–81 (Spring 1970).

Bicks, Robert A. "Corporate Mergers and the Antitrust Laws: Clayton Act, Section 7." In *The Corporate Merger,* edited by William Alberts and Joel Segall. Chicago: University of Chicago Press, 1966.

Binder, Denis. "Securities Law of Contested Tender Offers." 18 New York Law Forum, no. 3, 569–679 (Winter 1973).

Blair, John M. "Conglomeration in Food Industries." In *Economics of Conglomerate Growth,* edited by Leon Garoian. Corvallis, Oreg.: Oregon State University, 1969.

————. "The Conglomerate Merger in Economics and Law." 46 Georgetown Law Journal 672–700 (Spring 1958).

Blake, Harlan. "Conglomerate Mergers and the Antitrust Laws." 73 Columbia Law Review 554–92 (1973).

Bock, Betty. "Mergers and Reciprocity." *Conference Board Record* 2 (July 1965):27–36.

Bok, Derek. "Section 7 of the Clayton Act and the Merging of Law and Economics." 74 Harvard Law Review 226–355 (1960).

Bork, Robert. "The Rule of Reason and the Per Se Concept: Price Fixing and Market Division," I. 74 Yale Law Journal 775–847 (April 1965).

————. "The Rule of Reason and the Per Se Concept: Price Fixing and Market Division," II. 75 Yale Law Journal 373–478 (1966).

Bork, Robert, and Bowman, Ward S., Jr. "The Crisis in Antitrust." *Fortune* 68 (December 1963):138–40, 192–201.

Bowman, Ward. "Tying Arrangements and the Leverage Problem." 67 Yale Law Journal 19–36 (1957).

Boyle, Stanley. "Pre-Merger Growth and Profit Characteristics of Large Conglomerate Mergers in the United States 1948–1968." 44 St. John's Law Review, Special Edition, 152–70 (Spring 1970).

Briloff, Abraham J. "Accounting Practices and the Merger Movement." 45 Notre Dame Lawyer, no. 4, 604–28 (Summer 1970).

————. "Financial Motives for Conglomerate Growth." 44 St. John's Law Review, Special Edition, 872–79 (Spring 1970).

Brodley, Joseph. "Oligopoly Power Under the Sherman and Clayton Acts —From Economic Theory to Legal Policy." 19 Stanford Law Review 285, 325–29 (1967).

Brozen, Yale. "The Antitrust Task Force Deconcentration Recommendation." 13 Journal of Law and Economics, no. 2, 270–92 (October 1970).

————. "The Persistence of 'High Rates of Return' in High-Stable Concentration Industries." 14 JOURNAL OF LAW AND ECONOMICS, no. 2, 501–12 (October 1971).

Burck, Gilbert. "How to Fend Off a Takeover." *Fortune* 79 (February 1969):83–162.

———. "The Perils of the Multi-Market Corporation." *Fortune* 75 (February 1967):130–38, 184–88.

Burrus, Bernie R. "Tying Arrangements and Reciprocity: A Lawyer's Comment on Professor Ferguson's Analysis." 30 LAW AND CONTEMPORARY PROBLEMS 581–89 (1965).

Campbell, James S., and Shepherd, William G. "Leading-Firm Conglomerate Mergers." *Antitrust Bulletin* 13 (1968):1361–79.

Carr, Belinda B., and Browne, Stephen J. "Method vs. Myth in Measuring Merger Activity." *Mergers and Acquisitions, The Journal of Corporate Venture* 6, no. 3 (Fall 1971):5–15.

Cooper, Edward. "Attempts and Monopolization: A Mildly Expansionary Answer to the Prophylactic Riddle of Section Two." 72 MICHIGAN LAW REVIEW 373–462 (January 1974).

Curley, Anthony J. "Conglomerate Earnings Per Share: Real and Transitory Growth." *The Accounting Review* 46, no. 3 (July 1971):519–28.

Davidow, Joel. "Conglomerate Concentration and Section Seven: The Limitations of the Anti-Merger Act." 68 COLUMBIA LAW REVIEW 1213, 1264–70 (1968).

Dean, Joel. "Economic Aspects of Reciprocity, Competition and Mergers." *Antitrust Bulletin* 8 (1963):843–52.

Dean, Joel, and Smith, Winfield. "The Relationships Between Profitability and Size." In *The Corporate Merger,* edited by William Alberts and Joel Segall. Chicago: University of Chicago Press, 1966.

Dewey, Donald. "Mergers and Cartels: Some Reservations about Policy." *American Economic Review,* Papers and Proceedings 51, no. 2 (May 1961):225–62.

Donnem, Roland W. "Conglomerate Mergers and Reciprocity." *Antitrust Bulletin* 8 (1963):283–91.

Edwards, Corwin D. "Conglomerate Bigness as a Source of Power." *Business Concentration and Price Policy.* New York: National Bureau of Economic Research, 1955.

Elzinga, Kenneth G. "The Antimerger Law: Pyrrhic Victories?" 12 JOURNAL OF LAW AND ECONOMICS, no. 1, 43–78 (April 1969).

———. "Predatory Pricing: The Case of the Gunpowder Trust." 13 JOURNAL OF LAW AND ECONOMICS, no. 1, 223–40 (April 1970).

Ferguson, James M. "Tying Arrangements and Reciprocity: An Economic Analysis." 30 LAW AND CONTEMPORARY PROBLEMS 552–80 (Summer 1965).

Fotenos, J. F. "Accounting for Business Combinations: A Critique of APB Opinion Number 16." 23 STANFORD LAW REVIEW 330–48 (1971).

Goldberg, Lawrence G. "The Effect of Conglomerate Mergers on Competition." 16 JOURNAL OF LAW AND ECONOMICS, no. 1, 137–58 (April 1973).

Gort, Michael. "An Economic Disturbance Theory of Mergers." *Quarterly Journal of Economics* 83, no. 4 (November 1969):624–42.

———. "Diversification, Mergers, and Profits." In *The Corporate Merger*, edited by William Alberts and Joel Segall. Chicago: University of Chicago Press, 1966.

Gort, Michael, and Hogarty, Thomas F. "New Evidence on Mergers." 13 JOURNAL OF LAW AND ECONOMICS, no. 1, 167–84 (April 1970).

Hale, G. E., and Hale, Rosemary D. "Reciprocity Under the Antitrust Laws: A Comment." 113 UNIVERSITY OF PENNSYLVANIA LAW REVIEW 69–77 (November 1964).

Handler, Milton. "Emerging Antitrust Issues: Reciprocity, Diversification, and Joint Ventures." 49 VIRGINIA LAW REVIEW 433–47 (1963).

Harsha, Hugh. "The Conglomerate Merger and Reciprocity—Condemned by Conjecture?" *Antitrust Bulletin* 9, no. 2 (1964): 201–30.

Hausman, Robert M. "Reciprocal Dealing and the Antitrust Laws." 77 HARVARD LAW REVIEW 873–86 (1964).

Hayes, Samuel L. III, and Taussig, Russell A. "Tactics of Cash Takeover Bids." *Harvard Business Review* 45, no. 2 (March-April 1967):135–48.

Hibner, Don T., Jr. "Attempts to Monopolize: A Concept in Search of Analysis." 34 ABA ANTITRUST LAW JOURNAL 165–77 (1967).

Hill, Henry P. "Accounting Options and Conglomerate Growth." 44 ST. JOHN'S LAW REVIEW, Special Edition, 855–63 (Spring 1970).

Hindley, Brian. "Separation of Ownership and Control in the Modern Corporation." 13 JOURNAL OF LAW AND ECONOMICS, no. 1, 185–221 (April 1970).

Hinnegan, K. A. "Potential Reciprocity and Conglomerate Merger: Consolidated Foods Revisited." 17 BUFFALO LAW REVIEW 631–50 (Spring 1968).

Hogarty, Thomas F. "Profits from Mergers: The Evidence of Fifty Years." 44 ST. JOHN'S LAW REVIEW, Special Edition, 378–91 (Spring 1970).

———. "The Profitability of Corporate Mergers." *Journal of Business* 43, no. 3 (July 1970):317–27.

Jacoby, Neil. "The Conglomerate Corporation." *Center Magazine* 2, no. 4 (July 1969):41–53.

Jewell, George H., Jr. "The Tax Legislation Against Conglomerates— The Case Against the Tax Legislation." 44 ST. JOHN'S LAW REVIEW, Special Edition, 1073–80 (Spring 1970).

Johnston, J. "The Productivity of Management Consultants." *Journal of the Royal Statistical Association* 26 (1963):237–49.

Kamershen, David R. "A Theory of Conglomerate Mergers: Comment." *Quarterly Journal of Economics* 84, no. 4 (November 1970):668–73.

————. "The Influence of Ownership and Control on Profit Rates." *American Economic Review* 58 (June 1968):432–47.

Keeshan, Lawrence W. "Conglomerate Mergers and the Theory of Reciprocity." 22 STANFORD LAW REVIEW 812–46 (1970).

Knickerbocker, Daniel Candee, Jr. "Miching Mallecho: The Tax Reformers' Sneak Attack on Conglomerates." 44 ST. JOHN'S LAW REVIEW, Special Edition, 1047–72 (Spring 1970).

Kripke, Homer. "Conglomerates and the Moment of Truth in Accounting." 44 ST. JOHN'S LAW REVIEW, Special Edition, 791–97 (Spring 1970).

Larner, Robert J. "Ownership and Control in the 200 Largest Non-Financial Corporations, 1929 and 1963." *American Economic Review* 56, no. 4 (September 1966): 777–87.

Lee, Lawrence. "The Tax Reform Act and Convertible Debt Securities." 44 ST. JOHN'S LAW REVIEW, Special Edition, 1081–1113 (Spring 1970).

Lev, Baruch, and Mandelker, Gershon. "The Microeconomic Consequences of Corporate Mergers." *Journal of Business* 45, no. 1 (January 1972):85–104.

Levy, Haim, and Sarnat, Marshall. "Diversification, Portfolio Analysis and the Uneasy Case for Conglomerate Mergers." *Journal of Finance* 25, no. 4 (September 1970):795–802.

Lewellen, Wilbur. "A Pure Financial Rationale for the Conglomerate Merger." *Journal of Finance* 26, no. 2 (May 1971):521–37.

Lintner, John. "Expectations, Mergers and Equilibrium in Purely Competitive Securities Markets." Papers and Proceedings of the American Economic Association. *American Economic Review* 61 (May 1971): 101–11.

Loevinger, Lee. "How to Succeed in Business Without Being Tried." BNA, *Antitrust and Trade Regulation Report,* no. 496 (January 19, 1971):D-1–D-23.

Logue, Dennis E., and Naert, Philippe A. "A Theory of Conglomerate Mergers: Comment and Extension." *Quarterly Journal of Economics* 84, no. 4 (November 1970):663–67.

Lorie, James H., and Halpern, Paul. "Conglomerates: The Rhetoric and the Evidence." 13 JOURNAL OF LAW AND ECONOMICS, no. 1, 149–66 (April 1970).

MacAvoy, Paul W., McKie, James W., and Preston, Lee E. "High and Stable Concentration Levels, Profitability, and Public Policy: A Response." 14 JOURNAL OF LAW AND ECONOMICS, no. 2, 493–99 (October 1971).

McGee, John S. "Predatory Price Cutting: The Standard Oil (N.J.) Case." 1 JOURNAL OF LAW AND ECONOMICS, no. 1, 137–69 (October 1958).

McLaren, Richard W. "Statement to the House Ways and Means Committee." *New York Times,* March 13, 1969, p. 72.

Malott, Robert H. "The Control of Divisionalized Acquisitions." In *The*

Corporate Merger, edited by William Alberts and Joel Segall. Chicago: University of Chicago Press, 1966.

Manne, Henry. "Mergers and the Market for Corporate Control." *Journal of Political Economy* 73, no. 2 (April 1965):110–20.

Marcovits, Richard. "Tie-Ins, Reciprocity, and the Leverage Theory." 76 YALE LAW JOURNAL 1397–1472 (June 1967).

Markham, Jesse W. "Merger Policy Under the New Section 7: A Six-Year Appraisal." 43 VIRGINIA LAW REVIEW 489–528 (1957).

————. "Survey of the Evidence and Finding on Mergers." *Business Concentration and Public Policy.* New York: National Bureau of Economic Research, 1955.

Mellman, Martin, and Prisand, Norman. "That Complex Earnings Per Share Figure (A Product of the Merger Movement)." 44 ST. JOHN'S LAW REVIEW, Special Edition, 894–904 (Spring 1970).

Monsen, R. Joseph, Chiu, John S., and Cooley, David E. "The Effect of Separation of Ownership and Control on the Performance of the Large Firm." *Quarterly Journal of Economics* 82, no. 3 (August 1968):435–51.

Mueller, Dennis C. "A Theory of Conglomerate Mergers." *Quarterly Journal of Economics* 83, no. 4 (November 1969):643–59.

————. "Reply to: A Theory of Conglomerate Mergers: Comment and Extension." *Quarterly Journal of Economics* 84, no. 4 (November 1970):663–66.

————. "A Theory of Conglomerate Mergers: Reply." *Quarterly Journal of Economics* 83, no. 4 (November 1969):675–79.

Narver, John. "Supply Space and Horizontality in Firms and Mergers." 44 ST. JOHN'S LAW REVIEW, Special Edition, 316–40 (Spring 1970).

Neal, Phil C. et al. "White House Task Force Report on Antitrust Policy." Submitted July 5, 1968. Reprinted in BNA, *Antitrust and Trade Regulation Report,* no. 411 (May 27, 1969):A1–A6.

Nelson, Ralph L. "Business Cycle Factors in the Choice Between Internal and External Growth." In *The Corporate Merger,* edited by William Alberts and Joel Segall. Chicago: University of Chicago Press, 1966.

Penrose, Edith. "Biological Analogies in the Theory of the Firm." *American Economic Review* 42, no. 5 (December 1952):804–19.

Peterman, John. "The Clorox Case and the Television Rate Structures." 11 JOURNAL OF LAW AND ECONOMICS 321–422 (October 1968).

Phillips, Almarin. "Reciprocity Under the Antitrust Law: Observations on the Hales' Comment." 113 UNIVERSITY OF PENNSYLVANIA LAW REVIEW 77–79 (1964).

Posner, Richard A. "A Statistical Study of Antitrust Enforcement." 13 JOURNAL OF LAW AND ECONOMICS 365–419 (October 1970).

Preston, Lee E. "A Probabilistic Approach to Conglomerate Mergers." 44 ST. JOHN'S LAW REVIEW, Special Edition, 341–55 (Spring 1970).

————. "Giant Firms, Large Mergers and Concentration: Patterns and Policy Alternatives, 1954–1968." *Industrial Organization Review* 1, no. 1 (1973):35–46.

Rahl, James. "Applicability of the Clayton Act to Potential Competition." 12 ABA ANTITRUST LAW JOURNAL, § 143, 128–45 (1958).

Reid, Samuel R. "A Reply to the Weston/Mansinghka Criticisms Dealing with Conglomerate Mergers." *Journal of Finance* 26, no. 4 (1971): 937–46.

————. "Conglomerate Growth: Consistency With Economic Theory of Growth." In *Economics of Conglomerate Growth,* edited by Leon Garoian. Corvallis, Oreg.: Oregon State University, 1969.

Reiling, Henry B. "EPS Growth from Financial Packaging: An Accounting Incentive in Acquisitions." 44 ST. JOHN'S LAW REVIEW, Special Edition, 880–93 (Spring 1970).

Reinhardt, U. E. "Conglomerate Earnings Per Share: Immediate and Post-Merger Effects." *The Accounting Review* 47, no. 2 (April 1972): 360–70.

Robinson, Joan. "Rising Supply Price." *Economica* 8, no. 29 (1941): 1–8.

Schwartz, Samuel. "Merger Analysis as a Capital Budgeting Problem." In *The Corporate Merger,* edited by William Alberts and Joel Segall. Chicago: University of Chicago Press, 1966.

Seidler, Lee. "Mergers—The Accountant as a Creative Artist." 44 ST. JOHN'S LAW REVIEW, Special Edition, 828–47 (Spring 1970).

Shepherd, William G. "Conglomerate Mergers in Perspective." 2 ANTITRUST LAW AND ECONOMICS REVIEW, no. 1, 15–32 (Fall 1968).

Shors, John D. "Corporate Reorganizations: Some Current Developments Including the Tax Reform Act of 1969." 44 ST. JOHN'S LAW REVIEW, Special Edition, 1128–47 (Spring 1970).

Silverstein, Leonard L. "Impact of the Acquisition Indebtedness Provisions of the Tax Reform Act of 1969 on Corporate Mergers." 44 ST. JOHN'S LAW REVIEW, Special Edition, 1014–46 (Spring 1970).

Sinrich, Norman. "Tax Incentives and the Conglomerate Merger: An Introduction." 44 ST. JOHN'S LAW REVIEW, Special Edition, 1009–13 (Spring 1970).

Sloane, Leonard. "Reciprocity: Where Does the P. A. Stand?" *Purchasing* 51, no. 11 (November 20, 1961):70–79.

Smith, Keith V., and Schreiner, John C. "A Portfolio Analysis of Conglomerate Diversification." *Journal of Finance* 24 (June 1969): 413–27.

Smith, Noel I. "Attempt to Monopolize: Its Elements and Their Definition." 27 GEORGE WASHINGTON LAW REVIEW 227–44 (1958).

Stanger, Abraham M. "Accounting for Business Combinations: Choice or Dilemma." 44 ST. JOHN'S LAW REVIEW, Special Edition, 864–71 (Spring 1970).

Steiner, Peter O. "Conglomerates and the Public Interest." 14 LAW QUADRANGLE NOTES 14–21 (Spring 1970).

————. "Markets and Industries." *International Encyclopedia of the Social Sciences* 9 (1968): 575–81.

————. "Public Expenditure Budgeting." *The Economics of Public Fi-*

nance. Washington, D.C.: Brookings Institution, Studies of Government Finance, 1974.

Stigler, George J. "The Economics of Information." *Journal of Political Economy* 69 (1961):213–25.

———. "Monopoly and Oligopoly by Merger." *American Economic Review,* Papers and Proceedings 40, no. 2 (May 1950):23–34.

Stigler, George J. et al. "Task Force Report on Productivity and Competition." Submitted in January 1969. Reprinted in BNA, *Antitrust and Trade Regulation Report,* no. 413 (June 10, 1969):X1–X8.

Stocking, George, and Mueller, Willard F. "Business Reciprocity and the Size of Firms." *Journal of Business of the University of Chicago* 30, no. 2 (1957):73–95.

Swenson, J. Malcolm. "Action Against Conglomerate—Will It Hurt Small Business?" 44 St. John's Law Review, Special Edition, 1153–62 (Spring 1970).

Taft, Robert S. "Acquiring the Closely-Held Corporation." 44 St. John's Law Review, Special Edition, 1144–52 (Spring 1970).

Teberg, Richard L. "Of the Short-Swing Trading Rules in Mergers and Acquisitions." *Mergers and Acquisitions, The Journal of Corporate Venture* 6, no. 2 (Summer 1971):4–9.

Telser, Lester. "Abusive Trade Practices: An Economic Analysis." 30 Law and Contemporary Problems 488–505 (Summer 1965).

———. "Cutthroat Competition and the Long Purse." 9 Journal of Law and Economics, no. 2, 259–77 (October 1966).

Trier, Dana L., and Snider, Darryl. "United States v. Falstaff Brewing Corporation: Potential Competition Re-examined." 72 Michigan Law Review 837–68 (March 1974).

Turner, Donald. "Conglomerate Mergers and Section 7 of the Clayton Act." 78 Harvard Law Review 1313–95 (May 1965).

Wallace, Forrest D. "Some Principles of Acquisition." In *The Corporate Merger,* edited by William Alberts and Joel Segall. Chicago: University of Chicago Press, 1966.

Weiss, Leonard W. "Conglomerate Mergers and Public Policy." In *Economics of Conglomerate Growth,* edited by Leon Garoian. Corvallis, Oreg.: Oregon State University, 1969.

———. "An Evaluation of Mergers in Six Industries." *Review of Economics and Statistics* 47, no. 2 (May 1965):172–81.

Westerfield, Randolph. "A Note on the Measurement of Conglomerate Diversification." *Journal of Finance* 25, no. 4 (September 1970):909–14.

Weston, J. Fred. "The Determination of Share Exchange Ratios in Mergers." In *The Corporate Merger,* edited by William Alberts and Joel Segall. Chicago: University of Chicago Press, 1966.

Weston, J. Fred, and Mansinghka, Surenda K. "Tests of the Efficiency Performance of Conglomerate Firms." *Journal of Finance* 26, no. 4 (September 1971):919–46.

Whisler, Thomas L. "Organizational Aspects of Corporate Growth." In

The Corporate Merger, edited by William Alberts and Joel Segall. Chicago: University of Chicago Press, 1966.

Williamson, Oliver E. "Economies as an Antitrust Defense: The Welfare Tradeoffs." *American Economic Review* 58, no. 1 (March 1968): 18–36.

Wintrub, Warren G., Graichen, Raymond E., and Keidan, Harry W. "Tax Aspects of Corporate Acquisitions." 44 ST. JOHN'S LAW REVIEW, Special Edition, 1114–27 (Spring 1970).

Wyatt, Arthur R., and Spacek, Leonard. "Accounting Principles and Conglomerate Growth." 44 ST. JOHN'S LAW REVIEW, Special Edition, 805–27 (Spring 1970).

Yamey, B. S. "Predatory Price Cutting: Notes and Comments." 15 JOURNAL OF LAW AND ECONOMICS, no. 1, 129–42 (April 1972).

Zerbe, Richard. "The American Sugar Refinery Company, 1887–1914: The Story of a Monopoly." 12 JOURNAL OF LAW AND ECONOMICS, no. 2, 339–75 (October 1969).

Cases

Addyston Pipe & Steel Co. v. United States, 175 U.S. 211 (1899).

Allis-Chalmers Mfg. Co. v. White Consolidated Industries, 414 F.2d 506 (3d Cir. 1969).

Aluminum Co. of America v. FTC, 285 F. 401 (3d Cir. 1922).

Aluminum Co. of America, United States v., 148 F.2d 416 (2d Cir. 1945).

Aluminum Co. of America, United States v., (Rome cable), 377 U.S. 271 (1964).

Armco Steel, United States v., 1970 *CCH Trade Cases* ¶ 73,283 (S.D. Ohio 1970).

Armour and Co. v. General Host, 296 F.Supp. 470 (S.D. N.Y. 1969).

Beatrice Foods Co., In re, [1965–1967 Transfer Binder] *CCH Trade Regulation Reporter* ¶ 17,244 (FTC 1965); [1970–1973 Transfer Binder] *CCH Trade Regulation Reporter* ¶ 20,121 (FTC 1972).

Bendix Corp. v. FTC, 450 F.2d 534 (6th Cir. 1971); 3 *CCH Trade Regulation Reporter* ¶ 19,288 (FTC 1970).

Bethlehem Steel, United States v., 1970 *CCH Trade Cases* ¶ 73,376 (E.D. Pa. 1970).

Birnbaum v. Newport Steel, 98 F.Supp. 506 (S.D. N.Y. 1951); 193 F.2d 461 (2d Cir. 1952).

Brown Shoe Co. v. United States, 370 U.S. 294 (1962).

Butler Aviation Inc. v. Comprehensive Designers, Inc., 307 F.Supp. 910 (S.D. N.Y. 1969); 425 F.2d 842 (2d Cir. 1970).

California Packing Corp., In re, 25 FTC 379 (1937).

Columbia Steel Co., United States v., 334 U.S. 495 (1948).

Consolidated Foods Corp., United States v., 380 U.S. 592 (1965).

Continental Can Co., United States v., 378 U.S. 441 (1964).

E. I. duPont de Nemours & Co., United States v., 353 U.S. 586 (1957).

Electronic Specialty Co. v. International Controls Corp., 295 F.Supp. 1063
    (S.D. N.Y. 1968); 409 F.2d 937 (2d Cir. 1969).
El Paso Natural Gas Co., et al., United States v., 376 U.S. 651 (1964).
Falstaff Brewing Corp., United States v., 332 F.Supp. 970 (D. R.I. 1971);
    410 U.S. 526 (1973).
First National Bancorporation, United States v., 329 F.Supp. 1003 (D.C.
    Colo. 1971); 410 U.S. 577 (1973).
First National Bank & Trust Co. of Lexington, United States v., 376 U.S.
    665 (1964).
FMC Corp., United States v., 218 F.Supp. 817 (S.D. Colo. 1963).
Ford Motor Co. and The Electric Autolite Co., United States v., 286
    F.Supp. 407 (E.D. Mich. 1968); 315 F.Supp. 372 (E.D. Mich.
    1970); 405 U.S. 562 (1972).
Foremost Dairies Inc., In re, 60 FTC 944, 1084 (1962).
Fortner Enterprises v. United States Steel Corp., 394 U.S. 495 (1969).
GAF v. Milstein, 324 F.Supp. 1062 (S.D. N.Y. 1971); 453 F.2d 709 (2d
    Cir. 1971).
General Dynamics, United States v., 258 F.Supp. 36 (S.D. N.Y. 1966).
*General Dynamics (United Electric Coal Companies and Freeman Coal
    Mining Corp.), United States v.,* 341 F.Supp. 534 (N.D. Ill. 1972);
    1974 *CCH Trade Regulation Reporter* ¶ 74,967.
General Foods Corp. v. FTC, 386 F.2d 936 (3d Cir. 1967).
General Motors Corp., United States v., [1961–1970 Transfer Binder]
    CCH Trade Regulation Reporter ¶ 45,063 (Case 1733) (1963).
General Tire and Rubber, United States v., 1970 *CCH Trade Cases* ¶ 73,-
    303 (N.D. Ohio 1970).
Georgia-Pacific Corp., In re, 3 *CCH Trade Regulation Reporter* ¶ 20,147
    (FTC order 1972).
Griffith Corp., United States v., 334 U.S. 100 (1948).
Grinnell Corp., United States v., 384 U.S. 563 (1966).
Imperial Chemical Industries, United States v., 100 F.Supp. 504 (S.D.
    N.Y. 1951).
Ingersol Rand Corp., United States v., 218 F.Supp. 530 (W.D. Pa. 1963);
    320 F.2d 509 (3d Cir. 1963).
Inland Steel, United States v., 1970 *CCH Trade Cases* ¶ 73,197 (N.D. Ill.
    1970).
International Salt Co. v. United States, 332 U.S. 392 (1947).
ITT (Canteen), United States v., 1971 *CCH Trade Cases* ¶ 73,619 (N.D.
    Ill. 1971).
ITT (Grinnell), United States v., 306 F.Supp. 766 (D. Conn. 1969); 324
    F.Supp. 19 (D. Conn. 1970).
ITT (Hartford), United States v., 306 F.Supp. 766 (D. Conn. 1969).
Kennecott Copper Corp. v. FTC, 467 F.2d 67 (10th Cir. 1972).
Knight, E. C., United States v., 156 U.S. 1 (1895).
Ling-Temco-Vought, United States v., 315 F.Supp. 1301 (W.D. Pa. 1970).
Manufacturers Hanover Trust Co., United States v., 240 F.Supp. 867
    (S.D. N.Y. 1965).

Mechanical Mfg. Co., In re, 16 FTC 67 (1932).

Northern Pacific Railway Co. v. United States, 356 U.S. 1 (1958).

Northern Securities Co. v. United States, 193 U.S. 197 (1904).

Northwest Industries, United States v., 301 F.Supp. 1066 (N.D. Ill. 1969).

Pabst Brewing Co., United States v., 384 U.S. 546 (1966).

Penick & Ford and R. J. Reynolds Tobacco Co., United States v., 242 F.Supp. 518 (D. N.J. 1965).

Penn-Olin Chemical Co. et al., United States v., 217 F.Supp. 110 (D. Del. 1963); 378 U.S. 158 (1964); 246 F.Supp. 917 (D. Del. 1965).

Pennzoil Co., United States v., 252 F.Supp. 962 (W.D. Pa. 1965).

Philadelphia National Bank, United States v., 374 U.S. 321 (1963).

PPG Industries, United States v., 1970 *CCH Trade Cases* ¶ 73,373 (W.D. Pa. 1970).

Procter & Gamble, FTC v., 58 FTC 1203 (1961); 63 FTC 1465 (1963); 358 F.2d 74 (1966); 386 U.S. 568 (1967).

Republic Steel, United States v., 1970 *CCH Trade Cases* ¶ 73,246 (N.D. Ohio 1970).

Southern Pacific Co., United States v., 259 U.S. 214 (1922).

Standard Oil Co. v. United States, 221 U.S. 1 (1911).

Standard Oil Co. of California v. United States, 337 U.S. 293 (1948).

Sup't of Insurance v. Bankers Life & Casualty Co., 404 U.S. 6 (1971).

Susquehanna Corp. v. Pan American Sulphur Co., 423 F.2d 1075 (5th Cir. 1970).

Trans-Missouri Freight Assn., United States v., 166 U.S. 290 (1897).

Union Pacific Railroad, United States v., 226 U.S. 61 (1912).

United States Steel Corp., United States v., 251 U.S. 417 (1920).

United States Steel Corp., United States v., 1969 *CCH Trade Cases* ¶ 72,-826 (W.D. Penn. 1969).

United States Steel Corp. v. FTC, 426 F.2d 592 (1970).

Von's Grocery Co., United States v., 384 U.S. 270 (1966).

Waugh Mfg. Co., In re, 15 FTC 232 (1931).

Westinghouse Electric, United States v., 1972 *CCH Trade Cases* ¶ 74,053 (W.D. Pa. 1972).

White Consolidated Industries Inc. and White Motor Corp., United States v., 323 F.Supp. 1397 (N.D. Ohio 1971).

Wilson Sporting Goods and Nissen Corp., United States v., 288 F.Supp. 543 (N.D. Ill. 1968).

Index